S0-CFI-463

Lobbying and Policy Change

Lobbying and Policy Change

Who Wins, Who Loses, and Why

FRANK R. BAUMGARTNER, JEFFREY
M. BERRY, MARIE HOJNACKI, DAVID
C. KIMBALL, AND BETH L. LEECH

THE UNIVERSITY OF CHICAGO PRESS   CHICAGO AND LONDON

FRANK R. BAUMGARTNER is the Bruce R. Miller and Dean D. LaVigne Professor of Political Science at Penn State University. JEFFREY M. BERRY is the John Richard Skuse Professor of Political Science at Tufts University. MARIE HOJNACKI is associate professor of political science at Penn State University. DAVID C. KIMBALL is associate professor of political science at the University of Missouri–St. Louis. BETH L. LEECH is associate professor of political science at Rutgers University.

The University of Chicago Press, Chicago 60637
The University of Chicago Press, Ltd., London
© 2009 by The University of Chicago
All rights reserved. Published 2009
Printed in the United States of America
18 17 16 15 14 13 12   4 5

ISBN-13: 978-0-226-03944-2 (cloth)
ISBN-13: 978-0-226-03945-9 (paper)
ISBN-10: 0-226-03944-7 (cloth)
ISBN-10: 0-226-03945-5 (paper)

Library of Congress Cataloging-in-Publication Data

Lobbying and policy change : who wins, who loses, and why /
Frank R. Baumgartner . . . [et al.].
    p.   cm.
  Includes bibliographical references and index.
  ISBN-13: 978-0-226-03944-2 (cloth : alk. paper)
  ISBN-13: 978-0-226-03945-9 (pbk. : alk. paper)
  ISBN-10: 0-226-03944-7 (cloth : alk. paper)
  ISBN-10: 0-226-03945-5 (pbk. : alk. paper) 1. Lobbying—United States.
2. Political planning—United States. 3. United States—Politics and
government—21st century. I. Baumgartner, Frank R., 1958–
  JK1118.L577   2009
  320.60973—dc22

                               2008048343

♾ The paper used in this publication meets the minimum requirements of the American National Standard for Information Sciences—Permanence of Paper for Printed Library Materials, ANSI Z39.48-1992.

Contents

List of Tables and Figures

Tables

Figures

Acknowledgments

A s readers will discover in the pages that follow, conducting the research that produced *Lobbying and Policy Change* was a vast undertaking. In fact, in our initial request for funding to the National Science Foundation, reviewers had such strong reservations about the feasibility of what we were proposing that we were given only a small amount of funds and essentially told to demonstrate that we could do it. We worked for two years and reapplied for full funding, which, happily, was awarded. Thanks first to Frank Scioli of NSF for believing in the project. While the project was feasible, it was not easy, and we could not have done it alone. We had an enormous amount of help from a small army of students, and no words can adequately express our appreciation for all that they did to make this book a reality. Here, however, we can at least publicly thank them for their hard work and dedication.

Although the authors teach at four different schools, our project was headquartered at Penn State University, where Frank Baumgartner and Marie Hojnacki coordinated the work of most of our research assistants. Some students worked just for a semester; others worked with us for years. Some did work that was specialized; others became so valuable to us that we came to rely on them for many different tasks, including interviews in Washington, Web searching, designing the project Web site, checking the accuracy of work done by others, training new staff, developing coding schemes and then coding data, and even analyzing our results. In some cases, assistants became collaborators and their names appear on some of the conference papers and articles that grew out of the research.

Christine Mahoney began working for us at the very beginning of the project, when she was a Penn State undergraduate. She stayed on at Penn State for her Ph.D. and helped us until she left for Brussels to conduct fieldwork for her dissertation on lobbying. Christine was involved in almost every aspect of the project, including conducting interviews in Washington and supervising and training other staff. Christine is now running her own research projects at Syracuse University, where she is on the faculty. Her first book, *Brussels versus the Beltway*, published in 2008, provides an explicitly comparative dimension to the literature on lobbying, as she compares the results she got while working in Washington with findings stemming from her interviews in Brussels.

Timothy La Pira, then a doctoral candidate at Rutgers University, also conducted interviews for us during the summers of 2001 and 2002. He continued contributing to the project by taking on some coding tasks. Tim went on to work at the Center for Responsive Politics in Washington and then joined the faculty in the Department of Political Science at the College of Charleston.

Nick Semanko, who went on to law school at Boston University, was instrumental in designing our Web site and oversaw many aspects of the project during his last two years of undergraduate studies at Penn State. One Semanko was not enough, and Nick's brother Andy started working on the project even before enrolling as a freshman at his brother's alma mater. Andy worked on the project as the webmaster for three years. Matt Levendusky worked on Web design and coding issues while he was an undergraduate at Penn State, before going on to doctoral work in political science at Stanford. He's now on the faculty at the University of Pennsylvania.

Midori Valdivia worked on the project for over two years as an undergraduate and came to be one of the students we relied on for our most difficult coding decisions and tricky cases. She worked hard on many aspects of the project before entering the graduate program at Princeton's Wilson School.

Many thanks also to the following Penn State undergraduates, who helped with various aspects of coding and Web searching: Neel Aroon, John Baer, Josh Beail-Farkas, Brian Blaise, Lauren Cerminaro, Steven Dzubak, Darrin Gray, David Hall, Sarah Hlibka, Matt Iaconetti, Mary Lehrer, Michelle O'Connell, Susanne Pena, Carl Rathjen, John Riley, Katrina Romain, Sara Ryan, Julie Sandell (now a Penn State graduate student), Roberto Santoni, Alex Smith, Adam Spurchise, Jennifer Teters, and Phil Thompson. Mary Gardner helped us to edit our manuscript as it reached its final form. At Rutgers University, undergraduates Daisy Bang, Kristen Beckbissinger, Kelly Ferraro, Peter Geller, Diane Hickey, Lauren

Oleykowski, and Venesa Pagan assisted Beth Leech by transcribing interviews and compiling lobbying records. Similarly, at Missouri–St. Louis, Matt McLaughlin helped David Kimball collect campaign contribution data. At Tufts, Erin Desmarais worked with Jeff Berry. Please know that each of you was instrumental to the success of our research.

Other Penn State graduate students who worked on the project include Asma Abbas, Hugh Bouchelle, Amber Boydstun, Gretchen Carnes, Sushmita Chatterjee, Kevin Egan, Daniel Jones-White, Young Kim, Stephanie Korst, Heather Ondercin, Paul Rutledge, Jen Schoonmaker, and Josh Vermette. Patrick Hennes worked on the project under the supervision of David Kimball at Southern Illinois University at Carbondale. We thank you all for your professionalism, enthusiasm, and long hours.

Students in several courses were subjected to early drafts of the book manuscript, and the final version benefited greatly from their critiques and suggestions. We thank the graduate students in the fall 2007 American Proseminar at Rutgers University (and especially Sara Angevine for her close reading); Fred Barbash and his students from the fall 2007 seminar in the Washington Program of Northwestern University's Medill School of Journalism; and the graduate students in the spring 2008 Seminar on Organized Interests at Penn State.

We feel very fortunate that so many distinguished scholars took time away from their own work to read all or most of a draft manuscript, either at our request or for the University of Chicago Press. We profited greatly from suggestions from Laura Arnold, Lee Cronk, Kevin Esterling, Christoffer Green-Pedersen, Bryan Jones, John McCarthy, Andy McFarland, Kay Schlozman, Mark Smith, Garrett Sullivan, and a reviewer for the University of Chicago Press who chose to remain anonymous. We also profited from the advice of Sylvain Brouard, David Coen, Martial Foucault, Abel Francois, Rick Hall, Burdett Loomis, David Lowery, David Meyer, and Jim Stimson. We're also indebted to our colleagues in the departments of political science at the universities of Missouri–St. Louis, Penn State, Rutgers, and Tufts. They provided wise counsel to the endless stream of problems and questions we brought their way.

We also received useful feedback at talks where one of us spoke about various parts of this book. Thanks to Jan Beyers at the University of Antwerp, Virginia Gray at UNC–Chapel Hill, Jacob Hacker at Yale, William Maloney at Newcastle, Yves Meny at the European University Institute in Florence, Jennifer Mosley at the University of Chicago, Jan Van Deth at Mannheim, and Larry Bartels at Princeton.

The National Science Foundation supported this project through grants SBR-0111224 and SBR-9905195. We're deeply grateful to NSF and its reviewers for placing so much confidence in this project. Of course, NSF bears no responsibility for the analysis reported here. We also extend our thanks to the Robert Wood Johnson Scholars in Health Policy Research Program for the fellowship it awarded to Marie Hojnacki, which, in turn, facilitated the first stage of data gathering. Frank Baumgartner expresses his gratitude to the Camargo Foundation, which provided a residential fellowship in 2007, and to Cevipof/Sciences Po Paris and the University of Aberdeen, where he has been lucky to have productive visits on numerous occasions. Beth Leech thanks the Center for the Study of Democratic Politics at Princeton University during the book's final stages. The College of the Liberal Arts, the Department of Political Science, and the Miller-LaVigne Professorship at Penn State University, and the Graduate School at Rutgers University provided substantial material support for our project as well. We are grateful to all these sources for their support.

To the hundreds of lobbyists, legislative aides, bureaucrats, and others in Washington whom we interviewed, please accept our sincere and humble "thank you." You were all so gracious and generous in allowing us into your offices, taking time from your work to discuss the policymaking process with us. Quite literally, we could not have written this book without you. Because our interviews were conducted with promises of confidentiality, we cannot list our interviewees by name, but you know who you are!

Finally, we appreciate the care that went into the production of this book at the University of Chicago Press. We're grateful to Clair James, Michael Koplow, Megan Marz, Rodney Powell, Isaac Tobin, and editorial director John Tryneski.

Frank R. Baumgartner
Jeffrey M. Berry
Marie Hojnacki
David C. Kimball
Beth L. Leech

Advocacy, Public Policy, and Policy Change

Who wins in Washington? Do moneyed interests, corporations, and large campaign contributors use the goodwill and access to policy makers that their resources may earn for them to get what they want? Does partisanship or ideology determine the outcome of most policy disputes, flowing inexorably from election results? Do the same factors affect highly salient issues as well as those discussed only within specialized policy communities? How often do rhetoric and spin succeed in changing the way issues are discussed? How closely do organized interests and policy makers work together and how often do they come into conflict? Do elected officials act to protect the public interest against the demands of the powerful, recognizing that some constituencies have no lobbyist? Our goals are to understand how the policy process works, who wins, who loses, and why.

To answer these questions, we interviewed more than three hundred lobbyists and government officials about a random sample of nearly one hundred issues across the full range of activities of the U.S. federal government. We identified our issues and conducted our interviews over the last two years of the Clinton administration (1999–2000) and the first two years of the George W. Bush administration (2001–2002). Through these interviews and by searching systematically through publicly available documents, we were able to map out the constellation of which government officials and organized interests were mobilized on each issue, and, through follow-up telephone interviews and by monitoring news and official Web sites for four years after our initial interviews, we were able to find out who got what they wanted and who did not. Ours is the first study of its kind.

We have chosen this approach because much of the research on lobbying, as well as journalistic accounts of the impact of money in politics, is based on captivating examples that simply are not representative of what typically occurs. In fact, for a journalist, typical occurrences may be far less interesting or newsworthy than those egregious cases of influence peddling that occasionally hit the headlines. Good government, after all, can be dull (or at least a lot duller than corruption, mismanagement, malfeasance, or scandal). Political scientists, too, have had a difficult time generalizing about lobbying, because they often focus only on issues that reach the end stages of the policy process or that are well publicized. Our study shows that most issues do not reach those final stages and most are not highly publicized, even within the Beltway. To get a full picture of the world of advocacy and lobbying in Washington, we looked behind the headlines and beyond the roll call votes.

Studying Power in Washington

We began by looking at ninety-eight randomly selected policy issues in which interest groups were involved and then followed those issues across two Congresses, about four years. We were interested in all policy issues and potential policy issues in which interest groups were involved, whether or not those issues were already part of any formal government agenda. This posed a challenge, of course, since there is no list of such issues from which to draw a sample. Worse, most of the issues raised in Washington on any given day die from lack of attention, so we needed a way to include (in their proper proportion) even those issues to which no one besides the most devoted advocates would ever pay any attention. We sought a list of those issues on which at least one interest group was working, but one that was properly weighted to reflect the activities of the entire lobbying community. In order to reach valid conclusions about lobbying and the impact of lobbyists on the issues on which they work, we wanted a random sample of the objects of lobbying. Of course, it turns out that many interest groups are active on exactly those same issues that other groups are working on—the distribution of lobbying follows what has been called a "power law" or "the 80/20 rule" because a large percentage of all the lobbying occurs on a small percentage of the cases.[1] Whether groups were individually raising issues that they hoped others would eventually pay attention to or jumping on a bandwagon on a highly visible issue, we wanted a random sample of the objects of what groups were working on.

Here is how we solved this problem. By law, an interest group that is lobbying must file a quarterly disclosure report listing the issues on which it lobbied and how much it spent. Taking advantage of this, and to generate a random sample of the objects of lobbying, we weighted the issues so that those that generated more lobbying activity were more likely to fall into our sample. First, we started with a sample of registration reports drawn from previous filings under the Lobby Disclosure Act. Organizations must file a separate section in their report for each issue area in which they are active, and any public relations or lobbying firms that they employ must also file reports listing them as the client. In any given period, a large corporation or trade association may report activity in a dozen or more issue areas, with their lobbyists-for-hire also filing additional reports on their behalf. Smaller organizations, such as one of the universities that employ the authors of this book, might have a single report filed in their name, with one or two issue areas mentioned. Previous research by Beth Leech and colleagues showed that these lobby disclosure reports were relatively stable over time: If a certain number of groups were registered in a given policy area one reporting period, it was highly likely that a similar number would register again in the following time period.[2] These multiple filings in multiple issue areas allowed us to use each section of each report as a weighting system to identify the *most active lobbying organizations*. The sampling unit was a lobbying report on an issue area, and the most active lobbying organizations filed the most reports. (Our interviewing and other data collection procedures are explained in more detail in the appendix.) We used *Washington Representatives*, a directory of lobbyists, to identify a lobbyist who represented the selected organization.[3]

In interviews, we asked the selected lobbyists to name *the most recent issue* relating to the federal government on which they had been working—literally the last item that had crossed their desk, or had been the object of an email exchange or the topic of their most recent policy-relevant phone conversation.[4] The issue could be *any* policy issue *at any stage* of the policy process, as long as it dealt with the federal government. The result is a randomized snapshot of what interest groups in Washington were working on during the period of our fieldwork (again, 1999–2002).

Although our time frame had more to do with pragmatism—none of us live in Washington and we tended to go there for a month or two at a time—the consequence of not being able to complete the research in a short period of time adds to our confidence that the sample is representative. If the field research had been planned to take place entirely in the fall of 2001, for example, an unrepresentative number of homeland security issues would have fallen into the sample.

Can we be confident that this sample is truly random? We know theoretically that our sample is random because of our sampling technique, but how do we know that our theory worked in practice? One way is by looking at the results, which we will do later in this chapter: The results certainly are diverse, covering virtually all areas of the federal government and including issues ranging from front page stories to obscure little tidbits of federal policy arcana. For example, who decides just how much clinical social worker services are reimbursed when clients receive them in a skilled nursing facility under the Medicaid program? It may not matter much to you or to us, but it showed up in the sample because it matters to those professionals in the field a great deal, and they lobbied for a change in the reimbursement rates. And while it's an obscure issue, it's not a trivial one, as such decisions affect the quality and nature of services eventually received by the public. Readers of this book will become aware of the diversity of the issues we studied just by reading the pages that follow, but they can find much more, including a full range of overview materials as well as all laws, bills, hearing testimony, statements in Congress, news articles, interest group press releases, and other materials on each of our ninety-eight issues by looking at our Web site: http://lobby.la.psu.edu.

The more important way to be sure that our sample is a random sample of the objects of lobbying is to understand what that means and what it does not mean. It is not a list of the most important public-policy controversies in Washington. Many of our issues were relatively minor, in fact. Others were huge, such as President Clinton's proposal for permanent normal trade relations with China. It is not a list of what business wanted. Indeed, some were efforts to *undo* gains that businesses might have achieved in some previous round of the policy process. Nor is it a sample of the problems government is actively working to address. As we will see below, it is certainly not a sample of what the general public is most concerned about. Rather, quite simply, it is a sample of the issues on which organizational representatives were active, with greater weight accorded to those issues that were of interest to a greater number of organizations.

Note that the sampling actually had three stages: First, we selected organizations, with the most active the most likely to be chosen. Second, from each organization we selected an in-house lobbying representative. Third, each selected representative provided us with an issue. That means that if the organization we interviewed had been active on one hundred issues in the recent past, we took just one in one hundred of their issues. Smaller organizations had a lower probability of entering our sample, but if they did, their issues had a higher probability of being chosen. If a group had been recently active on only five issues, then each issue had a one-in-five, not a one-in-one-hundred chance. The net result of our sampling strategy is that we have, for the first time, a sample of the issues that are of concern to organized interests. Issues that were of concern to hundreds or thousands of interest groups during the time of our study were highly likely to fall into our sample, and indeed we did find that President Clinton's efforts to reform the health care system and ensure that China received long-term status as a favored trading partner were among our issues. However, issues that were more limited in their scope also fell into our sample, with the same proportion as there were organizations working on them.[5]

It's possible that if lobbyists were actually working on something that they preferred not to be made public, they may have told us about another issue. While we cannot, of course, get a firm estimate about this problem, we guarded against it in some important ways, notably not including lobbyists for hire in our initial sample. We feared that they often would not talk to us about their efforts on behalf of clients without the client's approval, so we only talked with so-called in-house lobbyists—those who work directly for the trade association or corporation that is registered as the lobbying organization.[6] In general, we found our respondents to be very open.

Our sampling procedures mean that our focus is on issues that in some way involved Congress, and issues relating to the judiciary and that are solely agency-related may be undercounted. This is because the lawyers who file public interest lawsuits or design the legal defense strategies of trade associations are not typically in the government relations offices of the organizations we sampled, and therefore we did not typically reach them in our interviews. Likewise, many lawyers, engineers, and other specialists who work on regulatory issues for companies do not consider themselves legislative lobbyists and are not required to register as such. Our respondents in the government relations department would be more likely to be familiar with an issue that involved Congress and might not have thought to mention a lawsuit or small, niche regulatory matter as "the most recent issue." But although most of our issues have at least some congressional connection, 56 percent of our issues involved an agency or agency official in a prominent advocacy role, and several of our issues involved the courts at some point in their recent histories. Despite these potential limitations, this remains the most representative sample that has ever been used in a study of lobbying.

Since we followed our issues for four years, we know a lot about what eventually occurred (if anything did). In fact, as we outline in the chapters to come, for the majority of our issues, little happened. If what they are supposed to be doing is producing change, interest groups are a surprisingly ineffectual lot. A focus by the media and many academics on explaining political change or sensational examples of lobbying success obscures the fact that lobbyists often toil with little success in gaining attention to their causes or they meet such opposition to their efforts that the resulting battle leads to a stalemate. Of course, many lobbyists are active because their organizations benefit from the status quo and they want to make sure that it stays in place. We will show that one of the best single predictors of success in the lobbying game is not how much money an organization has on its side, but simply whether it is attempting to protect the policy that is already in place.

Issues, Sides, Advocates, and the Mobilization of Power

We have an unusual approach to the study of lobbying and power, and it is helpful to offer more detail on what we did and to introduce some vocabulary that we will use throughout this book. (Our appendix provides much more detail on the material that follows, and our Web site even more than that.) During our interviews, we asked our respondents to identify the major players on each side of the debate. This typically elicited a list of government officials and other outside advocates who shared the goals of the advocate we interviewed, and a set of actors in opposition. Sometimes there were others mentioned as well, sets of actors who were not necessarily opposed to what the advocate was trying to accomplish, but seeking another outcome nonetheless. We have defined a "side" as a set of actors who share a policy goal. Note that these actors may or may not be working together; we call them a side if they seek the same outcome even if they do not coordinate their activities.

Table A.1 lays out the full set of sides on each issue, the number of major players we identified from each side, and the number of interviews we conducted. As the table makes clear, we identified 214 sides over our 98 issues. We attempted to interview a leading representative from each side on the issue, and in each interview we continued to ask the same questions about who was involved. After two or three interviews and after perusing documents related to the case, we usually had a complete picture of the issue and the advocates involved in it and further interviews typically added few new details and no new actors to our list. The most common single goal across our 214 sides is, not surprisingly, to protect the status quo from a proposed change.

The number of sides per issue ranges from just one to as many as seven, but typically is just two: one side seeking some particular type of change to the existing policy and another side seeking to protect the status quo. We will have much more to say about the relatively simple constellation of conflict that we observed in our cases in later chapters. The number of advocates on each side is determined by our count of "major players." We defined a major player as an advocate mentioned by others (or, occasionally, who was revealed through our subsequent documentary searches) as playing a prominent and important role in the debate. The number of major players per side, as shown in table A.1 ranges from just one to over fifty, but is typically in the single digits. Overall, we identified 2,221 advocates across our 98 cases, for an average of 23 actors per case. Note that to be included in a side, a major actor must be actively supporting the goals of that side; that is, they must be actively advocating either the retention of the status quo or some policy change. Government decision makers who play a neutral role but who may be the object of considerable lobbying by others are not included even though they may have come up many times in our interviews.

We discovered very few neutral decision makers. To be sure, we did observe situations where important roles were assigned to officials who were not actively promoting any particular policy outcome. The actions of these officials may have mattered greatly to others, and they may have even been the targets of active lobbying, but they are not a "major player" in our study because they were not advocates for any "side." These officials were most often agency officials or technical staff in such offices as the Office of Management and Budget, the Congressional Budget Office, or the Centers for Medicare and Medicaid Services (e.g., those whose technical cost estimates of proposed policy changes may have a large impact on the debate). But for the most part, when a government official was mentioned in our interviews as being involved in an issue, that official clearly had a preferred side in the debate and was actively working to further that side. Although much of the literature seems to promote a view on lobbying that presents governmental actors in relatively neutral positions as the targets, but not the sources, of lobbying, we found few such individuals, especially not in the ranks of committee chairs or other leaders.[7] Much more common than these neutral decision makers were government officials who themselves were policy advocates working hand-in-hand with other members of the same side, urging a particular policy outcome, and actively lobbying others. In fact, about 40 percent of the advocates in our study were government officials themselves, not outside lobbyists. That is why we typically use the term *advocate* rather than the more common term *lobbyist*. It turns out that many advocates are already inside the government, not on the outside looking in.[8]

For every major interest group actor we identified (including those whom we did not interview), we systematically gathered information from publicly available sources relating to their political and monetary resources. We explain these searches in detail in the appendix, but suffice it to say that we know everything it is possible to collect about their membership, budget, annual revenues, number of employees, hired lobbyists, lobbying and PAC expenditures, and more. We also know their positions and talking points on the issues, as we systematically downloaded all information about the relevant issues on which they were active from their Web sites and also looked for congressional statements, speeches, and hearing testimonies. Of course, we did newspaper and television searches as well, to find out what was being said about the issue in the press. In sum, we are able to record systematic information about each of over 2,200 major actors we identified across our 98 randomly selected issues.

Finally, through follow-up interviews and by tracking publicly available information (such as congressional dockets), we were able to find out what eventually occurred on the issue. Because a side is defined as a set of advocates who are seeking the same policy goal, we could then assign a value at the end of our study of that issue (approximately four years later) as to whether this side had achieved none, some, or all of its goals. Of course it gets more complicated than that, as there are different types of goals, but the general idea is simple. For each of our issues, we constructed as complete a map as possible of who was involved, what resources they controlled, what arguments and strategies they used, and what eventually occurred. Did they (and their allies) get what they wanted, or not? Before the reader asks the question as to why no political scientist has done this before, we hasten to point out that five of us have been working on this project, with dozens of student assistants, for more than eight years. The scope of the project has been daunting, but we believe it provides us with strong evidence for our conclusions.

Advocates, In and Out of Government

About 59 percent of the major actors were lobbyists from various organized interests, while 41 percent were government officials. Tables 1.1 and 1.2 give an overview of the types of lobbyists and government officials we found to be active on our issues.

Interest groups

Table 1.1 shows the distribution of the 1,244 lobbyists by the type of organization that they represent. The table shows that citizen groups are the most frequently cited type of major participant in these policy debates.[9] About 26 percent of the groups in our study are citizen groups, or organizations representing an issue or cause without any direct connection to a business or profession. Trade associations and business associations like the Chamber of Commerce represent 21 percent of the total mentions. Individual businesses lobbying on their own behalf make up 14 percent of the total; professional associations, which represent individuals in a particular

TABLE 1.1 **Major Interest-Group Participants**

Group type	Number	Percentage
Citizen groups	329	26
Trade and business associations	265	21
Business corporations	179	14
Professional associations	140	11
Coalitions specific to the issue	90	7
Unions	77	6
Foundations and think tanks	71	6
Governmental associations	38	3
Institutions and associations of institutions	20	2
Other	35	3
Total	1,244	100

profession (such as the American Medical Association or the American Political Science Association), constitute 11 percent of the total.

Formal coalitions specific to the issue at hand make up 7 percent of the total. Although unions are one of the most often mentioned "special interest groups" in the popular press, here (as in virtually all previous studies of advocacy in Washington) they make up a relatively small part of the total interest-group community: just 6 percent.[10] The seventy-seven mentions of unions reflected in the table, while small compared to mentions of other types of groups, actually overstates the number of unions that are active, because many of these are repeated mentions of the same unions. In fact, six unions make up more than half of the mentions of unions in our database.[11] By comparison, among large trade associations and peak associations like the U.S. Chamber of Commerce, the top six trade associations make up only 16 percent of the mentions of trade groups in our issues.[12] So while unions quite often play a prominent role in policy debates, it often is overlooked that the labor sector is really just a handful of organizations compared to the much larger number of businesses and trade associations that are represented in these same issues. The few union organizations that are active in Washington are well financed and highly professional, but those resources and skills must be spread across an exceptionally wide range of issues compared with other types of groups. In contrast, trade and corporate lobbyists typically have a much larger staff to focus on a smaller number of key issues.

Think tanks and foundations, like unions, represented 6 percent of the total, but it was rare to see a think tank or foundation mentioned in relation to more than one or two issues. Two other types of groups each represented less than 3 percent of the total: governmental associations such as the National Governors Association; and nonprofit institutions such as hospitals and universities, combined with associations of such institutions. The catch-all "other" category includes churches, individual experts, international NGOs, and two advocates whose type could not be determined.

The most striking feature of this distribution of interest group lobbyists is the predominance of citizen groups in these debates. Since our sample was weighted by activity, businesses were much more likely to appear as issue identifiers in our initial interviews than were citizen groups, as we will show in detail below. As we conducted interviews and researched the issues named by the businesses and others, however, citizen groups were routinely named as central actors in many issues. Citizen groups are thus more important to policy debates than simple numbers would indicate, because, like certain unions, they tend to be active and recognized as major players on many issues. Kay Schlozman and John Tierney's 1986 study, which weighted its interview sample by how active the organizations were in Washington, painted a picture of the Washington advocacy community that showed 30 percent businesses, 26 percent trade associations, and 18 percent citizen groups.[13] The 1996 federal lobbying disclosure reports, from which we drew our sampling frame for this study, showed that businesses make up more than 40 percent of the registrants, with trade associations second in number, and citizen groups a distant third, comprising only about 14 percent of the registrations. We were therefore far more likely to interview a lobbyist for a business or business organization in our initial issue-identification interviews than we were to interview a lobbyist for a citizen group. And yet table 1.1 shows that citizen groups were nearly twice as likely as individual businesses to be mentioned in our interviews as major participants. Citizen groups may spend less on lobbying and lobby on fewer issues than business organizations, but when they do lobby, they are more likely to be considered an important actor in the policy dispute. Jeffrey Berry, in his book *The New Liberalism*, found a similar pattern. Citizen groups—in particular liberal citizen groups—were dominant actors in the congressional issues and media coverage he examined.[14]

These findings are good and bad news for citizen groups and labor unions, the two types of groups who stand out for being involved in many issues per group. On the one hand, they show that the groups are active and are recognized by other players in Washington as playing a fundamental role in a great variety of our sample of issues. Further, they may indicate the degree to which other players in Washington take them seriously. The groups often have great public legitimacy. As journalists like to find a controversy in any story or to tell the drama of the underdog who comes out on top, citizen groups may provide the divergent perspective that gives the issue some punch.

On the other hand, with fewer resources than organizations from the business community, citizen groups are often spread thin. Like labor unions, they are often requested to become involved in many more issues than they have the resources to cover deeply. And when they do get involved in, say, an issue relating to consumer credit practices by banks, or an environmental dispute related to coal-mining practices, or automobile emissions standards, they often find themselves in a David and Goliath position, with a few staff members on their side facing sometimes hundreds of industry lobbyists or researchers who work on nothing but that one particular issue year-in and year-out. The American Petroleum Institute, for example, has about 270 staff and an annual budget of $42 million. All these people are not lobbyists, of course, and the budget goes for many things, to be sure, but the Institute deals only with petroleum issues. When the issue shifts to nuclear energy, the Nuclear Energy Institute, with 125 staff members and a budget of $34 million, may get involved. Electrical generation in general? The Edison Electric Institute will be there, with its 200 staff and $50 million annual budget.[15]

There is no question which side, producers or consumers, has more financial resources for Washington lobbying, so there is reason for citizen groups to be discouraged, and one might expect them to lose most of the time. But, as we will see, citizen groups often have resources that go beyond finances. In addition, organizations rarely lobby alone. Citizen groups, like others, typically participate in policy debates alongside other actors of many types who share the same goals. For every citizen group opposing an action by a given industrial group, for example, there may also be an ally coming from a competing industry with which the group can join forces. Further, ideological or public-policy agreements can give citizen groups powerful allies within government, at least on some issues. Putting together a strong coalition to work toward a policy outcome often involves recruiting some major citizen groups to come along. They play a much larger role than simple numbers would imply.

Figure 1.1 shows the frequency with which interest groups of various types were in two parts of our sample: the initial "issue identifiers" who were selected based on their frequency of lobbying activities, and the "major participants" in our issues, including not only those whom we interviewed first, but all those whom we identified as playing a major role on the issue.

Individual corporations, trade associations, and professional groups constitute 74 percent of the issue identifiers in our sample, but they collectively represent only 48 percent of the major participants. Citizen groups, representing just 15 percent of the issue identifiers, are 26 percent of the major participants. Because the initial issue identifiers were selected by a sampling procedure that weighted proportionately by the level of lobbying activity, those numbers reflect the lobbying community in Washington (and indeed, the heavy skew in favor of the business community is consistent with previous findings, as discussed above). In looking at the percentage of all major participants coming from different sectors of the interest-group community, on the other hand, we see who is more prominent. Citizen groups speak more loudly than their numbers suggest. There

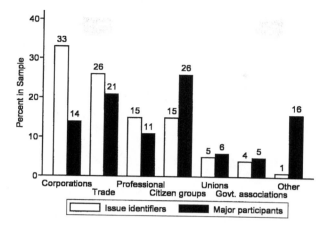

FIGURE I.I. Types of interest-group participants.

are two caveats to this, however. First, as suggested above, the citizen groups find themselves out-matched in terms of resources, as there are so many more occupationally based groups in Washington. Second, who is setting the agenda? The list of issues in our sample clearly reflects the occupational basis of much of the Washington lobbying community. Further, the issue identifiers tend to control significantly more material resources than others. Probably because of their corporate and professional background, the identifiers are systematically wealthier than others. We will detail in later chapters our efforts to summarize the control of various material resources by the advocates we identified in each of our cases, but suffice it to say that we have done a very complete job. When we construct an overall index of the control of resources (e.g., PAC contributions, lobbying expenditures, lobbying staff, and so on), we find that the identifiers, and the sides with which they are associated, are indeed wealthier than the others.[16] We will return to these issues of wealth bias in the agenda below and in later chapters.

Advocacy within government

Our list of major advocates includes nearly 900 government officials. As noted earlier, far from being merely the object of lobbying activity from outside interests, governmental advocates comprise more than 40 percent of the advocacy universe; table 1.2 shows the numbers of different types of government officials who were mentioned as leading advocates.

TABLE 1.2 **Major Governmental Participants**

Group type	Number	Percentage
Rank-and-file Republican	186	21
Rank-and-file Democrat	179	21
Republican committee or subcommittee chair or ranking member	172	20
Democratic committee or subcommittee chair or ranking member	151	17
Executive branch department or agency	100	12
Democratic leadership	23	3
White House	20	2
Nonnational government (e.g., governors, mayors, local officials)	10	1
Other congressional body	8	1
Total	873	100

Table 1.2 shows that the most frequently mentioned category of government official in the issues we studied was rank-and-file members of Congress. Reflecting the relatively close partisan division in Congress, Republicans and Democrats were mentioned in virtually equal numbers—21 percent each. It is not surprising that committee and subcommittee leaders from both parties (the chair of the committee or the ranking member of the committee) were also frequently mentioned—20 percent of the major participants were Republican committee leaders and 17 percent of the major participants were Democratic committee leaders. Executive branch department and agency officials were 11 percent of the total. Party leaders, on the other hand, are not mentioned often as major participants. Similarly, there were few mentions of the White House, other congressional bodies, or actors outside the federal government (governors, for example). These data make clear that issues typically are dealt with among specialized communities where members of Congress, relevant committee and agency officials, and only a few other government officials become involved.

We can look at these data in another way; instead of asking what percentage of the total participation each type of government official represented, we show in table 1.3 how many of our ninety-eight cases included at least one government official of each type. This clearly shows the specialized nature of most policy issues.

Table 1.3 shows that about two-thirds of all cases include rank-and-file members of Congress and committee and subcommittee leadership from both parties. Executive departments and agencies were close behind, mentioned as major participants in 56 of our 98 issues. House and Senate party leadership officials and members of the White House staff are involved in 20 or fewer of the issues, by contrast. Some of this may seem surprising—as

TABLE 1.3 **Number of Issues with Each Type of Governmental Actor**

Group type	Number of issues
Republican committee or subcommittee chair or ranking member	67
Rank-and-file Republican	67
Rank-and-file Democrat	66
Democratic committee or subcommittee chair or ranking member	59
Executive branch department or agency	56
Democratic leadership	20
Republican leadership	18
White House	16
Other congressional body	7
Nonnational government (e.g., governors, mayors, local officials)	7
Total Issues	98

Note: The numbers show how many of our 98 issues included the indicated type of government advocate. Government advocates are included only if they took an active role in promoting a certain position on the issue, not merely because they held a decision-making role regarding the issue.

we will note in chapter 11, few issues see a change in policy if party leaders oppose them. The party leaders were not central advocates for most of our issues, however. If agenda setting and advocacy were primarily a top-down process in Congress, we would see many more mentions of party leaders or party leadership as central figures in these debates. Instead, they are important primarily in their role as gatekeepers. By comparison, executive department personnel, rank-and-file members of Congress, and committee and subcommittee chairs and ranking members are each mentioned in similar numbers of issues, ranging from 56 to 67 of the cases. Policy making is a bottom-up process that is relatively porous for advocates.

The Lobbying Agenda and the Public Agenda

Our sample of issues is broad, ranging from a line item in the defense budget to such high-profile debates as late-term (partial-birth) abortion, trade with China, and health care reform. But for the most part our issues lay at neither of these extremes. Readers may want to take a moment to review the list of issues and the sides we identified for each issue, as reported in the appendix, table A.1. This table simply lists the name as well as the opposing sides of each issue in our sample. Only two of our issues—a defense appropriations bill line item that required no expenditures and an amendment to make federal safety officers eligible for an existing housing program for law enforcement officials—could be considered small, private issues without cost to taxpayers or broad policy implications. And only four of our issues were prominent enough to have been the topic of any interest-group televised issue advertisements.[17] Most of our issues were in the middle in terms of size and salience, for example, providing better access for commuter railroads, FCC rules for religious broadcast licenses, and changing the retirement age for commercial airline pilots.

The agenda of lobbying is significantly different from the congressional agenda overall or from the public's list of major concerns. Table 1.4 compares the issue areas where we found our lobbyists to be active with data taken from the Policy Agendas Project (www.policyagendas.org) showing for the period of our study the number of congressional hearings held, laws passed, presidential statements in the State of the Union Address, and public responses to the Gallup Poll question "What is the most important problem facing the nation today?"[18] The Policy Agendas Project makes available historical information about the activities of the U.S. federal government such as laws, bills, executive orders, and congressional hearings. All the data in the Policy Agendas Project are coded into a single classification system, based on nineteen major topics of activity (and further broken down into some 226 more precise subtopics). We have classified our ninety-eight issues by this same topic system, providing a simple way to compare the agendas of the Washington lobbying community with other agendas, most importantly perhaps with the concerns of the public as expressed in public opinion polls.

The table is sorted by the frequency of the cases in our sample, and in the right-most column we see the percentage of the public that identified that same issue area as containing the nation's "most important problem." Crime tops the list for the public, but not for the lobbyists. The state of the economy comes second for the public, but not for the lobbyists. International affairs (that is, the threat of terrorism and war) is third for the public, but lobbyists have a different agenda. In fact, the table shows that there is no single agenda in Washington.

About 20 percent of all of our issues fall in the area of health policy. This should not be a surprise to anyone who has followed politics in Washington over the past decade. Health care reform and health care related issues have been ubiquitous in national politics. Eighteen percent of all federal lobbying reports filed by interest groups in 2000 were on topics related to health, disease, Medicare, or prescription drugs, so our sample of issues reflects this mobilization of lobbyists quite accurately.[19] The second most frequent policy area was the environment, followed closely by

TABLE 1.4 **The Lobbying Agenda Compared to Other Agendas**

Policy topic	Lobbying issues in sample	Congressional hearings[a] (%)	Laws[a] (%)	Statements in the state of the union speech[a] (%)	Public opinion[a,b] (%)
Health	21	9	3	9	8
Environment	13	5	4	3	2
Transportation	8	5	3	0	0
Science, technology, and communication	7	5	2	3	1
Banking, finance, and commerce	7	8	4	1	0
Defense and national security	7	7	6	5	5
Foreign trade	6	2	2	3	0
Energy	5	4	1	1	2
Law, crime, and family policy	5	6	5	8	26
Education	5	4	2	12	10
Government operations	3	12	19	1	6
Labor, employment, immigration	3	4	4	6	2
Macroeconomics and taxation	2	3	1	12	19
Social welfare	2	2	1	9	7
Community development and housing	2	1	1	1	0
Agriculture	1	3	2	1	0
International affairs and foreign aid	1	11	5	18	10
Civil rights	0	2	1	4	3
Public lands and interior affairs	0	8	32	2	0
Total N	98	5,926	764	1,113	

Note: The table displays the distribution of our 98 issues by topic area and gives comparable information from the Policy Agendas Project. For each column, cell entries indicate the percentage of observations that fall within the 19 topic areas listed in the rows. Data cover the period of the 106th and 107th Congresses.
[a]Congressional, presidential, and public opinion data come from the Policy Agendas Project (www.policyagendas.org).
[b]Public opinion refers to the responses to the question of what is the most important problem facing the nation.

banking, finance, and commerce; defense and national security; and science, technology, and communication. Overall, the issues presented here represent a wide range of policy areas and our sample of issues covers 17 of the 19 policy areas used in the Policy Agendas Project. The only topics not represented are civil rights/civil liberties and public lands. Even those two issues arise as secondary aspects of two of our issues—one of our crime issues involves attempts at a civil rights framing, and one of our environmental issues involves logging roads in national forests.

The result of our method of sampling is a broad range of policy issues that provides a representative look at the role of interest groups in the policy process. We will return in our conclusion to the vast disparities between the lobbying agenda and other agendas, including that of the public. But our book is about what advocates are doing, and we are confident that our sample of issues reflects the broad range of their concerns. Most of these deal with professions, industries, and businesses.[20] To the extent that they engage the concerns of citizen groups, they largely reflect the postmaterialist values of the environmental movement, not the nitty-gritty worries of the poor and the unemployed.[21]

One aspect that may be surprising to many students of politics is how few of our issues were in the public eye. Although these were primarily active policy issues involving competing interest groups and multiple members of Congress, most of them received little or no news coverage in mainstream media outlets during the time of our study. Twelve of our 98 issues had no newspaper coverage, and ten had no news coverage of any kind. Even among those that had newspaper coverage—which was the most common sort of coverage—half of the issues had 15 or fewer news stories published in the 29 major U.S. newspapers indexed by Lexis-Nexis—so the average American would have likely seen little to nothing at all about them from any media source. More than 70 percent of our issues had no TV news coverage, and only about half were mentioned in the *National Journal*, a weekly policy magazine that is widely read by policy makers and lobbyists in Washington. Even an active political observer would likely be unaware of most of our issues, unless the issue happened to be in a policy area in which he or she regularly participated. Most of the time, on most issues, lobbyists work at very low levels of public visibility, and our sample reflects this.

Our sample may be full of low-salience issues, but these issues were central to the activities of scores of members of Congress, agency officials, and interest-group lobbyists during the period when we did our fieldwork. They almost uniformly were important policy issues, with the potential to have broad effects on taxpayers, businesses, and citizens. An average of nine congressional bills were introduced and three congressional hearings were held on each of our issues. Variation was wide, however, and 6 of our issues had no bills at all and 35 were the subject of no hearings. Only about half of our issues (51) reached the stage where a floor vote was held in either chamber, when all members would have the chance to weigh in on it. Many previous studies of interest-group influence have focused exclusively on issues that reached the floor-vote stage.[22] Most of our issues were focused on congressional activities, but substantially more than half of them included at least one executive department or agency as a prominent policy advocate—not just as a target of lobbying, but as an advocate, pushing a particular viewpoint on the issue. Our study clearly illustrates the idea of "separate branches sharing power"; the legislature and the executive are mutually involved in the vast majority of our cases.

Public Policy and Changes to Public Policy

To study lobbying is to study efforts to change existing public policies. This is the first of four basic observations with which we begin our book and from which we can deduce some of our most important findings. In this section we lay out these expectations. Our four starting points are not theoretical assumptions; in fact each should be completely uncontroversial. Further, they are borne out empirically by our study, not simply assertions with which we begin. However, these four factors alone go far in explaining some of our most important and most surprising findings, so we lay them out in some detail here. The four points are simple: First, lobbying is about changing existing public policies. Second, policies are complex, with multiple and contradictory effects on diverse constituencies. Third, following from the previous fact, "sides" mobilized to protect or to change the status quo tend to be quite heterogeneous. And, fourth, attention in Washington is scarce. Let us consider these in turn.

Changing an existing policy

Each of the cases in our sample features an existing public policy, not an effort to establish an entirely new policy from scratch. This fact has fundamental and perhaps surprising implications for the study of lobbying, however, implications insufficiently recognized in previous studies or journalistic reports. Most importantly, it implies that whatever bias in the mobilization of various social, business, and corporate interests may exist in Washington, this bias should already be reflected in the status quo. That is, existing public policy is already the fruit of policy discussions, debates, accumulated wisdom, and negotiated compromises made by policy makers in previous iterations of the policy struggle. Further, if the wealthy are better mobilized and more prone to get what they want in Washington, they should already have gotten what they wanted in previous rounds of the policy process.

No matter what biases may exist in Washington, any current lobbying activity starts out with these previous decisions as the starting point. Unless something important has changed in terms of the inputs to the decision-making process (e.g., a new set of policy makers, important new evidence about a policy alternative, a new understanding of an issue, a newly mobilized interest group), there is little reason to expect the outputs to change. If we assume that wealth or interest-group mobilization is related to power, then *changes* in power should be related to *changes* in mobilization and statistically uncorrelated to *preexisting levels* of power or mobilization.[23] This is as simple as its implications are profound for the study of lobbying.

We will explore in detail whether the wealthy typically win in Washington, and, to the surprise of many readers, we will show that they often do not. The reason, we think, is not because they lack power, but because the status quo already reflects that power. After all, if they are so powerful, why would policy be so distasteful to them? Logically, they should have mobilized to correct problems in the past. In any case, political scientists and journalists alike have typically studied the lobbying efforts of various interest groups as if there was no established status quo policy already in place. That simple fact has enormous implications.

We noted above that changes in policy should be related to changes in mobilization, not to levels of mobilization. Of course, there may be many times when levels of mobilization do change. Elections intervene, bringing new leaders into office. Committee chairs or agency heads resign or are replaced, putting the allies of different groups into power, thus changing their access and influence. New technical information comes to light, changing the parameters of a previously settled policy dispute. Demographic or economic trends evolve in such ways that policies get increasingly out of synch with the problems they are designed to address. Interest groups mobilize with greater vigor or focus on an issue they had previously not prioritized. We will address all of these possibilities in the chapters to come, and indeed we do find that they affect the policy-making equation. In the short term, however, such things do not vary much and do not necessarily correlate with the distribution of material resources. Sometimes, such trends or developments might help one side; sometimes, the other.[24]

Complex impacts on diverse constituencies

Our second starting point is that not only are existing policies virtually always in place, but these policies have complex impacts on diverse constituencies. Not a single one of the policies we studied could be considered to be one-dimensional in terms of substantive impact; each one had diverse effects on multiple groups. For example, the vast majority of the issues had some kind of budgetary implication with respect to the federal government, states and localities, or private businesses and consumers. In addition to whatever substantive impact the policy may have had, it also reflected people's diverse views on the proper size of the regulatory state.

The complexity of existing public policies is much greater than only this, however. Different policies differentially affect urban and rural areas or various geographical regions, professional groups, and ethnic constituencies. A policy that promotes freer trade with China may be argued from a dimension of its impact on growers of certain agricultural commodities, textile manufacturers, consumers, or retail sellers of shoes, or from a perspective focusing on human rights, international engagement, national security, or environmental protection. An issue relating to the disposal of used nuclear fuel rods may be argued from the perspective of sound environmental policy, whether the federal government can force a state to accept waste from other regions of the country, the possibility of predicting geological stability over tens of thousands of years, the safety of transporting nuclear waste over the nation's aging railway infrastructure, reducing terrorist threats, or the future of the nuclear power industry in the face of global climate change. Each of our cases was subject to a dizzying array of complicated and sometimes unrelated arguments. Indeed, the diverse impacts on such a wide range of potential constituencies that characterize all the issues we studied may well be the reason why the existing policies are in place. If they had only an isolated impact on a single policy community or political constituency, they may never have generated enough political support to have been enacted in the first place. Hence, a second common element in our cases, besides being about existing public policies, is their inherent multidimensionality.

The diversity of sides mobilized to work together

Third, following directly from the multidimensional effects on diverse constituencies of most public policies, the "sides" that mobilize, either to demand change or to protect the status quo, are likely to be highly diverse. In spite of journalistic accounts suggesting that much lobbying involves a single corporation attempting to get a single favor or contract with no broader implications for others, such "lone ranger" lobbying is far from the norm. More commonly, advocates are lobbying to change or to protect an existing public policy with diverse effects on a number of constituencies. The sides that get mobilized to protect the status quo or to demand change are rarely homogeneous.

The scarcity of attention

Our fourth point of departure, which like the ones above is also borne out in our data, is very simple: attention in Washington is scarce. The information environment in Washington is overwhelmingly complex, with thousands of bills being considered each year in Congress, hundreds of hearings occurring in more than a hundred different subcommittees, and public concerns moving from issue to issue at a rapid pace.[25] Evidence that follows in subsequent chapters shows that one of the most difficult tasks for many lobbyists is simply to gain the attention of other players in Washington. Considering the crush of important problems that the nation does face, merely having a reasonable solution to a problem is not usually enough; in order to merit the time and attention of a large number of Washington policy makers, the problem the policy addresses must be substantial. Even serious problems affecting small constituencies may face obstacles unrelated to any active opposition to the proposed policy improvement, but simply due to the scarcity of space on the public agenda.

Expectations

These four observations are enough for us to deduce a series of what may appear to be surprising expectations. In the following chapters we will test these hypotheses and show them to be largely borne out by our data. The ideas are as follows:

1. The relation between control over material resources and gaining the policy goals that one wants in Washington is likely to be close to zero.
2. Because the status quo already reflects the distribution of power in previous rounds of the policy process, the mobilization of resources to change the status quo versus to protect it is likely to be relatively equal in most cases.

3. Because of the complexity of most public policies, the distribution of forces seeking to change or to protect the status quo policy will typically be quite diverse. That is, the actors working on various sides of the issue are likely to be heterogeneous.

4. Because of the diversity of resources controlled by individual lobbying organizations (and the government officials with whom they are allied), the linkage between material resources and policy outcomes will be lower at the individual level (that is, considering individual lobbyists) than it is at the aggregate level (that is, considering the combined resources of entire "sides"). In neither case is it likely to be substantial.

5. Usually, policies will be stable. When policies do change, the change is more likely to be substantial than it is to be marginal.

6. In those cases where there is an imbalanced mobilization (e.g., where one side is much more highly mobilized than a rival side), the side with more resources will prevail. Further, the ability of a wealthy side to gain what it wants when opposed to a relatively weak side will be stronger when the wealthy side seeks to protect the status quo. We expect imbalanced mobilizations to be rare, however, because of points 1 through 3 above. On average, mobilizations are likely to be relatively balanced, sides to be heterogeneous, and outcomes to be unrelated to resources.

Readers may be surprised by these expectations, as they go against decades of study of policy change and lobbying and seem to fly in the face of the obvious assumption: of course the wealthy win in Washington. We would simply say: If the wealthy are so certain to win, they should already have won in a previous iteration of the process. Since the distribution of power should already be reflected in the status quo, there is no reason that *changes* to the status quo, which is what lobbying is about, would necessarily move in the direction of even further gains for the wealthy (nor systematically against them). After all, if the status quo reflects a rough equilibrium of power, and we believe it does (and a quite unfair equilibrium in many cases, with much greater benefits going to the privileged and the wealthy than to the needy and the poor), then changes to the equilibrium should reflect only changes to the mobilization of these interests. In the short term, such changes are likely to be random.

We described above how substantively complex most issues of public policy are and how they often have diverse effects on many different constituencies. This implies that proposed changes to such policies would stimulate diverse reactions from the various groups who might be affected by them, and there is little reason to expect these reactions to be all in the same direction. In those cases where we do observe a one-sided mobilization of wealth, then yes, of course, we do expect that side to win. But we expect that such lopsided mobilizations are rare. After all, if the policy was having an overwhelmingly terrible impact on such a broad range of powerful actors, how did it get enacted in the first place? Lobbying battles often pit sides of relatively equal mobilization and resources against each other, because many diverse constituencies are often affected by proposed changes to complex public policies. It is of course possible that the continued operation of a policy, unchanged, may have drifted over the years or decades to a point where it was having a substantially new effect on some constituency. Or new economic or technological developments may create inequities over time. In such cases, we could see relatively one-sided mobilizations of bias, with many organizations mobilizing to demand a change and few countermobilizing to protect the status quo. We do expect that this will occur from time to time, and when it does we would expect the wealthy side to achieve what it wants. However, there are two reasons why they might not. First, constituencies may mobilize before the disparities become so obvious; why would the aggrieved wait twenty years to right a wrong that has become patently obvious? In reality, the mobilization may come much sooner than that, and this means that the battles will be much more closely fought. Second, if they do mobilize prematurely, the scarcity of attention in Congress may make it difficult for them to gain significant space on the agenda.

One of our expectations, number five in the list above, may not be obvious given our set of starting assumptions; why would policy changes be substantial rather than marginal, once they do occur? We will explore these reasons in greater detail in chapter 2, but they relate mostly to the scarcity of attention and the general equality of resources expended on various sides of the lobbying equation. There are cases where mobilizations are uneven for reasons explored above. More importantly, defenders of the status quo benefit from many advantages in the policy process, perhaps the most important of which is simply the lack of time to address all issues that might deserve consideration. The friction associated with the scarcity of attention also implies that when things do find space on the agenda, it is often the result of quite large mobilizations, and when policies do change, the change is less likely to be slight tinkering, but rather to reflect more substantively important changes.

Challenging Assumptions

From the immediately preceding discussion, it should be obvious that the coming chapters are going to challenge many common assumptions about the nature of power and influence in American politics. While it may be better to be wealthy than poor when lobbying in Washington, we find surprisingly weak links between material resources and moving public policy in one's preferred direction. The causes for this are complex but interesting. For example, the wealthy often oppose the wealthy. Similarly, our results suggest that the impact of partisanship and elections may be significantly less than is often assumed, though again we find important nuances to this general conclusion. We begin in chapter 2 with a detailed discussion of the causes of policy change in general.

One particularly important aspect of the lobbying game that seems often to be overlooked is the fundamental role played by elected officials. We have already noted, of course, that these officials are rarely neutral, but rather are advocates themselves, actively using their influence to affect the terms of the debate and lobbying others.[26] Scholars since David Price, Robert Salisbury, and Ken Shepsle have emphasized the importance of individual congressional offices in creating policy initiatives.[27] Salisbury and Shepsle in particular conceive of the congressional office as an "enterprise" in which the member is looking for issues on which to make a reputation. In order to run for higher office, after all, one must point to a number of policy-related accomplishments, so elected officials are not simply following the dictates of the special interests, but also looking for the opportunity to advance public policy in some direction that they believe will be popular with voters or good for the country. Richard Fenno's ethnographic wanderings through congressional offices led to his conclusion that members of Congress have three goals: reelection, influence within the chamber, and "good public policy."[28] We should not discount the importance of the policy goals of elected officials themselves, and in later chapters we will see just how hard it can be for even wealthy interest groups to overcome the active opposition of key government officials.

We will argue that the sources of stability in politics are much broader than the political science literature suggests and point to the importance of the existing networks of policy makers, interest groups, and other experts in maintaining the status quo. The strength of the status quo means that when change occurs, it tends to be significant rather than incremental. Further, this stability rests not on a thin infrastructure of institutional rules and arrangements, but on a much firmer foundation. Entire professional communities, complex constellations of actors with different elements of concern, keep existing policies in place until pressures build for large numbers of them to change their positions. Institutional rules matter, but the stability stems from forces much larger than only this.

Of course, what is a "significant" policy change and what is not is often in the eyes of the beholder, as we discuss further in chapter 2. But when the choice is between the status quo and a policy that will make it harder to declare bankruptcy to protect assets, the change certainly feels significant to overextended consumers. When a new trade policy will potentially create billions of dollars in new investment in China, the change is certainly significant to the businesses it will affect. When a new policy will force all hospitals in the United States to buy a new type of needle for injections and will lead manufacturers to make millions more of those needles, the change does not seem insignificant to hospital accountants, the needle manufacturers, or the health care workers who now are better protected from HIV/AIDS. In most of our cases, the difference between the status quo and the proposed policy would mean important changes for the businesses and individuals covered by that policy. Many of the policies we discuss in the chapters to come involve policy changes that, if adopted, would impose billions of dollars of new costs (or open up the possibility of similar levels of new benefits).

We argue in chapters 2 and 3 that this tendency toward nonincremental change is in large part *caused* by the strength of the status quo. Because powerful forces—both social and institutional—protect the status quo, it takes an even more powerful set of pressures to produce change. The coalescing of advocates from within and outside of government is a start, but often external changes in the policy environment are required as well. Pressures build, but no change occurs until the pressures are sufficient to overcome the inertia of the status quo. When this threshold is passed, the momentum for change usually takes the policy response beyond a true incrementalist response.

In chapters 4 through 8 we review interest group resources, tactics, and arguments and the effects of partisanship and elections. The analysis shows tremendous skew in the resources available to individual interest groups, as many studies have found in the past. However, we also show a surprising tendency for sides to be heterogeneous, for reasons laid out earlier in this chapter. Further, our review of interest-group tactics and arguments shows the various ways in which those protecting the status quo are advantaged. Many arguments (such as one simply focusing on uncertainty and unknown consequences of policy change) and many tactics (such as maintaining close contact with relevant government officials) systematically differentiate those who would protect versus those who would change the status quo. Our review of the impact of partisanship and elections continues our review of the systematic differences between our competing sides. Chapter 9 presents some of our most surprising findings, those focusing on the difficulty of reframing policy issues, and our explanation for this. We found few cases of reframing, even though we followed the issues for four years. The large policy communities of experts and professionals surrounding each issue go far in explaining the stability that we observe for most issues most of the time.

There are many complications to the story of the impact of money in the lobbying process, and we deal with these questions in some depth in chapters 10 and 11. One of the more interesting twists on this argument stems from our use of the concept of lobbying "sides" in the policy struggle. As we discussed above, it turns out that sides are typically heterogeneous. That is, the rich do not just ally with the rich and the poor with the poor, but rather groups of allies are mixed. Interest groups with low levels of resources are as likely to be allied with interest groups with high levels of resources as with other low-resource groups. These mixed alliances help to temper the role of money in the political process. None of our findings should be interpreted to suggest that it is preferable to be poor than rich in Washington. But when we look for a direct and simple relationship between money and policy change, it is not there.

The power of the status quo extends not only to policies themselves, but also to the ways lobbyists, journalists, and officials think and talk about those policies, as we discuss in chapter 9. Politicians, elected officials, and interest groups spend huge amounts of time trying to spin new and more advantageous ways for others to view their issues, and we encountered these efforts repeatedly during our time in Washington. It turns out, however, that it is much easier to formulate a new frame—the political science word for spin—than it is to have that frame adopted by others in the policy community. Framing at the individual level goes on all the time. All it takes is for someone to turn a phrase and focus on a different aspect of a problem. But reframing at the macro level, at the level of the entire policy community—a process also known as issue redefinition—is actually quite rare. Generally accepted frames tend to endure for a long time.

We will go through these and other findings systematically in the chapters to come. However, at the end of this chapter we should introduce one fundamental element of our interpretation of our findings, one to which we will return in the conclusion. No matter what we find about the linkages between the mobilization of power on various sides of the issues we have studied, the hard fact is that this mobilization itself is heavily skewed. And it's skewed not just toward the wealthy, but more generally toward professional communities of corporations, professionals, and institutions and therefore away from average citizens. One need not adopt a class-based approach to the study of lobbying in the United States to recognize that K Street is full of well-paid representatives of corporate America. The airlines are more likely to be present in the lobbying community than the diffuse group of people who often suffer through terrible service as airline customers. The bias is not just a corporate one; this is an oversimplification. More accurately, it is a bias toward professions and occupations. Many Americans may share an opinion, an ideology, or a feeling. But they are dramatically less likely to mobilize and join an interest group with a powerful Washington presence on the basis of these shared interests than they are to be a member of a professional association or labor union or be employed by a company or an institution that has substantial representation in Washington.

There are only two ways to change these hard facts. Either such constituencies need to mobilize, or our elected officials must do a better job of recognizing whose voices are amplified through the corridors of power as reflected on K Street, whose voices are muffled, and whose voices are completely absent.

CHAPTER TWO

Incrementalism and the Status Quo

Nuclear power is the ultimate not-in-my-backyard (NIMBY) issue. These plants, sited at a time when the benefits of nuclear power were far more salient than any risks to safety, are something of a relic because NIMBY sentiments make it politically impossible to build new plants. Although for the foreseeable future the United States cannot do without the electricity generated by nuclear plants, the plants still in operation are controversial because they produce a waste by-product in the form of spent nuclear fuel rods. What to do with these depleted but highly radioactive fuel rods has proven to be an extremely difficult political task. Splitting the atoms that produce electricity turns out to have been the simple part.

Fuel rods have a useful life of about eighteen months. When they are removed from the nuclear reactor, they are literally too hot to handle and are put at the bottom of a large swimming pool within the nuclear facility. They must remain submerged for about three to five years. After that, they're still hazardous and therein lies the problem, because they remain hazardous for hundreds of thousands of years. The "temporary" solution has been to store the cooled fuel rods on the grounds of the nuclear power plants in thick, protective casks. This is hardly a satisfactory answer, and the nuclear industry has long pressed government to keep up its end of a tacit agreement to take responsibility for spent fuel. As an industry lobbyist explained to us, since the Atoms for Peace program in the 1950s, government has said to the commercial nuclear industry, "you burn it, we'll take care of it." Industry lobbying eventually paid off in 1982, when Congress passed a law providing for a national repository by 1998 for the hazardous, used fuel rods.

Despite sixteen years to study, site, and construct the repository, by 1998 the federal government had yet to build the facility. Overcoming local opposition to building something that would hold the entire nation's nuclear waste, for eternity, is no small challenge. At the time of our initial interviews on this case in the summer of 2000, a government panel had moved as far as selecting a waste site: Yucca Mountain, Nevada. Even though Yucca Mountain, 100 miles northwest of Las Vegas, was far from any significant population center, Nevadans were generally outraged at the thought of their state becoming the nation's nuclear dump. Responding to their constituents' concerns, the Nevada congressional delegation blocked construction. During the 2000 presidential election, candidates Al Gore and George W. Bush were pressed as to whether they would follow through and establish Yucca Mountain as the repository. Vice President Gore was strident in his opposition. Governor Bush, worried that he would lose the normally Republican state, sent his vice presidential candidate to the state toward the end of the campaign to reassure Nevadans that the Republicans had their best interests at heart. Candidate Cheney said that if elected, the administration would let the EPA, rather than the Nuclear Regulatory Commission, set the safety standards, thus ensuring that there would be very high safety standards if Yucca Mountain were eventually built.

Yet Bush and Cheney did not promise to kill the project, and in 2002 the administration gave the Yucca Mountain project the green light. The anger in Nevada over the decision gave Democratic nominee John Kerry an opening, and he made his opposition to Yucca Mountain a springboard to trying to carry the state in 2004. Kerry told Nevada voters, "Not on my watch."[1] Although voters decided that Kerry wouldn't have a watch, the defeat of Democratic Senate leader Tom Daschle in 2004 led to the promotion of Harry Reid of Nevada as the new Senate Minority Leader and then, after the Democrats' victory in the 2006 congressional election, Majority Leader. Not mincing words, Reid then said, "The proposed Yucca Mountain nuclear waste dump is never going to open."[2] In mid-2008 his U.S. Senate Web site still included prominent mention of his work in keeping the facility from ever seeing the light of day, including the opportunity for visitors to sign a "Stop Yucca" petition.

Incrementalism, the Status Quo, and Substantial Policy Change

Policy making over Yucca Mountain illustrates many of the main findings of this book. At the broadest level, the story illustrates the endurance of the status quo. Despite the seriousness of the problem—nuclear waste piling up at reactor sites, some near cities—the status quo has persisted for decades. Yucca Mountain remained on the drawing board and some of the planning hinted at incremental progress toward an eventual change. And then change came and it was anything but incremental. The Bush administration's green-lighting of the repository was a dramatic and fundamental change in American energy policy. And yet it's unclear at this writing whether the change will actually be implemented. If Harry Reid and the opponents of nuclear energy prevail, the status quo may stay in effect for several more decades, if not forever.

Although Yucca Mountain has had its own unique twists and turns, it represents many of the strongest patterns we see in our ninety-eight cases. Most of the time in most of the cases, the status quo endures. But it is also true that for a minority of cases, significant (nonincremental) change did materialize during the period we followed the issues. This enduring power of the status quo is evident in another way. During the fight over Yucca Mountain, the same basic arguments prevailed. For proponents, the case for Yucca Mountain has always been about the government's promise to dispose of waste and about the safety issues relating to current storage at reactors. For opponents, the arguments have been equally unchanging: transportation and storage at Yucca Mountain are unsafe and, more broadly, the country should be moving away from nuclear power. Like the fuel rods themselves, these arguments refuse to go away. They've always been the basis of the debate. One important element to the argument is also reflected in all of our cases: there is a status quo, so changing it requires special justification. After all, things have worked up until now, why must the policy be changed at all? This logic of "why change it?" or "why now?" is present in every issue, and it is a substantial hurdle for proponents of change. Those opposed to whatever proposal may be on the table have a range of arguments available which essentially add up to: At least we know what we have with the status quo. These turn out to be quite convincing.

The heated debate over nuclear waste continued in such a stable, durable manner because there was a stable, durable set of advocates on each side. Over time some of the individual legislators, aides, and lobbyists left the scene, but they were replaced by others with similar views. More importantly, the same organizations stayed involved. There was no changing panoply of congressional committees and interest groups. It is a long-running play with the same cast speaking the same lines. And each side has substantial resources. It turns out that such situations are not uncommon. It's quite typical for those concerned about an issue to stay involved over the long haul. They conscientiously monitor what their rivals are up to. They seek new opportunities to get what they want. And, most of the time, opponents hold each other in check.

The heart of our research in Washington was to examine the structure of the policy-making process in national politics, to try to better understand how interest groups fit into that structure in the modern day. To that end, we thought about our research in light of the most widely accepted theory of public-policy making, as well as alternatives to that theory.

Incrementalism

Although our research began with the hope of finding something new about the process of making public-policy, our starting point was what's old—the conventional wisdom about how government formulates policy. Unlike much of modern social science, this model, incrementalism, is rather simple. Indeed, its very simplicity is surely a large part of its lasting popularity.

The incrementalist model has its origins, of course, in Charles Lindblom's seminal article "The Science of Muddling Through."[3] Lindblom criticized what now seems like a straw man—the notion that decision makers search comprehensively through all available alternatives and evidence before reaching a decision on the most appropriate route to take. That this rational comprehensive model now seems hopelessly idealistic is testament, in part, to the power of Lindblom's theory. His idea was that the way people make decisions in the real world is to quickly limit their thinking to a small number of realistic alternatives and then choose a pragmatic course of action. And that course may not be the most effective solution, merely the one that most will agree to, the one that is most easily available, or one of several that is "good enough," even though it may not necessarily be the absolute best. The consequence of this process is that over time, policy making moves in small steps. When Congress or an agency deliberates over a policy, it builds on what is already in place rather than starting from the beginning and envisioning from scratch what the best possible system might be.

Lindblom's theory was warmly embraced by political scientists for a variety of reasons. Perhaps most importantly, incrementalism placed politics at the center of the governmental process. That is, policy making was not some technical set of procedures that needed to be perfected so that government could act rationally. Rather, at the heart of policy making were bargaining and negotiation among interest groups and government officials working from the same starting point: the policy currently in place. Further, it seemed to correspond to how bureaucrats and other policy makers actually do their work. They rarely invent entirely new programs; usually they stick with what is already familiar.

Despite its aging bones, incrementalism has persisted as a valid lens through which public-policy making can be viewed. Early research strongly supported its central contentions. Research on the budget was particularly persuasive. Works like Aaron Wildavsky's pioneering *The Politics of the Budgetary Process* document the incrementalist patterns in the development of the federal budget each fiscal year.[4] Wildavsky found that over time some functions of government would gain budget increases more than others, but that gains above and beyond the mean in any one year tended to be modest. The budget was the perfect example of incrementalism.

Lindblom's theory was also supported by sophisticated work on cognition, in particular the pathbreaking work of political scientist Herbert Simon that brought us the phrase "bounded rationality."[5] The human mind is capable of processing only so much information, of considering only so many alternatives. Although we may attempt to be rational in our thinking, to coolly weigh available evidence and then make an informed decision, our rationality is sharply bounded by limited processing power. We rely on cognitive shortcuts, limiting the work in making decisions to a comfortable level.

The cognitive model of bounded rationality has a close analogue in policy making. A government institution, like Congress, has limited capacity and can process only some of what is brought before it. Despite its enormous resources, many issues languish while Congress focuses on a small subset of problems. As a result of its limited processing power, it, too, takes short cuts, limiting its search for information and alternatives. Just as Congress can focus on only a small proportion of all the problems that deserve attention, governmental debate about any given problem tends to be limited as well. As we discussed in chapter 1 and will note in greater detail in later chapters, every issue that we studied here was conceptually highly complex. How to dispose of spent fuel rods is not an easy scientific or technical question; how do we know which site will be geologically stable for a million years? But, of course, it is not just a technical issue; many political factors are relevant as well. Do most state governors or those living near railroads relish the idea of tons of nuclear waste being transported all across the country?

Technical and political dimensions of the debate are intertwined, and the arguments are numerous. Public debate on the issue, however, is much simpler than what one might imagine from talking to the experts. A "bottleneck of attention" typically limits our attention to only a subset of all the possible issues and, for each issue, to only a few of the many possible elements of the debate. It's not so much that our capacity for reasoning is so limited, but that the complexity of the world around us—the swirling mix of complicated and poorly understood problems that rise and fall on the government agenda—is so tremendously complicated. Bounded rationality is the simple concept that attention is limited. This uncontroversial statement has many implications for the policy-making process.

Despite incrementalism's broad applicability and its resonance with our commonsense judgment of how government operates, a significant amount of criticism of the model has emerged. Perhaps the most frustrating aspect of the theory is that there is no agreed upon demarcation that divides incremental change from nonincremental change.[6] Incrementalism is not a concept that lends itself well to a bright line; every policy change is an increment more or less. A clear set of criteria to distinguish the small percentage of policy changes that exceed incremental change has never been established.

Punctuated equilibrium and friction

Criticism of the incrementalist model has not led to a great deal of theory building about the policy-making process. There is considerable theory development about parts of the policy-making process and about the behavior of sets of actors in the process, but broad, comprehensive theories of the entire policy-making process are few and far between. There is seemingly so much to account for that any relatively parsimonious theory of policy making runs the risk of being far too incomplete to be convincing.

In this vein one alternative to incrementalism is Frank Baumgartner and Bryan Jones's work on punctuated equilibrium. It is not a full-blown theory of policy making, but it goes right to the heart of incrementalism's broadest, most emphatic claim: that policy making moves in small steps because of inherent constraints in the political process. Baumgartner and

Jones first attempted to refute the belief that policy making is dictated by constraints mitigating against large-scale change.[7] They find, for example, that new ways of thinking about a complex problem can sweep through the government with surprising rapidity, as they show with examples such as nuclear power, pesticides, smoking, and other issues. To take one example, the nuclear power industry benefited from a tremendously positive public image in the 1950s as the "Atoms for Peace" slogan exemplified U.S. confidence in using our scientific and technical know-how to create electricity that would be so cheap to produce that we would give it away for free. This vision was reversed dramatically in the 1960s by a darker view, one focused on danger, radioactive waste, nuclear proliferation, and health concerns. Neither vision, they note, reflects the entire story. Bounded rationality and limited attention cause the political system to sometimes lurch from overwhelming enthusiasm to damning criticism very quickly. Of course, for most issues most of the time, the public image, like the public policy, remains stable.

Sometimes it can take decades for new information to have an impact or for the processes of dramatic change to develop significant momentum. The research on the link between cigarettes and cancer was around for decades prior to the landmark surgeon general's report on smoking and health in 1964. But it was not until a decade after the report that Congress was finally convinced that policy change was necessary. By that time, the decades of negative press stories about tobacco and health had reached a tipping point where Congress could no longer look at tobacco as strictly an agricultural issue. It was not until the 1990s that the states reached the "master settlement" by which tobacco companies paid hundreds of billions of dollars to the states and agreed to further restrictions in tobacco marketing procedures. In the early twenty-first century, states and communities are multiplying their antismoking regulations, marking a huge shift in the U.S. government's attitude toward smoking from encouragement to increasingly tight restrictions. The underlying facts of the smoking issue, on the other hand, have not changed a whole lot. Rather, attention now focuses on the health effects of second-hand smoke and not so much on individual smokers' rights or the agricultural and trade aspects of the tobacco industry. With a different focus, dramatically different policy orientations are supported.

Such sharp departures from existing policy, or "punctuations," may follow periods of equilibrium when policy making moved in the same direction for years. Such was surely the case for cigarettes. In contrast to incrementalism, the theory of punctuated equilibrium incorporates both stability and changes far greater in scope than a constant process of incrementalism could suggest. Baumgartner and Jones recognize the continuity, stability, and inertia of the normal circadian rhythm of policy making, but argue that large-scale change is not an anomaly. There is no iron law of equilibrium that restricts policy making to incremental changes once a policy is established. Further, they argue that the tendency to hew close to the status quo during long periods, a cornerstone of the incrementalist model, actually makes it inevitable that more dramatic shifts will occasionally have to occur.

Just as there is no definition of what constitutes an incremental change, there is no clear demarcation that identifies a change large enough to qualify as a punctuation. What is the magnitude of difference that separates a moderate change from something that truly punctuates an existing equilibrium? Baumgartner and Jones try to quantify the degree of change across a range of issues. Using a database of sixty-two categories of spending for each annual federal budget between 1948 and 2000, and looking across the full range of annual percentage changes, they determine that the typical case falls within a tightly constrained range of small adjustments. In fact, so incremental is this process that they criticize earlier scholars for *understating* the degree to which very small adjustments dominate the distribution of changes (even though those scholars did indeed focus on incrementalism), referring to the distribution as "hyper-incremental."[8] There is no doubt about the tendency to reproduce the status quo, or for the policy process to produce a large percentage of extremely small adjustments to existing policy, perhaps even more so than the original incrementalists suggested. But this is only part of the story; the other part of the story is that there are a great many punctuations. It's striking that moderate changes, somewhere between hyperincremental adjustments and sharp punctuations are uncommon. Figure 2.1 reproduces Jones and Baumgartner's analysis of all budget changes across almost fifty years of postwar history.

At first glance, the data form what appears to be a normal curve, familiar to all. But in fact the curve is not statistically normal; the central peak is much too high, and there are far more cases out in the extremes. Baumgartner and Jones observe: "For students of policy change, this distribution has a very important meaning. Many, many programs grew or were cut very modestly—that is, incrementalism was the order of the day for most programs most of the time. *Hyperincrementalism* might be a more

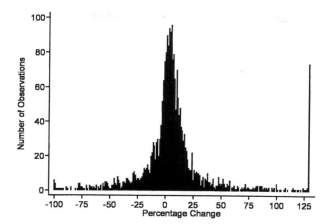

FIGURE 2.1. Annual changes in federal spending across sixty-two categories, 1948–2000. The figure shows the number of federal budget categories that changed by the percentage indicated on the horizontal axis. Across the entire period since 1948, 6 items were reduced by more than 99 percent, 20 items by –13 percent, more than 80 items each in the range of –3 to +8 percent, and 74 items increased by over 130 percent in a single year. (For the purposes of presentation, these observations are all grouped at +130 percent, but their actual values extend far out into the right tail.) The figure is adopted from Jones and Baumgartner, *Politics of Attention*, fig. 4.14, p. 111, and is based on a total of 2,416 annual observations.

accurate phrase for what happened in the vast majority of the cases. But sometimes programs received huge boosts, propelling them to double or triple their original sizes or more. Sometimes, but less often, programs lost half of more of their funding. Moderate increases or decreases were rather unusual, on the other hand."[9]

Although the bunching of data points in the middle reflects a normal distribution, the cases falling outside of the cluster in the middle do not tightly taper to a flat line just left and right of the central grouping of cases. Instead, the tails of the distribution are "fat" rather than tapering off to zero. In short, their distribution differs from the prototypical normal curve displayed in statistics texts. Although the overall portrait is one of incrementalism, it's evident that there are too many cases in the fat tails to write off as oddballs, exceptions, and idiosyncrasies. And that central peak, reflecting the power of the status quo, is just too high.

Jones and Baumgartner note that these processes are similar to many other processes in the physical sciences and that scientists have used a "friction" model to explain them. Imagine that the policy process involves pushing some weight along a sticky surface: It will not move at all until the pressure is greater than the friction of the surface. Once the pressure for movement becomes great enough, however, a dramatic change may occur as the friction is overcome. Pushing things along sticky surfaces produces not steady change, but rather a combination of no change interspersed with surges, dramatic movements when the friction is overcome. In such a model, moderate pressure is insufficient and thus, if the analogy holds, moderate policy change may be more difficult to enact than one might assume.

When the forces of friction are high, it is very hard to move an object even a little. Where pressures build up, no changes occur until the pressures are sufficient to overcome the "standing friction" (or the level of friction required to make the object move from a stationary position). When this threshold is passed, there may be a sudden jump as the object jerks to a new position. If the pressures continue, then it will keep moving, but the initial movement will be jerky even if the pressure is constant. Therefore Jones and Baumgartner argue that a friction model helps explain the *disproportionality* between inputs and outputs. The effect of constant political pressure can be almost zero until the pressure reaches a threshold, and over that threshold the degree of movement can be even greater than the degree of pressure. They argue that the political system alternates between underresponding to pressures and then occasionally overresponding as the forces of friction are finally overcome. They quote long-time Washington lobbyist Tom Korologos who quipped that "the things Congress does best are nothing and overreacting."[10]

The Sources of Friction

We have depicted a contrast between incrementalism on the one hand and a mixed system of largely incremental policy making and disequilibrating punctuations on the other. This model works well for the budgetary process, where inflation alone dictates that most existing budget lines will see an observable increase in funding. But in turning to authorizing or reauthorizing legislation, another model seems entirely plausible. It may be that the converse of large-scale change is no change at all. In fact, the stalemate or gridlock scenario is common in scholarly and popular accounts of government, in which Americans complain that government can't get anything done. Why is the status quo, or stalemate, so common? Where does friction in the policy process come from? There are a number of possibilities, each with an element of truth.

Partisanship and elections

In recent years the most prevalent explanation offered is that the nation is too divided, too partisan. In this view, ideologues have captured both parties and legislators reflect a hardening resistance to compromise and a preference for waging war against the opposition. If Congress allowed majoritarianism to rule, partisanship would not promote gridlock, as the party with the most votes could have its way and pass the policies it prefers. But of course there is no simple majoritarian system. A prerequisite for such rule is that a party controls both houses and the presidency. And even if a party did control both ends of Pennsylvania Avenue, internal procedures work against strict party rule except when majorities are quite large. The opportunity for filibuster, for example, means that a majority in the Senate is actually sixty senators.

Therefore, one possible explanation for the dominance of the status quo is partisanship. Perhaps elections bring into power new leaders, following perhaps a presidential lead or benefiting from a new majority in Congress, and these new leaders, along with their partisan allies outside of government, work together to enact new policies that differ from the policies enacted in the "old regime." During periods when partisanship and control of government do not change, on the other hand, there is little reason to revisit the status quo.

There is much to this explanation of policy change, in fact. Some of our issues were indeed dramatically affected by new elections. For example, in the last months of the Clinton administration, OSHA announced new regulations designed to reduce repetitive motion injuries in the workplace: the so-called ergonomics regulations. After the 2000 elections brought the Republicans to power, these regulations, already scheduled to be implemented, were scrapped amid much publicity and partisan credit-claiming (we discuss the ergonomics regulations in greater detail in chapter 6). Elections matter.

Partisanship can also matter if members of the different parties refuse to work together or simply have different priorities. We found that the inability of many advocates to construct a bipartisan coalition of support for their initiative in Congress effectively doomed their efforts. So partisan divisions can help enhance the status quo. If bills can't be passed except with the creation of a bipartisan coalition, or if party leaders enact a new series of policies reversing those that came before them, partisanship could be a major source of the typical bias in favor of the status quo, as well as the occasional dramatic departure from it.

On the other hand, if partisanship were the only force driving the structure that we see in politics, we would find little reason for any policy change except immediately after those elections that bring new majorities to power. In fact, we see a lot of policy change in interelection periods. There is only so much space on the political agenda, and, as we will see, the new Bush administration did indeed reverse a few of the issues that had been enacted under President Clinton. Yet the number of problems facing government is so great, with new ones constantly rising to demand attention, that a comprehensive review of all existing policies is out of the question. Thus, the status quo often survives in spite of shifts in partisan control. As our research project spanned the last two years of the Clinton administration and the first two years of the Bush presidency, we can look at these issues in great detail.

Special interests

A common scapegoat for stalemate or gridlock is interest groups themselves, or "special interests" as they usually are called when they are being blamed for some societal ill. As the number of interest groups in Washington skyrocketed after the "interest group explosion" in the 1960s, it seemingly became harder to get anything done. The logic is simple: with many groups on every side of an issue, policy making becomes more difficult and agreement is harder to negotiate. If corporations and the wealthy are highly mobilized in the political sphere, and they have large teams of highly paid lobbyists available to protect their interests, perhaps it is almost impossible to push policy changes that threaten the material interests of large corporations, trade groups, labor unions, and others with lots of money. An increasingly complex and contentious policy-making environment is hardly ideally suited for productivity. Although one study shows no relationship between the number of interest groups and gridlock, the results are not definitive and the belief persists that the proliferation of interest groups is a cause of stalemate.[11]

We explored the degree to which policy making was subject to gridlock. The end of the Clinton administration and the first years of the Bush administration were certainly partisan times. There was also divided government, with neither party firmly in charge during the period of our field research. But it became clear to us that a lack of movement on an issue that some legislators or lobbyists were pushing did not necessarily indicate that policy making was gridlocked. Rather, what was common was a lack of movement because one side was more powerful than any opposition. In such cases a coalition of groups and legislators had, at one time, succeeded in enacting a policy. Over time that coalition maintained its dominance over those who would shift policy in a new direction. In this situation, when the status quo prevails, it is not gridlock. Rather, it is one point of view dominating another. Gridlock, after all, would imply that no movement is possible *even if there were consensus* on the need for policy change.[12] As we argue at length in the chapters that follow, the benefits that accrue to defenders of the status quo are significant, but that should not mean that the desires of the status quo's defenders are not important. Certainly the multiplicity of interests in our complex society means that competition for attention is fierce and groups may often fight to a standstill, but there is no solution to this problem other than suppressing or ignoring the voices of people and groups who try to make themselves heard. Interest groups and advocates competing to a standstill, as powerful forces support different views, may well be one source of a bias in favor of the status quo, but such competition is not the same as gridlock.

Institutional gatekeepers

Much political science literature has focused on the power of institutional gatekeepers, congressional power barons who rule their fiefdoms with an iron hand.[13] Whether it is the majority leader who controls access of bills to the floor of the Senate for an eventual vote, the Rules Committee chair who determines whether amendments will be allowed in House-floor discussion of various bills, or a committee leader who refuses to report a bill out to the larger body, literature and folk wisdom abound concerning the monumental power of those who hold the keys to the next step in the policy process. Indeed, we find again that there is much to these explanations. In fact, the phenomenon may go even further than is sometimes discussed, as we found many lobbyists in our sample stymied at an even earlier stage: the inability to find even a few members of Congress with enough interest in their issue.

Institutional gatekeeping, like competing interests and elections, is an important element of the story we will tell. But it does not explain much on its own. Again and again, we find that significant changes occur with no shift in who was guarding the gates, or that shifts in gatekeepers lead to no change in the policy. Further, the causes of stability are often much broader than the institutional structure approach implies. In fact, we suggest in chapter 4 that entire professional communities of experts may be reluctant to embrace new policy initiatives most of the time. However, we also note that when they do shift, they can shift in a collective manner that makes possible dramatic policy reversals.

Passing the threshold

With hundreds of policies simultaneously being considered, policy makers may not want to tinker with complex programs and risk some unintended consequence, just because there is a small part of the policy that is slightly imperfect. This is especially true if the imperfection affects just a small constituency. There are only so many hours in the day, and the most urgent policy problems have to be addressed before dealing with issues that were addressed in any case just a year or two earlier during the last program renewal. The status quo policy is typically the result of the accumulated wisdom of decades of work and experience in the area. Proponents of change have the unenviable task of convincing others that existing policy is so far off the mark that a new policy is warranted. This is a tough sell. People resist change not only because they prefer the substance of the status quo, but also because they understand it and may fear unintended consequences of tinkering with the system.

An example can illustrate this prejudice against change. Consider the difficulties that clinical social workers had in correcting what they saw as an error in the 1997 Balanced Budget Act. Clinical social workers had not been included in a list of professions whose services were excluded from "bundled payments" to nursing homes; that is, they were not included in a list of professions such as physicians and other specialists whose work is reimbursed over and above any payments that the nursing home receives for general services to patients. All nursing homes are expected to provide certain services, and payment for those is "bundled" to cover normal operating expenses. The list of professional services excluded from these general payments, and therefore eligible for additional Medicare payments, has a direct impact on the cost of Medicare services, the likelihood that nursing homes will provide more of these services, and on patient care. When the list of professions excluded from these payments was developed in the 1997 Balanced Budget Act, a staff member took a list from previous legislation and inserted it in the bill; inadvertently, and without people noticing, this list excluded clinical social workers—a simple mistake.

Is the mistake important enough for Congress to take steps to fix? The issue is certainly no barn-burner; no member of Congress is likely to lose an election over it or even to hear much from any constituents about it. It affects only a single profession (though it affects them strongly). It requires Congress and the Centers for Medicare and Medicaid Services to admit that their original and very complicated legislation included a mistake and to argue that, even though those affected did not notice it at the time, this mistake is important enough that Congress should revise the law to fix it. In sum, the issue is complicated, it costs money, and it is not likely to mobilize large numbers of constituents or gain anyone reelection. Nothing happened. Advocates proposing change lost not so much because they faced active opposition or hostility in Congress, but more because their issue was tedious, somewhat expensive, and there was simply not enough pressure to overcome the friction associated with bringing attention to a small issue when there are so many seemingly more important matters being debated in Washington. This is not uncommon.

Even if policy makers recognize that the policy is imperfect or the result of an error, as with the clinical social workers above, it may still be a hard sell to convince others, especially those in leadership positions, that the current policy is working so badly that it must be overhauled. This threshold effect means that the vast majority of policies do not change at all. A few pass the threshold and may change substantially. (Ironically, it means that it is often easier to change big mistakes than to fix small ones, as by definition the latter affect fewer people.)

Students of agenda setting have long noted that dramatic policy changes do occur, sometimes through the efforts of brilliant policy entrepreneurs who reframe entire debates. Yet for most issues most of the time, individual policy makers fight an uphill battle to reframe their issues. One of the most important reasons for this is that the issues are not new and the status quo policy was probably the result of substantial thought, deliberation, and compromise when it was adopted. Those adversely affected by the proposed change in policy fight back, exposing whatever flaws in the arguments they can find. The friction model we have described here is due not only to a particular set of institutional rules (though it may be reinforced by them). Rather, it stems from more fundamental sources rooted in the complexity of the issues themselves, the scarcity of attention, the structure of professional communities surrounding most policy issues, and the reluctance of gatekeepers to admit mistakes.

Attention and critical mass

As we look across these possible sources of friction in the political system— each with a grain of truth—it becomes clear that the most important reason for the endurance of the status quo is that power is divided within the

American system and attention is limited. Because power is fragmented, many political actors must come together if policy change is to be made. The scarcity of attention identified by Baumgartner and Jones means that gathering those actors together is not easy. The typical two-year Congress, for example, sees close to eight thousand bills introduced, yet only about four hundred passed into law. The vast majority of proposals for policy change fall on deaf ears, and this may not be because people oppose them, but simply because they have other priorities. Since there are many more policy problems than there is time or money to solve them, some priorities have to be set, and those issues with lower priority, for whatever reason, are simply pushed down in the queue, perhaps to be considered at some time in the future. We saw this in the fact that seventeen of our issues had only a single side. Often this was because potential opponents knew the issue had such low salience or momentum that there was no need to work against it; friction alone, or the status quo bias, would do the trick quite nicely. So friction is well understood in Washington.

Divided power and limited attention mean that it is in the best interest of interest groups and members of Congress to be working on the same issue that everyone else is working on. The central question is which issues will attract enough other policy makers and advocates to make it worthwhile to spend time and effort on those issues. As we will see in chapter 5, advocates of a policy repeatedly told us that one of the most difficult obstacles they faced was simply trying to get other interest groups and government officials to pay attention to their issue. The problem of attention can seem like a Catch-22, in which an issue cannot go forward in the political process without more attention, but the issue cannot get more attention unless it goes forward. An issue becomes "important" and worth spending time on because others have decided that it is important and worth spending time on, and those decisions are in turn based in large part on the decisions of others before them. External events, or merely the build-up of participants, bring an issue to a critical state in which a sudden shift is possible, and change then can occur. The status quo is strong, but it can be broken.

Conclusion

The patterns we have found run against the grain of many common assumptions about how the U.S. national government works. Throughout this book we will see the constant force of the status quo at work, structuring outcomes. What are some of the possible causes of the patterns we see? Why is the status quo so strong? In the past, scholars have pointed to the importance of partisanship and elections, interest-group influence, and institutional gatekeepers. There is some truth to each of these answers, but they are not entirely satisfactory. Partisanship alone does not explain change—or lack thereof. Interest groups certainly help reinforce the status quo, as do institutional gatekeepers, but change often occurs without any change in the gatekeepers and in spite of the presence of many interest groups. To explain the patterns we find, we must look to the necessity of gathering a critical mass of advocates to an issue and the difficulty of doing so given the multiplicity of issues and the limited nature of attention. In the chapters that follow, we explain these patterns in policy making in more depth, including a closer look at the structures in Washington that do account for much of the stability. The strength of the status quo does not mean that nothing ever changes, but it does mean that change is never easy in politics. Long periods of effort by advocates of policy change may add up to nothing—or may finally be rewarded by an abrupt shift in policy.

Structure or Chaos?

O ne of the most complex and well-publicized policy controversies of the Clinton administration was the debate about granting permanent normal trade relations status to China. Championed by President Clinton and supported by many business groups and free-trade advocates, the proposal was bitterly opposed by labor unions, environmental groups, agricultural interests, and human rights groups. It involved many seemingly incomparable dimensions of evaluation: free trade, consumer prices, jobs, environmental impact, abortion, human rights, free speech, agricultural exports, military relations, and maintaining diplomatic relations with a rising world power. But at the end of the day, when the issue was debated in Congress, there were only two sides, for and against. An advocate for moving to include China told us, "The fundamental argument was that getting China into the WTO was not only good for companies and the American economy, but it was in the national interest as well." A lobbyist on the other side of the issue drew an equally simple conclusion: China was "not ready for a full WTO relationship with the United States because of China's egregiously bad record on human rights and workers' rights and also egregiously bad record on noncompliance with past trade agreements." If there were so many implications of the issue, why were there only two sides to the debate?

Policy issues are rarely straightforward debates about whether a certain goal is desirable or not. The typical policy debate in Washington involves uncertainty about how serious the underlying problem really is, who will be affected by any policy designed to address it, how much such a policy may cost (and who will pay), whether the policy will work as proponents claim, whether it might have unintended negative consequences, and even sometimes about whether the problem the policy is designed to address is really a problem at all. The typical case is ambiguous and complex, with a combination of considerations ranging from the philosophical to the technical. And yet, at the end of the day, the structure of policy conflict in Washington is usually very simple. One side proposes change; another attempts to protect the status quo.

What creates the structure of policy-making debate in Washington? We focus here on two interrelated causes: first, the continuing nature of public-policy debate, which leads to a strong tendency for conflict to simplify along the lines of changing the status quo or not; and second, the presence of large knowledge-based communities of experts surrounding virtually all policy programs, which means that new policies are rarely adopted without a full discussion of various effects they may have. This creates a kind of friction that prevents new dimensions of an issue from rising to the forefront too easily. These knowledge communities bear similarities to the gatekeeping structures and the concept of "structure-induced equilibrium" that have been observed in Congress,[1] but the effects of shared information within policy communities are much broader. These are powerful sources of status quo bias in most cases but also explain the occasional burst in policy that we observe from time to time. Perhaps surprisingly, we do not identify partisanship as a central source of structure in policy making, though we will see that it often has an indirect but important effect as the parties take different positions and as congressional procedures are dominated by partisan gatekeepers. In fact, as we will see in later chapters, partisanship and ideology are rarely explicitly the main points of argumentation, but they structure the process nonetheless.

The chapter is structured as follows. We begin by introducing a fundamental conundrum within the political science literature, in which one group of scholars emphasizes the inherently complex nature of the substance of most public-policy debates and another presents evidence showing the extreme predictability and low-dimensional structure of debates and votes in Congress. We then explain the complexity of our issues, in substantive terms, using our interviews to illustrate the deep and shared knowledge about policy issues and government programs that characterizes the communities of professionals which surround the policies we studied. Having established the complexity of the issues and the fullness of the information available to those involved, we move to the issue of the structure of conflict, and we show that extremely simple patterns of conflict characterize the vast majority of our issues. We end with a discussion of the importance of the shared-knowledge communities that surround each of our issues, what political scientists have called policy subsystems, iron triangles, policy communities, or, more recently, issue networks. Surprisingly, we show that these concepts have much in common with a more specific literature from studies of Congress, that on "structure-induced equilibrium." Our findings in this chapter clearly support our expectations from chapter 1 that our issues are indeed complex and that they affect diverse constituencies, creating heterogeneous sides. However, surprisingly perhaps, the structure of conflict itself is quite simple: maintain or change the status quo. In fact, the complexity of public policy induces simplicity in policy conflict.

Two Views

E. E. Schattschneider's *The Semi-Sovereign People* remains one of the classics of American political science.[2] In this work, still influential now almost fifty years since its original publication, Schattschneider develops the idea of the *expansion of conflict*. Political conflicts, he notes, are not like sports events with agreed upon rules of who is part of the battle and who is in the audience. Rather, they are like unorganized rumbles with no clear rules. Those involved in an initial dispute may follow a strategy of expanding the conflict to appeal to heretofore-uninvolved constituencies, or one of conflict containment if they think their interests are best served by limiting participation only to those currently involved. The underdogs, Schattschneider wrote, often appeal for government intervention in their disputes with more powerful rivals. (Schattschneider called this a strategy of "socializing" the conflict, or expanding it.) In his view, many public controversies and many established government programs regulating such things as labor relations had such a process at their root.

How does one expand or restrict a conflict? Mostly through reframing the issue. Those seeking greater involvement by others attempt to explain how the issue has broader implications than only the most obvious or direct ones. Their opponents seek to contain the issue, showing how it sets no precedent, does not affect others, and should be left only to the experts to decide. In sum, the outcome of a conflict, for Schattschneider, is largely determined by the degree to which the conflict expands.[3] Rules and procedures play little role in his theory.

Many scholars have built on Schattschneider's theories, publishing scores of books and articles that place rhetorical strategies and issue-definitions at the core of the political struggle. This has particularly been the case in the field of agenda-setting studies. Roger Cobb and Charles Elder, writing in 1972, further developed theories of conflict expansion by investigating how issues move from the informal public agenda to the systemic, or government, agenda.[4] John Kingdon followed in 1984 with his theory of "multiple streams" relating to how issues are defined in government and how they emerge on the political agenda, especially after windows of opportunity are opened.[5] Frank Baumgartner and Bryan Jones's work in 1993 focused on the dual processes of issue-definition and venue-shopping as they developed a theory stressing how issues are often routinely handled within a community of experts and follow a stable policy direction.[6] But they also emphasized how issues are, on occasion, dramatically redefined.

Anne Schneider and Helen Ingram described how various "target populations"—that is, social or political constituencies that are the objects of many policy programs—are framed.[7] Some (such as "family farmers") have positive associations, whereas others ("welfare cheats") carry negative connotations. Public policies follow predictably from these portrayals. Deborah Stone's work illustrated the importance of what she called "causal stories," explanations of the reasons for a given public-policy problem.[8] Where poverty is explained by a story emphasizing economic transformations, failure of the educational system, and racial stereotyping or discrimination in employment practices, more interventionist policies are justified. Where a causal story dominated by arguments about individual responsibility, morality, and hard work dominates, then different poverty policies seem to follow.

All these authors have in common a relatively fluid view of the policy process. Issue-definitions, they argue, are the result of lobbying efforts by social and professional groups on the policies that concern them. These change over time, and as they do, predictable shifts occur in the direction of public policy. *Control the definition of the terms in the debate, and you control the direction of public policy.* Thus, these scholars contend that strategic advocates can take advantage of the complexity of the policy processes and the multidimensional nature of policy debates.

The literature on the impact of institutional rules and procedures emphasizes a different set of questions and lays out much less hope for policy change or indeed for influence of actors outside of government in the policy process, particularly within Congress. The literature on congressional procedures and institutional processes also accentuates the gatekeeping ability of leaders. Because leaders are able to decide which kinds of amendments will be allowed, choose who may offer amendments, and determine the rules by which votes will be taken, they affect the outcomes of political debate. Ideology and partisanship play important roles, as arguments and roll-call voting are seen to follow relatively straightforwardly from core beliefs and partisan structures within Congress.

We want to square this methodological circle. Our goal is to bridge these two literatures, which so often fail to address each other, confronting both sets of ideas with our evidence. Do institutional procedures drive outcomes? Or do issue-definition and framing make things happen? Our approach, following individual issues that are the object of lobbying, allows us to investigate both institutional procedures as well as efforts to redefine debates.

Our results confirm and disconfirm different parts of both literatures. For example, in general we find that lobbyists cannot simply redefine issues when they please (see chapter 9), although they certainly try, and the use of arguments is highly structured (see chapter 7). Yet in our interviews there was little discussion of congressional rules. We heard virtually no strategizing about how to overcome a particular rule or of how to work within constraints established by existing rules. What we heard instead involved the guts of the legislative process: how to get enough key players to pay attention, how to get enough support to move legislation forward, or how to mobilize enough participants to kill a bill. For a typical lobbyist or legislative staffer thinking about the problem they're working on that day, strategizing about the rules seemed irrelevant. Rules are a given that an individual advocate (whether inside or outside of government) is unlikely to be able to influence. Surely at key junctures a rule might influence a strategic choice, but overall what we heard on K Street and on Capitol Hill was about coalition building. Further, because of the complexity of the effects of various policies on different constituencies, lobbying is profoundly structured by the simple orientation of status quo versus change. Further, the sides associated with these views tend to be diverse.

Simple Issues, Complex Implications

Some political conflicts, such as those on abortion or gun control, seem to involve disputes about the desired ends of a policy. Some favor abortion

rights; others disagree. Some support expansive gun-owning rights; others
favor restrictions on guns. There is no subtlety to these debates, little ambi-
guity, and little room for compromise. Even relatively stark debates, however, may be more complex than they appear on the surface. Individuals
may have diverse reasons for holding a given opinion, for one. Some may
support gun rights because they believe owning a gun makes them safer;
others because they don't trust the government; and still others because
they believe the Constitution guarantees it, and they don't like seeing that
guarantee whittled away. No matter what the diverse motivations may
be, all of these people are in fundamental disagreement with gun-control
advocates.

A second reason why debates may be more complicated than they appear is that even in those cases where disagreements seem considerable,
people may actually agree on some higher-level principles. When gun owners propose privacy and individual freedom justifications for their views,
they are evoking fundamental values with which virtually all Americans
agree. Similarly, when their opponents refer to child shootings and the
high level of violence in America, they also evoke concerns shared by the
vast majority of Americans. These are stark debates, however, and relatively clear in their structures because the focus of the debate is on the
substance of issue: One side wants to protect gun ownership, the other
wants to restrict it.

In spite of the clarity of many debates, the vast majority of public-policy
conflict does not involve such clear disputes. More common are much more
complicated fights, typically not about goals at all, but about the diverse
effects of the policy, its feasibility, alternative mechanisms of achieving the
same goal, cost, and unintended consequences. Nothing is simple when it
comes to the debate over the restriction preventing newspapers from owning a TV or radio station in the same market. On the one hand, people can
recognize the need to prevent a single company from owning too much of
the information marketplace. On the other, TV and newspapers are not
the only sources of information anymore, so one can question whether a
policy designed in an older era still serves its purpose. As one advocate
for change told us, when the rule was written "newspapers were seen as a
monopoly on local news. It's just not so anymore." He added, "With the
Internet and cable, there's a plethora of media voices." This convergence
of rapidly changing industries ensures that any discussion of newspaper
cross-ownership will run into a seemingly endless web of issues and considerations. Policies made at one time don't necessarily remain effective

forever. On the other hand, those opposed to the substantive purpose of the policy may just use "effectiveness" arguments to kill something they never liked in the first place.

Every one of our ninety-eight issues involved multiple dimensions of evaluation. Whether or not the overriding goal of the policy was in dispute, none of our issues could be understood along only a single dimension. Usually, these dimensions involved disagreements about the various effects of the policy, some of which may be universally recognized as valuable. In fact, for a given policy outcome, often there is no disagreement whatsoever about whether it involves a worthwhile social goal (in contrast to the abortion or gun control examples above). Rather, conflict erupts around questions surrounding the likely effects of the policy overall. Such was the case with computer export controls, one of the issues we investigated. Some of the largest and most influential information-technology companies in America were aligned in the Computer Alliance for Responsible Exports, and these massive companies worked hard to convince the government to change the way it identified "high performance" computers, the only ones subject to export limitations. The goal of government-imposed limitations on the highest performing computers is to stop rogue nations from using them to make bombs; no one disagrees with this goal! However, those who sell the computers affected by the policy make different arguments. Among other things, these groups note that computers actually used to design and test nuclear weapons are largely custom-made, whereas the export controls apply to off-the-shelf models. They also emphasize that computers with equivalent processing capacity could be purchased from manufacturers in other countries and that technology changes so fast that it outruns regulations. As one industry PR campaign put it, "Yesterday's supercomputer is today's laptop." Nonetheless, even such an impressive and well-heeled set of corporate heavy-hitters as Dell, Intel, Microsoft, IBM, Sun Microsystems, AOL-Time Warner, and others were not able to shake members of the Senate Armed Services Committee from a desire never to look "soft on defense." The corporate lobbying effort went nowhere.

No one disputes the goals of enhancing American exports abroad, building a stronger high-tech industrial base in America, protecting American jobs, enhancing profits, or beating foreign economic rivals. But, then again, no one wants to give the tools to design nuclear weapons to Iran, North Korea, or Libya. The problem, and the policy conflict, stems from the combination of incommensurate effects of the same policy; every one of our cases has this feature. The multidimensional nature of each of our issues means that they all involve trade-offs of apples to oranges. An important element of such debates is that the resource-rich do not always win, as in the Computer Export Control example. It also explains why seasoned policy makers may be reluctant to support a policy until they have had the opportunity to become familiar with all the arguments, not just those from one side.

Not only were the issues we studied invariably multidimensional, but they were characterized by uncertainty as well. Uncertainty refers to whether a given policy will produce a given outcome. How much market share would American companies gain if export restrictions were lifted? This matters, because if the number is large, that might represent a large number of jobs; but if it is small, then why bother? How much more likely would it be that a given rogue state would develop nuclear weapons if it had more advanced computers? Maybe the target country will develop them anyway, or maybe we have other ways of preventing it, so the policy is just not needed. Of course, the uncertainty associated with various outcomes makes the incommensurate trade-offs in many policies even more confusing: How much unknown lost market share is it worth for an unknown reduction in the probability that North Korea will develop or enhance its weapons, a reduction that may be equal to zero if they can simply buy the same computer from a foreign producer? As former Defense Secretary Donald Rumsfeld noted, "There are things we don't know we don't know." In thinking about the intersection of multidimensionality and uncertainty, one starts to understand the complexity of most lobbying in Washington.

The multidimensional nature of our issues has implications greater than mere uncertainty, since even if people reduced uncertainty to zero they would still disagree about whether positive results along one dimension outweighed possible negative consequences along some other dimension. For example, let's assume for the moment that we knew exactly how much freer trade would affect domestic consumer prices. That still would not tell us whether these potential benefits in terms of lower consumer prices would outweigh potential domestic job losses or the environmental dangers of moving factories overseas where standards are weaker. Different individuals might judge that trade-off differently. Most of our issues involve not just one but many trade-offs of this sort. Constituencies mobilize to ensure that their view on the debate is given substantial weight, that it is heard, loud and clear. As the debates themselves often involve such difficult comparisons, there is room for various political actors to give more weight to one dimension than to another. In sum, it is not easy to determine how a given issue will be discussed in the public sphere; many factors determine how much weight various actors will assign to the various possible relevant dimensions of evaluation and how they will make trade-offs among them.

All this implies that one would expect the structure of policy conflict to be quite complex, reflecting the multidimensional nature of the issues themselves. In fact, the conflict tends to be surprisingly clear-cut. If uncertainty refers to the likely results of a given policy proposal, and complexity refers to the multiple trade-offs that must be made on incommensurate dimensions of evaluation, then each of our cases is both complex and uncertain. In spite of the complex nature of every one of our cases, at the end of the day, when a vote is taken in Congress, there is tremendous regularity in who lines up with whom. Republicans typically line up on one side; Democrats on the other.[9]

How do policy makers move from the complex underlying multidimensionality that is inherent in all of our cases to an up-or-down decision on the final outcome? What causes a simple ideological structure to make a common "fit" in issues as diverse as the proposed US Airways–United Airlines merger, extending patent protection on certain pharmaceuticals, new regulations affecting the savings-and-loan industry, and the scores of different elements that were combined into the patient's bill of rights? Each of these issues raises complex economic, geographic, social, and environmental dimensions of debate familiar to those who are experts on the issue. Each is uncertain as well, since no one could say exactly what would be the impact of a given policy change. But in the end, when Congress votes, to a large extent these diverse issues are whittled down to a single structure. In explaining the sources of this structure, our first argument is simply that it does not stem from the clarity of the underlying issues. In fact, as we have already argued, the complex impacts on diverse constituencies may paradoxically be what keeps the structure of conflict so simple.

The Informational Richness of Lobbying

If an issue is complex, it is recognized by all concerned as having multiple and typically incommensurate dimensions. Even the simplest issue may have the consequence of increasing the purview of the federal government over the states, for example. Trade questions relating to China are inevitably linked to views about that country's human rights record, or abortion, or national security. Agriculture issues have environmental impacts. No matter what the substance of the issue, one way to look at any issue is who wins and who loses economically. Many issues have differential geographic impacts; for example, they may favor rural areas more than urban areas, or they may affect the Northeast adversely, or they may affect a single state or a particular social, racial, or economic sector of the population. The differential impacts of various policy choices may be completely unrelated to theoretical arguments about "good public policy." The best thought-out policy proposal that leads to job loss in a particular state will be a tough sell for at least two senators. If the policy will affect rural areas for the worse, then much of the Senate may be reticent. Woe to the Washington lobbyist who would overlook arguments about geographic impact. Interest groups and professionals surrounding the policy work to maintain or enhance attention to "their" dimension of the debate. This counteractive behavior reduces the ability of any other actors unilaterally to reframe or redefine the debate. Lobbying becomes a struggle for attention to one set of dimensions rather than another, and for the most part rival lobbyists and rival policy makers hold each other in check.

Different dimensions of evaluation lead different groups to support and oppose a given policy. Returning to the example of computer export controls, if the issue is evaluated on the dimension of promoting U.S. exports and the high-tech industry, then Republicans would naturally be in favor of liberalizing trade. But if national security trumps, then the same group may be in opposition. William Riker saw the importance of these questions and made it seem that strategically sophisticated policy makers should be able to manipulate arguments in order to promote the dimension of evaluation that leads to the right outcome.[10] But how easy is it to accomplish this? Can lobbyists determine the dimensions of debate that become salient? They would certainly like to.

Surrounding each issue that we studied is a community of professionals who spend their careers immersed in the details of a given issue, day-in and day-out. These people tend to have their opinions, of course, about what policies should be adopted and how serious the underlying problem is. But what is most striking about these communities of experts to a group of outsiders (such as those of us who did the interviews reported here) is their tremendous knowledge about the policy areas they work in. These people know their issues. They know their own viewpoint, of course, and they know the arguments of their opponents. They know the histories of the policies, the personalities of the original champions who created the policies in the first place, the justifications for and the problems with how the programs were originally structured, how these have evolved over time, and how similar policies have been tried (or not) in the states and in other countries. In short, they know whatever there is to know about their issues. Judging from our interviews, given the opportunity, many of these people could sit down and write a book about the history and develop-ment of their little corner of the U.S. federal government.

Many of the advocates we interviewed had been working in the area where they are active for decades. And even if they had not, in each policy area there are people, if not entire institutions, that have been involved in the ins-and-outs of the policy for a long time. Our interviews, typically three per case, became very repetitive after a while as people explained the background of the issue to us and the current disputes. While every respondent had their own particular arguments, of course, they also knew the arguments of the others, and they all were able to give a similar de-scription of the general background of the issue, what it was about, the rationale for the existing policy, various arguments for and against possible revisions to the policy, who is affected, who supports and opposes it, and so on. Among people who spend their careers dealing with a given social problem or government policy, they all know pretty much the same things, and they all know a lot.

The shared knowledge of all these people provides structure, and this structure rests much more broadly than on only a given set of institutional designs. Indeed, large parts of the structure associated with the policy process would remain even if institutional procedures changed, because they relate to the shared knowledge and information residing throughout a policy community. Single individuals typically do not have the ability to change the way an entire community of professionals looks at an issue. In response to arguments by one side that an issue is "really" about jobs and exports, others involved speak up: "No, it's not about that; it's an issue of national security," they might argue. Of course, the outcome of the debate depends on who wins this war of rhetoric, but the battle is never one-sided, and all sides are armed with pretty much the same, and very complete, understanding of the issue.

Through this process of informational richness, and mutual checks and balances, we can understand the extreme status quo bias associated with most issues in Washington, but also how things occasionally shift dramatically. What new information would be sufficient to redefine the complex debates that surround most Washington policies? Do elections do it? New scientific studies? Cultural shifts? Venue-shopping? Slick PR campaigns? Campaign contributions? Institutional rules? Leadership? Each of these has been proposed as the cause of important policy shifts, but as we will see, such shifts are very unusual. Typically no single factor determines a dramatic policy change. Even in combination, most of these are insufficient to overcome the extreme bias toward the status quo that we observe in our cases.

From Complexity to Simplicity

We noted in the beginning of this chapter how the underlying debate concerning permanent normal trade relations with China was highly complex, but the structure of conflict was very simple. Here we move to explaining the degree of simplicity that devolves out of the complexity present in the vast bulk of our cases. We look not at the substance of the underlying arguments, but at the structure of policy conflict. We look at the goals the various participants in the policy process were seeking. This simple factor explains a lot.

As discussed in chapter 1, we define a policy "side" as a group of actors attempting to achieve the same policy outcome. These advocates may or may not be working together, although it is typical that they do indeed coordinate their efforts. Sides include anyone attempting to promote the same goal, whether these advocates are within or outside of government. Across our ninety-eight issues, we identified 214 distinct sides, or just over 2 per case, on average. Table 3.1 shows how many were active in each case.

The table shows that a surprisingly large number of issues (seventeen cases) consist of a single side attempting to achieve a goal to which no one objects or in response to which no one bothers to mobilize. Ironically, the lack of countermobilization is a good predictor of failure. Many of these reflect efforts to put an issue on the agenda, but these efforts are either too early in the process for anyone yet to have reacted or they are clearly not moving so others have not gotten involved in the issue. We deal in more detail with the problem of the indifference of others in chapter 4.

One might think that with no opposition, those lobbyists working on behalf of the issues with only one side would rule the day in Washington. Reality is far from this, even when the "lobbyist" in question is the

TABLE 3.1 **The Simplicity of Policy Conflict**

Number of sides	Number of cases
1	17
2	58
3	14
4	8
7	1
Total	98

Note: The table shows the number of cases across our sample with the indicated number of distinct sides. A side is a group of policy advocates sharing a policy goal.

Defense Department. Our review of the Pentagon's efforts to upgrade the Chinook Helicopter, in service since the Vietnam War, shows that the proposal ran into no active opposition, but it was still not funded during the period of our study. Why? The real questions were how much of a priority a revitalized Chinook was for the Pentagon and what financial effort Congress was willing to make. The answer was that both sides had more important priorities. Similarly, efforts to regulate Medicaid and private insurance providers to require parity in reimbursement policies for expenses related to mental health disorders and expenses related to physical disorders aroused no opposition, and yet it made such limited progress that a lobbyist complained to us that his group was still "trying to get legislation that we've drafted introduced." Another advocate admitted that "a big problem for us is trying to get on members of Congress's screens." We will have more to say in chapter 4 about how hard it is sometimes to get on the agenda. But one reason for a lack of opposition in a policy debate is that the issue simply is not going anywhere, so opponents need not even bother to mobilize. Almost 20 percent of our sides were facing such a situation. A lack of opposition can be a bad thing.

A majority of cases—58 to be precise—had two sides. Just 23 cases involved what could be considered a complex structure of conflict (with multiple competing goals), and the bulk of these cases had just three or four sides. Typically, this consists of a status quo side and two or three sets of actors attempting to change the policy in slightly different ways. These groups may not be directly opposed to each other, but they are not working together, either. Only one case included five or more distinct sides.

One might expect that the multidimensional nature of the issues facing government would lead directly to an incoherent, overlapping, and confusing set of policy positions being held by various interested parties and that this, in turn, explains the policy stalemate and the extreme status quo bias that we observe in American politics. With advocates seeking multiple and conflicting goals, it might prove impossible to achieve consensus on anything. Although there is some intuitive appeal to this argument, the data in table 3.1 suggest that this is far from true. We found only a single case with five or more sides, while fully three-quarters of the cases had just one or two sides. Clearly, the causes of stalemate do not derive from the splintering of sides on the issues before government. Complexity can cause stalemate. But there is so much stalemate in Congress and so little complexity that most stalemate cannot be caused by complex patterns of conflict on most policy debates. Typically, debates are very clear, with just one or two sides active.

We did have one case in our sample with seven distinct sides; this related to the possible regulation of Internet prescriptions. Three different sides sought different types of regulations; two distinct sides argued either that the issues should be handled by the states or that existing federal law with voluntary measures could handle the problems; and two other significant sides weighed in on the issue with no proposed solution, but simply to protect their own separate and substantial interests on the matter.

Despite the seriousness of this problem, Congress was initially hesitant to act. Republicans in particular were hesitant to regulate the Internet, as they believe strongly in free-market principles that should result in consumers having broader choices and lower prices. Republicans also for the most part advocated allowing state governments to deal with the problem, since regulation of pharmacies is covered under state laws. Democrats were more outspoken in favor of additional federal regulations to ensure consumer protection. Work began in the 106th Congress with hearings, and a bipartisan compromise bill that contained some elements favored by both Democrats and Republicans was introduced just before Congress adjourned for the 2000 elections. Unfortunately for backers of the bill, there was little time left in the session and few strong believers in the feasibility of the bill's goals. The bill was introduced but never acted upon. A similar bill was introduced in the 107th Congress and again in the 108th Congress, but in each of these sessions members of Congress focused more attention on the issue of prescription affordability, and regulation of Internet prescriptions was never acted upon.

The inability to forge a new policy consensus in the complex environment associated with seven distinct policy sides, each with powerful actors fighting over various elements of a broad mixture of policies, is completely understandable. In this particular case, the relative newness of the Internet as a policy area may have helped make the multiple competing sides possible, because the policy subsystems at work are less set in their ways. But our data show that the proliferation of sides is extremely rare. The structure of conflict is typically crystal-clear, and this has a lot to do with the ongoing nature of public-policy disputes. Across all our issues, 133 sides (62 percent of the total) sought to change policy, and 81 (38 percent) worked to protect the status quo. Table 3.2 shows the number of "proactive" and "reactive" sides on each issue.

Looking first at the distribution of cases in terms of the groups attempting to protect the status quo, numbers here are typically quite low. First, a surprisingly high number (twenty-five cases) have no such side at all. This could be because all agree the status quo policy must be changed, and the only question is how to change it. However, the lack of organized protection for the status quo arises much more commonly because momentum for policy change is weak and fails to threaten anyone. Why waste scarce resources mobilizing to fight a scarecrow? If a real threat develops, there's plenty of time to mobilize to lobby such a slow-moving body as the U.S. Congress.

Second, two-thirds of the cases have exactly one status quo side. We saw only six cases with multiple status quo coalitions. (These would be where distinct groups mobilize to protect different parts of the status quo, as in a large piece of legislation affecting multiple constituencies, and where different groups mobilize to protect their own parts of it, not to kill the entire bill.) One key structure apparent in our data is that there is typically just one "coalition of the status quo." This may be because wherever there is a side attempting to change things, those who oppose it have a strong

TABLE 3.2 **Changing or Protecting the Status Quo**

Number of sides	Protect the status quo	Change the status quo
0	25	2
1	67	74
2	5	10
3	0	9
4	1	3
Total cases	98	98

Note: The table shows the number of cases with the indicated number of distinct sides attempting to change or to protect the status quo. There were 25 cases with no side actively attempting to protect the status quo, but just 2 cases with no groups actively seeking change. Overall, 81 sides were actively attempting to protect the status quo, with 133 attempting to change it. There can be more than one status quo side, because each may be concerned with protecting a different part of the status quo. Similarly, there can also be more than one side proposing changes if they seek different changes to the status quo.

TABLE 3.3 **The Structure of Conflict: Number of Sides per Case**

Number of sides seeking policy change	Number of sides defending the status quo			Total cases
	0	1	2 or more	
0	0	2	0	2
1	15	55	4	74
2 or more	10	10	2	22
Total cases	25	67	6	98

Note: The table shows that 55 of 98 cases had the straightforward situation of one side for change, one for the status quo. Only two cases had multiple sides on both sides.

incentive to simply coalesce into a single "kill-it" side — that is, when they bother to mobilize at all. Fully 92 of our 98 cases had one or fewer status quo sides. A lot of structure stems from the ongoing nature of most policy debates; there is always a status quo, and there are almost always some people who like it.

Looking at the distribution of proactive sides (i.e., those seeking a policy change), three-quarters of the cases show just a single one. There are strong incentives, apparently, to work toward a single goal rather than multiple ones. Of course, this is not always possible, and table 3.2 shows twelve cases with three or more distinct goals being sought. Still, these are not large numbers. Table 3.3 shows the overwhelming simplicity of the vast majority of issues.

Fifty-five cases, an absolute majority, had the simplest structure of all: one active set of participants attempting to change the status quo, and one set opposing them. Twenty-five cases involved one or more sides attempting to change things with no one mobilized on the other side. Ten cases involved more than one proactive side working against a single status quo side. Just 2 of our 98 issues involved multiple sides on both sides of the issue. The continuing nature of public policy structures much of the debate around it, and that structure is typically very simple.

Policy Communities as Sources of Structure

For more than a half century, political scientists have been describing policy making as a process that takes place within policy communities.[11] Lobbyists, legislators, and administrators with a shared interest in the same public-policy problem interact on an ongoing basis to shape relevant statutes and regulations. In scholars' minds the exact compositions of these communities and their implications for policy making have varied dramatically over the years. Whatever the scholarly model, however, policy communities have always provided much of the structure that we observe. No wonder political scientists have returned to a common set of ideas over the decades.

The initial conception of a policy community portrayed a very tight subsystem with limited participation and high levels of influence over policy making within a narrow range of public policy. The term "iron triangle" was popular in the postwar literature, suggesting a closed system with a three-legged stool of key committee chairs, lobbyists, and administrators. A broader and less dogmatic concept of "subgovernment" achieved more staying power, relaxing the assumption of just a handful of participants setting policy. But the basic idea of the subgovernment still held that a limited number of Washington policy makers and lobbyists controlled each area of public policy. A central claim was that policy making was consensual. What limited differences emerged among members of the subgovernments were easily settled because of the familiarity of the participants with each other, their history of working together, and the strong norm of compromise.

Remarkably, this literature removed conflict from policy making. The basic idea was that elections and presidents and congressional committee chairs may come and go, but policy communities endure. Analysts depicted a stable system, characterized by incremental policy making accomplished through quiet negotiations conducted behind the scenes.[12] Looking back, we know that not all policy making in the postwar period was consensual. Issues involving labor typically engendered conflict with business, and by the 1970s an active and resourceful public-interest movement changed Washington politics. Still, policy communities with limited participation did exist for a time after World War II, and if not all was quiet negotiation, policy making was more consensual and partisanship more muted than today.

Interestingly, this case-study-based literature on subgovernments has a conceptual link to the sophisticated formal modeling associated with Ken Shepsle and Barry Weingast's "structure-induced equilibrium."[13] This pioneering institutional analysis of Congress argues that the congressional committee structure and the associated rules and norms surrounding committee policy making work to produce stable policy outcomes. Who wants to be on the Armed Forces Committee in Congress? Naturally, those with particular concerns about the nature and health of the military.

In Congress, this often means those members with important military installations situated in their districts. Who wants to serve on the Agriculture Committee? It will always be those who represent farmers. That never changes. With shared interest comes a vested interest, as only those with a material concern with the issue have the incentive to become expert on the subject matter.

Because these "high demand" members systematically seek committee assignments where they can best protect their constituents, and because this affects the entire committee system in Congress, with few exceptions, the entire system can be seen as a giant "logroll," where high demanders in one area defer to their colleagues in other areas, expecting deference in return in those areas that matter to them. A structure-induced equilibrium keeps the committee system in place because it provides benefits to everyone, but the policies that result are heavily tilted to those with a special interest in the policy and thus often deviate from what the general views of all 435 members would be.

Of course, a key element of this system is that members actually defer to one another, but the incentives to do so are clear. Break the rules of mutual deference, and you may lose control over the policy area that is most important to your constituents and where you have special expertise. This view suggests that powerful structures and gatekeepers play a key role in the policy process, preventing most redefinitions from occurring, despite the efforts of those who may oppose the system. Thus, norms of deference to those with expertise could mean autonomy for those with a vested interest—the foxes guarding the henhouse, as it were.[14] Indeed, this explanation has been put forward for the growth in government over the decades; as each special interest finds itself in control of an autonomous policy subsystem, inevitably they extract more from the taxpayers and government grows through a system of mutual deference, each special interest in its own autonomous bailiwick.

Although developed as a theory of Congress, similar incentives are at play within the executive branch. It is not the Agriculture Department, after all, that is first to complain about the health consequences of smoking; they simply approach the question from a different starting point, concerned with how to help farmers. That is the institutional mission. So institutional missions mesh with electoral incentives to create the "giant logroll." Assumptions about the stability of the policy-making process in both the formal theory of Congress and the descriptive theory of policy making through subgovernments are built around the idea that norms and processes are designed to yield payoffs for all who cooperate. Thus, the two theories had much in common though they could hardly have been more different in terms of methodological approach.

The theory of structure-induced equilibrium continues to flourish while the concept of subgovernments fell by the wayside. The paradigm shift is marked by Hugh Heclo's seminal article on "issue networks."[15] Heclo argues convincingly that the policy communities he observes are much larger, much more open, and much less cooperative than the stereotypical subgovernment. He chides political scientists for stubbornly hanging on to a concept that had outlived its usefulness. Heclo notes that if we look "for the close triangles of control, we tend to miss the fairly open networks of people that increasingly impinge upon government."[16]

The fundamental change in the nature of policy communities came with the "advocacy explosion," the sharp growth in the number of interest groups in Washington that began in the 1960s.[17] As trade associations, corporations, professional associations, and citizen groups rapidly increased in number, policy communities in Washington were immutably altered. These new configurations were not just bigger versions of subgovernments. Rather, there is some imprecise but real threshold where small-group dynamics end and a different set of relationships emerges. Coordination becomes more difficult, bargaining becomes more complex, and opposition within the network becomes more likely. Modern issue networks are more prone to conflict, because expansion of such policy communities incorporates organizations with significantly different policy objectives.[18] Moreover, open disagreement can emerge along many different axes. Trade groups can be sharply opposed to one another because industries often try to poach on markets held traditionally by other industries. Despite the decline of labor, conflict between business and labor remains contentious. Citizen groups are often unwelcome by business-related lobbies, but they have become a fixture of Washington politics.

Paul Sabatier's work on "advocacy coalitions" has common elements with the issue-network view in that he focuses on long-lasting, stable conflicts among policy experts.[19] In this view, policy making surrounding important public policies is characterized by relatively stable coalitions of professionals and other experts who share a certain point of view. The larger issue network may be quite conflictual, as members of the different advocacy communities differ fundamentally on some core beliefs. But they have in common a shared and highly professionalized understanding of the underlying issues.

It is hard to describe contemporary networks in any detail, as they are characterized by indistinct boundaries. As John Heinz and his colleagues discovered, large networks may lack central players capable of coordinating advocacy.[20] Think of health care. With hundreds and hundreds of lobbies active in Washington, what organization has the breadth and muscle to mobilize and direct the entire network? Obviously alliances develop out of policy communities, but coalitions can emerge out of a network whose members actually oppose each other. In short, it's not so much that the networks shape policy as an institution, but that participants within a network coalesce and work together to try to shape policy. Different issues elicit different coalitions within the broader community.

Despite the sharp differences between the subgovernments of old and contemporary issue networks, there is continuity too. First, subsystems were not devoid of conflict and indeed were often organized around fundamental issues of disagreement. Second, even Heclo describes an issue network as a "shared knowledge group," but he failed to acknowledge that this was true of subgovernments as well. The participants in a subgovernment were experts in their policy area, and this eased negotiations. Another point of similarity is that, just like subgovernments, today's policy communities push Congress toward equilibrium. That is, the very structure of policy communities, which include key congressional policy makers and staffers as well as lobbyists, works in favor of the status quo. In fact, our central argument about the status quo policy reflecting an equilibrium value may help explain why the older literature is sometimes understood as one describing a lack of conflict. Rather, it was a literature focused on a lack of *policy controversy*, which may well have hidden important points where actors disagreed on core values, but where the status quo policy arrangement amounted to an equilibrium value arrived at after years of compromise and negotiation. So there is more in common in the policy literature than there are differences; generations of scholars have focused on the shared-knowledge communities that have long structured the policy process.

As shared-knowledge groups, interest-group advocates in contemporary issue networks possess the expertise to contend with policy makers in government. But the opposite is true too. A standard explanation of interest-group power is that many leading organizations possess data that Congress and agencies lack. It's often been argued that provision of hard-to-get information from groups to policy makers and staffers is a source of political power.[21] Over time, though, the advocacy explosion has been accompanied by an information explosion. Washington is saturated with interest-group and think-tank data. It flows like a volcanic eruption 24/7, surging down the halls of Congress and through the corridors of agencies. The informational advantages of the well-organized corporations and trade associations have diminished as competing groups came to Washington and institutionalized their own information capacity. Lobbyists walk around Congress and agencies with a new study appended to their body like a third arm. Facts compete in Washington, just like Democrats and Republicans. But the information competes in an environment which is tremendously rich in information, as we have discussed. Further, each lobbyist attempting to spin her issue in a new way is held in check by scores of other knowledgeable observers, common members of the same policy community who share a common understanding of the facts and justifications associated with "their" little area of public policy. In sum, the shared knowledge that characterizes all members of a policy community imparts considerable structure to the policy process. In our cases, this is a key explanation of the inability of individual policy advocates to spin their issues however they pleased. Thus, it helps explain the apparent paradox with which we began this chapter: each of our issues was substantively complex and multidimensional, but discussion of it was surprisingly simple.

Conclusion

There are many reasons for the structure of conflict we have observed. This structure is definitely not related to the substance of the issues, which are uniformly complex. Rather, the structure comes from the need to build coalitions "for" and "against" a particular proposal. Why don't these coalitions endlessly cycle, changing as fluidly and fluently as the language a given lobbyist might use? The most important reason is what might be called an "information-based equilibrium," by which we mean that communities of professionals keep each other in check, countering proposals and claims about the value of some new policy with pointed rejoinders about the flaws in the argument. With large communities of professionals and experts surrounding most public policies, it is rare that a new consensus suddenly emerges across the board. Further, because of the diverse impacts of the public policies we have studied, the sides mobilized to protect or to change the status quo are highly diverse, a point to which we will return in later chapters.

The simplicity of the structure of policy conflict that we observe is due not to the inherent clarity of the underlying issues being debated, but to the great difficulty for any advocate in pushing the collective attention of all those involved in the policy process to dimensions of the debate that have been overlooked in the past. One might wonder why they even try, since the odds appear so strongly stacked against policy change. The dilemma for advocates seeking change is illustrated by criminal justice reform, one of our cases that went absolutely nowhere during the time of our study. This case represented a broad effort by civil rights and other progressive advocates to bring attention to systematic racial biases and other flaws in the justice system. According to proponents of this new way of thinking about the "war on crime," the war is flawed by differential sentences for crack and powder cocaine, more aggressive police behavior in minority communities, racial profiling, and mandatory sentencing guidelines and "three strikes" laws that have taken discretion away from judges and sometimes led to tremendous penalties for relatively small offences. Toward the end of the Clinton administration, advocates were just beginning to bring attention to this series of issues, including some success in noting the alleged crime of "driving while black," in which patrol officers were much more likely to monitor the behaviors of minority drivers than whites. When the Bush administration came to office, Attorney General John Ashcroft showed little interest in these arguments. The war on terror after 9/11 made racial profiling seem like recommended police practice, in fact. So the effort seems like a complete failure.

So what do advocates gain from promoting new policy paradigms that do not catch on? In our example, advocates understand the long-term nature of their goals. While they got no immediate policy response, they have indeed managed to get some of these background ideas into the policy community. Many states have adopted moratoria on the death penalty after so many flaws and wrongful convictions have been pointed out. High-level attention to the "driving while black" phenomenon led to some investigations and revised procedures. Disparate sentences for crack and powder cocaine have become the object of official review. Mandatory sentencing laws have become the object of discussion within legal circles. While no one would say that the issue has been fully engaged or that advocates have overcome the friction that all policy communities impose on new ideas, who knows what impact these ideas may have at some point in the future? It could be quite substantial. The political system deals with issues as they are presented from the communities of professionals and experts. Changing these cultures and the shared knowledge within these large communities may take time, but it can have substantial policy impacts in the long term.

CHAPTER FOUR

Opposition and Obstacles

Reform of the United States Postal Service (USPS) is not an issue that helps members of Congress gain points with their constituents or establish their reputations on the national stage. Nonetheless, few (if any) policy makers would claim that the postal service is a well-functioning operation. Over the years, decision makers in government, government watchdog groups, businesses, and the public have variously decried the inefficiency, ineptitude, or insularity of the USPS. This was certainly the case in January 1995, when the Republicans took over as the new majority in Congress. Against the backdrop of Republican calls for reform, the new chair of the House Postal Subcommittee of the House Government Reform and Oversight Committee, Representative John McHugh (R-NY), began to hold hearings in order to learn what he could from the USPS's customers, competitors, and labor unions about how best to fashion a bill that would help the USPS remain relevant, functioning, and competitive. With assistance from organizations representing those who are heavy USPS users (e.g., direct marketers and nonprofit mailers), McHugh developed and introduced a measure in both the 105th and 106th Congresses that would allow the postal service greater discretion in developing new services for competitive consumers while also controlling rate increases for universal mail service. By the 106th Congress, McHugh had the support of Representative Dan Burton, Chair of the Reform and Oversight Committee, as well as a coalition of bulk mailers, Federal Express, Pitney Bowes, and various small newspapers. The primary opponents to this measure were the United Parcel Service (UPS), who argued that any efforts to prop up the USPS further imbalanced an already uneven playing field, and members of Congress who generally agreed with the position of UPS.

Both sides in the debate sought to reach out directly to members of Congress and to mobilize their grassroots to do the same. But even with the involvement of the grassroots, the conflict on this issue was not very visible outside of Washington. Indeed, even as a member of Congress, it was not especially difficult to ignore the efforts of reformers and their opponents, because there was little chance that the bill, despite its success in the postal subcommittee, would pass the full committee. In addition to the committee-level opposition from Republicans who preferred privatization, Democrats on the committee decided that they would seek to block the movement of any bill from the committee in order to deny Chairman Burton, a Republican, any measure of legislative success. By the end of the 106th Congress, H.R. 22 had faded further into the legislative background, and its primary congressional advocate, John McHugh, was prevented by Republican rules on term limits from continuing his leadership of the postal subcommittee in the next Congress. Postal service reform and modernization, despite the engagement of relevant parties in and out of government and general recognition of the need for reform, never attracted sufficient attention to gain a place on the public agenda.

A similar outcome awaited clinical social workers in the 106th Congress, as discussed in chapter 2. As a result of a small provision contained in the Balanced Budget Act (BBA) of 1997 and an administrative rule enacted in 1998 by the Health Care Financing Administration (now the Centers for Medicare and Medicaid Services), clinical social workers would no longer be reimbursed for the counseling services they had been providing at skilled nursing facilities. Initially, organizations representing the interests of clinical social workers thought this would be a relatively easy problem to fix. This initial optimism was due to the circumstances surrounding the legislative and administrative changes that produced the new situation. Specifically, one goal that Congress had for the BBA was to minimize the number of individual reimbursements that Medicare would provide for services provided in skilled nursing facilities. To save costs, the BBA required that reimbursements for services at these facilities be bundled together, not reimbursed separately. Doctors objected to their inclusion in the bundled payment and, prior to passage of the Act, committee staff in the House and Senate sought out a list of specialty providers that could be excluded from bundled payment. The list they found was the government's price list for various medical procedures. Clinical social workers were not on this list, because they are not service providers in hospitals and they were not recognized as legitimate providers of service under Medicare until 1989, after the list was developed. Clinical social workers providing services in a skilled nursing facility, then, would be paid only through the bundled payment from Medicare to their employer.

On its own, this provision of the BBA would not prevent reimbursement of clinical social workers for their services in skilled nursing facilities. The bundled payments might be lower, but payment could continue. Organizations of clinical social workers presumed—initially—that an appeal to the fact that this was potentially an inadvertent exclusion would mean that they might be able to get a quick legislative or administrative "fix." But HCFA complicated matters by proposing a rule in 1999 that Medicare would not make any additional payments for social work services performed in skilled nursing facilities, because these nursing homes are required to have social workers on staff and, thus, the general reimbursement by the government covers such costs. Importantly, this proposed rule did not differentiate traditional social workers from clinical social workers. Only the latter provide mental health and psychological services that are not covered in the general reimbursement agreement between skilled nursing facilities and Medicare. This proposed rule complicated the situation that resulted from the BBA, but, again, the clinical social workers thought some type of fix to (now two) "inadvertent errors" would not be too difficult to achieve.

However, despite HCFA's willingness to delay the proposed rule and the active assistance of two members of the health subcommittee of the House Ways and Means Committee—Representatives Pete Stark (D-CA) and Jim Leach (R-IA)—the clinical social workers could not get the remedy they sought. Instead, they encountered an array of obstacles both to addressing what they perceived as unintended policy consequences and to returning to the status quo. For example, the Congressional Budget Office estimated that rectifying the problem would increase Medicare costs because it would once again be paying for clinical social workers' services. In addition, the clinical social workers and their advocates faced an information problem. As one advocate explained, "It's not easy to explain what clinical social workers do, how they differ from other social workers, and why this bill needs to be passed in two sentences or two minutes—

often you don't have any more time than that. There's a huge education problem." The clinical social workers also had few allies in their effort, as nursing homes were reluctant to revisit the bundled payment issue for fear that additional service providers would also seek exemptions. And, if this were not enough, the clinical social workers, who generally had worked with Democrats on most issues, were facing a Republican Congress not interested in increasing costs to government, especially as so many interests affected by the numerous provisions of the BBA—including hospitals, doctors, and other service providers—sought relief from "unintended consequences" of the Act. Despite the absence of active opponents, hope for a quick or not-so-quick fix faded as the hurdles to policy success became apparent. As with reform of the postal service, there was little to compel policy makers to take up this issue when there were many other issues to choose from that provided greater potential for claiming credit. The status quo remained in place.

In order to achieve their policy goals, organizational advocates seek to draw the attention of policy makers and to encourage their action on the organization's behalf. Likewise, government decision makers who are interested in policy change try to enlist organizational allies to help them build support for the initiatives they seek. But, as these two examples illustrate, getting others to pay attention to your cause is not an easy task. To be sure, there are issues that emerge onto the agenda of government very quickly in response to external events (state and federal emergency preparedness in response to Hurricane Katrina, for example). But most of the time, advocates compete for scarce space on the political agenda.

Like Congress, the media—whether print or broadcast—have a limited agenda.[1] Time and page constraints limit what becomes "the news." Even with Web sites, news organizations have only a limited number of reporters to assign to different issues. Organized interests typically have to prioritize issues based on the preferences of their members and supporters and their perceptions about what issues are most likely to be acted upon in a given political environment (e.g., Republicans generally avoid policy proposals that raise the operating costs of businesses). In the case of Congress and administrative agencies, policy makers must choose to allocate their time among the myriad different issues they are called upon to address.[2] In other words, even if media, interests, and government have significant resources of time, staff, and money at their disposal, these resources are inadequate to the many demands that are or could potentially be placed upon them. All actors in Washington are faced with more issues they could spend time on than they have hours in the day. This scarcity of attention has a big impact.

If an issue does both attract attention and become part of the public agenda, advocates still face additional challenges. Consider the efforts during the 106th Congress to repeal the federal estate and gift tax, or "death tax" as it is characterized by those who oppose it. Unlike postal service modernization or the reimbursement of clinical social workers, repeal of the estate tax commanded considerable public attention. Indeed, this issue illustrates the kind of situation that everyone can easily call to mind—a public battle between highly mobilized opposing sides. The case for repeal was made by an alliance of business groups (including those representing minority business owners), Republican members of Congress, and also some Democrats. On the other side were labor organizations and congressional Democrats who argued that repealing the tax would amount to a big tax break for the wealthiest Americans and lost tax revenues from what they argued was a "truly progressive tax." The ensuing campaign to repeal the tax played an important role in casting doubt on the claims of opponents and in building public support for repeal. Indeed, there is evidence to suggest that many Americans, including those who were unlikely to amass assets that would subject them to the tax, began to accept repeal supporters' claims that the average American was doing what he or she should to get ahead only to find the estate tax standing in their way.[3]

The active opposition encountered by both supporters and opponents was not the only obstacle preventing them from achieving their objectives. Proponents of a repeal faced President Bill Clinton's promised veto if the repeal measure, H.R. 8, passed both the House and the Senate. Moreover, Democrats had been given the opportunity to offer ten amendments to H.R. 8, through which they sought an exemption increase in lieu of repeal, support for various unrelated matters (e.g., one amendment pertained to prescription drug coverage under Medicare), and consequently, a bill that would need to be sent to conference before being sent to the president (because it would differ from the bill the House passed, H.R. 8). The delay became meaningful, because Republican supporters of H.R. 8 sought passage of a "clean bill" that would go straight to the president, making it possible for Republicans to "use this measure to negotiate with the president on some spending bills that have to pass." If repeal supporters were not successful in their negotiations with Clinton, their plan B was to have these events unfold "right before their convention so they can say that they tried to work on this issue but Clinton held them up."[4] Presidential priorities, presidential campaign politics, and the intricacies of legislative process played a considerable role in both the failure of estate tax repeal in the 106th Congress, as well as the eventual demise of the estate tax in the 107th Congress after President Bush was named the winner of the 2000 election.

As the estate tax debate makes clear, if advocates care about an issue salient to others, they are likely to encounter opposition. This opposition might come from policy makers, the public, and interest groups. One strategy for advocates is to figure out how to mute or overcome this opposition. But even if it is possible to do this (which, as we will see in chapter 11, is unlikely given the array of resources available to different sides on an issue), advocates, as the three examples make plain, still encounter many other obstacles.

Of course, advocates who prefer to maintain the status quo benefit from the hurdles that frustrate advocates of change. When issues that status quo defenders do care about attract attention, these advocates will try to keep the issue off of the public agenda so as to prevent any further momentum for change, but other obstacles to change are almost certain to lie ahead.

The issue of physicians seeking exemption from antitrust laws provides an excellent illustration of how proponents of the status quo policy can try to prevent an issue with some momentum from moving forward. Current antitrust law treats physicians as independent contractors who, therefore, are not allowed to engage in collective bargaining with health plans. But many doctors would prefer to have greater leverage in their relationships with HMOs, which have increasingly required physicians to justify their treatment plans and referral decisions. During the 106th Congress, Representative Tom Campbell (R-CA), an antitrust expert, introduced legislation (H.R. 1304) to exempt doctors and other health care professionals from antitrust laws, allowing them to form collective bargaining units when negotiating fees, coverage, and other issues with HMOs and insurance providers. Campbell's bill was greeted as a "neutron bomb" for the health care industry, giving "doctors a free pass to be above the law, to collude and fix prices." But largely through Campbell's personal efforts with the House leadership and Rules Committee, a vote on the measure was scheduled. The measure passed by a vote of 276 to 136 in the Republican-controlled House. But the Republican leadership was "none too fond" of the bill, which was strongly opposed by business organizations and insurers. Although members of Congress would rather have been seen as supporters of doctors than HMOs, the fact that not a single member of the Senate would be associated with a companion measure is striking. Aside from the business and insurance industry opponents who would have appealed to Republicans to stay away from the issue, Senate Democrats reportedly opposed the measure because it would have provided Campbell—a challenger to Senator Dianne Feinstein in the 2000 election—with a measure of legislative success to tout in his campaign. So, even in the case of a measure that passes handily in the House, supporters of the status quo can put a halt to a proposal's momentum.

In this chapter, we consider obstacles and opposition. We begin by discussing the types of opposition and obstacles that underlie conflict in policy debates, focusing not only on an advocate's active opponents but also on passive forms of opposition and other hurdles. Next, we describe how we came to learn about the obstacles advocates experienced, and we present the patterns of opposition and distribution of obstacles that are faced by different advocates active on different issues in different political environments.

Attention and Mobilization

Gaining attention is not easy. Consider, for instance, the frustration voiced by a representative of an industry association who during the 106th Congress was seeking an accelerated depreciation schedule for computer equipment to bring it more in line with the typical two- to three-year replacement cycle, a significant issue for businesses and industries that are heavily computerized: "The only tax bills getting serious attention [in this session] are the estate tax and the 'marriage penalty,' which affect lots more people than our issue. It's hard to get people in Congress to pay attention to our issue and get involved in passing it."

Indeed, there are forms of opposition that are passive but nonetheless formidable to those advocates who are trying to change current policy. These derive from the unwillingness, inability, or indifference of others to engage or consider an issue. This unwillingness may lead relevant others—decision makers and organizational allies—to opt not to allocate time, resources, or effort to an issue. In some circumstances, this lack of engagement may reflect a practical decision by an organized interest or decision maker to allocate their limited resources only to their highest issue priorities or to those issues they believe are most likely to gain some legislative or administrative traction. Consequently, if an advocate has difficulty engaging others and bringing together a coalition to press its demands, it may be difficult to get the attention and interest of those in government.

In other circumstances, the indifference may be rooted in a desire on the part of groups or decision makers to ignore those problems and matters of policy that would have adverse consequences for their preferences and interests if they did become part of the public agenda.[5] For instance, as we will see, supporters of the status quo often may choose to do nothing when advocates challenge their interests; they know that the odds are in their favor that nothing will happen regardless of advocates' efforts to seek change.

This indifference also may have pernicious effects, as when a lack of willingness to engage a problem serves to marginalize the concerns and interests of a particular segment of society. An obvious example is the failure on the part of policy makers to deal effectively with proposals related to health care, housing, and income support for those with little to no political visibility, such as an urban underclass. By ignoring such groups, decision makers and organized interests can develop policy and allocate limited resources in ways that serve their interests (e.g., setting time limits on receiving income support or devising plans for health care assistance that require employment or the filing of tax returns) without having to address complicated, longer term solutions and a politically unpopular use of resources. Even for those interests with significant mainstream support, it may be difficult to move on policy matters that serve a stigmatized set of individuals or groups. As one advocate supporting parity for mental health coverage explained, "You have to deal with the stigma that society assigns to mental illness. . . . Just when you're reaching people, some poor mentally ill patient shoots up the White House. It's not what a diabetic or cancer patient does when they get upset."

Whatever the motivation for the unwillingness, inability, or indifference of others to consider an issue, one key principle should be stressed. The absence of countermobilization to those challenging the status quo does not necessarily signify the success of the challengers' efforts. In fact, the lack of countermobilization is a good predictor of failure, as potential opponents can often sit back and wait, confident that the scarcity of attention will make it unnecessary for them to voice their active opposition. Of course, if they do see momentum for change developing, they can mobilize at that point.

Encountering Opposition

Advocates who are able to draw attention to their concerns have cleared
an enormous hurdle. But numerous potential sources of opposition and
additional obstacles remain. The type of opposition that comes to mind
most readily to observers of the policy process is active opposition: direct
mobilization by advocates on the other side of the issue. These competing advocates may have different policy goals on an issue, or they may
only disagree about the means to achieve a particular end. Regardless,
their presence changes the character of a policy debate. Most simply, the
existence of conflict immediately increases the chances that others will
be drawn into or begin to observe the policy debate. Conflict attracts attention. As interested others—including members of the public, journalists, organizations, and government decision makers—become aware that
an issue is contested, they too may "choose sides," thereby increasing the
chances for greater and more visible conflict. As Schattschneider argued,
conflict begets conflict, and makes the outcome of the policy debate much
less certain.[6] Conflict of this type, among active opponents, is quite common among the very salient public-policy issues that are the frequent focus
of scholars' and journalists' attention. On a number of issues in our study,
such as the estate tax (mentioned earlier), managed care reform, NAFTA,
late-term abortion, and reauthorization of the farm bill, it is relatively easy
to observe the governmental actors and organizational advocates who associate themselves with different sides on the issues and work actively to
advance their policy goals.

Although uncertainty no doubt increases when advocates face greater
active opposition, it would be premature to conclude that policy success
is less likely when there is greater opposition. Just as resources are not
clear predictors of policy success (as we demonstrate in chapter 11), the
presence of active opposition alone is likely to be a similarly inadequate
predictor. If the presence of active opposition can attract other participants into a debate and increase conflict, each side may have supporters in
roughly equal balance. Strong opposition is likely to be countered.

Moreover, in any policy debate, opponents may include organized interests, members of important committees in Congress, other members of
Congress, administration officials, unorganized individuals, and so on. The
constraints imposed by these opponents and the uncertainty their opposition introduces for an advocate are highly variable. For instance, opposition from members of Congress who do not sit on relevant committees

is likely to be perceived as less of a constraint than is opposition from the party leadership. In addition, an advocate who encounters opposition from organizations but not from government decision makers would have a relatively easier time advancing his or her preferences than would an advocate who faces opposition from government decision makers. However, organizational opponents may publicize the conflict in a different way than government officials might. The presence of more sources of opposition increases the possibility that the stakes in the policy debate will change.[7]

Reconsidering Opposition

Certainly it is important to know whether the side an advocate supports has attracted active opponents. But for some of the issues we followed, it was not always clear to us (or, more importantly, to the advocates we interviewed) who else, if anyone, was actively opposing their position. Yet virtually every advocate we spoke with could describe hurdles or obstacles that stood in the way of their success. In this way, an exclusive focus on active opposition will certainly overlook other obstacles that some advocates encounter. Obstacles may derive from the characteristics of the issues and policy alternatives advocates care about (e.g., their cost, the populations they target), aspects of congressional policy making (e.g., the need for a supermajority of support, the majority party's control of the agenda), electoral politics, and the partisan structure of government. For example, issues may be linked to stigmatized or otherwise unpopular target populations whose interests, for whatever reason, are relatively easy (or politically acceptable) to ignore (e.g., the stigma associated with mental health problems that we mention above may make it difficult for advocates to draw attention and resources to problems affecting this population). Aspects of the policy-making process also may create difficulties for advocates, such as when unclear jurisdictional boundaries make it difficult to determine precisely who should deal with (or who is likely to be most supportive of dealing with) a particular problem. Additionally, advocates may encounter difficulties that arise when coalition-building strategies are shifted by election outcomes. For instance, making progress on any issue in Senate sessions requires the ability to put together a bipartisan coalition of support, an ability that is unlikely to be equally shared across advocates or issues. Indeed, the partisanship that structures government provides advantages for some and obstacles for others. The inability to engage members of the majority party in Congress may provide an insurmountable hurdle for some advocates.

Overall, then, advocates may experience different forms of opposition as they try to achieve their goals: a lack of interest, effort, support, concern, or attention from relevant others; active opposition; and obstacles that derive from the issues of interest, the process of making policy, electoral politics, and the partisan structure of government. These forms of opposition, while not entirely independent, each provide distinctive information about the nature of the opposition associated with a policy issue. To focus on only a subset of the various types of opposition that advocates face is to risk misrepresenting the challenges and opportunities they encounter in Washington. For instance, although there may be no active conflict, advocates facing issue-specific or electoral obstacles most certainly perceive these as hurdles to achieving their goals. This form of opposition is simply different in nature from the tangible presence of active opponents. For example, advocates seeking funding for the AIDS Drug Assistance Program (ADAP) explained that they "really don't have any opposition except in that there's competition for a fixed pool of money. . . . Some [members of Congress] might not be inclined to lend support, but this is a rare thing, as it is really about providing treatment for a disease that now responds to the new treatments." Here, it is not active opposition but the competition for financial support that constrains an advocate's ability to achieve its objectives. Indeed, such obstacles—as well as the indifference discussed earlier in the chapter—may be especially important in preventing issues from becoming part of the public agenda and in maintaining the status quo. Importantly, these forms of opposition would not be detected by most studies of policy and advocacy because most studies typically consider only those issues that are already under consideration by Congress or regulatory agencies.

We interviewed advocates about the difficulties or hurdles they encountered in achieving their objectives. Their responses included references to organizational adversaries and members of Congress who had taken opposing public positions on the issue; the cost of achieving an objective; difficulties convincing organizations to devote time and effort to an issue; and a lack of a suitable legislative vehicle to translate a measure into law. We categorized these responses in terms of whether they referenced the following: active opposition (realized or expected) from various sources; indifference or inattention from those same set of sources; or one of eight

TABLE 4.1 **Types and Sources of Opposition by Intent**

Type and source of opposition	Status quo defenders (%)	Status quo challengers (%)	All sides (%)
Experienced active opposition from:			
Organized interests***	85.7	63.0	71.4
Congressional leadership	7.9	4.6	5.9
Members of Congress	49.2	38.9	42.7
Executive branch/administration	22.2	17.6	19.3
Mass public/voters	3.2	0.0	1.2
Lack of attention, interest, or support from:			
Organized interests	4.8	11.1	8.8
Congressional leadership	3.2	2.8	2.9
Members of Congress**	4.8	15.7	11.7
Executive branch/administration***	6.4	14.8	11.7
Mass public/voters	1.6	4.6	3.5
Expected active opposition from:			
Organized interests*	1.6	8.3	5.9
Congressional leadership	0.0	0.0	0.0
Members of Congress	0.0	2.8	1.8
Executive branch/administration	1.6	0.0	0.6
Mass public/voters	1.6	0.0	0.6
Number of sides	63	108	171

*Difference between defenders and challengers is statistically significant at $p < .10$.
**Difference between defenders and challengers is statistically significant at $p < .05$.
***Difference between defenders and challengers is statistically significant at $p < .01$.

obstacles (cost or budgetary concerns; insufficient or inappropriate data; divisiveness among allies; a stigmatized target population; disputes about the appropriate venue or jurisdiction for an issue; legislative logistics; electoral politics; and partisan or ideological concerns). The measurement appendix provides additional detail about these categories.

Table 4.1 shows the distribution of active opposition as well as the relative lack of attention or support from various governmental and nongovernmental sources reported by advocates associated with each of 170 sides across our ninety-eight issues. The table shows the overall percentage of sides encountering each type of opposition; the percentages for those who are defending the status quo; and the percentages challenging the status quo.

The most common source of active opposition is not surprising: organized interests. According to the advocates who are associated with the sides of the issues identified in our study, organized interests are their most typical opponents regardless of a side's policy goal. That being said, active opposition from organized interests is much more likely to be cited by sides that are defending the status quo than by status quo challengers (85.7 versus 63.0, a difference of 22.7 that is statistically significant at the .01 level). This difference likely reflects the different ways in which status quo defenders and challengers experience opposition. For those who seek change, there may be many obstacles to overcome before any tangible opposition is realized. Indeed, organizational opponents may not be apparent to some advocates who are promoting change, because those opponents may not have mobilized. Organized interests that are defenders of the status quo may have reason not to actively engage those working toward change; doing so would simply draw more attention to the latter's concerns. Advocates who prefer to maintain current policy are likely to be more inclined to wait to expend resources to oppose changes in policy until it appears that the challengers' actions are gaining ground with decision makers, the public, or relevant others.

Given that opposition from organized interests is mentioned by nearly two-thirds of sides challenging the status quo, there appear to be many cases in which challenges to status quo policy—regardless of their prospects for success—do mobilize organizational opponents. Relatedly, even if organizational advocates who support the status quo are willing to remain inactive until challengers' efforts gain attention, they are not likely to continue this stance indefinitely—a point that is not lost on sides seeking change. According to the data in table 4.1, expected opposition is of relatively greater concern to challengers than to supporters of the status quo (a 6.7 percentage point difference that is statistically significant at the .10 level). Yet even for challengers, the percentage of sides mentioning expected opposition as a concern is less than 10 percent. Overall, the organizational nature of active opposition experienced by most advocates suggests that organized interests may play a significant role in the policy process as initiators of change. This, of course, is no surprise.

The next two most common sources of active opposition also are unsurprising. More than 40 percent of the sides identified a member of Congress as a source of opposition, and 19 percent similarly identified executive branch officials as their opponents. However, unlike organizational opposition, these sources of opposition were cited to a similar extent by defenders of the status quo and proponents of change (49.2 versus 38.9 in the case of Congress and 22.2 versus 17.6 in the case of the executive branch, respectively). Thus, regardless of policy preferences, opposition from government decision makers is a common concern.

The lower proportion of sides mentioning opposition from government officials as compared to organized interests may reflect the different operational tendencies of groups and government officials. Because organized interests exist to protect and advance the interests they represent, they have relatively more reason than do governmental actors to engage opposing interests even when those interests may be working on issues that have little chance of moving onto the public agenda. In fact, organized interests may opt to be active (perhaps to a relatively limited extent) as a way of showing their members and supporters that they are on the watch, protecting and advocating for their concerns. For government decision makers, especially those elected to office, there are greater incentives to oppose actively only those initiatives that are likely to be taken up by the government and media. Elected representatives can most effectively claim credit for their accomplishments when they are engaged with issues that are in the public eye. Further, why engage in conflict when it may not (yet) be necessary?

It is somewhat surprising that fewer than 10 percent of the sides identified in our study, regardless of their objectives, encountered notable opposition from the congressional leadership, as we see in table 4.1. It was far more common for advocates to mention active opposition from committee chairs, ranking members, and regular committee members, who in our coding scheme were all coded simply as members of Congress. The relatively low salience of many of the issues we study helps to explain why we see so little opposition from the party leadership in Congress. The leadership has little need actively to oppose issues that reflect only a challenge from opponents to the status quo, as those issues are unlikely to move forward. (Of course, that the leadership opt not to be involved on certain issues will likely contribute to the lack of momentum observed on these issues.)

The greater emphasis on committees and rank-and-file members of Congress relative to congressional leadership also suggests that the relevant sphere of congressional activity for advocates is almost exclusively limited to those legislators with substantive concerns about the issues; most issues are decided within communities of specialists. As we discuss later, there are certainly some instances when advocates need to be concerned about the distribution of a chamber's policy preferences, such as when matters come to the floor for a vote. But given the rarity of floor events, it is clear from the data shown in table 4.1 that most sides concern themselves with opponents who are more immediately engaged with the issue.

Also notable is the infrequency with which advocates mention opposition from members of the public. It is surely the case that the public had not yet given attention to many of the issues advocates spoke about to us, making opposition from the public an unlikely prospect.

We turn next to the tendency for sides to note a lack of support or attention from governmental and nongovernmental actors as an obstacle. Table 4.1 shows important differences between status quo challengers and defenders for this type of opposition. Specifically, no more than 6 percent of sides supporting the status quo mention inattention from organized interests or government decision makers as an obstacle to achieving their goals. This is to be expected, because the objectives of those defending the status quo are probably best met when other advocates are *not* mobilized. Thus, defenders of the status quo are not trying to attract attention to the policy they hope will remain unchanged. Yet inattention can still pose a problem for status quo defenders, as when organizational or governmental allies are not sufficiently engaged to oppose the efforts of challengers. In most circumstances, however, activity, not inactivity, is a problem for status quo defenders.

In contrast, inattention from members of Congress, members of the administration, and organized interests provides few, if any, benefits for sides challenging the status quo. Attention, most especially from those in government, is a necessary commodity in order to realize change. As shown in table 4.1, relative to supporters of the status quo, status quo challengers are more likely to cite inattention as an obstacle, and they are more likely to mention inattention from governmental actors than from organized interests as a problem. In the case of members of Congress, the 10.9 percentage point difference between status quo challengers (15.7 percent) and defenders (4.8 percent) is statistically significant at the .05 level. But that so few sides challenging the status quo cite a lack of attention as an obstacle is surprising given the necessity of attention for movement on policy. Most likely, these results reflect the heterogeneity of those sides challenging the status quo. Some of these sides are engaged in issues that are being contested and considered on the public agenda (e.g., business interests and Republican members of Congress who support repealing the estate tax), whereas others are focused on issues that are well below the radar of other advocates (e.g., clinical social workers and their congressional allies who are attempting to alter the rate at which these workers are paid by Medicare).

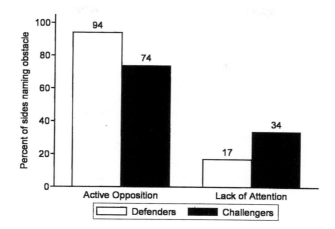

FIGURE 4.1. Active opposition and lack of attention, by policy intent. N = 171 sides.

Given the data presented in table 4.1 on both inattention and opposition, it is not surprising that the number of different sources of opposition is fairly small for all sides. The vast majority (84.9 percent) of those sides who mention active opposition cite only one or two sources, and of those sides who mention inattention or a lack of support as a problem, 97.9 percent identify no more than two sources.

Figure 4.1 aggregates the information about active opposition and inattention that we present in table 4.1 to show the proportion of sides that cite active opposition or a lack of interest from at least one of the following sources: members of Congress, members of the congressional leadership, executive branch officials or agency personnel, and organized interests. Sides supporting the status quo are almost certain to experience active opposition. Over 90 percent of these sides cite active opponents as impeding their ability to achieve their policy goals. In contrast, only 17 percent mention a lack of support or attention from government decision makers or groups as posing difficulties.

Status quo challengers also are quite likely to mention active opposition as an obstacle to achieving their policy goals, but, unlike status quo supporters, a sizable proportion of those sides seeking change (26 percent) encounter no active opposition to their policy goals. Moreover, a third of those sides seeking change note that inattention or a lack of support from

TABLE 4.2 **Types of Obstacles by Intent**

Obstacles	Status quo defenders (%)	Status quo challengers (%)	All sides (%)
Concerns about cost/budgetary impact	3.2	27.8	18.7
Logistics of the legislative process	19.1	15.7	17.0
Partisanship/ideology	0.0	13.9	8.8
Divisiveness among allies	9.5	6.5	7.6
Data to support position is insufficient/ inappropriate	4.8	6.5	5.9
Disputes regarding venue/jurisdiction	1.6	6.5	4.7
Electoral politics	3.2	5.6	4.7
Stigmatized target population	0.0	1.9	1.2
At least one obstacle	30.2	52.8	44.4
Number of sides	63	108	171

organized interests and government decision makers have adversely affected their chances for policy success.[8]

Table 4.2 presents information about additional obstacles mentioned by advocates seeking and opposing policy change. Of the obstacles shown in table 4.2, only those that are associated with the logistics of the legislative process are of concern to relatively similar proportions of both status quo defenders and challengers. Logistical difficulties include various characteristics of congressional policy making that can either stall or accelerate a measure. These characteristics include the lack of an appropriate legislative vehicle to which a measure can be attached, inadequate numbers of sponsors or cosponsors to bring a measure under consideration, loss of control over a measure when it moves out of committee to the floor, the need for a supermajority to secure passage of a measure or to override a veto, and the need to resolve inconsistencies between House and Senate measures that have been sent to conference.

For any advocate, these aspects of congressional policy making can seem insurmountable. As one advocate who was interested in maintaining current policy explained, "Being on the floor . . . makes educating Congress more difficult and . . . it can tend to be a lot more emotional. When members get before the camera on C-Span, things get emotional and are based on emotion rather than on an argument based on fact." Similar frustration was expressed by a congressional advocate who supported extending some existing energy tax credits: "Just trying to find the right tax bill. . . . The frustration really was more trying to find a vehicle to put them on, that would pass muster in the Senate too and go into law, because we were getting a little frantic. . . . We were really scrounging to make sure there was a tax vehicle out there that was acceptable. Nobody had a problem with extending these tax credits, the problem was that they were perceived as sweeteners for other tax measures . . . just sort of as honey in the pot, and it wasn't enough honey to get people to vote on."

Beyond the concerns about logistical hurdles, there are few similarities between status quo challengers and defenders regarding obstacles. Most notable, perhaps, is the fact that few status quo supporters mention *any* such obstacles. As we saw in table 4.1, for these sides, policy success is hindered primarily by active opposition from organized interests, members of Congress, and officials within the executive branch. Although active opposition does not preclude the presence of obstacles, the only additional hurdle that is mentioned (beyond the logistical aspects of congressional policy making that are described above) is divisiveness within a side or among allies. According to the advocates we interviewed, this divisiveness tends to impede both active support of a policy goal and the communication of a consistent message.

For those sides challenging the status quo, two obstacles in addition to those associated with the logistics of the legislature are mentioned fairly frequently: cost (mentioned by 27.8 percent of all sides challenging the status quo) and partisanship (mentioned by 13.9 percent of those sides). As table 4.2 illustrates, the chances of successfully challenging the status quo are adversely affected by the real or perceived costs that policies would impose on taxpayers, the government and/or the private sector. That cost-related hurdles are experienced by status quo challengers almost exclusively is perhaps not too surprising. Extensive research is not required to claim that something other than the status quo—something less well-known and certain—costs more than current policy. Indeed, a statement made by the advocate quoted above who sought an accelerated depreciation schedule for computer equipment is illustrative: "There are no real opponents to our position. The main impediments are (1) the difficulty in getting a tax bill through Congress and (2) the cost to the Treasury." In chapter 7 we present data about the policy arguments made by status quo challengers and supporters, and illustrate the frequent use by status quo supporters of arguments about the high cost of proposed policy changes. These arguments can clearly resonate.

More surprising, perhaps, is that partisan concerns—while relatively important among the set of obstacles reported by status quo challengers in table 4.2—are not mentioned more often.[9] (Recall that our study encompassed a period that included both former President Bill Clinton's struggles with a Republican-controlled Congress and an election that put the government under single-party control but produced a highly partisan atmosphere.) But while there are certainly many issues in our study that revealed the polarized atmosphere in Washington that so many journalists and scholars have pointed to, we also have many issues that simply were not of this type. Indeed, given that about a third of status quo challengers were concerned about a lack of support and attention to their interests, the lack of partisan obstacles becomes less surprising.

Yet there are times when even relatively small, low-salience issues are burdened by partisan division. This was certainly the case for those advocates trying to change the payment rate for clinical social workers. Several advocates seeking change spoke of the challenges they faced because theirs was "not a Republican issue." Specifically, "clinical social workers are very liberal and have no history of working with or contributing to Republicans, [and the proposed measure] will cost money." To make matters worse for those seeking policy change, no one other than the social workers was complaining. As one advocate explained: "There are few complaints from patients to members [of Congress] so far because services haven't been affected much yet. . . . When people start getting denied care and begin to complain . . . that Medicare is not covering services they used to receive, then it will be easier to get Republicans to pay attention to this bill." This example illustrates an important point about the idea of partisanship as a source of obstruction. When issues are described as partisan, we generally think of the polarizing battles between Republicans on one side and Democrats on the other. But given the organization of Congress and the agenda-setting powers of the president, partisanship can also prevent certain battles from ever taking place; that is, it can function as a form of agenda denial, a means of taking off the table those issues considered "Republican" or "Democrat" when the opposition party is in power. In this way, some change seekers are dealt a double whammy. First, they can't get support or attention because their issue-related concerns do not have implications that are sufficiently broad-based or urgent (the low salience mentioned above). In addition, if their positions on these issues clearly reflect the quintessential divisions between Republicans and Democrats, the party in power can easily and without consequence ignore advocates' concerns when it opposes the change they seek. We have much more to say about partisanship in chapter 5.

TABLE 4.3 **Types of Obstacles Experienced by Opposing Sides on the Same Issue**

Obstacles	Not mentioned by any side	Cited by one side	Cited by opposing sides	Number of issues
Active opposition	1 (2%)	6 (11%)	49 (88%)	56
Lack of attention, interest, or support	33 (59%)	22 (39%)	1 (2%)	56
Lack of attention, interest, or support	40 (56%)	31 (42%)	1 (1%)	73

Note: Data reported in the first two rows are limited to those 56 issues for which information about obstacles and opposition were available for opposing sides. Data in the final row include these 56 issues plus the 17 with only a single side.

In table 4.3 we turn our focus away from side-specific opposition and obstacles to consider the patterns of opposition between different sides on the same issue. As the table demonstrates, of the 56 issues for which we have information about opposition from at least two (opposing) sides, there are 49 (88 percent) where active opposition is reported by the sides in conflict. These cases reflect the type of opposition most often discussed by researchers and other political observers. In four of the seven remaining cases, only a side challenging the status quo reports active opposition. Intentionally or not, those sides protecting the status quo may not yet recognize the challenge to their preferences. Table 4.3 also shows that nearly two-fifths of the 56 issues we mention above are characterized by only one of two opposing sides mentioning a lack of support or attention. In all but one of these cases, there is also active opposition.

But to look solely at those issues for which we have data on at least two opposing sides does not fully represent the extent to which opposition as a lack of attention or support is problematic to interested advocates. Instead, we also need to examine the opposition reported for the seventeen additional issues that are characterized by a single side. Once these additional cases are considered, we find that 42 percent of the issues are characterized by a side citing a lack of attention as an obstacle. Thus, the battles between opposing advocates that are featured in most studies and most popular accounts of the policy process do not fully account for the nature of the opposition that is characteristic of many policy matters of concern to advocates. Where there are two sides to an issue, active opposition is obviously of concern. However, whether or not there is active opposition, the lack of attention by others is cited in almost half the cases. This, of course, is bad news only for those seeking change.

Conclusion

In this chapter we have argued that an exclusive focus on active opposition does not offer a complete picture of the difficulties faced by advocates in Washington. For the vast majority of advocates, particularly those who support the status quo, some active organizational or congressional opposition is the norm. But for a significant portion of the advocates we interviewed, there was no active opposition to speak of. One might conclude that a policy consensus had developed on these issues, but this is an optimistic view. A less sanguine interpretation of these data is that there was little need for opponents to assert themselves or even to register their disagreement on many issues. This is because the "unopposed" advocates are primarily those who sought to change status quo policy, which, as the previous chapters have argued, is a difficult feat. Moreover, and perhaps more important, challengers to the status quo also were more likely than status quo defenders to report that a lack of attention to their concerns created a hurdle. For these advocates, a lack of attention from governmental actors proved to be particularly challenging. The prospects for success for those advocates seeking to change the status quo were further dampened by the real or perceived costs of the policies they support, the partisan nature of the legislative agenda, and the logistics of the legislative process. In the case of status quo defenders, legislative logistics and active opposition define quite completely the obstacles they encounter.

Viewed narrowly, the recognition that inattention is a significant obstacle for many advocates, that other obstacles are apparent even for those who can attract attention, and that a lack of active opposition does not signal policy consensus may seem unsurprising. Most observers of the policy process recognize how few potential issues actually find their way onto the public agenda. But viewed more broadly, the ubiquitous reports of organizational opposition and the lack of attention noted by many status quo challengers underscore just how different the process of advocacy is for those who seek to change and those who defend current policy. In many ways, advocates with different goals are navigating very different waters, so that the strategies and tactics they use to achieve their policy goals are likely to be quite different. That being said, the precise means by which various obstacles affect advocates' chances for policy success become particularly important to consider given that so many advocates—both challengers and defenders of the status quo—report organizational and congressional opposition, as well as hurdles imposed by certain features of the legislative process, as the primary impediments. In the chapters that follow, we consider how advocates' objectives affect their actions, as well as how particular forms of opposition and obstacles shape the outcomes they realize.

CHAPTER FIVE

Partisanship and Elections

Reforming legal procedures for class-action lawsuits has long been high on the policy to-do list for many business interests in the United States. Huge jury awards for civil damages and the legal expenses of defending against time-consuming lawsuits in multiple states can greatly increase the cost of doing business. In this quest, business groups usually find ready allies in Republican legislators, while strong opposition comes from Democrats and trial lawyers who typically represent plaintiffs in class-action lawsuits.

For many years, business groups tried to persuade Congress to pass legislation capping the damages for pain and suffering in product liability lawsuits, but they were not able to overcome opposition from Democrats. In the 1990s they hit on a new legislative proposal: move class-action lawsuits involving plaintiffs from multiple states into federal court. This would significantly reduce the number of legal venues where companies need to prepare for trial (from thousands of state and local courts to dozens of federal courts). Furthermore, federal courts are less likely to rule in favor of plaintiffs than many state courts.

Since the new approach did not cap jury awards for damages, it was supported by some business-oriented Democrats, and passage in Congress looked possible. However, two important obstacles remained during the 1990s. Democratic President Bill Clinton opposed shifting class-action lawsuits to federal courts and prevented its passage while he was in the

White House. In addition, there were enough Democratic opponents to prevent passage of the legislation in the Senate. Business fortunes changed when Clinton was succeeded by Republican President George W. Bush in 2000. Bush made legal reforms, including the class-action provision, an important part of his domestic agenda. The final obstacle fell in the 2002 elections, when Republicans gained a 55-seat majority in the Senate. Legislation moving many class-action lawsuits from state courts to federal courts passed Congress and was signed into law in 2004.

Political parties contest elections to gain power over the policy-making process and political agenda that comes with holding elected office, and ideological divisions between the major parties have become more pronounced in the last few decades. Thus, it is no surprise that partisanship and elections shape interest-group advocacy in Washington. Intense partisan disagreements often produce stalemate that maintains status quo policies, but elections sometimes enable one side to overcome partisan stalemate and enact significant policy change.

Partisanship and Policy Making

Partisanship has become a more important feature of the policy-making process because of the increasing party polarization in American national politics, particularly in Congress and in relations with the president. Over the last forty years, the Democratic caucuses in the House and Senate have become more uniformly liberal, while Republicans have become more conservative.[1] The result is increased voting discipline and policy success for the majority party, especially in the House.[2] Ideologically moderate politicians (such as conservative southern Democrats and liberal northeastern Republicans) are gradually disappearing from Congress. The decline of a political center in Congress has made it more difficult for the two parties to find common ground on many critical issues.[3]

At the same time, there appears to be a resurgence of partisanship among American voters in the last thirty years. The correspondence between ideology and party identification has increased—conservatives and liberals have increasingly found their way to the Republican and Democratic parties, respectively.[4] In addition, the public has grown more aware of policy differences between the parties, and public evaluations of the parties and top government officials have become more polarized along party lines.[5] Finally, the influence of party identification in voting decisions has increased.[6]

The heavy role of partisanship in campaigns and in government helps explain how issues with multiple potential dimensions of conflict tend to get compressed into a one-dimensional conflict with two opposing sides (Republicans versus Democrats). Research on Congress tends to emphasize the procedural powers used to serve the interests of the majority party.[7] Neither party wants to see its membership closely divided on an important issue, for it is perceived as a sign of weakness in the party leadership. Thus, party leaders in Congress use their control of the agenda to prevent consideration of bills that might undermine the majority party coalition.[8] For example, in his widely discussed "majority of the majority" declaration, House Speaker Dennis Hastert announced that he would not bring to the floor any legislation that was not supported by a majority of Republicans, regardless of the level of support for the measure from Democrats or the Senate.[9]

Policy advocates can reinforce partisanship in the policy-making process. There are a wide range of mutually reinforcing relationships between interest groups and the congressional parties. As we note in chapter 1, government officials often act as policy advocates in concert with a coalition of interest groups. Similarly, some scholars argue that interest-group advocates help subsidize the activities of legislators.[10] Finally, there are ubiquitous links between organized interests and political parties in national politics. For example, labor unions and liberal citizen groups are often allied with Democratic politicians, while conservative citizen groups and business peak associations tend to work with Republicans. The group MoveOn.org has been active in raising money for Democratic candidates and running advertisements criticizing Republican politicians for supporting the war in Iraq. Additional examples include recent alliances between the GOP leadership in Congress and politically conservative lobbying organizations, such as the K Street Project, an effort by Republican leaders to persuade interest groups not to hire Democratic lobbyists, and the Wednesday group meetings for conservative activists and politicians organized by Grover Norquist's Americans for Tax Reform.[11] Lobbies will sometimes push legislators not to work across the aisle because they don't want to cooperate with interest groups pursuing opposing electoral goals. In an interview, one business lobbyist told us, "Why should we do anything legislatively to help groups that want to unseat [Republicans]?"

For all these reasons, we expected parties and elections to be important factors for some issues in our sample. What is less clear is just what proportion of issues is characterized more by partisanship than cooperation between the parties. As a first cut, we summarize data from interviews with policy advocates about a particular issue. Our interviews included a question about partisan conflict and elicited detailed narratives about the history of each issue. We regard an issue as partisan if most Democrats are on one side of the issue while most Republicans seem to be on the opposite side. For example, on one highly partisan issue in which some interest groups were pushing for additional government regulation, an advocate trying to generate bipartisan support vented her frustration by explaining that "many Republicans said it's a Democratic issue—we're not interested, we're against government intervention." Overall, slightly less than half of the issues in our study (43 out of 98) were described as partisan by at least one advocate in our interviews. Partisanship does not appear as pervasive as one might think.

We recognize that some advocates might have an incentive to understate partisan conflict. As a second cut, we created a finer measure of partisanship based on a closer examination of interest group and government activity on the issues in our study. We coded some issues as "strongly partisan" where the two parties in government were organized on opposing sides of the issue. For example, on these issues committee and floor votes split primarily along party lines. These tend to be issues that pit key party coalitions against each other (such as business/labor disputes or debates over abortion). Thus, partisan divisions provided the primary source of conflict on these issues.

We coded other issues as "somewhat partisan" where disagreement between the two major parties was more subtle. These issues did not always strike at the heart of ideological disputes between the parties, but such disagreements often lurked not far below the surface. In addition, there tended to be disagreement among advocates about whether to describe these issues as partisan: on the vast majority of the "somewhat partisan" issues, at least one policy advocate described the issue as partisan, but other advocates on the same issue may not have seen the issue in partisan terms.[12] Finally, we coded some issues as "nonpartisan" where we found little or no sign of partisan disagreement and where all advocates agreed that the issue was nonpartisan.

With the more refined measure, we find 23 strongly partisan issues, 31 somewhat partisan issues, and 44 nonpartisan issues in our sample. This finding requires some discussion. Much of the literature on Congress and the presidency tends to emphasize partisanship as one of the defining features of these institutions.[13] If partisanship is such an important feature of

national government, why are so many of the issues in our study nonpartisan? Part of the difference is a matter of scholarly perspective. Studies of
national government institutions tend to focus on the official (legislator or
president, for example) or official actions (such as roll call votes or presidential vetoes) as the unit of analysis. These politicians have clear party
affiliations and obtain their offices in partisan elections. Thus it is often
natural to compare officials of different parties. In addition, the executive
and legislative branches have institutional structures (such as Cabinet ap-
pointments and congressional committees) that lend themselves to partisan organization.

In contrast, we take a policy-making perspective where the issue is the
unit of analysis. Rather than comparing different government officials
and their actions, we are comparing issues. This is an important distinction
when looking for patterns of partisanship. While roll call votes in recent
decades tend to map onto a single dimension closely related to party affiliation, policy outputs in Congress have multiple dimensions.[14] One of our
main arguments is that certain types of issues, which tend to be partisan,
get more attention in Congress, the news media, and the scholarly literature than other issues that tend to be less partisan. Attention and partisanship tend to reinforce one another. Parties help generate attention for the
issues they choose to promote, but party leaders in government can devote
their energies to only a relatively small number of issues at one time.

Partisanship and Salience

We analyze the role of parties and elections by comparing the policy-
making process on the partisan versus nonpartisan issues in our sample.
As Schattschneider observes, the policy-making process tends to pivot depending on whether an issue maps onto partisan divisions. Political parties
tend to "socialize" conflict, increasing public attention to policy disputes.
In chapter 3 we point out that the number of competing sides can vary
substantially from one issue to the next. In fact, seventeen issues in our
sample feature only one side (typically pushing for policy change) and no
organized opposition. Issues with just one side tend to receive little news
coverage and relatively little open debate in Congress. Most of the issues
with just one side (12 of the 17) were nonpartisan.

Given the polarized political climate in Congress, we expected that partisan issues tend to be more salient than nonpartisan issues. Our evidence

TABLE 5.1 **The Salience of Partisan versus Nonpartisan Issues**

Type of issue	Floor statements	Bills	Congressional hearings	TV news stories	National Journal articles	Number of issues
Strongly partisan	45.7**	13.3**	7.7**	7.5**	8.1**	23
Somewhat partisan	25.8**	10.2*	3.2*	1.1	6.3*	31
Nonpartisan	13.6	6.6	1.7	0.9	1.5	44

Note: The table shows the average number of statements on the floor of the House or Senate, bills introduced in Congress, congressional hearings, television news stories aired, and *National Journal* articles published regarding the 98 issues in our study.
*Difference from "nonpartisan" category significant at $p < .10$.
**Difference from "nonpartisan" category significant at $p < .05$.

supports this hypothesis. As table 5.1 indicates, partisan issues received substantially more attention in Congress and the news media than nonpartisan issues. Issues marked by partisanship tend to attract significantly more government and advocacy activity than nonpartisan issues. For example, the partisan issues in our sample are more frequent subjects of congressional bills, hearings, and floor statements than nonpartisan issues. In other words, on average, more legislative activity was directed toward issues where partisan combat was involved. This is no surprise given the relatively high levels of partisanship in Congress and is consistent with much of the literature on Congress. At the same time, issues receiving a lot of public attention (such as high gas prices) offer parties an opportunity to contrast their positions with the opposition.

Nevertheless, we still have a large number of issues not characterized by partisan conflict. The nonpartisan issues are so numerous that the sum of overall legislative activity on the nonpartisan issues is almost equal to the sum of legislative activity in either partisan category on all three legislative measures in table 5.1. Ignoring less salient, nonpartisan issues is to ignore a lot of action.

In addition, the more partisan issues in our sample receive significantly more news coverage than the nonpartisan issues. This pattern is partly the result of more legislative activity, on average, on the partisan issues. Partisan conflict also provides a convenient frame for "objective" news reports striving to provide both sides of an issue. Journalists cultivate drama to attract an audience to news products, and partisan disagreements are hardy perennials for dramatic news content. Finally, partisan conflict has become an increasingly attractive frame for news coverage that often portrays politics as a "strategic game."[15]

Furthermore, it is not just that nonpartisan issues tend to generate less activity and attention. The degree of partisanship matters as well. On many of the salience dimensions, strongly partisan issues attracted more action and interest than somewhat partisan issues. The unmistakable result is that higher levels of partisanship are associated with higher salience.

Some authors have argued that one factor contributing to increased partisan polarization in the United States is increased attention to cultural issues such as abortion and gay marriage.[16] However, the large majority of registered lobbyists in Washington represent corporations or trade associations, so the culture wars are only a small part of the lobbying agenda we describe in chapter 1. In fact, only five issues in our study involve issues that pit traditional versus modern cultural and religious values. Thus, one source of partisan conflict is reduced when examining the lobbying agenda.

This difference in salience helps explain why our finding of substantial nonpartisanship on many issues contrasts with large segments of the literature on national institutions which emphasizes the primacy of partisanship. Some of the literature emphasizing partisanship in Congress focuses on the most salient policy debates. For example, the latest edition of Barbara Sinclair's book *Unorthodox Lawmaking* includes new case studies of the Medicare prescription drug legislation in 2003, energy legislation in 2005, and President Bush's tax cut proposals.[17] All were important policy debates, and all were highly partisan issues that received tremendous amounts of news coverage.

Our evidence indicates, however, that in addition to those highly salient issues there are many less salient nonpartisan issues being considered by the government. We believe that these less partisan issues are also less frequent subjects of scholarly inquiry. It is certainly understandable that low salience issues receive comparatively little scholarly attention, except hidden as quantitative data in large databases. Some of the disparity is related to the magnitude of policy change being proposed and the number of people who will be affected by the policy. Among the issues in our sample are an alternative process for contracting with independent vendors who provide moving services to military personnel, and funding for cystic fibrosis research by the National Institutes of Health. Legislation providing a new Medicare prescription drug benefit will directly affect more people than legislation funding cystic fibrosis research. A study that focused on such minor issues would likely be ignored (if published at all). Thus, a book of case studies about policy making in Washington is going to analyze issues such as the Iraq War, health care reform, or tax cuts. And on such issues partisanship is sharp, as the two major parties offer competing views and harshly denounce each other's position.

If the goal of research is to be able to *generalize* about policy making, then such research should be about cystic fibrosis research as well as health care reform, about the Iraq War as well as moving services for military personnel. And it should be about all the issues that fall in between the most salient and least visible of matters before government. That is, such research should be about the entire range of issues that come before government. And by looking at a random sample of issues, we see not so much a partisan contemporary Congress but a selectively partisan body with salience as a key correlate of partisanship.

Another difference between the institutional and policy-making perspectives involves the stage of the policy process that is examined. For example, many studies of Congress examine roll call votes on the floor or in committee, and these studies find strong evidence of partisanship.[18] However, roll call votes take place near the end of the policy-making process, and partisanship appears to be less prevalent at earlier stages of the process.[19] As Berry observes, advocacy often involves lobbying for attention, simply trying to get government officials to take an interest in an issue.[20] In the previous chapter, we demonstrate that inattention is a key impediment for advocates on many issues in our sample.

Given the way we measure policy salience, reaching a vote on the floor of the House and Senate is synonymous with high salience. Almost half of the issues in our study (47 out of 98 issues) never reached the floor of the House or Senate for a roll call vote. Not surprisingly, the issues that did reach floor votes tended to be partisan issues. Almost 80 percent of the strongly partisan issues in our sample reached a floor vote, while less than half of the nonpartisan issues reached a floor vote. If more of the nonpartisan issues had progressed further in the legislative process, perhaps some of them would have been subject to more partisan conflict.

This is not to imply that the nonpartisan issues in our sample are disproportionately stuck in earlier stages of the policy-making process. As we show below, a substantial number of nonpartisan issues in our study progress far enough that significant changes in public policy are made. Furthermore, roll call studies typically exclude unanimous or near-unanimous votes.[21] Nevertheless, some of our issues include legislation that passed the Senate by unanimous consent or passed the House by nearly unanimous votes. For example, legislation to appropriate funds for the AIDS Drug

Assistance Program passed unanimously in both houses. A resolution to end United States membership in the World Trade Organization failed in the House Ways and Means Committee by a unanimous 36 to 0 vote and failed on the House floor 363 to 56.

In addition, even when we examine the issues that progressed to a floor vote, we do not always observe partisan conflict. Of the 51 issues in our study that were subjected to a floor vote, slightly more than half (27) produced a "party vote" with a majority of one party voting against a majority of the opposite party. Put differently, 24 issues in our study were the subjects of roll call votes that did not feature much partisan conflict. Thus, while policy salience helps distinguish partisan from nonpartisan issues, the nonpartisan issues do not seem to suffer entirely from lack of government action.

Some might argue that the distinction between partisan and nonpartisan issues is somewhat irrelevant given the growing use of omnibus legislation in Congress.[22] Perhaps many of the nonpartisan issues get attached to omnibus bills that are sources of partisan conflict. Only twenty-seven issues in our study (less than one-third) were a relatively small portion of a larger omnibus bill, such as appropriations legislation. The proportions were similar for nonpartisan and partisan issues, although the strongly partisan issues were almost always stand-alone bills rather than part of an omnibus package.

Since partisan issues are more salient, it is reasonable to hypothesize that partisan issues are more likely to revolve around basic philosophical differences. One way to test this is to examine the potential budgetary and regulatory impact of the issues in our study. A key aspect of partisan conflict in the United States involves debates over the size and scope of the federal government. Perhaps the partisan issues are more likely to involve proposed changes in federal spending, in federal programs, or in federal regulation. However, as table 5.2 shows, partisan and nonpartisan issues are fairly similar in terms of their broad impacts on the federal government. For example, ten of the strongly partisan issues (43 percent) involve plans to increase or decrease federal spending. By comparison, a slightly larger number of nonpartisan issues (64 percent) include proposals to change federal spending (although the difference is not statistically significant). By the same token, similar proportions of partisan and nonpartisan issues include plans to cut or expand an existing program, to create a new government program, or to broaden or diminish federal regulations. Many issues in our study would alter the size and scope of the national government, changes that animate many philosophical disputes

TABLE 5.2 **Budgetary and Regulatory Implications of Partisan versus Nonpartisan Issues**

Type of issue	Issue includes plan to:				
	Raise or lower federal spending (%)	Substantially enlarge or cut an existing federal program (%)	Create a new federal program (%)	Increase or decrease federal regulatory authority (%)	Number of issues
Strongly partisan	43	35	30	74	23
Somewhat partisan	48	45	23	68	31
Nonpartisan	64	41	30	57	44

Note: For each column, entries indicate the percentage of strongly partisan, somewhat partisan, or nonpartisan issues with the programmatic feature described in the column heading. The number of cases is listed in the right-hand column. None of the differences within columns is statistically significant.

between the two major parties in the United States. However, partisanship does not appear to go hand in hand with issues that have potential impacts on the programs and powers of the federal government.

Some of the issues in our study were directed at executive branch agencies or the courts, rather than Congress, and thus never became the subject of legislative debate. It is possible that the nonpartisan issues were more likely to be handled in government venues such as federal agencies or courts where there is less overt partisanship. However, there does not appear to be a pattern of nonpartisan issues being handled outside of Congress. While some of the nonpartisan issues in our sample were the subject of court or agency deliberation, many partisan issues in our sample (such as prevailing wage regulations, late-term abortion, and licenses for religious broadcasters) also involved significant court or agency activity.

In sum, the main difference between partisan and nonpartisan issues is salience. As the visibility of issues increases, so do the stakes for the legislative parties as they search for ways to promote their policy solutions while differentiating themselves from the opposition. A false calculation may hurt them in the next election, while a shrewd and carefully constructed position may gain them an advantage and lead to the election of more members running under their banner.

Elections and Policy Making

Due to the growing role of partisanship in national government, electoral change is an important source of policy change in the United States. A shift in party control of Congress or the White House can have a dramatic impact on the policy-making process. Our study provides a natural experiment to examine the impact of elections and critical events on advocacy and policy making. Our process for selecting issues for case studies began in 1999 and continued until 2002. Three important events occurred during this period. First, a Republican president was elected in 2000 to succeed a Democratic president. As a result, 58 of the issues in our study were identified during the 106th Congress, when Bill Clinton was president, while 40 issues were identified during the 107th Congress, after George W. Bush became president. The shift in party control of the White House also shifted the political agenda in Washington.

Second, the 2000 elections brought Democrats to parity with Republicans in the Senate, with each party holding fifty seats. Initially, the GOP maintained control with Vice President Cheney's tie-breaking vote as president of the Senate. However, the defection of Senator James Jeffords from the Republican Party led to a short interregnum of Democratic control of the Senate from June 2001 to the end of 2002. Democrats in the Senate used their agenda control power during this period to stymie some Republican initiatives. As a result, Republicans did not effectively gain majority control of the Senate until 2003.

Finally, on September 11, 2001, hijackers commandeered commercial jets and crashed them into the World Trade Center and the Pentagon. The September 11 attacks fundamentally changed American politics. In the aftermath of the attacks, the political agenda shifted sharply toward national security and foreign policy, and American-led wars were launched in Afghanistan and Iraq. In addition, after the September 11 attacks, American public opinion rallied around the national government and boosted the approval ratings of President Bush just eight months into his first term.

These critical events took place while we were in the field gathering cases to study. In some cases, it may be difficult to isolate the effect of the 2000 election from the events of September 11 on the issues in our study. How much would President Bush have been able to shape the policy-making agenda and influence Congress if the September 11 attacks had never occurred? Although it is impossible to definitively answer this question, there are some issues in our study that were affected by the election of President Bush. We examine the shift in party control of the White House in several ways. First, we look for cases of accelerated policy change after the 2000 elections. These cases involve issues where policy change was stymied under President Clinton but moved forward under President

Bush. Second, we look for cases of policy reversal, where a policy adopted under President Clinton was later reversed under President Bush. Third, we examine our issues for examples of a shifting policy agenda as a result of the 2000 election. These are mutually exclusive categories.

Accelerated policy change

One way in which elections affect public policy is by increasing opportunities for policy change that did not exist under the previous elected leaders. There are seven issues in our sample where policy change accelerated after George W. Bush replaced Bill Clinton as president. All are cases where opposition from Democrats stymied policy change prior to the 2000 election.[23] There were clear policy conflicts between President Clinton and the Republican-controlled Congress. At least four of the issues in our study were vetoed by President Clinton during the 106th Congress (1999–2000). Once President Bush assumed office and the veto threat disappeared, policy change on many issues moved forward. In fact, President Bush did not veto any legislation until his sixth year in office.

As an example of policy change that accelerated after President Bush took office, consider the dispute over the proposed disposal of nuclear waste at Yucca Mountain, Nevada, described in chapter 2. President Clinton vetoed legislation to designate Yucca Mountain as a nuclear waste storage facility, and Congress was unable to override his veto. However, after replacing Clinton in the White House, President Bush lobbied Congress to pass the Yucca Mountain legislation and signed it into law.

Another policy that changed under President Bush after being stymied by President Clinton was repeal of the federal estate tax (described in chapter 4). In 2000, the Republican-controlled Congress passed legislation to repeal the estate tax, over the opposition of most Democrats. Nevertheless, Republicans were unable to override President Clinton's veto. In 2001 a newly elected President Bush, who campaigned on a pledge to lower taxes, signed legislation to phase out the estate tax.

Policy reversal

We also count three cases where President Bush reversed a policy change that had been enacted by President Clinton. One example involves proposed ergonomics regulations designed to reduce workplace injuries. At the very end of the Clinton administration, the Occupational Safety and

Health Administration (OSHA) proposed new regulations to force businesses to take steps to reduce the chance of injuries on the job. Organized labor and many Democrats in Congress strongly supported the new regulations and emphasized the benefits of improved workplace safety. Many business groups and Republicans in Congress opposed the proposed regulations because of the extra costs they would impose on employers. They understood the stakes in the election. Barely concealing his contempt, a business lobbyist said OSHA is "moving at breakneck speed to get this done. They want to get it done before the next administration. I'm sure the Department of Labor would prefer Gore. A Bush administration would be less likely to go through with these regs." At the time we spoke with him, this lobbyist and others in his trade group were working hard to raise money for the Bush-Cheney ticket. The business lobbyists working against the ergonomics standards were rewarded. In 2001 the Republican-controlled Congress voted to repeal the regulations on largely party-line roll call votes. President Bush then signed the ergonomics legislation into law to complete the repeal.

Agenda shift

Finally, we examine other cases, where the election of President Bush appears to have changed the policy agenda in Washington. We identify two types of changes in the policy agenda: (1) cases that dropped off the policy agenda after President Bush was elected and (2) cases that received no serious attention until after President Bush was elected. In identifying the policy agenda, we define issues as being on the agenda if they were the subject of congressional hearings or reached the floor of at least one chamber of Congress.

We count five issues that received serious political attention under President Clinton but then effectively dropped off the political agenda after the 2000 election. One such issue involved a failed effort to change the way antitrust laws apply to physicians (described in chapter 4). In the 106th Congress the American Medical Association worked with Representative Tom Campbell (R-CA) on legislation to allow doctors to bargain collectively when negotiating fees and treatment issues with insurers. The issue has partisan undertones. Democratic administrations tend to use antitrust law to investigate alleged monopolies and corporate mergers to prevent undue concentration of economic power. The Clinton administration, while officially opposing the Campbell legislation, had basically stopped bringing antitrust enforcement actions against physicians while turning its antitrust energies on proposed mergers and large companies like Microsoft. Republican administrations tend to be less concerned about mergers (generally regarding them as manifestations of economic efficiency) and focus antitrust enforcement on price-fixing or other forms of collusion between firms or individuals. Thus, Republican leaders in the House opposed Rep. Campbell's legislation.

Despite the opposition from Republican leaders in the House, the legislation passed the House by a wide margin. However, the legislation stalled in the Senate. For all intents and purposes, the issue of exempting doctors from antitrust legislation dropped off the national agenda the next year. In 2001 the incoming Bush administration professed little sympathy for the doctors' position, and Rep. Campbell was no longer in Congress, having run unsuccessfully for the U.S. Senate in 2000. Although similar legislation was introduced in the House in 2001, it garnered only forty-two cosponsors and died a quiet death in committee without so much as a hearing.

By the same token, some issues in our study that were absent from the policy agenda under President Clinton received more serious attention after the inauguration of President Bush. For example, consider the ongoing debate over stem cell research and human cloning. The debate has moved beyond the hypothetical since scientists in Scotland cloned a sheep in 1996. Some advocate a complete ban on human cloning, including a ban on "therapeutic cloning" such as certain types of stem cell research in which cells are extracted from embryos in an attempt to develop cures for diseases. Much of the organized opposition to therapeutic cloning comes from anti-abortion organizations that view the destruction of human embryos as immoral. On the other side, there are scientific organizations and nonprofits that fight for stem cell research as a possible route to treatments for devastating diseases such as diabetes and Parkinson's.

With President Clinton firmly opposed, legislation introduced in the 106th Congress to ban cloning went nowhere. Two separate bills were introduced to ban human cloning, including therapeutic cloning, but each bill was supported by no more than a handful of cosponsors and neither bill even received a hearing in Congress. Things changed when President Bush, a strong ally of the pro-life movement, took office. In his first year as president, Bush made a nationally televised address in which he announced a policy of limiting federally funded stem cell research to existing lines of embryos that had already been harvested. In addition, President Bush vowed to veto legislation that allowed any type of cloning. Legislation

TABLE 5.3 **The Impact of the 2000 Presidential Election**

Type of issue	Effect of presidential election			Unaffected	Percentage of cases affected	Total
	Accelerated policy change	Policy reversal	Agenda shift			
Strongly partisan	6	2	1	12	43	21
Somewhat partisan	0	1	6	21	25	28
Nonpartisan	1	0	0	37	3	38
Total	7	3	7	70	20	87

Note: Eleven of the 98 issues we studied were resolved before the 2000 election and so could not have been affected by it; we include only 87 "continuing" cases here.

to ban human cloning received more serious attention in the 107th Congress. A bill prohibiting most types of therapeutic cloning reached the floor of the House of Representatives, where it passed, with most Republicans voting for the ban and most Democrats voting against it. Said one advocate for the ban: "Therapeutic cloning is essentially cloning your twin just to disembowel it. We think, and the president has used these same words, that it is wrong to create life just to destroy it." Although the legislation did not pass the Senate, President Bush significantly raised the profile of issues relating to stem cell research.

The election of a new president altered the course of policy making on a substantial number of cases in our study. In examining cases of accelerated policy change, policy reversal, and agenda shift, we find that more than 15 percent of the cases in our study that continued from the 106th Congress to the 107th Congress were substantially affected by the 2000 presidential election. Not surprisingly, as table 5.3 indicates, partisan issues were much more likely than nonpartisan issues to be affected by the 2000 election. Almost all of the issues affected by the election were initially categorized as partisan issues based on the coding described above. Only one of the nonpartisan issues experienced accelerated policy change or policy reversal as a result of the presidential election. This involved a dispute over whether to initiate procedures to impose tariffs on imported steel, an issue where President Bush ultimately bucked economic conservatives in the GOP by proceeding with the tariff process. Overall, a larger portion of strongly partisan issues (43 percent) than somewhat partisan issues (only 14 percent) in our study were affected by the presidential election. This is consistent with recent studies indicating that partisan factors better explain the winnowing of legislation on highly salient issues.[24]

Partisanship and Policy Change

If partisan issues tend to be more salient, then perhaps partisan issues are more likely to experience policy change. Put differently, if partisanship is a key feature of roll call voting (one of the latter stages of policy making), then perhaps partisan issues are just closer to the end of the policy process where change occurs. On the other hand, some observers equate partisanship with policy gridlock.[25] Table 5.4 indicates the number of issues experiencing policy change within four years during our study period, for each category of partisanship. Cases with incremental change from the status quo, usually the result of negotiation and compromise, are coded as having "modest" policy change. Issues with nonincremental change, where the new policy is a dramatic break from the status quo, are coded as having "significant" policy change.[26] On issues with "significant" change, there is little negotiation or compromise. For example, there was no compromise on the issue of moving class-action lawsuits to federal courts—business advocates pushed the issue until it was passed into law.

Overall, the status quo usually prevails. After four years, policy changed on roughly 40 percent of the issues in our sample. Policy change was slightly more likely on nonpartisan issues (though the differences are not statistically significant). In many of the strongly partisan cases described above, the presidential election of 2000 influenced the outcome of the issue. As a result, explaining policy change for many of those issues comes down to understanding which political party held power at the time. In contrast, policy change occurred on most of the nonpartisan and somewhat partisan issues without a direct assist from the elections.

Partisanship and elections are important features of policy making. However, the fact that policy change was as likely to occur on nonpartisan issues as on partisan issues means that other elements of the policy-making

TABLE 5.4 **Policy Change on Partisan versus Nonpartisan Issues**

Type of issue	No change	Modest policy change	Significant policy change	Percentage with modest or significant changes	Total
Strongly partisan	14	2	7	39	23
Somewhat partisan	22	4	5	29	31
Nonpartisan	22	7	15	50	44
Total	58	13	27	41	98

Note: None of the differences in the table is statistically significant.

process must come into play. Why are so many of these issues unaffected by partisanship and elections? What explains policy change on those issues? There are, of course, a variety of sources of conflict that cut across party lines. For example, military procurement issues tend to pit regional coalitions of legislators, representing the hubs of competing contractors, against each other regardless of party affiliation. Other issues may feature different industries or trade organizations facing off. For example, a proposed regulation by the Federal Communications Commission to allow new radio licenses for low-power FM radio stations provoked a lobbying battle, with the National Association of Broadcasters and the National Religious Broadcasters opposing the new regulations. On the other side was a coalition of local governments and several other religious organizations. When Congress considered legislation to overturn the regulations, different Republican leaders were pitted against each other.

As chapter 4 indicates, there are other important impediments to policy change besides partisanship. One is budgetary constraints. On a substantial number of issues in our study, advocates cited the federal budget deficit and budget pressures as major obstacles to any proposal for increased spending (whether the spending was for a liberal or conservative initiative).

And as the following chapters indicate in more detail, the power of the status quo and challenges in attracting the attention of government officials are common obstacles facing policy advocates. The privileged position of the status quo is a challenge for policy advocates on partisan and nonpartisan issues alike. In addition, policy advocates frequently describe the struggles to get government officials to pay attention to their issue or position. As Berry explains, this means that lobbying typically is a long-term commitment requiring steady and methodical effort.[27] The fruits of policy advocacy typically are not enjoyed for quite a while. Almost nine of out every ten issues in our sample involved continuing advocacy and policy-making activity two years after our initial interviews. Similarly, the vast majority of policy sides in our study had been lobbying on the issue in prior years, and a large majority of them expected to continue lobbying on the same issue in future years.

Since many policy advocates take a rather long-term view of policy making, they often try to build bipartisan coalitions of supporters in government. As chapter 8 indicates, the policy advocates we interviewed frequently reported contacting legislators of both political parties, especially when they were advocating policy change. Thus, in some cases the advocacy community may act as a countervailing force against the partisanship conventionally believed to reign in national politics.

Conclusion

In chapter 2 we discussed the power of the status quo and reviewed both the incrementalist model of policy making along with the critiques of that theory. Furthermore, we indicated that analysis of the ninety-eight issues in our sample might shed light on the validity of this enduring theory. Some may see the evidence in this chapter on partisanship and elections as an endorsement of incrementalism. After all, if 90 percent of our issues continued on during the period of the next Congress, and if most had emerged as issues before the time we were in Washington, what better evidence is there of incremental policy making? Moreover, almost half of our issues didn't have a partisan dimension and another quarter were only somewhat partisan, which can be interpreted to support Lindblom's argument that parties are not very relevant to policy making.[28] One might expect that on most issues, most of the time, cooperative policy making through bargaining and negotiation is the norm.

Yet we don't read this evidence on partisanship and elections as an endorsement of incrementalism. In comparing the frequency of significant policy change, incremental change, or no change in our sample of issues, incremental change is the smallest category. We simply do not observe much incrementalism. Rather, we conclude that this random sample of issues demonstrates that policy making is influenced by several forces that provide the friction to reinforce the status quo. Partisanship and partisan stalemate provide part of the glue that reinforces the status quo in American politics. Elections, and the changes in political representation they produce, are one source of punctuation that can produce significant policy change.

In particular, we find that the election of a Republican president in 2000 to succeed a Democrat changed the direction of seventeen issues in our study.[29] These punctuations, such as the reversal on ergonomics and on the nuclear waste repository, are fundamental changes in policy. Incrementalist theory holds that policy making transcends elections. Instead, we find that in a significant minority of cases a single election helped produce policy punctuation. Moreover, election-related policy change occurred almost entirely on issues characterized by partisan conflict. Elections matter.

This is why interest groups are increasingly moving into electoral politics to help elect candidates that share their policy views.[30] The two parties differ in essential ways, and those differences are sometimes the trump card in policy making—policy making that is discontinuous.

Nevertheless, we also observe many issues lacking partisan disputes. One of the main correlates of nonpartisan issues is a lack of attention from government and the news media. Attention is a scarce commodity in policy making, and party leaders in Washington cannot devote substantial attention to many issues. As we note in chapter 1, most issues in our study receive relatively little attention, and party leaders are rarely identified as major players in our sample of issues. Thus, partisanship and policy salience tend to go hand in hand.

However, a lack of attention is not the only source of nonpartisanship in the policy-making process. Most public-policy debates are shaped by a community of knowledgeable advocates in which both political parties are often represented. In this study, we examine many sides, groups of advocates pursuing a shared policy goal. We identify 169 policy sides including at least one government official as a major policy advocate, and 100 of them (59 percent) include at least one official from each major party. If we use a more stringent measure of bipartisanship, 40 percent of policy sides in our study include multiple government officials from each party. Thus, many of the policy sides in this study are bipartisan. Groups trying to build support for their policy goals often find major advocates from both parties.

Finally, let us return to the findings of this chapter in light of a substantial literature on Congress and the president that emphasizes the central role of partisanship. On closer inspection, our observation of substantial nonpartisanship is not wholly at odds with this literature. One of the main theories of parties in Congress emphasizes the conditional nature of partisanship. The conditional party government theory notes that policy debates often involve multiple dimensions and argues that only issues that divide voters and officials on party lines motivate legislators to invest power in their party leaders. In addition, the theory posits that the agenda-setting process in Congress tends to produce issues on the floor that divide along party lines.[31] This seems consistent with our findings that partisan issues receive significantly more attention in Congress and are more likely to be the subject of a vote on the floor of the House or Senate.

It is just as important to note that other studies of Congress emphasize alternative influences on policy making. For example, John Kingdon's influential study of lawmakers argues that constituent interests tend to trump partisanship when the two considerations are in conflict.[32] In several issues, we observe government officials who buck their party to push an issue important to their constituents. For example, GOP Representative David Dreier opposed a significant segment of his party in arguing for fewer restrictions on exporting powerful computer technology, largely because of the importance of the high-tech industry in his home state of California. Other studies note that regional alliances sometimes overcome partisan differences. Finally, another recent study emphasizes the personal, and often nonpartisan, considerations that often motivate government officials. For example, in one of our issues, Senator Pete Domenici, who has dealt with mental health issues in his family, has been a leading advocate for Medicare coverage of mental health treatments.[33] Policy advocates often monitor constituent and regional needs and opinions, and they develop relationships with government officials that may nurture personal investment in an issue. Thus, interest groups and their policy advocates can serve as a mitigating force against rampant partisanship in policy making.

And for those issues that do evoke partisan division, there is still the possibility that they are characterized by incrementalism. Inaction is often politically unacceptable, and the inability of either side to have enough votes to overcome a filibuster, a presidential veto, or other obstacle to enactment can force adversaries into negotiations—negotiations that lead to policy only incrementally different from what existed before. Ideologues taking half a loaf—it still happens in Washington.

Strategic Choices

When political scientists observe lobbyists in action, they typically write about them as if their behaviors emerge from a deliberate plan, well thought out in advance. The advocate chooses the issue that is the most propitious for action, targets the policy makers who are likely to be the most receptive or open to persuasion, selects tactics that will best serve the organization's interests, and formulates arguments that will be the most compelling to those they will be lobbying. Armed with a creative and convincing argument, perhaps some new evidence or at least an anecdote, money to donate to political campaigns, and easily mobilized supporters, advocates gather support for their policy preferences according to a logical plan of action. This may be a simplistic description, but it is not too far removed from both popular and academic descriptions of the advocacy process. Lobbyists are portrayed as powerful because they can move so many levers in the policy process.

Lobbyists, of course, do shape policy debates and policy outcomes in important ways, but this does not mean that all lobbyists are usually successful or that any given lobbyist usually is. In fact, they often have little control over the policy process, and many of their actions are reactive rather than proactive, forced upon them by the actions of other policy makers and advocates. In short, advocates are often swimming upstream, trying to make the best out of a situation they do not control. This was abundantly clear to the advocates with whom we spoke but is strangely absent in most academic and journalistic writing about them.[1] One suspects that there are incentives, especially for journalists, to write of the cases where lobbyists have influence over policy. In our interviews, we found the situation to be much more complex—sometimes they do have influence, of course, but they are far from able to control the situation in most cases. Consequently they make do as best they can, reacting to the ever-changing policy environment.

Indeed, as the two previous chapters demonstrate, lobbyists' actions are shaped by partisanship and the outcomes of elections, as well as by myriad obstacles and forms of opposition they encounter. Lobbyists are not free to do as they please; they must adapt their strategies to the situation at hand. Yet advocates in Washington are strategic and purposive, and we can see clear patterns in how they behave. In this chapter we discuss many of the forces that affect the strategic choice of arguments and lobbying tactics. The following two chapters detail our evidence.

Two of our cases illustrate the constraints on (and opportunities for) advocates' decision making that we have in mind. Consider the first issue. Back in 1999, many clinical pathologists were aware that the Medicare rate of reimbursement for a Pap screening—a tool for diagnosing cervical abnormalities—was lower than they thought it should be, given the cost to doctors and technicians of providing the service. The Centers for Medicare and Medicaid Services (CMS), then known as the Health Care Financing Administration (HCFA), was the agency responsible for the Medicare program and for regulating payment rates. In 1999 HCFA—preoccupied by a series of budget cuts and growing health expenses—was in no hurry to increase the reimbursement rate. Yet one impatient pathologist decided he wanted to see some movement on this issue. He enlisted his member of Congress, Representative Neil Abercrombie (D-HI), to introduce legislation that would mandate an increase in the payment rate. Following a tour of a screening facility, Abercrombie became active on the issue. With the legislative ball beginning to roll, organizations representing the interests of clinical pathologists took notice. Various professional organizations representing pathologists and other health care providers had already been attempting to negotiate with HCFA over the rates. To their frustration Representative Abercrombie was a Democrat in a Republican-controlled House who did not sit on any committee that would play a role in establishing such an increase. Yet, like it or not, the effort to raise the reimbursement rate for Pap screenings had taken on a legislative rather than a regulatory focus. Lobbyists made the best of a situation that had been initiated by a single constituent and his member of Congress. As a lobbyist for one association put it, "This isn't a strategy [we] would have pursued, but once the bill was out there, we had to support it." The precedent-setting nature of a congressional mandate, if it were followed up in other areas, was truly frightening to many other interest groups, raising fears of detailed legislative involvement in other areas of Medicare rate-setting. (A modest increase in Pap smear screening rates was included in a budget agreement in the 1999–2000 session.)

Around the same time as Neil Abercrombie was being recruited to assist a constituent, members of the Business Roundtable—160 CEOs of Fortune 500 firms—saw an opportunity to secure favorable access to a new market. They wanted to do away with annual congressional review of China's trade status as a "most-favored-nation" (MFN), establishing permanent normal trade relations (PNTR) instead. (Most-favored-nation status simply means that trade with the country in question will benefit from the most generous tariff rules that the United States grants to any country. Countries not on this list may be subjected to punitive or discriminatory tariffs.) The United States and China had long had most-favored relations, but Congress insisted on annual reviews of this policy, hoping to maintain greater leverage over China if it could threaten, in any given year, to revoke the status. Though the Roundtable had long been involved in trade issues, it had never been very involved in the debate over China's MFN status. By 1998, however, it had made this a major legislative objective. Yet changing the status quo by securing permanent MFN status for China would not be easy given both public and governmental concern about the implications of PNTR on China's human rights abuses. Why should Congress relinquish its leverage? On the other hand, freer and more predictable terms of trade with China promised to help open up a huge and growing market.

How did the Roundtable prepare to enter this new, highly visible, and contentious arena of debate? Actually, some of the preparation had been in the works for a few years, long before this particular issue became a priority for them.[2] This allowed the Roundtable to hit the ground running in 1998. Specifically, the organization made a conscious decision in the mid-1990s to raise their dues so that they would have resources for any legislative effort they sought to undertake. As the Roundtable began to focus on China and PNTR, some of the resources were used in a number of congressional districts to establish local networks encompassing companies and individuals who were keenly interested in access to global markets. These networks were augmented by the individual grassroots operations that member companies of the Roundtable had developed. Moreover, since the 1990s, the Roundtable had made it a practice to hire legislative consultants who acted as liaisons with Congress and served as external whips to keep track of progress and coordinate interactions with the Hill. Many of these preparations were not directed toward China trade per se but rather to any issue given priority by the member CEOs.

The question of what strategy to use on this issue appears to have been answered in part before the prospect of permanent normal trade relations with China emerged. With these resources in place, the Roundtable was able to devote considerable energy to what became a highly visible (and successful) fight to enact PNTR for China. It had the support of the Clinton administration, though it faced active and vocal opposition from labor unions, environmentalists, and human rights advocates. While the Roundtable certainly did not control the debate, it did execute a plan and it took strategic advantage of a large group of allies. And these allies devoted more of their own resources because they saw the lobbying muscle already devoted to the issue.

These two examples illustrate a few of the points on which we will focus in this chapter. Advocates in both cases sought changes to a status quo policy, but strategic considerations, beginning with the very decision to lobby, developed quite differently. In one case the issue was of considerable interest to the public, to major interest groups such as the entire labor movement, and even to the president himself. In the other, most Americans would have little knowledge or concern about the details of the policy, though it was of great professional interest to those directly affected. Lobbying strategies were clearly chosen with an eye toward a particular goal and with reference to the resources each organization controlled. However, choices were highly constrained as well by factors beyond the control of the advocates themselves.

Three Constraints on Choice

In this section we describe how forces external to organizations and policy makers—namely, the power of the status quo, the degree of change sought, and issue salience—can affect adjustments to their advocacy strategies.

The power of the status quo

In chapters 2 through 4 we described a fundamental problem for advocates seeking change: the inability to attract sufficient attention to the issues they care about. This scarcity of attention represents one source of friction in the policy process; it ensures that advocates and their problems will compete for space on an agenda that reflects only a subset of the myriad potential problems that could attract the attention of those in and outside of government. A great number of worthy policy proposals go nowhere not because of active opposition but because agenda gatekeepers and their allies have more urgent concerns. Attention scarcity and the other sources of policy friction that we describe in chapter 2 go a long way toward helping us understand the difficulties that arise for those who seek to change the status quo. For instance, because no one can ever know precisely what the consequences and implications of a new policy will be, advocates seeking change must work to overcome the aversion of most policy makers to actions that may generate unintended and deleterious consequences. Relatedly, because the communities of advocates engaged on particular issues have shared understandings of the justification for the current policy, knowledge of its shortcomings, information about alternatives that have been previously proposed (and the reactions to them), as well as policy options that have been previously tested in the states or overseas, they are likely to be in no hurry to exchange the status quo that they may have had a hand in shaping for the uncertain consequences of a new approach. Resistance to changing the status quo for an alternative associated with uncertainty also comes as a result of individuals' tendency to weigh the prospect of potential losses more heavily than the possibility of gains.[3]

The case of criminal justice reform provides a striking example of the hurdles facing those seeking changes to the status quo. In this case, dozens of civil rights organizations had formed several coalitions, some of them with the help of funding from the Soros Foundation. Several of the organizations had conducted major research reports that showed racial disparities in criminal prosecutions and punishments. The research included a report sponsored by the American Civil Liberties Union, "Driving While Black," that exposed the problem of racial profiling. A range of related issues were highlighted in these various studies, all of which added up to some serious problems in the delivery of justice. For a time, the issue appeared poised to emerge on the national agenda. While the organizations received a great deal of press coverage for their efforts,[4] they received almost no serious political attention. No major bills were introduced in Congress, and participants in the coalition were not sure, when we interviewed them in the summer of 2000, exactly what their strategy should be or what aspect of criminal justice reform they should try first to address in the political arena. Despite media coverage, the issue was so far off the formal political agenda that opponents of changes to the criminal justice system didn't even bother to organize. But the absence of organized opposition didn't mean that advocates of reform were optimistic. Far from it. As a member of one of the civil rights organizations said, "The opposition is everywhere, so strong that it doesn't need to be organized. It is every politician who argues for tough-on-crime attitudes. It's the entire current criminal justice system." In fact, as discussed in chapter 4, sometimes the lack of an organized opposition is the surest sign that a proposed policy change is going nowhere. If it were going somewhere, some opposition would likely form.

More generally, policy change requires more than the attention of policy makers. It requires at least one alternative to the status quo that a large number of advocates and decision makers find appealing and can support.[5] Devising such an alternative often requires a substantial multiyear investment. Given all this resistance in the policy process, advocates who desire to change current policy readily admit that they are usually embarking on a multiyear effort. A corporate lobbyist working on food quality told us matter of factly, "The bills won't go anywhere . . . but they give us something to talk about." In essence, he was acknowledging the difficulty of overcoming the status quo, even with his industry's large resources, and the hope of easing resistance to status quo alternatives step by step.

To be sure, those protecting the status quo cannot ignore efforts to change current policy. Just as individual incumbents are seldom comforted by the advantage they are said to enjoy, advocates realize that the context may be just right for a change to take place. But relative to those challenging the status quo, the odds are generally in favor of those who defend it. Across our ninety-eight cases, we have no examples in which an advocate who supported the status quo took no action and was then surprised by a change that took place. The status quo tends to remain the status quo, despite organized efforts to change it. Because of this, we expected to see that the intent of a policy advocate—whether they are playing defense, attempting to protect the status quo, or offense, proposing a change in policy—would be the single most important determinant of their behavior. It will affect the types of arguments they use, the tactics they choose, their overall level of effort, and the success they can expect to enjoy.

Degree of change sought

The types of change advocates seek can vary tremendously. Some advocates may attempt to create new policy or change an existing policy, while

TABLE 6.1 **Extent of Change Sought by Sides to Existing Government Programs**

Effect of preferred policy on established government programs	Percentage of sides
Substantially reduce	13.6
Little or no effect	56.5
Substantially expand	29.9

Note: $N = 214$ sides. "Effect of preferred policy on established government programs" measures whether the policy objective supported by a particular side would substantially reduce or expand an established government program, or whether it would maintain the status quo or does not deal with an established program of the federal government.

others, like the civil rights organizations mentioned above, may seek to build public support for a long-term goal. The civil rights organizations were working primarily to raise public consciousness about the seriousness of an issue; they had not (yet) translated this into any specific legislative proposals. Indeed, the policy objectives of many of the advocates in our study were intended to have little or no effect on established government programs. Table 6.1 shows the percentage of sides across our ninety-eight issues that were seeking to reduce or increase the size or scope of an existing government program and those that sought no change in any established program.

The table shows that 57 percent of the sides were seeking no change to established government programs. Only a minority of these, in fact, were simply mobilized to protect the status quo, but the changes they sought did not involve any changes to established programs. Perhaps more in keeping with conventional understandings of advocacy, the table shows that nearly a third of the sides sought to expand existing programs, and another 14 percent sought significant reductions in them.

Two of our issues, providing health insurance to the uninsured and funding of graduate medical education, illustrate what the degree of change sought can—and cannot—tell us about lobbying strategy. In the late 1990s, many advocates working on health policy thought that circumstances were ripe for expanding health coverage to those who do not qualify for Medicaid but who also could not afford to purchase coverage on their own. Most everyone agreed that there was a problem: the number of uninsured was increasing, and the existing system of providing coverage was not sufficient to reverse this trend. In addition, with federal budget surpluses replacing years of budget deficits, advocates could once again promote policies that were not budget neutral. As one advocate we interviewed explained, "The argument for doing nothing can't be made anymore. It's understandable that when trying to reduce the deficit it isn't possible to do what's needed. But you can't say that we can't do it now, because we can . . . , and we cannot keep saying that a growing economy will help reduce the number of uninsured." To be sure, there was disagreement about what aspect of the system needed to be fixed and how big a fix was needed, but there was virtually no disagreement that the growing number of uninsured represented a problem in need of a solution.

The case of funding for graduate medical education centered upon the federal government's payments to hospitals through the Medicare program for the training of doctors and other health professionals, such as pharmacists and nurses. In 1997 a congressional appropriation significantly reduced both payment levels and the number of residencies per hospital. As one hospitals lobbyist put it, "That was a big hit" to the bottom line. Throughout the 106th Congress, organizations representing health professionals and hospitals worked to try to convince Congress to increase the payment levels, at least restoring them to their pre-1997 levels. Their arguments were compelling. Hospitals train residents who, at the completion of their rotations, typically leave for private practice, an HMO, or another health care facility. In short, the training hospital prepares doctors to work elsewhere. Such hospitals believe that their work for the greater good should be supported adequately by the federal government.

In comparing these two issues, what struck us was that medical associations focused on graduate education mounted a much more vigorous campaign to achieve their goal than did the associations focused on expanding insurance coverage. The reason, we suspect, is that a change in the medical training stipends seemed much more "doable." There were no advocates working against the health groups, though budget constraints were an important countervailing force. In contrast, efforts to extend health care coverage drew the attention of numerous advocates both in and out of government. These advocates tended to see this issue through the prism of previous battles involving health insurance, perhaps most notably the debate over President Clinton's health care plan in the mid-1990s. Relatedly, among those seeking change, there were those for whom the only credible solution was universal coverage through a single-payer (government) system as well as those who advocated a relatively modest extension of tax credits to the so-called working poor. In the end, however, these two proposed changes, to extend coverage to the previously uninsured and to maintain or increase the medical training stipend, achieved the same result: no change.

In thinking about the wide variety of advocacy campaigns, we have tried to puzzle out the calculations that advocates make regarding what to push, what to leave for another day, and how much effort should be applied to those issues which are not their first priorities. Large changes—like those associated with extending coverage to the uninsured—can seldom be achieved quietly. The only way to produce big change is to get many people to engage the issue. If this does not occur, nothing may happen, at least in the short term. Individual organizations and individual policy makers are certainly likely to reach out to their allies both in and out of government in an effort to draw attention to their concerns, but getting others to engage the issue, to make it a true priority, is never easy.

Different organizations and different policy makers all have different priorities, of course, and the limited time available to pursue all worthy priorities may prevent even sympathetic allies from adopting as a priority the concerns of other advocates. Here, as elsewhere in the advocacy process, the efforts of a broad coalition focused on the same goal may be more effective in attracting attention to an issue than would be those of a single advocate acting alone. As we have seen in chapter 4, coordination of issue priorities with allies within and outside of government can be a major impediment to change. One critical calculation by advocates in a coalition concerns the allocation of scarce resources: Why should an ally work on an issue that appears to have little chance of passage? As an advocate considers how to spend his or her time and the precious organizational resources at his or her disposal, there is the temptation to offer symbolic support to the coalition and focus instead on an issue that has a good chance of passage and is a high priority for that organization alone. For this reason, those seeking substantial policy change rather than only small adjustments face a high hurdle to convince their own allies that the time is ripe to push for the big change they may all desire.[6]

Of course, relatively small changes—like restoring funding for graduate medical education—are not necessarily easy to achieve either. For one, as mentioned above, policy makers and other advocates often are invested in the status quo that they developed, making them reluctant to consider even relatively small changes. Although in some cases it may be easier to predict the consequences of small changes, there is always the possibility (as the advocates we interviewed frequently reminded us) that a relatively small change in some area of policy might establish (or raise the possibility of establishing) a precedent for change elsewhere.

For legislators the calculation regarding their involvement with an issue inevitably leads them to weigh political benefits against the opportunity costs of doing less in other areas. They are regularly asked to address a whole host of issues, and one might guess that they allocate their time to those they deem most important in terms of policy impact or to a key constituency. If a change is too small, it may simply not be worth the time. Although an outside observer may see a small problem as easy and quick to address, time and focus are still required, and the matter may not be sufficiently visible to make it worth a legislator's effort since they would have to work hard to get recognition for their efforts.[7] Is there really a significant political benefit to trying to push through a change in the bundling rules for Medicare charges that exempt social workers? Who back in the district or state is watching? It's likely that even many social workers would be oblivious to the change, and certainly most would be oblivious to their own legislator's role in trying to effect that change.

Advocates continually find themselves in the position of weighing what is doable against what is really needed. Large-scale change is more difficult, and it's understandable that advocates will often focus instead on smaller parts of a policy problem and try to fix them one by one. Yet, while small changes may be simpler to accomplish in practical terms, it is no easy task to motivate advocates in government to expend their time and effort on matters that may have minimal payoff in terms of reputation building. And yet there are times when both types of change are possible: advocates risk large investments of their time and energy for broad new policy, and they work far less extensively outside of the spotlight to affect policy they or their constituents deem important.

Salience

Part of making assessments such as those just described is judging whether an issue's level of visibility is likely to change. Over the years the AARP, with enormous resources at its disposal, believed it could raise the visibility of Medicare's lack of a prescription drug benefit. The organization was wealthy enough to run television commercials on the issue, and its overall advocacy is surely one of the reasons that legislation creating such a benefit was passed in 2003. In contrast, a lobbyist for a large corporation responded to our question as to what he was working on by saying, "an archaic issue relating to the Mining Law of 1872." We knew immediately we weren't going to hear about TV commercials his group was airing or, indeed, about any effort to significantly raise the salience of the issue. In both cases the judgments as to whether to expend organizational resources to raise salience were sound. In many instances, though, the decision on relevant resource allocation is more difficult to make and the outcomes of such efforts harder to judge.

Considering salience is essential for understanding the uncertainty advocates face on issues they care about as well as the efforts they undertake to advance their preferences.[8] When issues are especially salient to the public, an advocate's actions are more likely to be observed and the issue is more likely to engage other advocates. When issues are less salient, existing scholarship suggests that advocates benefit from operating under the radar and out of the public eye, for instance by adding language to an existing bill or by making available arguments or analyses to suggest the infeasibility of an opponent's proposal.[9]

Of the ninety-eight issues that we follow in this study, few attracted much attention from Congress or the media. Indeed, as figure 6.1 illustrates, most of the issues we tracked across the 106th and 107th Congresses barely registered, either with policy makers in Congress or with reporters and editors at national and local newspapers. The objects of most advocacy efforts in the years of our study were unlikely to be familiar to the public or to have attracted widespread attention from advocates in Washington. Only three of the ninety-eight issues we studied are the type of high salience issues that typically draw scholarly and journalistic attention.

Figure 6.1 shows the distribution of salience across our issues. We looked at how many newspaper stories, TV news segments, floor speeches, and other activities took place surrounding each of our issues and combined the data into an overall index of salience. The result is highly skewed. The vast bulk of the issues received little attention, while a few got the lion's share of it. Indeed, if we look at one measure of salience, the number of newspaper articles on the issue, we find that just eight issues had more than one hundred articles published (and one, medical coverage for the uninsured, had over two thousand). The distribution of news stories is just as skewed as the overall salience indicator we show in figure 6.1. The low level of salience of most issues, but the extremely high salience of a few, has many implications.

Supporters of the status quo often benefit from a lack of attention to policy that they have no desire to alter. Those seeking change, on the other hand, are at a considerable disadvantage. If the change they seek is broad in scope, visibility is essential; an issue will go nowhere if no one takes it seriously enough to engage it. In this way, greater salience may be critical in order to create enough momentum to overcome the friction in the policy process. Yet a relatively more salient issue creates a less predictable

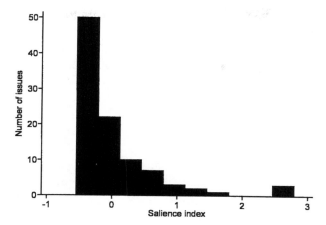

FIGURE 6.1. The distribution of salience. Salience is represented by a continuous index based on congressional and media coverage of each issue, with higher values reflecting more public visibility. The index has a mean value of 0, reflecting the average level of salience. $N = 98$ issues.

context for an advocate, because the audience is both bigger and more diverse than on less visible issues.

The linkages between salience, uncertainty, and conflict stem from the fact that salience is partly endogenous to the process—that is, the issue becomes salient not solely on its own but also because of events or the advocacy of lobbyists. Advocates who are disadvantaged by the dimensions of conflict associated with the status quo may benefit from broadening the scope of attention to an issue; these advocates may use outside or grassroots lobbying in an effort to increase salience, particularly as they attempt to move an issue onto the public agenda.[10] All that being said, a given advocate is more likely to be reacting to a growth in salience generated by events or by other advocates than he or she is likely to be successful in rendering an issue salient. For each advocate who prefers to see the issue in the daily papers, after all, there are likely others who would like to see the issue forced back into obscurity. So salience is both a result of lobbying and a powerful constraint on available lobbying strategies, once greater salience is achieved. No individual lobbyist determines the level of salience associated with an issue, however.

The issue of whether and how to apply and collect taxes on Internet sales provides an example of how salience evolves in response to the actions of advocates. When Congress first took up this issue during the late 1990s, lawmakers came close to passing a permanent ban on taxing sales made on the Internet. At the time, the issue of an Internet sales tax was not especially salient and the "e-Freedom Coalition" nearly had its day. But as bricks-and-mortar retailers and county and state governments (who would have faced a fiscal crisis if they could no longer collect sales tax on an ever-increasing share of consumer purchases) began to mobilize on this issue (forming, naturally enough, the "e-Fairness Coalition"), the momentum in Congress for a permanent ban came to a halt. Eventually, Congress did pass a temporary moratorium on Internet sales taxes, but they saw this short extension as an opportunity for states to make changes to their sales tax codes to facilitate application and collection of taxes from Internet sales. Here, the conflict expansion strategies of the e-Fairness Coalition were successful, thus upsetting what was almost a huge policy victory for the antitax advocates and online retailers of the e-Freedom Coalition. Increased salience was related to increased attention to a new dimension of the issue—from promoting the rise of Internet commerce, the issue became one of protecting the fiscal health of state and local governments.

In some cases, a highly unusual event or crisis (e.g., a blackout, a riot, a popular book, a terrorist attack) provides a focal point that may speed changes that are already being pushed. Advocates of change can use these events not only to justify the seriousness of a problem but also to generate support for a particular solution. However, if efforts to change the definition of an issue or to attract the attention of allies in government were not already in the works, crises or focal events might pass by without any policy change. Such crises do offer opportunities for the advocates of change, and if they are ready to seize on them, then major change becomes far more likely.

Choosing Arguments and Tactics

How policy arguments are used by advocates to build support for their objectives may appear straightforward. An advocate—the representative of an organization, a member of Congress, a member of the president's cabinet—offers a rationale or justification for a particular goal, seeks to explain the positive implications of some action, or undermines the goals of a rival perspective by explaining its negative implications. The advocate is defining or framing the issue in a way that is consistent with his or her goals. But we know surprisingly little about the content of advocates' appeals, how successful they are in attempting to redefine debates, and how their own opponents react when they see a rival's efforts to reframe the debate.

In terms of content, a wide range of recent studies, indeed a growing research consensus, focuses on the roles of providing information and on technical expertise in affecting the terms of a policy debate and the reactions of decision makers to the appeals of advocates. Many portrayals of lobbying are rooted in the notion that the currency of lobbying is the costly information that lobbyists provide to decision makers.[11] In this context, information is valuable because of the uncertainty that pervades the political and policy processes. When little is known about a proposal, policy makers attach greater value to information that minimizes uncertainty, presuming, of course, that they would incur some cost for acquiring that information. If advocates had unlimited time and resources to collect information, there would be little value in the information exchanged. But because time, money, staff, and other resources used to gather and sort through information about a particular issue or proposal are time, money, and staff not used to do something else, value is attached to information that lobbyists provide; the information reduces policy makers' search-related costs.

Costly information might relate to the social or economic impact of a policy being considered, its political consequences for a policy maker or his or her party, or information about the breadth or narrowness of support for a proposal and its chances of gaining momentum or going nowhere. Yet within the body of work that emphasizes the role of information in lobbying, there is considerable variation in opinion regarding the *nature* of the information provided and its intended effect. Scholars such as Hansen and Austen-Smith and Wright emphasize that the information conveyed by a lobbyist to a policy maker is private—it is information that is acquired by the lobbyist that is not available to or uncovered by other sources of information.[12] Information in this category could include estimates obtained from a privately commissioned study of the costs a proposal would impose on businesses, as well as information about constituents' attention to and attitudes about an issue that is emerging on the congressional agenda. Indeed, this idea of private information is critical to Hansen's theory that the most influential advocates are those who have a "competitive advantage" over others in providing information to meet the reelection needs of members of Congress.[13] For Hansen and others, private information linked to legislators' desires to be reelected is *the* information that advocates can provide.

But more recent work on lobbying illustrates how other types of information, including publicly available information about policy proposals, may be important in relationships between advocates and policy makers. In particular, Hall and Deardorff focus on the transmission of "information that legislators require for their work in influencing legislation," including policy analyses, research reports, and other expertly developed information as well as "political intelligence" that is designed to assist policy makers who seek to shepherd a measure through the legislative process. Hall and Deardorff argue that, unlike constituency-related information, expert policy information and political intelligence are of value to legislators who seek to be active on policy matters that are important to the information-providing lobbyists, because it subsidizes the legislators' efforts and activities. Although some of this information may be privately held and acquired, even publicly available information can be valuable to a policy maker if lobbyists "analyze, synthesize and summarize—in a politically user-friendly form, information to promote the policy goals that their group and the legislator share."[14] In addition to affecting effort, there is evidence that organizational advocates are often successful in getting Congress to make policy decisions that are informed by research and the technical expertise that they provide.[15]

The idea that publicly available information can be a valued commodity in exchanges between advocates and policy makers may seem counterintuitive. If information about policy proposals and their implications are available to any citizen, interest group, or policy maker who seeks to obtain it, how could it possibly be of value to a policy maker to receive that information from an advocate? The answer lies in the fact that precisely because there is an enormous amount of policy-relevant information out there, policy makers and their staffs would (and do) incur considerable costs to sort through and locate what is relevant, credible, useful, or being used by others. Indeed, as Jones and Baumgartner argue, the problem for most policy makers is not how to get more information but how to make sense of the avalanche of information that comes at them from every direction.[16] Given the multidimensional nature of most policy debates, advocates' arguments may be designed not so much to provide new information but to emphasize one dimension of the debate or one implication of a proposal over another. Advocates' efforts to focus attention on the cost element of a proposal, its fairness to particular socioeconomic groups, its technical feasibility, or to any of a range of possible dimensions of evaluating a proposal, reduce the time and effort required by legislators and their staffs to sort through the many implications of a proposal. Indeed, Smith has shown that legislators' interpretations or understandings of an issue can have implications for the support a policy receives.[17] Advocates assist with these interpretations and help focus policy makers' attention on a particular dimension of debate. This reduces the uncertainty associated with an issue, allowing legislators and their staffs to hone in on an issue from a particular vantage point or definition, thus reducing the costs they would otherwise incur in sorting through and digesting the sea of available information.[18] In short, policy makers may find valuable both privately held information that advocates convey as well as information that is available but costly to locate, synthesize, or interpret.

That being said, there is also research to suggest that policy makers are responsive to symbolic or valence appeals that are unlikely to convey information that is difficult for policy makers to acquire for themselves. Several studies highlight the importance of symbols in politics and their use and misuse by decision makers and advocates to achieve public-policy goals.[19] Although there is no single definition of what constitutes symbolic rhetoric or symbolic arguments, such arguments are commonly portrayed as relatively simple, emotional narratives that involve accessible images or appeals to widely accepted social values.[20] In a sense, if a group begins a media campaign emphasizing a powerful emotional symbol, and if a member of Congress believes constituents might be affected by that symbol, the fact that the symbol contains little in the way of new or costly information may not matter. In the abortion debate, a mobilization campaign emphasizing the evils of "partial-birth" abortion may have greater impact than a new study that examines the incidence and effects of teen pregnancy. Symbolic appeals, at least in the case of some high-salience issues, may be emphasized even if those appeals are well known to those participating in the issue debate.

Like arguments, tactics are another means of transmitting information. Direct contact between advocates and between advocates and policy makers conveys information regarding the policy implications of the issue being considered, as well as how debate surrounding the issue might be affected by the policy process itself (e.g., partisanship in a chamber of Congress or reluctance of an agency official to move on a matter of policy). Grassroots activities communicate to policy makers the salience of an issue as well as whether there are likely to be electoral implications associated with activity on the issue.[21] On many issues, a number of different tactics are observed, presumably because a variety of information—about policy implications, the salience of an issue, and so on—is needed by and is useful for policy makers.[22]

Given our understanding of how advocates' goals and the salience of policy issues affect advocacy, how might these forces be expected to shape arguments and tactics? Generally speaking, advocates who support the status quo can be expected to highlight not the virtues of the status quo but the tremendous uncertainty and potentially negative implications of any alternative to it. This is not to suggest that questions will not be raised about the operation of the status quo and its consequences. Indeed, there can be tremendous uncertainty about the true effect of even established policies—are they working as intended, are they effective, do they have added benefits in other ways, do they have unintended negative consequences? Challengers may raise these issues in an attempt to redefine the debate and raise doubt regarding the current justification for the status quo. Yet there is always more uncertainty with alternatives to the status quo, providing status quo supporters with an advantage that challengers can never have.

We also expect that support for or opposition to the status quo will affect an advocate's use of tactics. Advocates of change typically start a round of debate. Defenders of the status quo, virtually by definition, react to the efforts of others. In fact, since many efforts to change the status quo go nowhere, one of the most common tactics of those who support the current state of affairs is simply to do nothing. Monitor the environment perhaps, but sit tight.

We mentioned above that salience is partly endogenous to the policy process. Often, defenders of current policy benefit from keeping an issue out of the public eye and limited to as small a group as possible. Therefore, we expect to see relatively few instances of status quo defenders engaging the public or the media in their efforts. In contrast, those challenging the status quo are more often expected to engage in activities that raise the visibility of their concerns. In some instances—especially when the change that is sought is small—operating under the radar may be more beneficial, even for opponents of the status quo. But relative to defenders of the status quo, challengers will benefit more from tactics that increase visibility.

Salience also may have implications for the information advocates contribute to the issue debate. According to Bacheller, advocates who are dealing with issues that are controversial and more salient to the general public will engage in more "nonspecialized" activities, such as contacting other advocates to "argue in support of a legislative position."[23] In addition, West and Loomis are quite direct about the relationship between the arguments of advocates and issue visibility, predicting that the scope of conflict and the number of interests affected by an issue shape the type of narratives that will be used to define that issue. "As the scope of the conflict broadens, narratives become less complex and their meaning more frequently conveyed by metaphor and symbol."[24]

Finally, we expect that some types of information are better conveyed through verbal argument, while other types of information are better demonstrated through action. For instance, personal contacts are likely to be an effective means for advocates to ensure that their contacts in and out of government remain involved and are aware of the most up-to-date arguments about the likely implications of a particular policy alternative. However, electoral ramifications are probably better demonstrated through action. After all, grassroots efforts can be viewed by policy makers as indications of an advocate's ability to mobilize constituents on election day.[25] In this way, advocates who seek to affect the traceability of issues and a policy maker's actions on those issues may be far more effective turning out the grassroots than in describing to a policy maker that their actions on an issue may have electoral implications. Similarly, Kollman argues that grassroots mobilization serves as a powerful signal to policy makers about the state of public opinion and the intensity of interest-group preferences.[26] Costly public mobilization campaigns may be effective if and only if they show a membership willing to take action. If they do, policy makers may take note of the salience members of the public attach to the issue. If they do not, policy makers may conclude that although lobbyists are all worked up, the public is not.

Conclusion

Policy advocates face many hurdles and encounter different opportunities as they work to advance their preferences. Uncertainty prevails as advocates try to anticipate reactions to their actions, predict and process responses to their policy preferences from different audiences, and make plans for how to operate in a policy environment that is often driven by actions and events that are out of their immediate control. Yet amidst the dynamic context in which lobbyists operate, we expected certain patterns to emerge in the arguments and tactics that advocates select.

For one, we anticipated that advocates' support for or opposition to the status quo would significantly affect the arguments and tactics they employ. The uncertainty that surrounds new proposals provides an advantage to status quo supporters such that the arguments they use are likely to focus less on the benefits of the status quo than on the many possibilities for the proposed policy to do harm, impose costs, or otherwise make at least some portion of society worse off. In contrast, challengers to current policy will be generating support for the proposed policy whose uncertain consequences are being highlighted by the other side. Indeed, status quo challengers may seek to use their arguments to redefine an issue, a task we expected to be made difficult by the communities of specialists who are quite familiar with the current and previous efforts to change the status quo. Additionally, supporters of current policy are unlikely to act on an issue until there is a reasonable expectation that those challenging current policy have some momentum behind their actions.

Second, we expected that the magnitude of the policy changes advocates seek and the salience of the policy issues they care about also would affect advocates' choices of arguments and tactics. Given the advantages associated with supporting the status quo, we also expected that the effect of salience and the degree of change sought on the arguments and tactics an advocate uses would differ depending on the advocate's goals. For instance, we anticipated that status quo challengers, more often than supporters of current policy, would use arguments and tactics that have the potential to attract attention to the issue, although challengers to the status quo might be less likely to engage in such attention-expansion strategies when the change they seek is relatively small. Moreover, previous research suggests that advocates will tend to use more simplistic arguments and position-taking tactics when the issues they take an interest in are relatively salient.

Whether the evidence supports the expectations we have presented here about argument and tactic use is the subject of the next two chapters. In chapter 7 we examine arguments, and in chapter 8 we report on tactics.

CHAPTER SEVEN

Arguments

Advocates seemingly choose their arguments from a tremendous range of possibilities. We saw in chapter 3 that each of our issues was highly complex, raising many possible dimensions of debate—feasibility, cost, fairness, federalism, and so on. We also saw that the structure of conflict surrounding the issues was, somewhat surprisingly, relatively simple. Consequently, even though each issue was characterized by just a few sides, usually one urging some kind of policy change and another defending the status quo, the policy justifications offered by advocates associated with those sides could refer to many of the different ways of engaging the issue. In this chapter we focus on how advocates tailor their arguments to their goals and how they react to the arguments of their rivals.

By design, we gained a lot of information about the issues on which advocates were working when we conducted our interviews. Our primary goal was to get the advocate to talk as much as possible about the issue. For this reason, our first question was quite broad: "What are you trying to accomplish on this issue and what type of actions are you taking to make that happen?" An excerpt from an interview with the representative of a medical professional association about an issue we introduced in the previous chapter, providing health insurance to those without insurance, illustrates a typical response:

> In [the 106th] Congress it is unlikely that any entitlement will be expanded to cover all the uninsured, so we chose to target [our] plan to . . . those who may

have low-wage jobs who are not likely to receive health coverage and people without resources to purchase supplemental insurance. . . . The budget surplus that is available gives us the means to provide coverage to the population. . . . The plan has four components. The first provision is a tough sell because it expands an entitlement and includes an unfunded mandate to states. This provision involved expanding Medicaid to cover those at or below 150 percent of the poverty level. . . . The second provision is the one getting the most attention now. It involves a refundable tax credit for individuals with incomes between 100 and 150 percent of [the federal poverty level] that would allow them to purchase health insurance coverage. . . . The third provision expands funding for Medicaid outreach. States aren't trying very hard to locate those who are eligible for Medicaid—they aren't devoting resources to this. . . . Finally, the fourth provision would provide temporary subsidies for up to six months for unemployed individuals to cover the cost of their extending their health insurance benefits. . . . As people start making commitments about the size of the tax bill and what should be included, we want our proposal to be a consideration. . . . We've been saying it's important that if you do provide a tax cut or credit, a credit for the uninsured to purchase coverage should be in the mix. . . . We are saying we want it to be high enough to be worth something and to target the correct population. . . . We may end up walking away if the proposal that moves forward isn't what we support.

This account provides us with a wealth of information about the association's rationale for taking up this issue at the time of our interviews; it also demonstrates the ways in which the political environment and policy context affected both the development of the proposal and how this association sought to broaden support for that proposal. But what we did not have in this description was an argument: a clear statement of a goal and a justification for it, or a statement of what would happen if a stated goal were not accomplished. In order to gain this information, we asked the question: "What's the fundamental argument you use to try to convince people to do this [or not to do this]?" For our purposes, only those statements that either justify a given policy goal or discuss its implications can serve as arguments. In response to this latter question, the advocate cited above had the following to say:

One of the main arguments we've made to people on the Hill is it's not the case that the market, when the economy is good, will take care of the uninsured. . . . For a long time many claimed that with a growing economy, the number of uninsured would decrease. But this hasn't happened. Instead, the number of uninsured has increased. . . . This argument for doing nothing can't be made anymore. . . . We have been saying that something should be done to address the problem of the uninsured and that something can be done now because we have a budget surplus. It's understandable that when trying to reduce the deficit it isn't possible to do what's needed. But you can't say that we can't do it now, because we can.

In this response, the representative offers a clear justification for extending insurance to those who lack it, indicating that the government needed to step in to fix a problem that the private sector had failed to correct. Moreover, the representative stressed that the problem of the uninsured had gotten worse in the face of government inaction. As these two excerpts illustrate, statements of problems associated with the current policy without linkage to a new policy goal simply describe the issue context as it is understood by an advocate. Arguments, on the other hand, represent that subset of the possible dimensions of engaging an issue that are actually the object of discussion and active debate.

In this chapter, we look closely at the arguments that were used by the advocates we interviewed about our ninety-eight issues. Of particular interest is how the use of different arguments is affected by advocates' support for or opposition to the status quo, the salience of the issues they care about, and the magnitude of budgetary and programmatic change they seek. Our clearest expectations, drawn from existing scholarship, were that advocates defending the status quo would play to their advantage and offer arguments intended to raise the level of uncertainty about proposed policy changes. We also expected that advocates would resort to relatively simple arguments when issues were more salient. Our expectations about how argument use is shaped by the amount of change advocates seek were less precise. We expected only that the degree of budgetary and programmatic change associated with advocates' policy preferences would affect argument use differently for advocates with different goals and for those who were active on less versus more salient issues.

Argument Types

Because so little is known about the types of arguments that advocates typically make, we begin with a simple look at the nature of argumentation observed in our study. To that end, table 7.1 shows the distribution of argument types made by advocates associated with each of 172 sides across our

TABLE 7.1 **Types of Arguments Used, by Intent**

Argument type	Status quo defenders (%)	Status quo challengers (%)	All sides (%)
Problems/no problems with implementation or feasibility	68.8	74.1	72.1
Promotes/inhibits some goal	59.4	64.8	62.8
Imposes/reduces costs on nongovernmental actors	48.4	56.5	53.5
Equality of treatment/discriminatory impact	39.1	41.7	40.7
Positive/negative noncost consequences	43.8	34.3	37.9
Imposes/reduces costs to government***	17.2	38.9	30.8
Big precedent/modest change	23.4	21.3	22.1
Government procedural or jurisdictional issues	18.7	16.7	17.4
Appropriate/inappropriate for government to solve problem*	20.3	11.1	14.5
Problem bigger/smaller than estimated or is misunderstood	17.2	11.1	13.4
Supported/opposed by constituency or other group	10.9	12.0	11.6
Crisis/no crisis is looming	3.1	8.3	6.4
Has partisan or electoral benefits/costs	3.1	1.9	2.3
Necessary for national security or public safety	0.0	1.9	1.2
Number of sides	64	108	172

Note: Entries show the percentage of sides making use of each type of argument.
*Difference between defenders and challengers is statistically significant at $p < .10$.
***Difference between defenders and challengers is statistically significant at $p < .01$.

ninety-eight issues.[1] Table A.2, in the appendix, gives a complete list of the argument categories we coded.

The arguments are listed in order of the frequency of their use. Positive and negative arguments are combined for the purpose of this table, so we see, for example, that advocates representing 72.1 percent of the sides made arguments relating to feasibility or implementation of the policy under question. These could have been reassuring arguments that feasibility would be no problem, that the program could be implemented successfully, or they might have been the opposite. In any case almost three-quarters of all the sides made such arguments. (Table A.2 shows how we break these arguments down further into positive, negative, and neutral categories.)

The table shows the overall percentage of sides making each type of argument as well as how this may differ between those who are defending versus challenging the status quo. Perhaps the most notable aspect of the figures in table 7.1 is the diversity of argument types that are employed. Eleven basic types of arguments, touching on topics as diverse as feasibility, the appropriateness of government action, cost, and equality of treatment, are each used by more than 10 percent of the sides; seven of these types are used by over a fifth of them. Three types of arguments are especially common. More than half of all sides offer arguments that raise concerns or offer reassurance about the feasibility of policy options, suggest that certain policy options promote or inhibit some shared goal, or emphasize the costs or cost savings that particular policy alternatives offer to nongovernmental actors. Feasibility and implementation arguments are the most common themes articulated by our advocates, used in fully 72.1 percent of sides. For example, legislation introduced in the 106th Congress was designed to weaken the Food Quality Protection Act of 1996, a law that created a regulatory framework for setting exposure standards for pesticides. Farm groups attacked the law. As a lobbyist recounted, the main arguments to legislators were that, although regulations under the law were "supposed to be based on sound science, the data was not available to make [sound] judgments, [and] the time was not being provided to get the information to make sound judgments."

A large proportion of sides (62.8 percent) used an argument that the policy at hand promoted a widely shared goal or, alternatively, stood in the way of achieving some broad, appealing goal (e.g., public safety, improving the economy, improving rural health care). Who could really argue with the lobbyist for a group representing the elderly when he told legislators, "The rise in prescription prices has forced many seniors to choose between buying the drugs they need to stay healthy and the food they need to survive"? Another common argument (53.5 percent) involved imposing or reducing costs on nongovernmental actors. A bill that provided a subsidy to money-losing commuter rail from freight haulers made lobbyists for the freight industry go ballistic. One of them got a bit agitated when he told us, "These costs, if imposed on the freight railroads, will have to be passed on to their customers. The railroads will have to charge more to ship widgets, or whatever commodity. . . . Why should a widget manufacturer and the consumers of widgets have to subsidize commuter-rail operations in maybe a state that they don't even live in?"

For all three of these types of arguments, there are no significant differences in relative usage between supporters and challengers to the status quo. Although challengers are somewhat more likely to discuss policy feasibility and how policy options affect the costs borne by nongovernmental actors, the differences between these two groups are statistically indistinguishable.

The next most commonly used arguments are those that link policy options to equality of treatment or discrimination (40.7 percent); to various noncost consequences (37.8 percent); and to costs imposed upon or to be saved by government (30.8 percent).[2] Among this group of arguments, statistically significant differences are seen in the tendencies of challengers and defenders of the status quo to emphasize cost-related consequences. Challengers to the status quo tend to emphasize the costs borne by government at more than twice the rate of those defending the status quo (38.9 percent versus 17.2 percent). As we explain in more detail below, the emphasis on cost by status quo challengers provides insight into how advocates with different intentions tend to try to build support for their policy goals.

Less-frequently used arguments include those that refer to the magnitude of change proposed, the procedural or jurisdictional issues at stake, the appropriateness of government involvement, the size of the underlying problem, or the link between a policy alternative and some target group or set of constituents. As shown in table 7.1, no more than about a fifth of the sides in our study sought to justify or explain their preferences in these terms. Here again, relatively minimal differences emerge between status quo defenders and challengers, although status quo defenders are significantly more likely than challengers to make arguments that point to the appropriateness of government involvement in policy.

Given the overheated rhetoric of politics that citizens are exposed to in the media and the widespread belief that we live in an unusually partisan time, it may seem surprising that arguments relating to a looming crisis, partisan differences, national security, and public safety are quite rare. References to crises were made only by about 6 percent of our sides, though the table shows that when a crisis is mentioned, it is more often raised by challengers rather than by defenders of the status quo. One such plea we heard came from a union representative recounting the organization's efforts to convince the government that "a steel dumping crisis had begun." In meetings with high-ranking Bush administration officials, he emphasized that "18 to 19 [American] companies were in bankruptcy." This type of argument is a reasonable (and not unexpected) one for status quo challengers to make, given the hurdles they face in generating motion for change. Still, such arguments are unusual. The electoral implications of a policy choice are hardly ever mentioned as policy arguments. It's likely that electoral considerations are communicated more effectively through actions—mobilizing grassroots or grass-tops supporters—rather than words. In light of the popular view of lobbyists as mere conduits of money between well-heeled interests and policy makers, however, it is notable that few appeals reference campaign contributions as a rationale for supporting or rejecting the preferences of a side (references to campaign contributions are included as an electoral benefit/cost type of argument; see table A.2).[3]

Finally, it is surprising to see so few efforts to link policy goals with national security. The interviews for our project continued for more than a year following September 11, 2001, a period marked both by heightened security concerns and widespread acknowledgement that the political landscape and debate was dominated by national security. Perhaps the effort to link issues, generally, with national security concerns was relatively short-lived. We were not in the field between September 2001 and May 2002. When our interviewing resumed in May, some of the advocates we interviewed were working on issues related to the Bush administration's "war on terror" and its corollary efforts in Afghanistan and Iraq—terrorism reinsurance for airlines, maritime security, restrictions on foreign students' work in university laboratories, and efforts to increase and fund airline security. But advocates had begun to work on many other issues, and, based on our interviews, it appears that they sought to justify and explain their policy preferences in terms that were not explicitly related to the national security issues that were dominating the public agenda.[4]

Not only are the most dramatic arguments used the least, but the most commonly used argument, implementation or feasibility, is the rhetoric of the policy wonk. The other two most frequently used arguments, costs on nongovernmental actors and inhibiting or promoting some basic goal, are equally mundane. Why is it that advocates, particularly the lobbyists that dominate our sample, rely on ordinary arguments instead of those involving partisan or cataclysmic consequences? The difference we see between the hot rhetoric of political debate before the public and the mundane language of lobbying is that the audience is different. Lobbyists pitch their arguments to a sophisticated audience: policy makers. Telling the top counsel on a congressional committee that a crisis is looming or that a particular course of action is a great opportunity to stick it to the Democrats on the committee does little to enhance the lobbyist's credibility. Lobbyists want to be "players"; they want to be the ones policy makers call for help or advice. To that end, they want to promote their policy expertise. When they meet with policy makers or other lobbyists within a coalition, they want to show a mastery over the issues. For lobbyists a strong principle of behavior is that "credibility comes first."[5] Promote the policy, but promote one's career at the same time. By looking at a random sample of issues and systematically looking at what lobbyists do across the board, not only when they are quoted in the newspapers, we get a different view on the process than that which is sometimes promoted in both journalistic and in some academic accounts. Lobbyists are pretty dull a lot of the time. They have to be in order to be taken seriously by others who are just as expert on the subject matter as they are.

Further analysis of the specific arguments we encountered shows patterns that speak to the strategies used by advocates to push for change or defend the status quo. For one, within the category of goal arguments (used by 62.8 percent of all sides), claims that emphasize how a policy alternative promotes a shared goal are made much more often than are claims emphasizing how the policy or proposed change to it inhibits a goal (44.8 versus 27.3 percent). That being said, the positive argument about shared goals is much more common among status quo challengers (49.1 percent) than defenders (37.5 percent). In other words, advocates from both sides are much more likely to argue about how their preferred solution (be it the status quo or some alternative) promotes widely shared values such as economic growth, better education, or saving family farms than they are to focus on how the proposal of their rivals will diminish such goals. To the extent there are differences here, the challengers are more positive than the defenders. Defenders of the status quo can raise doubt, suggesting that any changes will have deleterious consequences; proponents of change focus more on the benefits.

In addition, when sides use arguments about unfair advantage or equality of treatment (just over 40 percent of all the sides used such arguments), they are almost always critical rather than supportive. About 38 percent of our sides voiced claims that the current policy (or the alternative proposal) provides or would provide an unfair advantage to some group. Typical was the argument of a bank lobbyist fighting a bill that would allow credit unions to expand more easily: "Credit unions, even if they have a community-based membership, don't have to serve their entire community, but a bank does. So it's a different playing field." Only 5.8 percent of the sides made the counter argument that the policy was in fact equitable. Equality of treatment is a fundamental argument; it is almost always a complaint, rarely a justification. Professional groups seeking exemption from a policy, for example, face systematic attack that any concession is simply "not fair"—these fairness or equitable treatment arguments can be made either about the status quo or about a proposed policy change, but they are almost always negative.

Moreover, when advocates talk about cost, they tend to focus more on the costs that policy options impose on private actors and institutions (42.4 percent) than on how the costs they bear will be reduced (21.5 percent). However, when cost reduction claims are made, they are significantly more likely to be made by challengers rather than defenders of the status quo (27.8 versus 10.9), while defenders of the status quo are slightly more inclined to talk about how the policy options supported by challengers impose costs on those outside of government (46.9 versus 39.8). In the case of costs to government, arguments tend to focus both on how policies will add to and also reduce those costs. But here again we see the much greater tendency on the part of those challenging the status quo to make claims about the cost savings of their policy preferences. While only about 5 percent of the sides supporting the status quo talk about its cost efficiency for government, 22 percent of the status quo challengers emphasize the cost savings that their policy options offer to government, a difference that is statistically significant.

The emphasis that advocates give to matters of cost when they make their appeals echoes the cost-focused structure of conflict that was described in chapter 3. Indeed, a close look at a type of cost-related argument that is used relatively frequently makes clear how the structure of conflict affects the context in which advocates try to achieve their goals. Consider, for example, the way in which cost-related considerations were raised by advocates for mandatory infant hearing screenings. These advocates argued that spending money early in an infant's life to detect hearing problems was a wise investment that would produce savings in the future: "If hearing problems are detected in the first three months of life, and there is intensive treatment by six months, children can communicate and develop language skills on par with other children their age.... Early detection and treatment can assist children's . . . development." In this case, the immediate costs were borne by the federal government in the form of grants to states to carry out the screenings, and (to a lesser extent) by private insurers who could be asked to cover the screenings as well. Savings in the future would be realized by a broad range of beneficiaries, including parents, children, school districts, as well as private insurers, not all of whom were mobilized into the fight. In this way, the cost concerns that structure the conflict associated with this issue manifest a substantial bias in favor of the status quo. Collective action problems, uncertainty about economic and financial estimates, and other factors mean that those who might benefit in the future are unlikely to be fully mobilized, whereas those threatened with immediate financial losses are almost certain to be moved to action. Kahneman and Tversky's insights into the imbalance between risk and reward are clearly evident in the realm of Washington politics.[6]

Within the category of noncost consequences, the pattern of argument use is similar to what we described above for the arguments about costs borne by nongovernmental actors. Specifically, there is a far greater tendency by status quo defenders to emphasize the negative consequences of opponents' policy preferences as opposed to the positive consequences of advocates own preferences (39.1 percent versus 7.8 percent, respectively). And status quo defenders are significantly more likely to make these claims (39.1 percent) than are challengers (25.0 percent). In the enduring debate over fuel economy standards, lobbyists for the car manufacturers consistently focus on painting a frightening scenario if the environmentalists get their way. Their argument to legislators is blunt, increasing the fuel economy (CAFE) standards puts "U.S. jobs at risk to the advantage of foreign jobs." It is to the advantage of status quo defenders to "go negative" to torpedo any proposals for change, whereas advocates of change must show not only that the status quo is flawed but also that their proposal for change would improve the situation.

A number of other differences in the more detailed arguments used by challengers and defenders of the status quo are apparent among the arguments that are used less frequently than those arguments mentioned above. These differences provide evidence consistent with the differences already noted—status quo defenders need not explain the benefits of the status quo, they need only cast doubt on the policy alternatives being proposed. For example, status quo defenders are more than three times more likely than status quo challengers to emphasize the need for more study about the feasibility of alternatives (17.2 versus 4.6 percent), and they are more than twice as likely to suggest that a large precedent will be set by any changes that are made to the status quo (17.2 versus 6.5 percent). It is also interesting that when the status quo involves the government not addressing a problem, status quo defenders appear to emphasize the insignificance of the underlying problem as well as the inefficiency that would result if the government did address it. All this adds up to suggest how easy it is to play defense in Washington: go negative. Raise doubts and fears, especially about cost to government, costs to private sector actors, and the feasibility of any government solution to what is probably an exaggerated problem in any case.

Making the Case for Policy Change or Arguing in Support of the Status Quo

We get some additional purchase on the use of arguments by status quo challengers and defenders of the status quo in tables 7.2 and 7.3. In table 7.2, the argument data are aggregated into categories that reflect more clearly some of the major themes noted above: doubt and uncertainty, optimism, increased costs, decreased costs, and prudence.

Table 7.2 shows that the relative use of arguments that underscore the costs that will result if their opponents' policy preferences are adopted is similar for both supporters of and challengers to the status quo. In addition, both defenders and challengers are almost equally likely to use arguments that raise doubts or uncertainty about the preferred policy of the opposing side. In the case of status quo challengers, these arguments are almost exclusively focused on the unworkability of the status quo. But there are far more substantial differences between status quo challengers and defenders in the use of the remaining categories of arguments. Claims about the cost reductions that would result from the preferred policy options are more than three times more likely to be made by challengers, a difference that is statistically significant. Other significant differences between status quo challengers and defenders are observed in terms of the level of optimism that pervades their claims and their tendencies to emphasize the relative prudence of the policy they support. As table 7.2 indicates, status quo challengers are much more likely than status quo defenders to emphasize what is positive about their policy preferences, and challengers are also more likely to emphasize the prudent or incremental nature of the policy changes they seek.

TABLE 7.2 **Categories of Arguments Used, by Intent**

Argument category/tone	Status quo defenders (%)	Status quo challengers (%)	All sides (%)
Raising doubts/uncertainty	67.2	63.9	65.1
Optimism about alternatives***	42.2	63.0	55.2
Costs will increase	54.7	48.2	50.6
Costs will decrease***	14.1	43.5	32.6
Preferred policy is prudent*	6.3	15.7	12.2
Number of sides	64	108	172

Note: Entries show the percentage of sides making use of each type of argument.
*Difference between defenders and challengers is statistically significant at $p < .10$.
***Difference between defenders and challengers is statistically significant at $p < .01$.

TABLE 7.3 **Positive and Negative Arguments Used, by Intent**

	Status quo defenders (%)	Status quo challengers (%)	All sides (%)
Argument tone			
Positive***	45.3	73.2	62.8
Negative	79.7	85.2	83.1
Strategy			
Positive only	10.9	12.0	11.6
Mix of positive and negative***	34.4	61.1	51.2
Negative only***	45.3	24.1	32.0
Neither*	9.4	2.8	5.2
Number of sides	64	108	172

Notes: Entries show the percentage of sides making use of each type of argument or strategy. The strategy "neither" means that the side used arguments that could not be classified as positive or negative in tone. Positive arguments include: policy promotes a shared goal, policy is equitable, policy reduces costs to government or to private actors, and policy has some secondary beneficial consequences. Negative arguments include: policy inhibits shared goals, policy is not equitable, policy imposes costs on government or private actors, policy has some secondary negative consequences, and policy does not work. The unclassified arguments are things such as "needs more study."
*Difference between defenders and challengers is statistically significant at $p < .10$.
***Difference between defenders and challengers is statistically significant at $p < .01$.

In table 7.3 we aggregate the arguments according to whether they are positive or negative in tone. Positive arguments include: policy promotes a shared goal, policy is equitable, policy reduces costs to government or to private actors, and policy has some secondary beneficial consequences. Negative arguments include: policy inhibits shared goals, policy is not equitable, policy imposes costs on government or private actors, policy has some secondary negative consequences, and policy does not work.

Most striking in table 7.3 is the tendency of both status quo defenders and challengers to "go negative." At least four-fifths of the sides make use of negative claims. Some of these, such as "small mom-and-pops are going out of business because they can't afford this insurance" and "there will be some unintended consequences that will probably outweigh the good," are quite simple and could effectively be used for any number of different issues. Other negative arguments present more complicated, issue-specific claims but nonetheless effectively raise concerns about policy alternatives. For instance, an airline representative explained that certain provisions of the airline security measures they were facing after September 11 were just not doable: "The December 31st deadline for [baggage] screening and the [other] initiatives on security . . . there was no way [the hub airports] were going to make this December 31st deadline." In the case of efforts to alter the provisions of Title IX, an advocate explained how the current policy inhibited the widely accepted goal of equal opportunity: "'Instead of promoting . . . equal opportunity, it's caused enforced equal outcomes' is just the basic argument for any Title IX issue we deal with. Equal outcomes first, even if that doesn't make sense."

Also of note is the disparity between challengers and defenders in terms of their use of positive arguments. Fewer than half of the sides defending the status quo make any positive claim, whereas over 70 percent of the challengers use that type of argument (a statistically significant difference). The bottom rows of table 7.3 bring these differences into sharper relief. For status quo defenders, there is a tendency not only to use arguments that are negative in tone but also to use negative arguments exclusively (45.3 percent of all sides defending the status quo). And while few sides of any type rely solely on positive arguments, a majority (61.1 percent) of the status quo challengers mix it up, as it were. These results add to our understanding of the basis of the status quo advantage. Affirming Kahneman and Tversky, losses loom larger than gains in Washington, and defenders of the status quo benefit greatly from raising the prospect of a negative consequence or otherwise portraying any alternative to the status quo as a risky choice.[7] Students of framing know that a given option or alternative can be portrayed in different ways, so the savvy status quo defender need not explicitly engage in outlining the virtues of the status quo policy. Rather, it is sufficient (and not too terribly difficult) to suggest that certain costs and negative consequences *might* result from a policy option being proposed. Indeed, "the status quo defines the reference level for all attributes. The advantages of alternative options will then be evaluated as gains and their disadvantages as losses . . . [and] the decision maker will be biased in terms of retaining the status quo."[8] In short, it is typically not sufficient for challengers to the status quo to say positive things about their new policy; they must also point out the flaws in alternative approaches including the status quo. Status quo defenders, on the other hand, can dwell on their opponents' flaws and may not have to worry about defending the status quo.

Engaging Opponents

Do advocates engage in debate along a single dimension of evaluation, or do they ignore one another? How do they respond to the claims of their rivals? In table 7.4, we consider how frequently advocates on different sides of the same issue use the same types of argument. That is, when one

TABLE 7.4 **The Degree to Which Arguments Are Directly Engaged or Ignored by Rivals**

Argument type	Raised by at least one side	Also engaged by another side	Percentage "issue engagement"
Problems/no problems with implementation or feasibility	51	33	64.7
Imposes/reduces costs on nongovernmental actors	45	21	46.7
Equality of treatment/discriminatory impact	35	15	42.9
Policy promotes/inhibits some goal	48	20	41.7
Imposes/reduces costs to government	20	8	40.0
Appropriate/inappropriate for government	15	6	40.0
Government procedural or jurisdictional issues	19	5	26.3
Positive/negative noncost consequences	35	9	25.7
Big precedent/modest change	24	5	20.8
Crisis/no crisis is looming	7	1	14.3
Problem bigger/smaller than estimated or is misunderstood	14	1	7.1
Policy supported/opposed by constituency or other group	9	0	0.0
Policy has partisan or electoral benefits/costs	0	0	0.0
Necessary for national security or public safety	0	0	0.0

Note: Data reported here are limited to those 57 issues for which argument data were available for challenger and supporter sides on the same issue.

side says the proposed policy will be inequitable, does the other side also address equity or does it shift the focus to, say, cost?

Overall, table 7.4 illustrates that there are some types of arguments on which the sides appear to engage one another—but not many.[9] The arguments are listed in order from those with the highest "percent engagement" to the lowest. As table 7.4 illustrates, arguments that raise concerns or offer reassurance about the feasibility of policy options are the only type to generate more than 50 percent engagement. Direct engagement also is fairly common when advocates emphasize costs to nongovernmental actors (46.7 percent engagement) as well as when they raise issues about equal or discriminatory impact (42.9 percent engagement). In all, table 7.4 gives us a sense of the competitive nature of the framing process. Although there is often some form of loose engagement with rivals, it is much more common for each side to focus on its best arguments. For those seeking to protect the status quo, these are often simply that the new proposal will not work as advertised, will cost more than the other side says, and may not be appropriate for government action.

Given the complexity of the issues and the need for advocates to justify a policy on the basis of the most compelling arguments available, it is no wonder that each focuses on different themes. But the result is a series of debates where each side often speaks past the other. One says a proposal will cost too much or will not work as advertised. The other says that in fact the policy will promote early childhood development. Better to focus on that widely shared goal rather than to get bogged down in a lengthy and technical debate about cost estimates, feasibility studies, and pilot programs. Mucciaroni and Quirk found the same dynamic at work among members of Congress.[10] When members of Congress spoke, they often focused on their own best points, not directly engaging the arguments of their colleagues who presented different opinions. The incentives for individual advocates to talk past the opposition are clear. However, we should not lose sight of some more important facts. Policy makers may be hearing arguments from both sides. The larger policy community which may be following or engaging in this debate will indeed be exposed to a range of conflicting sides on the issue. The debate, even if cacophonous, is rich.

Beyond Intent: Explaining Patterns in the Use of Arguments

We have argued that salience, intent, and the degree and type of change sought by advocates affect the choice of arguments. Here we provide a simple multivariate analysis to see whether there are any systematic patterns in the use of certain types of arguments as a function of these variables. For example, are arguments that invoke widely held values systematically more likely to be used on high salience issues, as some have suggested? Do links between the salience of an issue and the arguments used change as other relevant variables are held constant? For instance, when we take into account whether the side making the argument supports or opposes the status quo, do the linkages between arguments and salience remain robust? How is the choice of arguments affected by other characteristics of the issue, such as how a policy affects the federal budget, established programs, or private cost when salience and a side's support or opposition to the status quo are held constant?

A simple probit analysis allows us to predict the relative use of each type of argument. We focus specifically on how the choice of arguments is shaped by issue characteristics and the preferences and goals of a side: (1) *salience* (a continuous index based on congressional and media coverage of the issue, with higher values reflecting more public visibility); (2) *intent* (coded 0 for those that support the status quo and 1 for those seeking change); (3) *impact on the federal budget* (coded 1 if a side's objective would affect the budget of the federal government, 0 if it would maintain spending or have no budgetary impact); (4) *impact on private costs* (coded 1 if a side's objective would affect costs to private businesses or individuals, 0 if it would maintain costs or have no cost impact); and (5) *impact on established programs* (coded 1 if a side's objective would substantially change an established government program, 0 if it would minimally change an established program, maintain the status quo, or did not deal with an established program of the federal government).

Table 7.5 presents these results for argument types used by at least 10 percent of all sides. The signs that appear in each of the five columns indicate which of the variables are significantly associated with the use of each type of argument. Thus, glancing down the columns of the table shows which types of arguments were systematically associated with which of the five factors listed, while controlling for the other four characteristics.

Looking first at salience, the three negative signs in the second column of table 7.5 indicate that when issues are highly salient, advocates are less likely to use arguments about the magnitude of policy change (prudent, small change, sets a precedent, etc.), jurisdictional issues, and the size of the underlying problem. The first of these arguments justifies low salience (and may be an effort to keep the issue from attracting too much attention), and the other two are "inside baseball"— of interest within the Washington beltway but not likely fodder for broad public debate. When an issue receives greater governmental and media attention and is visible to the public, it is quite reasonable to expect that advocates would not bother to argue that the underlying problem was big enough to merit attention, because that hurdle had presumably been cleared. Similarly, it would not seem effective on such issues to make the counterargument that they issue did not, in fact, merit all the attention it was receiving. Claims about the magnitude of the policy itself also are likely to be a bit out of place in the context of a salient issue. That jurisdictional or procedural arguments are unlikely to be used on more salient issues is a bit surprising, because this category of argument includes constitutional claims and issues of federal-

TABLE 7.5 **Probit Analysis of the Use of Arguments**

Dependent variable	Independent Variables				
	Salience	Intent	Federal budget	Private costs	Established program
Problems/no problems with implementation or feasibility					
Promotes/inhibits some goal					+
Imposes/reduces costs on nongovernmental actors				+	
Equality of treatment/ discriminatory impact				+	
Positive/negative noncost consequences					
Imposes/reduces costs to government			+		
Big precedent/modest change	–		–		
Government procedural or jurisdictional issues at stake	–			+	
Appropriate/inappropriate for government to solve problem			–	+	
Problem bigger/smaller than estimated or is misunderstood	–		–		
Supported/opposed by constituency or other group					–
Raising doubts/uncertainty					
Optimism about alternatives	+				
Costs will increase				+	
Costs will decrease	+	+			
Preferred policy is prudent	+	–			
Positive arguments	+				
Negative arguments				+	

Notes: Eighteen separate equations were estimated to determine the probability of using each type of argument shown in column one as a function of the five independent variables that define the columns. Because the arguments are clustered by issues, we use robust standard errors calculated by applying Huber's formula to each cluster of observations that are identified with a single issue (Peter J. Huber, "The Behavior of Maximum Likelihood Estimates under Non-Standard Conditions," *Proceedings of the Fifth Berkeley Symposium on Mathematical Statistics and Probability* [Berkeley: University of California Press, 1967], 1:221–33). Cell entries are the signs of the significant ($p < .10$) unstandardized probit coefficients. If the coefficient is not statistically significant, the relevant cell is blank. Each type of argument is coded 1 if at least one advocate associated with a side used the argument, 0 if the side did not use the argument. Sample size is 172 for all estimations.

ism (see table A.2). But this is a relatively uncommon type of argument in our random sample of issues generally. What is perhaps most surprising in these results is that sides do not appear to be more likely to make appeals about how a policy promotes or inhibits a shared goal or appeals that highlight the discriminatory or equal impact of the policy when the issue of interest to them is relatively more salient. Salience, in general, has little relation to the choice of argumentation.

The results for intent—whether the set of advocates who comprise a particular side of an issue support or oppose the status quo—largely confirm the results presented above.[11] Specifically, table 7.5 shows that challengers are significantly more likely to use positive arguments, arguments that are optimistic in their claims, arguments about cost reductions, and arguments that characterize their policy goals as moderate, prudent, or trivial. On the other hand, challengers are significantly less likely to make arguments about the appropriateness of government action; this tends to be reserved for the defenders of the status quo, as we saw earlier in this chapter (although the status quo challenger seeking insurance for the uninsured who is cited at the outset of this chapter illustrates an exception to this general pattern).

The three remaining variables shown in table 7.5 provide information about whether and how the type of change that is associated with a side's policy preference affects the type of argument used. When the policy alternative supported by a side will affect the federal budget, arguments related to that impact, and to budget savings in particular, are much more likely to be used. In contrast, arguments regarding the size of the underlying problem and the magnitude of the change resulting from imposition of the policy are significantly less likely to be employed.

Issues that affect costs to be borne by private actors elicit a range of specific negative arguments. Not surprisingly, arguments directly related to those costs are more likely to be used, as are arguments that emphasize cost increases. In addition, the data demonstrate that when private costs are affected, advocates are significantly more likely to make arguments about the policy alternative's equality of treatment or discrimination (largely that it is unfair to raise costs on private actors), the appropriateness of government activity (government may have no business engaging in this activity), as well as jurisdictional or procedural claims (rules are not being followed). When private costs are set to increase or decrease, negative arguments generally increase. It is noteworthy that when a policy may affect private sector costs, the counterarguments against the policy tend not to focus on costs. They are negative, but those opposed to the policy find other ways of explaining their concerns.

Finally, table 7.5 shows that goal-related arguments are much more likely to be used by sides whose policy preferences entail substantial changes to current programs. That those seeking major change would link their policy preferences with the promotion of shared values makes sense given the difficulty of such change and the easy appeal of value-laden claims. On the other hand, sides that promote policies involving big change to established programs are much less likely to link those policies to the support or opposition they engender from particular groups. Particularized support or opposition would not seem to be an effective claim when the change at stake is considerable.

Conclusions

The strategic choice of arguments is made within the context of a great number of constraints. Advocates are certainly purposive in their choice of arguments, and we see that those proposing new policies are systematically more optimistic in their style of argumentation than those opposed to the changes. Yet advocates do not have free rein in their choice of argumentation strategies. Cost issues have to be discussed, like it or not. Feasibility issues cannot be ignored. Broad appeals to shared social values are common, but rivals are highly likely to counter such arguments by making use of a conflicting social value. The most prominent theme we can see in these data is, as in previous chapters, the tremendous advantage realized by those who seek to protect the status quo. Advocates actively attempting to push back a proposed policy change can go negative, cast doubts, focus on the uncertainty of the possible outcomes and the possible hidden or overt costs of the proposal, and raise questions about feasibility. Often they also question whether government is, after all, the proper solution. This is a strong complement of powerful arguments, readily available for most situations.

Challengers to the status quo in American politics are more positive in their arguments than their rivals; they focus on the possibilities of social or economic improvement that they expect from their proposals. But even these advocates do not entirely eschew negative arguments about the dangers of continuing with the status quo policies.

In sum, both sets of actors operate under heavy constraints on their actions, constraints that come mostly from the immediate and forceful reactions of their rivals. Neither side typically has the power single-handedly to determine the structure or focus of the debate, as it was typically set in previous rounds and is widely understood within a professional community in certain terms. Like it or not, advocates of both sides on a given issue must address important questions of cost and feasibility if these are raised. There is precious little evidence that strategic entrepreneurs can choose freely their arguments without constraints imposed by the nature of the issue or the actions of their rivals.

Chapter 6 outlined a number of reasons why political scientists believe that issues of high and low public salience tend to lead to dramatically different types of argumentation. Highly salient issues should be rife with broad appeals to shared values, whereas low-visibility issues deep within policy communities may see more technical or detailed types of arguments. In fact, we observed few differences. Broad appeals to shared social values are, actually, common on most of our issues, ranking second only behind feasibility and implementation issues as the most common type of argumentation overall. This does not mean that salience does not matter, but it certainly shows that even low-salience issues are commonly linked to broad values. Thus, contrary to what the literature led us to expect, we found here that the advocates' position with respect to the status quo was far more important than salience in shaping argument choice. Further, issues of cost affect the logic of argumentation.

Intent and cost to private actors structure much of the argumentation, just as we saw that these variables structure the nature of conflict overall. Issue debates are simpler as a result of this. Whereas every one of our issues was complex and affected many different dimensions of possible evaluation, actual debate as described by the arguments being used by the various sides was quite limited in variety. No more than a few fundamental issues, often focused on shared values, cost, and feasibility, dominated discussion. While other dimensions of evaluation were possible in almost every case, and came up in some, the overall structure of the rhetoric of the advocacy process is surprisingly centered on just a few questions. The issues, as debated, are not that hard to understand. The issues, in reality, are much more complex. But their entireties are not debated, because all actors may not contest most of the possible elements of discussion. Instead, debate centers on only those few dimensions of dispute. Overall, our observations point to constraints on strategy, minimal individual control, and a considerable advantage to those who support the status quo.

CHAPTER EIGHT

Tactics

We saw in the previous chapter that advocates choose different types of arguments depending on their intent. Defenders of the status quo sow doubt, raise concerns about the feasibility of proposals to change complicated policies, and attempt to focus discussion on the unintended consequences and cost overruns that may ensue if the carefully crafted status quo is changed. Here we examine the tactics that advocates use to achieve their goals. In our study, we were interested in how tactic use was affected by advocates' support for or opposition to the status quo, the salience of the issues they cared about, and the magnitude of budgetary and programmatic change that advocates sought. In general, we expected that challengers more so than defenders of the status quo would engage in tactics that had the potential to increase the visibility of their issues. Yet we recognized that neither defenders nor challengers would use such tactics when they sought to minimize both the conflict surrounding an issue and broader attention to their efforts. In addition, because status quo defenders are reactive rather than proactive on issues, we expected that they would typically be less active than those advocates challenging the status quo.

Overall, we find great similarity in the use of various inside, outside, and grassroots advocacy tactics—groups of all kinds attempt to remain in close contact with their congressional allies, for example. But we see important differences as well. Those seeking to protect the status quo maintain numerous advantages over those proposing changes. Across the board, defenders tend to be less active, engaging in fewer activities, strategically holding resources back unless it becomes apparent that they are threatened with a realistic challenge. In addition, those few activities where defenders do show greater involvement are defensive ones, such as showing the results of research, with the goal of demonstrating how any changes to the status quo are fraught with uncertainty and peril. As we have already emphasized, defending the status quo is not a difficult lobbying problem compared to building support for a new policy proposal. In general, the most striking difference between the two types of advocates is simply that the defenders of the status quo can often sit back and do very little.

Differences in lobbying tactics based on intent are much stronger than those based on the visibility of the issue or the type of change advocates are attempting to achieve. We find surprisingly little difference in the use of tactics across issues of high and low salience or across issues with different types of budgetary or programmatic impact. As we saw in chapter 5, the ease with which the status quo can be protected may be upended completely, however, if electoral results bring a new majority to power. We conclude our analysis in this chapter with these striking results—uncertainty about which policies may be reversed by a new president or a new majority in Congress makes defenders of the status quo engage in many more activities, just as proponents of change must do in normal times. Clearly, advocates are sensitive to the odds that policies may change; normally, chances are low, so defenders of the status quo can sit back and monitor while proponents of change must be much more active, fighting against powerful status quo biases.

The Choice of Tactics

In the course of our interviews, we asked each respondent about the various lobbying tactics they used in the case at hand, probing to elicit a complete list of their actions, which we later coded into categories so that we could compare across interviews. (Our appendix describes our interviews in detail.) Table 8.1 shows the percentage of sides using each of the thirty most commonly employed tactics we identified.[1]

For each tactic, we show the percentage of sides using it, separately for those defending and challenging the status quo. The last column shows the percentage use of the tactic across all sides. Inside, outside, and grassroots

TABLE 8.1 **Tactics of Advocacy**

Tactic	Status quo defenders (%)	Status quo challengers (%)	All sides (%)
Inside advocacy			
Personal contact with rank-and-file members of Congress or staff*	73.3	85.3	80.6
Work with legislative allies***	56.7	76.8	69.0
Disseminate in-house research to policy makers	65.0	59.0	61.3
Personal contact with majority committee/ subcommittee member or staff	56.7	63.2	60.7
Personal contact with majority committee/ subcommittee leadership or staff	48.3	57.9	54.2
Personal contact with minority committee/subcommittee member or staff**	43.3	60.0	53.6
Send letter/fax to member of Congress or staff	51.7	53.7	52.9
Personal contact with minority committee/ subcommittee leadership or staff	45.0	46.3	45.8
Disseminate external research to policy makers	53.3	41.1	45.8
Personal contact with agency official	45.0	40.0	41.9
Outreach/coalition building	36.7	41.1	39.4
Draft legislative language***	23.3	48.4	38.7
Testify at congressional hearing	40.0	31.6	34.8
Hire consultants to help with lobbying	28.3	36.8	33.6
Submit written comments to agency	31.7	22.1	25.8
Personal contact with White House official	15.0	21.1	18.7
Work with agency allies	16.7	19.0	18.1
Personal contact with majority leadership or staff	15.0	15.8	15.5
Testify at agency hearing	18.3	12.6	14.8
Draft regulatory language	11.7	11.6	11.6
Work with White House allies	6.7	13.7	11.0
Outside advocacy			
Press conferences/press releases	35.0	34.7	34.8
Public education/relations campaign**	8.3	22.1	16.8
Op-ed/opinion pieces	11.7	14.7	13.6
Pay for ads	15.0	12.6	13.6
Disseminate in-house research to the public	8.3	12.6	11.0
Grassroots advocacy			
Mobilize mass membership	40.0	52.6	47.7
Mobilize elite membership	15.0	22.1	19.4
Organize a lobby day	15.0	20.0	18.1
Mobilize general public*	11.7	22.1	18.1
Number of sides	60	95	155

Notes: Entries show the percentage of sides using each type of tactic. Tactics were coded solely for the organizational advocates who were interviewed (i.e., government officials were not included in our enumeration of tactics).
*Difference between defenders and challengers is statistically significant at $p < .10$.
**Difference between defenders and challengers is statistically significant at $p < .05$.
***Difference between defenders and challengers is statistically significant at $p < .01$.

tactics are grouped separately, with the most commonly used tactics at the top of each section. Most notable is the wide range of tactics used and the high frequency with which advocates on all sides work with congressional staff, members, and legislative allies in general. More than half of the sides report using a wide range of Congress-focused inside lobbying tactics. Over three-quarters work through personal contacts with rank-and-file members of Congress and their staffs. One experienced lobbyist said his professional association's first step is always "to try to get members of Congress to sign letters to the appropriations committees." More than two-thirds work with legislative allies, over 60 percent report disseminating policy research, and over 50 percent make contact with committee or subcommittee members from both parties, as well as with committee or subcommittee leaders from the majority. In sum, lobbyists place a priority on working closely with their legislative allies and nurturing contacts with those in gatekeeping positions. They also keep in close contact with their own membership, with just under half of all advocates mentioning mobilizing their own mass membership, the most frequent form of outside or grassroots lobbying.

A second noteworthy characteristic of the data presented in table 8.1 is how they differ from, and are significantly lower than, similar figures reported in previous research. Frank Baumgartner and Beth Leech reviewed a series of findings from the literature on the use of lobbying and found numbers often approaching complete saturation (e.g., 99 percent) for many of the tactics reported here, and almost always percentages were substantially higher than what we see here.[2] This can be attributed to our methodology; we asked about tactics used *on the particular issue at hand*, whereas most previous studies have focused on tactics used in general or "over the past twelve months." Logically, then, our numbers are lower. An important advantage of our methodology is that it identifies which types of advocates are more likely to use which types of tactics, as well as how this use varies according to the characteristics of the issue. The table shows that tactics are indeed different according to intent.

Across all three categories of tactics—inside, outside, and grassroots advocacy—defenders of the status quo are less likely than challengers to report activity. The only specific activities that status quo defenders engage in more often than challengers are disseminating research, testifying before congressional committees or agencies, contacting and submitting written comments to agency officials, and paying for policy-related advertisements. This pattern of activity illustrates one of the advantages accruing to advocates of the status quo—they can husband their resources, allocating them to those issues on the front burner. More often than not, they need not respond to the activities undertaken by challengers. To be sure, they must be attentive to efforts to change policies they support. But this requires only that they monitor the activity of other advocates and gauge whether the climate appears ripe for change. Unless there is a sense that some idea or proposal is gaining momentum, the defenders of the status quo need not act.

An example of this "watchful waiting" strategy comes from one of our cases. The Air Line Pilots Association (ALPA) has long backed the mandatory retirement of commercial pilots at age 60. With a strong retirement plan, most pilots are happy to trade the grueling work for the financial security they worked so long for. ALPA always kept an eye out for any legislative initiatives on behalf of the minority of pilots who want to keep working past 60, but otherwise they did little work on the issue. When dissident pilots found support from an important Republican senator and legislation began to move in the 107th Congress, ALPA swung into action and arranged meetings with all the senators and representatives on the key committees. Proponents of change periodically raise the issue when opportunities arise, at which point ALPA has to mobilize in order to swat the proposal down.

One of the primary activities used by all groups, but one of the few tactics used more by defenders of the status quo than by challengers, is sharing research with policy makers. The dissemination of in-house research is mentioned by 65 percent of those defending the status quo and external research is mentioned by 53 percent; these are common activities. Status quo defenders may use research reports to sow doubt about policy proposals, augmenting the arguments they make about the unintended consequences, cost, or feasibility of proposed policy changes that we described in chapter 7. Similarly, the distribution of research on a given topic, where the advocate is not proposing any change to current policy, may be a useful mechanism for lobbyists to maintain regular contact with government policy makers with whom they generally agree and with whom they want to maintain close ties. The research need not be offered in conjunction with a specific issue debate. A new report offers an excuse to stop by a key congressional office and spend time with a top aide exchanging intelligence and gossip about the issue. Similarly, these status quo defenders are active in working with agency officials, presumably discussing pending regulatory action, possible legislative changes, or new research.

These findings for status quo defenders are consistent with Heinz and colleagues' emphasis on the importance to lobbyists generally of "monitoring." It seems clear that those protecting the status quo remain prepared to act without necessarily having to actively defend their interests.[3] Our research also confirms Carpenter and colleagues' stress on the value to advocates of access to a broad range of acquaintances ("weak ties") as opposed to only close contacts ("strong ties").[4] Clearly, lobbyists of all kinds, but especially those working with their allies within government in a defensive posture, spend a lot of time maintaining contact, casting doubt on rival proposals, and keeping informed of activities surrounding their issues. This would seem particularly useful where lobbyists seek to protect the status quo and need to know where challenges may be coming from. Status quo defenders spend a lot of time listening, talking, monitoring. Challengers, on the other hand, have to be much more active.

Inside Tactics

It is surely not surprising that the most commonly used tactic overall is personal contact with rank-and-file members of Congress and their staffs. The quintessential lobbying tactic emerges as the most common means of advocacy for both status quo defenders and challengers alike. Over and over again, we heard lobbyists tell us how critical personal contact was. A corporate lobbyist working on an energy bill joked that he relied on "traditional shoe leather lobbying" so much that members of Congress "would jump under their desks" to avoid having to talk to him again about the issue.

However, table 8.1 also shows that the relative use of this tactic is quite different for status quo defenders and challengers. Indeed, the data show that it is unusual for a side challenging the status quo *not* to contact members of Congress or their staff—85.3 percent of challengers reported working in this way on the particular issue of concern. For status quo defenders, personal contact of rank-and-file members or their staff is common, but 27 percent do not bother even with this. (This difference, 85.3 to 73.3 percent, is statistically significant.) The difference we observe is certainly underestimated. Our research approach excluded any status quo defenders who felt there was so little threat to their interests that they never even mobilized. If we were to include those "potential sides," we would find that activity defending the status quo was even lower. A similar story can be told about work with the entire range of legislative allies. Over three-fourths of the sides challenging the status quo engage in this form of activity, whereas just under 60 percent of the sides defending the status quo do so (a statistically significant difference). As described above, defenders of the status quo do not usually need to engage in explicit campaigns to build support for their preferences. Their basic preference is current policy, and they are well aware of the hurdles that others must overcome to bring a shift to that center of political gravity. These distinctions between status quo challengers and defenders are apparent through other patterns of tactic usage that are presented in table 8.1. For example, status quo challengers are much more likely than defenders to work with committee and subcommittee members from the minority party in Congress (a statistically significant difference, 60.0 versus 43.3 percent); challengers are more than twice as likely as defenders of the status quo to draft legislative language (a statistically significant difference of 48.4 versus 23.3 percent); and challengers also may be more likely to work with their allies in the White House (13.7 versus 6.7 percent, a statistically significant difference using a one-tailed test).

That so many advocates work closely with their legislative allies should come as no surprise given the literature on the topic and given our own findings in previous chapters. Lobbyists need allies inside of government to introduce legislation, to propose amendments, and to work actively for policy change. Even if legislation has no chance of passage in the current session of Congress, a symbolic bill is part of the "softening up" strategy designed to educate potential allies and to push supporters to initiate action that will convey some sense of momentum.[5] As one bank lobbyist told us, "It helps just to build awareness." Ultimately a subcommittee or committee chair may determine that the time is ripe and will move decisively on the legislation. Another lobbyist said that after years of work on an issue involving private planes, the key committee chair "got us into a room and said, 'Let's work this thing.'" So maintaining close legislative contacts is fundamental to all lobbying.

Outside and Grassroots Tactics

The bottom part of table 8.1 shows the frequency of use of those tactics we group together as "outside" or "grassroots" tactics. Here we see much lower levels of usage across the board, with only two tactics reported by

more than 20 percent of our respondents: press conferences or press releases (used by 34.8 percent) and mobilization of the mass membership of
the organization (used by 47.7 percent). Clearly, inside tactics are used on
all kinds of issues, but outside and grassroots tactics are used more rarely
or only in certain circumstances. While a given organization may engage in
a variety of outside or grassroots tactics over the course of a year, on any
given issue they may or may not find it helpful to mobilize the grassroots
at all. Even press releases, often seen as a basic (and low-cost) Washington
activity, are used by only about a third of all advocates. Many organizations, of course, are actively seeking to avoid publicity or salience for the
issues with which they deal. In their cases, outside lobbying activities may
be necessary, but only if they lose control of the situation and the issue
begins to gain salience.

Patterns of usage by both challengers and defenders of the status quo
emerge even more strongly in the case of outside and grassroots tactics.
Differences are not always large, but challengers are more active than
defenders on all but one of the nine outside and grassroots tactics. (Defenders pay for advertisements more often than do challengers but the
difference between the two sets of advocates is both substantively and statistically insignificant.) Indeed, challengers are more likely than defenders
of the status quo to follow Schattschneider's advice and attempt to expand
the scope of conflict.[6] Specifically, challenging sides are significantly more
likely to organize a public relations campaign (22.1 versus 8.3 percent,
respectively) and to mobilize the general public (22.1 versus 11.7 percent,
respectively). There is also some evidence that challengers are more likely
to mobilize their rank-and-file members (52.6 versus 40.0 percent, a statistically significant difference using a one-tailed test). Although conflict-
expanding strategies are fraught with uncertainty, challengers are already
in a more uncertain position than status quo defenders and therefore must
accept additional risk in exchange for the possibility of building some momentum behind their policy objectives. In sharp contrast, the defenders of
the status quo have little reason to engage in conflict expansion except in
response to a viable challenge by rivals.

With public attention a scarce resource, expanding the conflict can
be quite difficult. A lobbyist who played a key role in putting together a
broad coalition of professional associations to work for expanded math
and science education funding ticked off the large numbers of members
they could use to expand awareness with a grassroots campaign: "We have
160,000 chemists . . . 40,000 physicists. . . . Collectively we may have 800,000

to 1,000,000 members. If just 5 percent of those folks are writing their members of Congress, that's going to be a big impact." But later in the interview he acknowledged that they never tried for the "big impact." Surely the obscurity of the issue was a disincentive to try to mobilize such a broad swath of the various associations' members. In the end, they just relied on asking 7,000 individuals they regarded as activists to write letters to members of Congress. Even with a large membership, mobilizing the grassroots is not that easy. And if an organization announces a plan to mobilize its membership but few respond to the call, this is a clear signal that the issue is not a major concern, a point that rivals will be sure to exploit. Mobilizing the grassroots is expensive, risky, and relatively rare.

Salience

Although conflict expansion strategies also tend to be associated with more salient issues, the overall relationship between salience and choice of lobbying tactics is rather complex. In table 8.2, we examine whether the use of outside advocacy, grassroots mobilization, and committee member or leader contact (as tactics representative of inside advocacy) are greater for sides active on more salient issues. In this table, we use an ordinal measure of salience ranging from low to very high, where the categories correspond to quartiles of the distribution of the general salience measure described in the appendix. (This measure of salience includes both Congress-based actions such as hearings as well as newspaper and television stories designed to capture attention outside the beltway.)

TABLE 8.2 **Salience and Advocacy Tactics**

	Lobbying tactic			
Level of salience	Committee-level contacts (%)	Outside advocacy (%)	Grassroots mobilization (%)	Number of sides
Low	63.4	31.7	58.5	41
Moderate	83.8	48.7	54.1	37
High	73.0	40.5	51.4	37
Very high	65.0	57.5	65.0	40
All levels	71.0	44.5	57.4	155

Note: Cells contain the percentage of sides using the tactic within each level of salience. The use of any one or more of the outside advocacy tactics shown in table 8.1, the use of committee-level contacts, as well as the use of grassroots mobilization are each statistically independent of issue salience.

In spite of what one might expect, table 8.2 shows that there is no systematic relationship between salience and tactics. Even grassroots mobilization varies only between 59 and 65 percent when we move from the least to the most salient issues. Similarly, the degree to which advocates engage with contacts on relevant congressional committees shows no relation to salience. Outside advocacy tactics do show some slight relation with salience, as the numbers rise from 32 to 57 percent when we move from the least to the most salient issues, but even here the relationship is uneven (and statistically insignificant), as the table makes clear. The choice of tactics may have more to do with one's policy goals (as we saw above) than with the visibility of the issue. It may also be that mobilization has more to do with where an issue is on the governmental agenda than with its general visibility. In other words, sides—particularly those challenging the status quo—may make use of mobilization campaigns when they sense that an issue is beginning to move or has some prospect of movement. At this point in the process, the involvement of grassroots supporters might provide a means of sustaining movement that could otherwise not be maintained. Indeed, the advocates we interviewed frequently spoke about their hesitance in stirring up the grassroots and grass-tops unless there was a relatively good chance that an issue would move; they fear mobilizing their members for an effort that fails even to engage.

It is important to keep in mind that advocates are not free to choose their advocacy strategies completely at will; sometimes they may be forced to engage in outside advocacy actions because of the high salience of the issue even if they might prefer to see the issue treated off the front pages. The mixed results we see here suggest that the choice of tactics cannot be expected to relate directly to any single characteristic of the policy process, even salience.

Policy Impact

One might well expect (as we did) that the choice of lobbying tactics would be clearly related to the degree of program-related or budgetary change sought by interested advocates. For example, it seems reasonable to expect that when the policy alternative supported by a side involves a dramatic break with the status quo rather than only a marginal adjustment from current policy, advocates associated with that side would make more use of outside lobbying or grassroots mobilization. Mobilizing support for a

TABLE 8.3 **Advocacy Tactics across Diverse Types of Issues**

	Rate of Use of Tactic			
	Outside advocacy (%)	Grassroots mobilization (%)	Committee-level contacts (%)	Total N
Affects federal budget?				
Yes	44.4	63.5	85.7***	63
No	44.6	53.3	60.9	92
Affects private-sector costs?				
Yes	47.5	55.9	67.8	59
No	42.7	58.3	72.9	96
Brings substantial change to estab- lished program?				
Yes	47.5	67.5	75.0	40
No	43.5	53.9	69.6	115
All issues	44.8	57.1	71.4	155

Note: Cells show the percentage of sides working on issues with or without the impact shown in the first column using the various tactics indicated. Sides' use of committee-level contacts is statistically dependent on whether the issue affects the federal budget; all other bivariate relationships between tactics and issue characteristics are not statistically significant.
***Pearson chi-square = 11.203; $p < .01$

larger change would seem to require a broader coalition and more public pressure. Similarly, one might expect that when the policy alternative supported by a side will affect the federal budget, advocates associated with that side would use specific lobbying efforts over and above those used by advocates supporting policy alternatives with little or no budgetary impact. Finally, advocates who promote alternatives which will impose costs on private-sector actors might well be expected to make greater use of outside lobbying, so as to make it clear that there is a consumer or environmental interest at stake. With one exception, as we show in table 8.3, *none* of these expectations is borne out by our study. The choice of lobbying tactics is not clearly related to any of these factors except to some extent by whether the federal budget is affected.

Looking first at the predictors of outside lobbying, we see no relationship between the use of outside lobbying and sides whose policy preferences affect the federal budget, affect private sector costs, or substantially affect existing government programs. Considering what leads to efforts to mobilize one's own grassroots membership, the relations are similarly nonexistent. Finally, looking at the correlates of committee-level inside lobbying contacts, neither the degree of change to current programs associated with a side nor the effect on private-sector cost of the policy alternative supported by the side has any discernible impact. The only statistically significant relationship we do observe in this series of bivariate relationships is between committee-level contacting and whether the federal budget is affected by the side's policy preference. If the budget is affected, 85.7 percent of the sides are in contact with appropriate committee-level officials, as compared to 60.9 percent of the time for those supporting policy options that do not affect the federal budget.

Although it makes perfect sense that advocates supporting sides affecting the federal budget would work in close contact with congressional committee gatekeepers, all in all the most remarkable thing about our findings is the paucity of systematic relationships among these variables and various lobbying strategies. The choice of lobbying tactics cannot be explained by ostensibly critical variables, including salience, degree of programmatic change, and budgetary impact. If substantial policy changes in American politics were dependent solely on advocate-generated visibility, it would be reasonable to see linkages between programmatic and cost changes and the use of conflict-expansion strategies. However, we see virtually none of this.

Partisan Turnover

As illustrated in table 8.1, linkages between nongovernmental advocates and those working on the relevant congressional committees are key. Here we explore these ties in more detail, noting the different strategies followed by proponents of change and by those defending the status quo. Finally, we note some dramatic differences in these behaviors induced by the change in partisan control of the presidency at the beginning of the 107th Congress.

Table 8.4 shows the relative frequency with which the sides supporting and challenging the status quo contact committee members and leaders (or their staff) from one or both parties. Among the patterns apparent in these data is the tendency, noted above, for defenders of the status quo to engage less often with policy makers. The table shows that status quo supporters appear to have less contact with the members and staff of relevant committees, either at the rank-and-file or the leadership levels (although the differences we observe are not statistically significant). Indeed, the most frequent strategy for defenders of the status quo is no contact with committee leaders (45 percent), and either no contact of rank-and-file members at

TABLE 8.4 **Committee Contacts by Intent**

Level of committee or staff contacts	Status quo defenders (%)	Status quo challengers (%)	All sides (%)
Committee leadership			
Both majority and minority	38.3	40.0	39.4
Majority only	10.0	17.9	14.8
Minority only	6.7	6.3	6.5
Any leadership contact	55.0	64.2	60.7
Committee membership			
Both majority and minority	41.7	53.7	49.0
Majority only	15.0	9.5	11.6
Minority only	1.7	6.3	4.5
Any membership contact	58.3	69.5	65.2
Number of sides	60	95	155

Note: Entries show the percentage of sides engaging in each type of contact. Leadership contacts include committee and subcommittee chairs and ranking minority members and their staffs. Membership contacts include all other members of the committees and subcommittees and their staffs. None of the differences between defenders and challengers are statistically significant.

the committee level (41.7 percent) or contact with rank-and-file members of both the majority and minority parties (41.7 percent). For status quo challengers, the most common strategy is to contact members or leaders of both the majority and minority parties (53.7 percent and 40.0 percent, respectively). This is a reasonable approach given that challengers to the status quo are likely to make every effort they can to construct coalitions of support that could help to move the legislation they seek to pass.

More surprising is the relatively low proportion of sides defending the status quo who contact committee members or committee leaders from the majority party exclusively. Because status quo defenders need only suppress legislative activity to achieve their goals, they could be expected to look to members of the majority party to make that happen. Even if a full-scale lobbying campaign is not warranted, keeping in touch with key gatekeepers on an ongoing basis would seem logical. Apparently doing so is not as necessary as assumed.

Finally, the data show that few sides rely exclusively on members or leaders of the minority party. In general, single-party strategies are rare across the board. Of course, it makes sense that little can be accomplished through exclusive contacts with the minority, but we find that few organizations rely exclusively on their contacts with the majority party, either. Lobbying in committee is typically bipartisan for both advocates of change and supporters of the status quo. But the advocates of change are much more active.

TABLE 8.5 **Committee Contacts by Intent, 106th and 107th Congresses**

Level of committee or staff contact	106th Congress		107th Congress	
	Status quo defenders (%)	Status quo challengers (%)	Status quo defenders (%)	Status quo challengers (%)
Committee leadership				
Both majority and minority	31.3	37.3	46.4	44.4
Majority only	6.3	18.6	14.3	16.7
Minority only	9.4	6.8	3.6	5.6
Any leadership contact	46.9	62.7	64.3	66.7
Committee membership				
Both majority and minority	34.4	54.2*	50.0	52.8
Majority only	12.5	6.8	17.9	13.9
Minority only	3.1	5.1	0.0	8.3
Any membership contact	50.0	66.1	67.9	75.0
Number of sides	32	59	28	36

Note: Entries show the percentage of sides engaging in each type of contact. Leadership contacts include committee and subcommittee chairs and ranking minority members and their staffs. Membership contacts include all other members of the committees and subcommittees and their staffs. None of the differences between defenders and challengers are statistically significant.
*Difference between defenders and challengers is statistically significant at $p < .10$.

Given our expectations about the importance of elections as facilitators of change, we might expect that the shift in control of the presidency from Democratic to Republican in 2001, at the start of the 107th session of Congress, would have implications for the type of contacts advocates make in Congress. For instance, proposals challenging the status quo in the 107th Congress were probably more likely than proposals in the 106th Congress to challenge policy supported by the Clinton administration. Further, those proposals probably stood a greater chance of success. A closely divided Senate and a Republican-controlled House, working in conjunction with newly elected Republican President George W. Bush, would certainly stand a greater chance of enacting change than would a second-term president facing a Congress controlled by a hostile opposition party, as occurred in the 106th. With change in the air, advocates defending the status quo in the 107th Congress could be expected to be more active than they might otherwise be when the "usual" obstacles to change are present. The data presented in table 8.5, which shows the information presented in table 8.4 separately for the 106th and 107th Congresses, support this expectation.

The data for the 106th Congress mirror the patterns presented in table 8.4. Namely, status quo challengers are much more likely to contact committee members or their staffs and committee leaders from the majority party than are status quo defenders. For the defenders, the norm is no committee-level contacts. In the 107th Congress, however, the defenders of the status quo are just as active as the challengers. It appears that defenders of the status quo could no longer confidently assume that inertia was working in their favor.

We saw few other significant differences in lobbying strategies between the 106th and 107th Congress. The differences observed between status quo challengers and defenders in their use of conflict-expanding strategies disappear in the 107th Congress. In all, the onset of the Bush administration affected lobbying strategies in committee by altering the expectation of the power of the status quo. An education lobbyist spoke of the problem her group faced: "It is challenging, because most of us who are working on this issue have our connections with the Democrats and no one [on our side] wants to say this is a Democratic issue."

While it was clear to all involved, as it is in every new administration, that most public policies will not be changed, the arrival of a new president induces great uncertainty among lobbyists. They mobilize to protect the status quo just as much as they do to take advantage of new opportunities to change it.

Conclusion

Policy advocates face many hurdles and encounter different opportunity structures as they work to advance their preferences. Uncertainty prevails as advocates anticipate reactions to their tactical moves, predict and process responses from different audiences to their policy preferences, and plan for operations in a dynamic policy environment not under their control. In examining the work of advocates, we find patterns to the advocacy process in Washington that help explain the policy change or lack thereof that we observe.

The clearest pattern found is that advocates of all types work closely with their legislative allies. Committee-level contacts (in both the minority and the majority) are fundamental to most advocacy campaigns and working closely with allies within government is the single most common lobbying tactic observed. At the same time, the means of navigating the process of advocacy differ substantially by intent. In general, supporters of the status quo need to do much less than do status quo challengers. Defense is a winning game in Washington.[7] But status quo challengers cannot sit back—they must be aggressive. Challengers make more direct contacts with policy makers, and they engage in more conflict-expanding strategies designed to draw attention to the issues they care about. These differences in activity levels are particularly interesting to consider in light of Salisbury's arguments about interest groups' tendencies to monitor the policy environment. Salisbury argued that organizational advocates had responded to the increasing number of "externality" groups and the fragmentation of the organizational community in Washington, DC, by expending less effort persuading policy makers and more time monitoring or "keeping track of what is happening in the policy process." According to Salisbury, monitoring provides organizations with a way of minimizing uncertainty about "developments relevant to their interests."[8] But our data suggest an alternative view of this lack of activity. Those advocates who operate from a context about which there is less uncertainty—the status quo—can afford to engage in watchful waiting. Defenders of the status quo work much more quietly, maintaining close contacts with congressional and agency-level allies, distributing studies that justify a cautious approach, and generally keeping the lines of communication open.

Of course, there are forces that can disrupt the environment in which status quo defenders typically operate. The election of 2000 appears to have provided precisely this type of disruption. The change in partisan control of the presidency, along with the closely divided Senate and Republican-controlled House reduced some of the barriers for advocates who sought to challenge the policies that were implemented or in place during the Clinton years. The uncertain environment mobilized both camps—some sought to take advantage of opportunities to push through new proposals, and others mobilized to protect themselves.

Another notable conclusion from our analysis is the limited impact of salience on tactic use. Specifically, as shown in table 8.2, the expected use of conflict-expanding tactics on issues of greater salience was not apparent.

What, then, do these patterns tell us about the advocacy process and the policy outcomes that emerge from it? They suggest that if change is to be effected, challengers must create a sense of momentum and either build pressure to overcome the friction that exists in the policy process or be poised to take advantage of circumstances outside of their immediate control that offer opportunities to move forward. To the extent that challengers can say or do enough so that some critical mass of interested parties begins to pay attention (or can take advantage of the situation if the interested audience becomes more receptive), they may alter the context for defenders and force them to behave more like challengers—to become more active, to justify the policy alternative they prefer. Some of these elements, such as the choice of tactics (and the choice of arguments), are within the control of organized interests and government officials involved in the policy process. However, many of them, such as the opportunities presented by partisan shift after an election or the priorities and actions of those in gatekeeping positions, are outside of the control of any lobbyist. In the end, advocates do what they can and they make do when they must.

CHAPTER NINE

Washington: The Real No-Spin Zone

S peaking at a Judiciary Committee hearing, Senator John Cornyn (R-TX) argued passionately in support of a proposed constitutional amendment banning gay marriages. Yet rather than attacking the basic validity of such marriages, Cornyn contended that the underlying question was the need to protect children. Senator Patrick Leahy (D-VT), who opposed the amendment, rebutted Cornyn, declaring the issue was clearly one of states' rights. Surprisingly, perhaps, neither focused on the surface issue, whether gays and lesbians should have the legal right to marry.[1] It's not that Cornyn and Leahy were trying to hide the basic conflict over gay marriage; everyone knew what the debate concerned. Rather, each thought it advantageous if the nation viewed the issue through the prism that they offered. Knowing that public opinion stood against gay marriage, Leahy believed that it was strategic to try to shift debate to states' rights, an enduring principle of federalism traditionally championed by conservatives. For his part, Cornyn thought that it would be more appealing for conservatives to be seen as protecting children rather than trying to crack down on an oppressed minority wishing to marry.

Social scientists refer to this process as "framing." Framing can be thought of as a competition among perspectives describing the same underlying phenomenon. Both Cornyn and Leahy were talking about the identical constitutional amendment, but each wanted the public to give greater weight to one of the considerations that related to the fundamental issue.[2] Frames are no small matter. In the words of Donald Kinder and Thomas Nelson, frames "live inside the mind; they are cognitive structures that help citizens make sense of politics. . . . Frames provide order and meaning, making the world beyond direct experience seem natural."[3]

The emergence and success of a new frame on an existing issue can sharply alter public perceptions. To reframe is to try to raise the salience of a particular aspect of a problem or of a particular solution to a problem.[4] Conservatives' aim in promoting the term "partial-birth abortion" was to make people understand exactly what happens during a late-term abortion. The term evokes a gruesome image: a fetus moving down the birth canal, only to have its life brutally terminated by a physician. Virtually all Americans find this upsetting, and no one needs specialized medical training to have an opinion about the matter when it is presented in these terms. Standing in stark contrast is the technical term "intact dilation and extraction," which conjures up a medical procedure about which most people would have no opinion and which would imply that perhaps only those with medical training should be making these decisions. "Partial-birth abortion" is not merely more evocative, but it pushes people to think of the larger issue in a particular way. For anti-abortion activists, gaining acceptance of their frame was a brilliant tactical victory in this ongoing and bitter conflict. Those who defend a woman's right to choose lost that skirmish in the framing wars and have never succeeded in reestablishing the widespread use of a more neutral term. This example surely supports George Lakoff's contention that "reframing *is* social change."[5]

Several things are clear. One is that framing can have huge impacts on policy outcomes. Second is that a given issue is often associated with dramatically different frames. Third, it is easy to point to individual cases, such as "partial-birth abortion," where a given debate has indeed been redefined. Finally, we know that lobbyists and political leaders of all kinds *attempt* to reframe issues all the time—they are masters of spin.

Still, there is much we don't know about framing and reframing. Most importantly, we know very little about the ability of individuals or organizations to affect frames. How difficult is it for lobbyists or government officials to successfully reframe an issue? If such an attempt is made, don't the opponents fight back? Are there particular conditions that make reframing more or less likely? Are there structures or institutions that affect this process, limiting the ability of actors to reframe? We utilize the case studies, including the initial and follow-up interviews with advocates, to try to answer some of these questions.

Strategic Politicians

The belief that framing is central to modern politics is grounded in both scholarship and in the conventional wisdom that underlies contemporary journalism. We turn here first to scholarship and then discuss journalism in the section that follows. The study of framing is no small academic niche, but rather has attracted attention from researchers across the social sciences, including social psychologists, economists, and political scientists. At a very basic level laboratory experiments have demonstrated unequivocally that subjects can be influenced in their opinions by framing effects. In one simple experiment, for example, subjects were given information on the risks of two alternative treatments for lung cancer, surgery or radiation. One group was told that out of 100 surgeries, 68 people are alive at the end of the first year. For the alternative, radiation therapy, 77 are alive at the end of the first year. Another group is told that out of 100 surgeries, 32 die by the end of the first year. For radiation, this same group is told that 23 die during the first year. Odds at the end of five years were similarly expressed. Even though both groups receive the exact same statistical odds for both treatments, many more in the second group opt for radiation. Apparently, people judge risks differently when they are expressed in terms relating to the chances of dying rather than to the chances of living.[6]

Recent research has focused on identifying the conditions under which framing is most likely to succeed or fail. For example, James Druckman found that the credibility of the source of information has a significant impact on the chances for the successful framing of an issue with the public.[7] Consider the credibility conferred by post-9/11 stories on Iraq in the *New York Times* and *Washington Post*. Although President Bush's own standing was high at that point, those papers' tacit support of his contention that Iraq possessed weapons of mass destruction (WMDs) burnished the credibility of the few fragments of flimsy evidence concerning WMDs that the administration put forward. Both papers would later issue unprecedented public apologies for their failure to examine critically the claims made by the administration. Nevertheless, at the time Bush was framing a proposed invasion of Iraq as an appropriate response to worldwide terrorism, the papers' acceptance of the case he put forth was crucial. The Bush administration's reliance on Secretary of State Colin Powell, who presented his devastating indictment of Saddam Hussein's ostensible weapons program at the United Nations General Assembly, was not coincidental. Secretary Powell had enormous personal credibility on the issue, much more than others within the administration more personally connected with the hard-line stance on Iraq. Source credibility matters, and Powell had great credibility.

William Riker's pioneering analysis of reframing claims that argumentation is far more than the art of rhetoric. Rather, reframing considerations are critical to the strategy of advocacy. He calls this process *heresthetics*—a neologism so awful it gives jargon a bad name.[8] Whatever the label, Riker called attention to a little appreciated aspect of political life, especially in the context of legislative policy making. In his slender classic, *The Art of Political Manipulation*, he offers readers a dozen cases where clever tacticians successfully reframed an issue. In one of these cases he recounts the efforts of Senator Warren Magnuson (D-WA) to stop the shipment of nerve gas from Okinawa to the United States. The gas was initially to be shipped through Seattle, but even when the Pentagon abandoned that idea, Magnuson kept fighting to make sure the gas never got anywhere near the Northwest. As the issue developed, the savvy, experienced Magnuson recognized that he did not have the votes to kill the revised plan on its merits (no matter where the gas was to be transported, there would be far more Senators pleased that their state or region had been spared than upset that they had been targeted). He then switched from an argument about the inherent dangers of nerve gas to one instead focused on senatorial prerogatives. His new argument claimed that the Nixon administration had ignored a previously passed resolution requiring the president to consult with the Senate on both issues relating to Okinawa and to the existing peace treaty with Japan. Magnuson implored his colleagues to stand up for their institution and to send the president a message about his need to consult with them. After closely examining the vote on some cognate issues, Riker concluded that Magnuson's introduction of a new frame won over enough votes to ban the shipment of the Okinawa nerve gas into the United States.[9]

Riker describes heresthetics as "structuring the world so you can win."[10] In his mind, such strategic efforts are common as legislators and other policy makers constantly rework their arguments to introduce new dimensions. Riker says that "accomplished herestheticians maneuver every day as part of their ordinary business."[11] This is very much a Madison Avenue view of human nature: even policy makers can be sold an old product repackaged as new. Riker does not deny the importance of partisanship or ideology but encourages readers not to consider decision making as a static set of choices dictated by standing positions or cleavages. In fact, the cleavages themselves are not fixed—each issue relates to many different dimensions, and each of those may divide the voters along a different cleavage, creating a majority on some dimensions but not on others. Determining what the fight is going to be about—setting the terms of the debate—has long been recognized by both practitioners and theorists alike as fundamental to determining the outcome of a legislative vote, a debate, or an election. We agree with Riker that *attempts* at strategic reframing are indeed part of the everyday work of policy makers and advocates around government. Success, however, is a different matter.

It is important to distinguish Riker's contention about the manipulation of arguments and issue frames from real-world changes in the external environment. Riker focused on alternative frames for an otherwise stable issue. It is a somewhat different situation when outside events alter the underlying issue. At any given time, the salience of an issue can rise or fall for reasons having little to do with the frames advocates are using in their effort to gain support. Bryan Jones uses the example of a proposal to build a superconducting supercollider, which was endorsed by the House of Representatives in 1991. A year later the same body of legislators turned around and voted against the supercollider. What had changed in the intervening year was that national concern over the budget deficit grew. As Jones explains, the underlying preferences of legislators didn't change, but the national environment led a number of representatives to pay more attention to the budget implications of building the expensive supercollider. In short, what happened outside the House of Representatives enabled opponents of the project to utilize a budgetary frame with more effectiveness.[12]

Scholarship has thus concentrated on two related but still distinct dynamics. In some cases a new dimension is introduced by advocates to try to reframe an otherwise unchanged, underlying condition. In other instances events and societal trends have altered the policy-making environment and advocates use the opportunity to reframe the issue. In both cases, either working alone or by taking advantage of windows of opportunity, policy entrepreneurs inside and outside of government sometimes succeed in their efforts to reframe debates.

Shadow or Substance?

Those who follow politics closely might scratch their heads at this literature, wondering about the value of research seemingly designed to docu-

ment the obvious: that politicians and their press aides constantly try to
shape stories. Is *heresthetician* anything more than academese for *spin doc-
tor*? These terms are, in fact, two sides of the same coin. It's not often that
serious academic research has a journalistic analog, but framing surely
qualifies as just such a case.

Journalists are not late to this game. Joe McGinniss's *The Selling of the
President 1968* was an early exposé of those trying to shape the coverage
of politics, but savaged journalists as well.[13] But the common knowledge
that all sides do it does little to reduce the efforts of spinners to spin and
journalists to identify spin for what it is. Sometimes the effort to spin the
story is the story itself. In a *New York Times* article about the Bush administration's Medicare drug benefit plan, reporter Robert Pear wrote not of
the program's actual performance, but of the efforts of the two parties to
spin their version of reality. Pear lampooned Republicans because they
"manipulated enrollment figures" and ridiculed Democratic leader Nancy
Pelosi for her hyperbole in claiming the law wasn't working because "a
Republican culture of corruption has infected our government."[14]

The norms that direct journalists to be wary of spin, the spoon-feeding
of information shaded to frame a story toward a particular perspective,
are now well entrenched in the profession. Journalists must also try to
understand the broader efforts of large-scale campaigns that extend far
beyond a single story. Typical of this genre is Bob Thompson's article in the
Washington Post dissecting the marketing analysis that led conservatives
to use the term "death tax" instead of the conventional "estate tax." Use
of the term "death tax" was shown by a party pollster to generate greater
anger among voters, convincing Republican lawmakers and lobbyists to
change their vocabulary.[15]

The behind-the-scenes stories focusing on the strategizing and mechan-
ics of political spin machines offer valuable insight into modern politics. At
the same time, a steady diet of newspaper and magazine articles can easily lead a reader to the conclusion that politics is shallow and susceptible
to the basest manipulation.[16] For whatever level of cynicism is truly warranted, it's important to recognize that the frames that are spun are often
connected to powerful, central ideas about the nature of government. The
problem with both the academic and journalistic literature on this topic
is that we have no baseline. That is, we can point to examples of successful reframing or spinning, but we have no idea whether these represent 1
percent, 50 percent, or 99 percent of what takes place on a typical day in
Washington. If spin were all that mattered, there would be no structure to
politics. If underlying structures were the whole picture, then there would

be no spin. We need to pin down some basic points of comparison. How common is successful spinning? Or to put it more precisely, how often do spin or framing change the generally understood definition of an issue? Anyone can push a new frame, but how often is such an effort successful in gaining broad acceptance of that frame?

Issue redefinition is clearly a challenge. By way of illustration, consider four major endeavors to frame broad-scale policy change: the Republican Contract with America, the Clinton health care proposal, the invasion of Iraq in 2003, and the Bush proposal to create private Social Security accounts. Each was accompanied by a major public relations campaign emphasizing a new frame that was a bold departure from the prevailing conventional wisdom. In the wake of the Republicans' landslide in the 1994 House elections, the new Speaker, Newt Gingrich, claimed that the voters had knowingly endorsed the Contract with America, ten broad policy planks supported by over three hundred Republican candidates for Congress that year. Even though polls showed only a small minority of the population knew of the Contract prior to the election, the frame offered by Gingrich and the Republicans' claiming an electoral mandate for this set of policies gained widespread acceptance among policy makers, journalists, and other observers. President Clinton proposed a revolutionary new health care system, managed competition, arguing that the existing system was broken and inefficient. The Republicans beat back this effort by emphasizing a familiar frame, that the government is too inefficient to be entrusted with health care.[17] The Bush administration's spinning of the need to invade Iraq is best symbolized by his chief of staff's explanation of why they waited until the fall of 2003 to push a war against Iraq: "From a marketing point of view, you don't introduce new products in August."[18] Bush's push for a new Social Security system was launched with an effort to convince Americans that there was a crisis in the system, one so urgent that it demanded immediate attention. Ironically, as the proposal began to sink, the White House scrambled to try to alter the frame that it had helped to develop, that the president wanted to "privatize" the system. The public reacted quite negatively to the idea that Social Security would be privatized. The White House's switch in terminology to "personal" accounts from "private" accounts never gained traction.

These four massive framing efforts all involved fundamental principles about the role of government, and all mobilized the nation's top leadership, including in three cases the president, armed with that most powerful of spin machines, the bully pulpit. All but the invasion of Iraq centered on the appropriate scope of government, the most basic of all differences between liberals and conservatives. The proposed war against Iraq forced citizens to consider the use of American military power in a world where terrorism presents a much greater threat than conventional warfare. For all the spinning on these issues, the frames pushed by advocates and opponents put a fundamental idea about the role of government front and center. Should we have a responsible party system? To what degree is government responsible for those who can't take care of themselves? What is more important, freedom or equality? Should America use its power to promote democracy in other countries? The manifestations of these debates, these contentious ideas, are the policies that affect people's lives.

No one disputes that ideas in the political arena have real-world impact. What should be emphasized, though, is that the framing of public-policy proposals is typically designed to evoke a broader political or ideological position. As Jacobs and Shapiro note, "A priming approach concentrates on raising the priority and the weight that individuals assign to particular attitudes already stored in their memories."[19] But priming is challenging, as the messages sent must break through the clutter of all the other messages that bombard us on an average day. And priming can easily stimulate opponents to launch their own efforts at persuasion.

Spin Rates

What is evoked by a particular effort at framing may disturb those on one side of a divide while pleasing others. What is used to prime may be false or misleading, as were President's Bush's claims about why it was necessary to invade Iraq. Frames can be used to stigmatize groups of people as undeserving of government assistance.[20] During the heated debate over immigration reform in 2007, some of the critics of the bipartisan legislation argued that illegal immigrants brought infectious diseases from their home countries into the United States.

Even if they are not purposefully misleading, frames are almost always, by definition, partial; they never tell the whole story. Thus, the question is which part of the story one prefers to put out there. Although it is evident that frames can be of great consequence, what is less certain is how often the introduction of a new frame has such an impact. It could be that cases where the emergence of a new frame succeeds, like the partial-birth abortion frame, are relatively uncommon. It could be that initial perspectives characterizing an issue may be rather durable, altered only incrementally over time, if at all. Another possibility is that frames change in response to things that are beyond the control of any single actor; these policy advocates may attempt to take advantage of them if they occur, but they cannot make them happen.[21] And even if issues are reframed because of the rhetorical skills of individual policy entrepreneurs or because of surprise events beyond the control of any single actor, we still know very little about how often this occurs.

To answer our question about how frequently reframing occurs, we asked our interview subjects about the arguments they were using. Thus, we know for each case what frames were being pushed and by whom. Further, because we went back to study what happened to our ninety-eight issues, typically 18–24 months after our initial interviews, we are in a position to make some judgments about how framing may evolve over time.

As we proceeded through our initial round of research on the ninety-eight issues, we certainly came across issues that seemed ripe for a talented heresthetician, issues where one side had not achieved dominance and where at least one of the sides would find it advantageous to change other participants' or observers' perceptions. Take, for example, opening up trade with Cuba. This issue has been around literally for decades, as fervently anti-Castro Cuban expatriates have blocked agricultural interests and others who lobby for open trade with Cuba. The three sides we heard in interviews—free trade with Cuba, expanded trade of pharmaceuticals and food only, and no broadening of trade—were perspectives that advocates have plied for years. No one we talked to expected any movement, and no new sides emerged during the following two years we tracked the issue.

Another case, one where we did observe policy change, involved new EPA regulations to reduce the sulfur content of gasoline. Like free trade with Cuba, gasoline-related air pollution is an issue of some years' standing. Our period of field research caught the end of one policy-making cycle, during which time the EPA published new low sulfur regulations. The two basic sides we heard were an environmental, clear-air position and a probusiness, antiregulatory viewpoint. This second view was pushed by smaller refiners, as large refineries were less concerned about additional costs to be incurred from reformulating gasoline. Large refiners may have even welcomed additional costs placed on their small competitors. The initiative for the new regulations came from an EPA review of the problem and from policies adopted by the state of California to reduce sulfur pollution there. During the period of the research, no new side and no new her-esthetics appeared to have played a significant role. The issue itself arose only because of the possibility of dramatic action. Research findings sug-gesting the effectiveness of a sulfur-reduction approach made movement in this direction all but inevitable. There was some new evidence attesting to the feasibility of a new approach, but there were no new arguments.

These cases offer cautionary observations about the widely accepted view that public-policy making is commonly shaped by framing and re-framing. One caution is methodological. In the Cuba case, there had been some change over the years. At some point, before this research took to the field, the ban on trade was modified, and limited amounts of drugs and food were permitted to be sold to Cuba. It was an incremental change—proponents of trade want much more—but it was a change. Because in-cremental change doesn't come out of thin air, one can only assume that advocates began pushing for a humanitarian opening to Cuba and that this view eventually influenced policy. The Cuba trade case raises a sim-ple question: At any time policy is modified, is there reframing? Nothing in the abundant literature on framing makes a distinction between incre-mental modifications and larger-scale change.[22]

Stable Frames

The sample of issues collected for this research is well suited for a broad analysis of framing. The random sample is particularly important, as most research on framing done outside the laboratory takes the form of case studies. As Druckman points out, selecting cases is dangerous, because "nearly every time scholars look for a framing effect, they tend to find it."[23] Aside from avoiding a selection bias, the random sample offers a wide array of policies at various stages of the policy-making process. The issues range from the nearly invisible to the highly salient, across virtually all major sectors of public policy.

Let us emphasize as strongly as we can that ours is only an analysis of *reframing*. The research design for this study did not allow for an analy-sis of initial *framing*, because our random sample comprised the issues lobbyists were working on the very week we interviewed them. Although some of the lobbyists were trying to push issues on the periphery forward, they mostly identified issues that were already far along in the legislative process. Overall, a significant proportion of the sample of issues related to long-term problems. Yet to study initial framing requires observations at the beginning, and the true beginning of an issue is difficult to fix. In this respect, some of the literature on reframing suffers from the same problems that we have noted in the literature on lobbying in general. Just as in lobbying there is almost always an existing policy that establishes a status quo, so too in framing studies. In the policy process, there is virtually always an established, status quo frame that dominates discussion.[24] Reframing, like lobbying, is about changing the status quo. But the status quo achieved its status usually for many reasons, and these may not easily disappear.

In reviewing each of the ninety-eight cases, coding revolved around a simple question: Over the time we followed each issue, did a new frame emerge by stage two of the research (that is, in the subsequent Congress, as much as two years after our initial interviews)? Each issue was coded as being characterized by stable framing, partial reframing, or complete reframing. A complete reframing was defined as the emergence of a new, dominant frame that reoriented debate over an issue. A partial reframing meant that a new frame altered the fundamental debate but that it did not become a dominant side. In practical terms this would reflect a new argument coming to the fore, joining the mix of other arguments that remained viable. An issue coded as having stable frames was still being debated in the same general terms as it was when we first interviewed participants. Our coding decisions were guided by comparing the original interviews with a follow-up interview during the next Congress, reviews of stories in the media, and any other pertinent information that we came across during the time we studied the issue.

The results are surprising. Of the 98 issues that fell into our sample, we judged just 4 issues to have undergone some degree of reframing over the period studied. One of those we coded a complete reframing, and three were partial. This is just 4 percent. (If issues that appeared to have reached a conclusive termination point at the time of the initial interviews are removed from the calculation, it is 4 issues out of 85, or 5 percent.[25]) One example of partial reframing came at the end of the Clinton administration when the Forest Service issued regulations banning further road building in the national forests. Proponents of the ban argued that the environmental degradation that came from the roads and the lack of funds to maintain existing roads dictated putting a stop to additional road building. Opponents from the timber industry were concerned about limiting access for logging. After it took office, the Bush administration was faced with a set of regulations it did not like, but believed the law constrained it from simply tossing out the Clinton rules. Instead, Bush administration officials fashioned a new policy that offered local control, so that officials at each site could determine what was best at that location.[26] The competing frames were not pushed aside, but this local-control perspective was successfully added to the mix by the administration.

In another case of partial reframing, a bankruptcy bill was tied up when Republicans hostile to abortion put in a provision exempting anti-abortion groups from civil claims that were the product of protests of violence at abortion clinics. The virulently anti-abortion group Operation Rescue declared bankruptcy rather than pay restitution to abortion clinics. Senate Republicans sympathetic to the anti-abortion movement believed that as a matter of conscience, such groups as Operation Rescue should not be required to distribute their assets to Planned Parenthood or other pro-choice organizations.

The third case of partial reframing involved Internet taxation, or more accurately, the lack of taxation on items purchased over the Internet. Initially the debate was argued on the basis of no new taxes versus the need for revenue by cities and states, which were losing revenue as consumers moved some of their purchases to Internet providers. A new argument came into play as so-called bricks-and-mortar stores began to emphasize fairness to all businesses. An identical product found both online and at a store at the mall can be sold more cheaply by the Internet supplier because no sales tax need be assessed. As one lobbyist working for a national retail chain put it, "All channels of commerce should be tax neutral. The government should not be in the business of picking winners and losers."

The one issue undergoing a complete reframing was a minor matter concerning the excise tax on telephone bills. The tax actually goes back to the time of the Spanish-American War and was justified as a luxury tax, because only the upper class had phones at that time. At the beginning of our research, phone companies were pushing Congress to eliminate the tax. At a later point in time, when the case was updated, the declining economy had effectively killed the proposal. Deteriorating economic conditions made legislators reluctant to give up the $5 billion a year the tax generated. The government's need for revenue was a new perspective and one that dominated what little discussion there was on the issue at the time of the follow-up research. (After this legislative defeat, advocacy turned to the courts, and, in a series of decisions, the application of this tax to long-distance phone calls was invalidated.)

Why is reframing so uncommon? Nothing in the literature offers an estimate of just how frequently reframing occurs, but that work certainly implies that it is not rare. Although there is work which is cautionary, citing barriers to reframing, the literature as a whole clearly suggests that reframing is a common strategy and sometimes succeeds.[27] It's not clear from the data gathered here as to how often reframing is tried, but our judgment is that when it is attempted it is aimed at a partial reframing and not at a wholesale reorientation.

The denizens of Washington continue to believe that reframing works but not because they've read William Riker or any of the others who have written on this subject. Rather, a central part of the culture of Washington is spin. Spin and reframing are certainly overlapping concepts, but in colloquial language *spin* usually refers to immediate and more transitory contexts—in particular the story being written that day by journalists. Spinning and public relations are so much a part of the day-to-day life of Washington, that it's easy to assume that reframing, efforts aimed at more enduring change in the way an issue is perceived over the next policy-making cycle, is often successful. Also, recent party history is often linked to success at such public relations skills. The triumph of conservatives and Republicans' success since the 1994 congressional elections has been widely attributed in large part to abilities to package their policies in an appealing and benign way.[28] Conversely, liberals are excoriated for their inability to match the conservatives on this score. George Lakoff, for example, argues stridently that the liberals' problems are not with their basic policies but with the way they're presented to the American people.

We're confident that our finding that reframing is rare is correct, not only because we used a random sample instead of selecting out cases, but also because our interviews with advocates left us with an indelible impression of just how difficult reframing is. In talking to lobbyists, legislative aides, and administrators, we observed people with little, if any, control over the definition of the problem at hand. In looking back at the sample of cases, many obstacles to reframing become evident. We group these explanations into three general categories: resources, political realities, and lobbyist skills and strategies.

Resources

Fights over public policy are not contests of ideas alone, but of resources as well. We focus our analysis here on resources related to the opposition, sunk costs, and coalitions. The most fundamental reason why reframing is difficult is that the advocates who want to reframe will very likely run into an *opposition side* that will fight any effort contrary to its interests. For example, on the issue of CAFE standards (which set miles per gallon thresholds for automobile manufacturers), both sides on this issue have substantial resources and many friends in Congress. Environmental organizations and auto manufacturers are both well represented in Washington and are savvy, aggressive lobbies. In our interviews on this case, we observed lobbyists fully engaged in watching the opposition's every move. Each lobbyist we spoke with went into enormous detail about the other side's arguments. Neither side is going to sit idly by and let the other redefine the issue without a concerted attempt to push such efforts off to the side.

Summary statistics from the completed interviews illustrate this point. The median issue had nineteen separate advocates who were identified during the research. That's a fair number of policy experts on an issue (and, of course, these represent only the most prominent advocates, not the even larger policy communities, often consisting of hundreds or thousands of professionals who are knowledgeable and concerned with the issue). Would they all be willing to support a new policy frame proposed by one of them, or even half of them support a new frame? The ability of the opposition to combat redefinitions is aided by the slow gears of Washington's policy-making machinery. Redefinition efforts are not tactical strikes but part of long-term strategy. Thus, opponents can't be caught off guard by an overnight sneak attack, as might happen with a new sweetener to be proposed as an amendment just for a floor vote.

A second resource-related constraint on reframing is *sunk costs*. Here we refer to tangible costs only, excluding psychological commitment, which we take up below. The arguments put forward by interest groups are more than the rhetoric of conversations or the theme in a memo left in the office of a member of Congress. Those arguments reflect an investment by an interest group or government office in supporting that line of advocacy. People working for interest groups are assigned to work on a particular problem from a particular viewpoint. Individuals may even be hired for their expertise on a particular aspect of a policy problem.

Over the years lobbyists and executives from Lockheed Martin have continued to argue as hard as they can that the C-130 transport plane is vital to the nation's defense. There is, of course, fierce competition for weapons purchases from the Pentagon, and the C-130 is not cheap. Nor is it sexy, as it lugs cargo around rather than attacking the enemy. And, weapons-wise, it is an aging senior citizen dating all the way back to the Korean War. It is not as though Lockheed Martin would refuse to use other arguments to try to promote the plane, but it's hard to imagine that anything would be as strong as arguments about the plane's success, functionality, and cost-effectiveness. The Lockheed Martin office in Washington works continually to develop evidence to support this basic story line. Every budget iteration requires that its lobbyists go forward with data to support the enduring arguments about the C-130. Frames themselves have histories and often large institutional investments that make them relatively stable.

The third and final resource constraint is participation in *coalitions*. Interest-group coalitions are ubiquitous in Washington, and, given the limited room on the congressional agenda and opposition from other interest groups, lobbies are eager to find allies with whom to fight. But with allies come compromises and reduced autonomy. Although a coalition isn't limited to a single argument that all participants must parrot, it makes sense for coalitions to coordinate their messages. Significant changes from that message may need to be negotiated. Since politics can make for strange bedfellows, some arguments may be tempered to keep opponents on other issues civil, if not friendly, on the matter at hand. On the regulations designed to reduce the sulfur content of gasoline, environmental groups and car manufacturers found themselves on the same side. The environmentalists surely had to agree to arguments that avoided their differences of opinion with auto manufacturers on other clean air issues. As one lobbyist told us, his coalition was "not this huge lockstep no-cracks phalanx." But he added, "there is an interest on our part in how we develop better relationships" with other groups, even those with which his organization is sometimes "at loggerheads."

The subject of coalitions suggests a broader point. As discussed in chapter 3, interest groups operate in a community of organizations with whom they commonly work. While coalitions of strange bedfellows are always striking, most coalition partners, most of the time, are like-minded organizations. Thus, one community of advocates typically monitors another community of advocates.[29] These policy communities are communication networks, and the regular interaction of advocates with their regular partners facilitates quick strategizing and mobilization. Again, our summary statistics are telling: the median number of advocates per side is eight. This multiplicity of actors and the resources they aggregate in policy communities make it all the more difficult for one set of participants to quickly or dramatically change the terms of debate. Thus, the very structure of issue networks supports the stability of frames over time.

Political Realities

For many issues, a reframing effort is a waste of time and resources. Given the difficulty of reframing under the best of circumstances, members of the Washington community will think long and hard about the political realities of such an endeavor. Our time spent with lobbyists and policy makers led us to reflect on three types of political realities that can deter reframing: political alignments, ripeness, and media norms.

By *political alignments* we refer to those who are in power and those who are in the minority. It is always the case that for some interests in Washington, the wrong people are in power. And for all practical purposes, those interests need to wait until an election brings change. One lobbyist told us that he's always asking, "What's the climate like?" and "Is the climate going to change?" These may seem like obvious questions, but they're ones that bear consideration in the context of reframing. A lobby, even as wealthy as some are, must rationally allocate its resources. In plain English, each lobby must put its money and staff where they are going to do the most good. And contrary to popular misconception, most lobbies in Washington are constrained by budgets and staffing limitations.

If the wrong people come to power, lobbies may rethink the arguments they've been presenting. In some instances a new argument might be a good idea. If the conservatives are in power, for example, an environmental group might want to shift argumentation toward market-based reasons, if there are any, for a particular goal. But even so, it is more likely that the disadvantaged group is instituting a change in emphasis rather than trying to reframe. Other counterstrategies may be considered, such as looking for a legislative trade in which allies in Congress logroll with the opposition, giving up something to gain something. But similarly, this is a strategic choice, not reframing.

Leaving aside changes in emphasis and legislative maneuvering, efforts to truly reframe may be too problematic for the typical Washington lobby. To begin with, the people who are in power and who don't share a lobby's goals must be assumed to be just as politically savvy. Is the opposition going to be swayed by a new argument, even one that is closer to its own philosophy? If a lobbyist wanting to reframe cannot convince himself that it is likely to work, why would he expend his scarce resources on it? Instead of a reframing effort, attention might turn to another, more promising issue. Or the organization might sponsor research that might create a more favorable environment for the issue when an opportunity presents itself sometime in the future. Or it might work the grassroots to strengthen itself and keep the issue alive with members of Congress when they visit home.

The largest group of lobbyists interviewed for this study worked for corporations and trade associations. Given the tax-cutting focus of the first term of the Bush administration, it is interesting that we came across relatively few tax cut proposals being worked on by lobbyists interviewed during the Clinton administration's last year. It seems clear that they had strategically decided on other issues as their priorities, issues where they might find the administration receptive, since tax cuts were not a major focus of the Clinton White House. What we didn't run across were efforts to reframe tax cut issues. Yet tax cut interests were there under the surface, and business lobbyists brought them forward in abundance when George W. Bush came to town.

Independent of who is in power, new issues that lack urgency must be nurtured through the governmental process until the time is right for action. We term this evolution *ripeness* to acknowledge that there is huge variation in the opportunity structure of public policy making. It may take years for an issue to develop, as advocates work to build support over the long-term. John Kingdon calls this a "softening up" period to educate policy makers so that "when a short-run opportunity to push their proposal comes, the way has been paved."[30] One of our issues, legislation aimed at obtaining federal funding for infant hearing screening, had been circulating in Congress for a decade before a program was incorporated into an omnibus piece of legislation. This is not unusual in Washington, where there are a limited number of bills that get enacted each year. Organizations like the American Speech-Language-Hearing Association and the National Association of the Deaf persevered over the years, pushing the same basic argument that it is much more advantageous to diagnose a hearing problem at infancy rather than waiting for it to be diagnosed when a child starts school. There was no reframing that could push this basic argument into the background. Eventually this long-term effort bore fruit.

But the ebb and flow of politics does not evolve in predictable cycles. Sometimes opportunities suddenly emerge, what Kingdon metaphorically describes as the opening of policy windows.[31] Sometimes long-term stability can be disrupted by events, intellectual developments, and greater media attention. Such opportunities may lead to reframing, as established truths have been shattered and everyone is considering the issue in a new light. After 9/11, for example, there was a mad rush in Washington to reframe all issues as related to national security. This sometimes reached the levels of farce. The American Traffic Safety Services Association, a trade group for road sign manufacturers, lobbied for more federal funds for street signs on the grounds that Americans would need better street signs to prevent traffic jams in the aftermath of a terrorist attack.[32] Nevertheless, some lobbies did successfully link a proposal they had been working on to post-9/11 security legislation before argumentation returned to more normal advocacy.[33]

Lobbies thus live in a world that rewards patience. Those that work to build support over time while they wait for the right party to win an election may sometimes find that fortune shines upon them. The reward may come with the sudden emergence of an opportunity, as was the case with 9/11. Generally, though, lobbies facing a hostile or apathetic government must be prepared to work for years to get their proposals enacted—if they're enacted at all.

Another facet of the pragmatism that guides Washington lobbying is that advocacy must contend with a *skeptical media*. Reporters and editors will consider new frames presented to them with a jaundiced eye, being sophisticated enough to understand that lobbies push that which is to their advantage, not what is objective and true. It is part of the professional training of reporters that they try to resist spin and to balance all views in their reporting. A reporter who prepares a story with a novel frame runs up against the norms of the profession and the vetting structure of a newspaper or broadcaster.

The greatest obstacle for lobbies needing media attention to help them persuade policy makers is to get the media to pay attention in the first place. Many of the issues in our sample were invisible to anyone outside of the specialists in the field. As a consequence, most efforts to persuade the media are not efforts to convince reporters that they should view the relevant issue through a new frame, but that they should regard the issue as worthy of their attention. To get any kind of coverage is a major victory for many lobbyists around town. For the American Optometric Association pushing Congress to fund residency training for newly graduated optometrists, any publicity would have been a godsend. The problem wasn't the frame but that the *Washington Post* didn't regard the issue as important. When we asked a lobbyist working on this issue to outline what he would be doing to advance his cause, we noticed that mention of media was conspicuous by its absence. When we asked specifically, he responded simply, "No PR." What was left unsaid was obvious: it was unrealistic to think that journalists would be interested in covering the issue.

But even for those lobbyists considering a new effort to reframe an issue that the *Washington Post* does cover, they must develop a realistic strategy to convince an experienced and talented beat reporter that he or she has the story all wrong. This is no small challenge. Since this is so difficult to do those lobbies with the resources may try to change the environment around a story rather than influence reporters directly. Tactics such as paid advertising, histrionics, protests, photo ops with prominent celebrities, media events on Capitol Hill, sponsorship of research, appearances on talk shows, and the like may over the long run result in more attention for a lobby's cause. Most likely, however, such advocacy is really aimed at shifting attention to an argument that is already present in the debate over an issue and not at reframing.[34]

Lobbyist Skills and Strategies

A third set of constraints on reframing derives from beliefs about what is right and about how an advocate succeeds at her vocation over time. Discussion here is organized around advocacy decisions influenced by conviction, credibility, and commitment over time. Although many lobbyists are happy to work for whoever will pay for their services, there are many others who work out of *conviction*. This is especially true of lobbyists for citizen groups and labor unions, who are typically fueled by ideology and are passionate about the righteousness of the issues they work on. Certainly labor union lobbyists are flexible on legislative strategy, but are they ever going to make arguments about justice and equality for workers a minor part of their advocacy? Is an environmental lobbyist ever going to be swayed from a primary argument that we must do more to clean the air or preserve the wilderness?

Such lobbyists are surely open to additional frames. The environmental lobbyist who is unyielding on matters of nuclear safety would not be averse to bringing forward the financial risks associated with nuclear power if she saw that it was advantageous. Nevertheless, ideological arguments endure over long periods of time and are not dropped just because they are out of fashion or the wrong party holds office. Commenting on an issue centered around tariffs on imported steel, the industry representative couldn't have been more emphatic: "Our argument? That's easy. . . . We believe in the free market." The labor lobbyist saw things differently but was equally direct: "These are good-paying jobs at stake." Their arguments were so basic that we could have been talking to Adam Smith and Samuel Gompers. Even when it seems that the time is propitious for a lobbyist to look for additional frames, the ideological core of their advocacy is never completely pushed aside.

Although conviction may be more important for some lobbyists than others, all lobbyists must be concerned about their *credibility*. Advocates know that to maximize their effectiveness with key staffers, legislators, and administrators, they need to develop a relationship with those individuals. This process is nurtured over the years, through a variety of interactions, where the lobbyist tries both to build support for their position and to build respect for their work ethic and trustworthiness. In the words of one lobbyist, "my reputation is my most valuable asset."[35] Part of building trust comes from when a lobbyist makes an argument about what is critical to the organization and then stays with that argument for some time. To come back to an office a few months or even a year later with a whole new frame can work against one's reputation.

This is not to argue that lobbyists should be unyielding and refuse to compromise. Lobbyists, even the most idealistic of the bunch, are ultimately pragmatists who are open to compromise. But, again, it's important to distinguish between strategic considerations as to how to move a proposal forward and efforts to reorient an argument through reframing. For a lobbyist to jump around from argument to argument, trying to find a frame that works, is counterproductive. When a lobbyist meets with a legislative staffer and asks her to buy into an argument, that lobbyist is, in effect, asking the staffer to go to her boss and ask the legislator to push that argument forward. After making that pitch to the legislator, is that same staffer going to want to hear the lobbyist try to reframe the issue on his next visit? It's conceivable that a lobbyist who would love to catalyze a reframing would have to make such a pitch to staffers whose boss actually wrote the original legislation now at issue. In short, continuity is often part of credibility.

Finally, *staying the course* turns out to be an effective strategy. In his study of interest groups and the legislative agenda Jeffrey Berry found that there is much to be said for continuity in issue advocacy. Berry did not use arguments or frames as a unit of analysis, but what he did observe over decades is that a key ingredient of the liberal citizen groups' success was to stay in the trenches, working on the same issues, year after year. By investing organizational resources into the development of expertise by staffers, the lobbies enhanced their influence by investing in people who developed reputations as leading experts on particular issues. When legislative staffers, administrative agency officials, or reporters need information about a problem, they know who to call for reliable intelligence.[36]

Is such an organizational development strategy incompatible with reframing? In theory, no. One's expertise on an issue could be broad enough to be able to adapt it to different frames. However, expertise on complex public-policy matters can be highly technical. Reporters may call a particular person at an environmental group precisely because she has a great deal of expertise on emissions from steel mills. It is the data that is offered and the proven reliability of that expert over the years that makes her so valuable. If that person has been documenting for years that particulate emissions at a specific level are harmful to public health, she may not be the best lobbyist for arguing a new frame about the economic inefficiency of such steel mills. In sum, people invest in frames, and this investment pays dividends.

Change and the Status Quo

The central finding on framing is not that nothing ever changes. Forty-one percent of the issues in the sample underwent some policy change during the four years of our research. Rather, the data demonstrate that change is rarely the consequence of the emergence of an entirely new frame. Thus, policy change is likely to originate from other sources (including increased attention to a frame that may have long been present in the debate).

Change can evolve from long-standing work by advocates, who build support over time by educating policy makers, reaching out to constituents, supporting research, and then publicizing the results. External events can make some proposals more or less appealing. Occasionally an external shock is so great that an issue can be reframed, such as was the case with civil liberties after 9/11. Other times trends and events move policy in less dramatic fashion, as was the case with the telephone excise tax. The decline in the economy simply made Congress less interested in tax cut proposals unrelated to the president's fiscal agenda. Most obviously, change can also come about from elections.

What are the implications of the rarity of successful reframing? At the broadest level, we must recognize the power of the status quo. As we have documented in so many other parts of this book, in a policy debate defenders of the status quo side typically possess enormous advantages. In the national policy-making system, there are many obstacles to overcome to enact change—it's just plain difficult to climb that mountain. In the Congress there are structural obstacles—two separate houses, divided control, and the filibuster among others—that change agents must overcome to succeed in achieving their goals. As we discussed in chapter 7, defenders of the status quo can use simpler and often more convincing arguments; they often need only to raise doubts about "untested schemes."

Much of the advocacy we observed was oriented toward what Bryan Jones and Frank Baumgartner have called "attention shifting."[37] The limited space on the political agenda pushes advocates to select strategies that call attention to their issue, to their priorities, and to the severity of the problem as they see it. When we spoke with a business lobbyist working to try to amend the Food Quality Protection Act of 1996, he complained that "in Congress, the enviros wear the white hat, and the farmers and business wear a black hat." He then conceded that "it's hard to argue that you shouldn't be looking at exposure from products." In his own way, he was acknowledging the dense structure on policy making on food safety. He knew that consumer interests and powerful consumer arguments on food safety could not be dismissed, so his focus was to get legislators and their aides to pay attention to the problems of his industry. It wasn't possible to alter the fundamental frames associated with his issue, but it was possible that modifications in the law might help the industry reduce regulatory costs.

It's also the case that reframing can emerge incrementally. Beyond shifts in attention that, over time, yield more weight to particular arguments, there are transformations that are qualitatively different than a re-weighting of attention.[38] In the case of capital punishment, for example, an "innocence frame" emerged over the course of many years. As more and more death sentences were overturned by DNA tests and other exculpatory evidence, press coverage became dominated by stories emphasizing wrongful convictions of death row inmates. In turn, public opinion was influenced.[39] Unfortunately, the research design of our study did not allow for an analysis of incremental reframing. Or perhaps we should say that a major finding of our study, based on our extensive fieldwork, is just how long it takes for this incremental reframing to occur. A much longer time frame than two elapsed Congresses would be necessary to adequately measure such change. Given the infrequency of reframing found in this study and all the constraints on reframing identified here, our best guess is that change over time is more typically a matter of slow attention shifting than dramatic reframing.

On a methodological note, it should be acknowledged that we have no measure of how many issues may have gone through some reframing before we initiated our interviews. Thus, it's possible that we missed a significant reframing that altered an issue before we identified the arguments and sides surrounding it. We did gather information about each issue's recent history, however, and we doubt that previously reframed issues form any significant portion of the overall sample. Analysis of each issue's sides typically reveals a rather basic set of arguments. Recall that 17 of the 98 issues had only one side and fully 58 of them had just two.

Given the infrequency of reframing, why is it that journalists, pundits, politicos, and not a few political scientists have assumed that it is widespread? Certainly part of the reason is that reframing, beneath the surface of the academic language, embodies a popular, cynical view of the policy-making process. Teena Gabrielson captures this view succinctly, noting, "In the marketplace of American politics, the packaging of political issues is often as important as the product."[40] For all of us, there is the tendency to believe that the objective virtue of our own policy positions is a victim of the other side's success at confusing the public with deceptive marketing of their positions. Beyond cynicism, however, is the reality that when reframing does take place, it can be of enormous importance. Although that wasn't the case in our sample of issues, there are examples of reframing making a huge difference. As noted above, the partial-birth abortion reframing had such a profound influence in that policy area that it became iconic evidence of the power of reframing. And, of course, the nation is at war in Iraq partly because of the great success of the Bush administration in presenting the case for the war in terms that were misleading. The use of capital punishment in America has been seriously eroded because of increased attention to problems and errors in trials.

Since reframing is so unusual, it appears that adjustments in the "packaging" of issues may not be nearly as important as is commonly thought. Initial frames tend to be enduring, and over time debate revolves around the core, not the surface. Assumptions that policy making is highly influenced by the superficiality of advertising, public relations campaigns, test marketing, and well-designed sound bites finds little support in the history of the ninety-eight issues tracked for this study. There is, of course, change over time as modest alterations move policies in one direction and the other. Surely, enduring frames can adjust incrementally to accommodate evolutionary change, but this is not the result of the kind of strategic effort to reframe envisioned by Riker. Instead, policy changes over the years are likely to reflect the long-term investment of resources by interest groups in conventional advocacy, the accumulation of research, and the impact of real-world trends and events.

CHAPTER TEN

Does Money Buy Public Policy?

In the early days of 1999, representatives from a large telecommunications company and two large trade associations made a visit to a relatively junior member of Congress. They had an issue that they thought he would be interested in hearing about. It involved cutting taxes in a time of tax surpluses, promoting consumer interests, and rolling back a policy that no longer had any reasonable justification. It had the backing of nearly one hundred groups, both within the business community and within a wide array of citizen and consumer groups. The backers had money, and their diverse membership seemed to assure that they would have legitimacy in the public eye as well. The issue had no organized opposition and seemed unlikely to develop any, since the issue had no natural enemies. Given all this, would the congressman be willing to serve as the issue's champion in the House? The interest groups would provide the organizing skills and media push outside Congress, but they needed someone inside Congress to bring the issue forward. The primary benefit to the junior member of Congress was a chance to be seen as a person who could get things done— a mover and shaker who led a popular bill through to fruition, later taking credit, perhaps, for saving consumers millions of dollars in taxes. The junior member said yes, and the fight to eliminate the 3 percent federal excise tax on telecommunications began in earnest.

Sometimes a policy proposal seems to have it all, yet still fails to pass. The effort to end the 3 percent excise tax was just such an issue. Telecommunications companies hated the tax because it was costly to collect and made their customers irritable, and efforts to eliminate the tax dated back more than fifteen years. The tax—which was applied to all phone bills, cell phone bills, and cable television bills—began in 1898 as a luxury tax on a newfangled invention. Its proceeds were to help defray the costs of the Spanish-American War. More than a century later, the fund created by the tax was not dedicated to any specific program, and, in a time of budget surpluses, it seemed like a good time to let it go. Proponents of eliminating the tax were well connected, gave plenty of campaign contributions, and had hired Jack Quinn, a former Clinton White House counsel who headed the prominent lobbying firm Quinn and Gillespie. Their issue was popular with the public, garnered respectable press coverage, and had no organized opposition. It was "good for the poor and old people," because it eliminated a regressive tax. On May 25, 2000, the bill passed the House with only two members voting against it. Time, however, was not on its side. Postponed on the Senate schedule because leaders had other priorities, the bill languished until the end of August, and with elections approaching, the session was essentially over. A last-minute attempt was made in October to attach it to the general Treasury appropriations bill, but that bill was vetoed on other grounds. Supporters hoped to reintroduce the bill and pass it during the 107th Congress. When the next session arrived, however, the federal budget surplus had evaporated—and with it any chance of the excise tax being eliminated. The issue died in committee.[1]

Resources are important to interest groups hoping to change policy, but even substantial resources do not guarantee a policy outcome. The groups supporting change here had all kinds of resources—staff, budgets, membership, diversity, bipartisanship, good connections. They had an issue that was sure to be popular with the public and that no one actively opposed. They failed nonetheless.

About the same time that the fight was underway to remove the 3 percent federal tax from consumers' telephone bills, another lobbying battle was underway, this one pitting banks against credit unions. In the popular press, advocacy by bankers evokes images of big-buck lobbyists, cozy relationships with members of Congress, millions in campaign contributions, and guaranteed results. But in the decades-long effort by banks to limit expansion by credit unions, banks have repeatedly ended up on the losing side. Credit unions traditionally can offer many banking services to employees of certain institutions (for example, federal employees or employees of a given school district, university, or hospital), but just what defines the "field of membership" for a given credit union? From the credit unions' perspective, they are often happy to take on additional members, even those whose connection with the original group might be tangential at best (e.g., spouses and children of members or people who formerly were connected with the institution but who no longer are). Because credit unions are nonprofit and offer low-cost services to members, banks see them as rivals and want the "field of membership" to remain as restricted as possible. But credit unions were merging and opening more branches in multiple communities and sought rule changes that would make it easier to complete many of these mergers. Hence, the dispute over the expansion of credit union services and membership emerged again in Congress in 1999. On the one side stood the American Bankers Association with all of its money, wide contacts in every congressional district, a huge PAC, many lobbyists, and a reputation for getting things done. On the other side, however, stood the credit unions with their consumer-friendly, small-town image. "You have the traditional, small, mom-and-pop type thing," a lobbyist for the banking industry said with regret. "That's the image that people associate with credit unions, like the Bailey Building and Loan in *It's a Wonderful Life.*"

Besides their hometown, popular image, credit unions have another asset money can't buy: a regulatory agency that exists primarily to ensure the financial stability and viability of their industry. With the National Credit Union Administration and public opinion supporting them, credit unions often win their battles against the bankers, both concerning regulatory matters and actions before Congress, in spite of the power and wealth of the banking industry, their natural competitors. The only place bankers have ever gotten a toehold on this issue is in the courts, where rulings favorable to the bankers have served only to kick the issue back before Congress to fix the authorizing legislation. The bankers have long been frustrated by this situation and have tried their best to change it, but to little avail. One banking lobbyist described his organization's attempts to raise the issue of what they see as the unfair competitive advantage that credit unions enjoy because of their tax-exempt status: "And so what occurred was that we realized that we could not win by going to the public. We decided to try decision makers. So what we focused on was newspaper editorial boards, but that didn't work either, because no one wants to tax mom and pop." The U.S. banking industry is one of the most powerful, well-connected, and politically savvy actors in national politics; they win many of the battles in which they engage. Why aren't they able to win all the time? Why were they not able to beat out the credit unions in the issue we studied, limiting the field of membership of growing credit unions as the credit unions encroached on a market bankers believe should be rightfully theirs?

Much has been written about the impact of money in politics. In this chapter we look carefully at the impact of material resources in achieving policy outcomes. In one sense, it is obvious that the wealthier the group, the more advantages. But policy making is a continuous process, with many issues already having been settled in previous rounds. Could the wealthy simply continually accumulate more wealth and policy advantage, winning more and more each time Congress considers their issue, continually expanding the distance between them and the also-rans? In this chapter we see that there are many complications to the rich-get-richer story as it relates to the policy process.

Looking beyond the Money

Popular accounts of the interest-group system often focus on the monetary resources that advocacy organizations possess: lobbying staffs, financial reserves, and campaign contributions. There certainly is a lot of money in the system—interest groups spend about $2 billion lobbying the federal government every year and about $500 million every two-year election cycle in campaign contributions.[2] Nonetheless, the relationship between money and political outcomes is far from simple, largely because where large amounts of money come into play on one side, others often mobilize as well. Scholars have struggled to document the impact of campaign contributions on policy decisions, but with inconsistent results. Donations from political action committees sometimes seem to have swayed legislators and equally as often seem to have had no effect. Since most of these studies have been based on one or a handful of issues at a time and since vote outcomes must be either yes or no, the results could very well be attributable to random fluctuations rather than any systematic effects of donations.[3] Further, the studies have been bedeviled by the problem that groups often contribute to members of Congress known already to agree with them or to those who have institutional gatekeeping positions related to the issues of interest to the group, so the money could be simply a wise insurance policy, an effort to keep access open and not to antagonize, or an attempt to keep friendly faces in Congress, not an issue-by-issue quid pro quo. After all, there are many issues in any given congressional election cycle, but groups can only contribute a certain amount. If a group wins some of its battles and loses others (as is typically the case), then how can we say that money was helpful or not, if the money typically cannot be connected to one or another of the specific issues? In any case, scholars have found no smoking gun, no systematic relationship between campaign contributions and policy success, a fact that might be surprising to readers of the press, where it seems that campaign contributions are equated with lobbying power across the board.[4] While no one doubts that money matters, and while there is no question that the wealthy enjoy greater access to policy makers and political leaders than other groups in society, whether this means that they can necessarily write their ticket in Washington, getting the policies they want when they want them, is another question. One reason why it may not be so is that the policy process is so hard to control. Very few government officials have the authority unilaterally to produce the policy changes that lobbyists might desire. Engaging in a lobbying initiative is inherently uncertain.

While it may be true that scholars have not found a systematic link between campaign contributions and policy outcomes, PACs are far from the only sort of political resource an interest group may have at its disposal. There are other material resources, including the size of an organization's budget or the extent of a corporation's assets. There are differences in staff size, number of lobbyists, and number of members. There are intangibles as well, such as public legitimacy and reputation. Any review of the impact of money in politics should review these factors as well, not just campaign contributions.

Material resources can sometimes be trumped by sheer numbers—organizations with many members may be heeded just as rapidly as organizations able to make large campaign contributions. Large numbers of members not only provide some democratic legitimacy to a cause—"look at how many people are represented by that organization; look at how many constituents agree with this argument"—but also can serve to put pressure on elected officials who are concerned about reelection. The number of members in a group, the degree to which public opinion supports a particular idea, and the number of other organizations that are willing to join a group in a given policy fight all are resources that can be of great help to an organization, even an organization that may not control large financial resources or have a large PAC.

Perhaps most important of all, however, is the degree of support an organization or its cause already enjoys among policy makers. In popular accounts these relationships are often attributed solely to linkages from campaign contributions, but these are far from the only tie that binds in Washington. There is also the simple fact of an organization and a policy maker sharing the same policy goal. Such allies are perhaps the most valuable resource in Washington. Policy makers and organized interests frequently work in tandem to advocate policy goals that they both share. Each can do things that the other cannot; officials within government can set agendas, meet with colleagues, and so on. Organized interests outside of government often have more staff time available, the ability to do research and publicize findings, and the luxury of working on just one or a few issues at a time. Both insiders and outsiders share an interest in getting others to pay attention to their cause, because without widespread interest within government in acting on a policy question, a bill will languish and die. Government officials are themselves central actors in these questions, not mere receptacles for interest-group influence, as they are sometimes modeled in the interest-group literature. As a result, most lobbying consists of working with allied government officials rather than only trying to convince them to support some policy option. Virtually all of the applications of the other sorts of resources are made in an effort to increase an organization's supply of these allies.[5]

Interest groups often work in such close collaboration with friendly government officials that the most accurate depiction of their relationship is that of members of a team. The advocacy organizations and the officials work together rather than in opposition. The links that bind the team members may be geographical (as in the stereotypical case of legislators who represent, say, corn-growing areas, who would naturally work to protect the interests of their constituents, often in concert with the relevant agricultural interest groups), professional (when a legislator's previous profession gives her a particular expertise in the issues relating to that profession), or ideological or partisan, crossing professional and geographic lines. We can get some sense of the importance of close working relations between outside advocates and sympathetic members of Congress from our interviews. The following passages stem from the same case; one from an outside organization and the next from staff members in Congress. The links here are ideological rather than geographical or professional, and the teamlike structure of the process is clear; each member of the team has specific roles based on what they can do better than others. This particular example involves an organization with exceptional access (including to the White House), but the strategy of enlisting congressional supporters and legislative leaders (referred to as "whips") is clear. We have deleted specific names and references to the particular issue:

> We always begin [a legislative effort] by breaking members of Congress down in terms of their support for [our policy]. Prior to the effort to get [our policy], we had 223 solidly anti, 131 solid pro, and 81 mixed in the House. . . . We give this information to the whips, because they need counts. We also want the vote count because the White House will want it. They want to know how much or how little support they can expect on the Hill. If the president is going to veto something, they'll want to know if there are enough votes to sustain the veto. Then we contact the solidly pro, undecideds, and lean-tos to see where people are. Then we re-sort and then there are member-to-member conversations [getting key supporters and the whips to contact others in the House]. There's lots of feedback about who needs what to be supportive. Then there is communication to members of Congress from our boss. We also have conversations not with staff but with members—sometimes staff don't know where their member is on our issues. We talk to the members to say, "What we want from you is x."

Now, most interest groups certainly cannot walk into the office of a member of Congress and say, "What we want from you is x" (or if they do they may not get the response they hope). But this group is obviously working closely with allies, and if they share the same goal and the group is asking the member to assist the larger coalition by targeting three specific colleagues and finding out what it might take to move their vote, then the reception might be quite different. A lobbyist on another high-profile issue described his group's close relations with his legislative allies this way: "Each member has a different take on the issue, and we always tried to tailor our arguments. This is the type of information where [the member's] whipping operation was so important: We traded information every day about who was leaning, which arguments to use with them, and the like." Coalitions thus sometimes involve very close working relations among groups inside and outside of Congress, each playing a different role, making the best use of their staff, resources, and contacts.

Here is how the same process looks from inside the Congress, according to the lead staff person of one of the whips from the quote above: "[My boss] was a natural to take the lead; it's right within her value system, and she takes the lead on most" issues in this area. A staff member from another legislative whip on the same issue said, "A lot of people consider him *the* Republican in the House [on this issue]. He takes a lot of stands on issues related to [this topic], . . . so he was viewed by a lot of outside groups as the person to go to on this." The legislators here are clearly ideologically committed to the issue—it corresponds to their idea of good public policy. When there is the opportunity for a major legislative push, with substantial outside support, they are more than happy to play a leading role inside Congress.

The staff member continued on concerning the tactics and close working relationships his office had with the outside organization. The outside group provided target lists, and the member of Congress and his staff did much of the direct lobbying: "We worked with [the outside group] to develop a list of members that [my boss] met with and talked to, and I specifically met with the staff and said, 'Your boss [supports this issue] and this would be a good issue for you.'"

Another staff member, this one in the House Democratic leadership, described the whipping operation relating to another issue, permanent normal trade relations with China, a case we have also discussed in previous chapters. The members-only whip meetings might start with a presentation from an outside expert who would focus on one aspect of the issue:

So we'd have the presentation, we'd hand out assignments for members to talk to some of their colleagues, and so they'd go out and talk to five or six of their colleagues and find out how they were going to vote on this or what issues mattered to them so we could tailor strategy to a particular member. Say there was a member from New Jersey who was undecided who had a pretty big labor presence in their district but also had a tech presence as well and was really split on what to do, but you kind of talk to them—"What kind of information do you need, what would be helpful to you?" "Well, the thing that would be helpful for me would be to talk to people from China about this." And so, knowing that, we tried to get Wei Jing Sheng in to see that member and give them help that way.

Lobbying sounds quite different from the popular conception when the target is a congressional staffer, the "lobbyist" is a staff member from a congressman of the same party, and the message is "Here is an issue that will make your boss look good." Groups with the resources, connections, and allies to work so closely with congressional leadership may well see different outcomes than groups without these connections. Coordinating with high-level allies inside government, especially a House or Senate party whipping organization, certainly helps. Is internal member-to-member lobbying really lobbying? Whether it is or not, it certainly is advocacy, and in the advocacy process outsiders and insiders often work together.

These quotes give a sense of how close working relations between interest group advocates and congressional offices can be in certain issues (especially high-profile ones, as these were). They also suggest the possibility of countermobilization, a point to which we will return later. If working with allies within government is an important determinant of what happens in Washington (and we believe that it often is), then one important question is who can get high-level government allies. Perhaps large corporations can do this but citizen groups cannot. We will look at all these questions in the next sections, as we attempt to map out as completely as possible who controls what resources and how this affects a group's ability to gain the policy outcomes that it seeks.

Examining Group Resources

As we analyze these resources, we compare efforts by organized interests and government officials not only as individual actors, but also as part of the group of organized interests who are on their "side" of the issue. After all, groups rarely lobby alone; they have friends to help them both inside and outside of government. Incorporating the collective nature of lobbying as we do allows us to evaluate whether certain types of groups are more able to take advantage of access to powerful government allies, for example. Looking at who is on a given side of an issue, rather than only looking at groups individually, also allows us to incorporate the actions of rivals. Strangely, this is relatively unusual in studies of lobbying. But lobbyists are certainly aware that they often face opposition, so it makes sense to include the competitive nature of lobbying in our analysis. We can ask: Which side wins? Was it the side with greater resources? Greater access to government allies? Larger memberships? More Fortune 500 corporations? In sum, we can lay out the distribution of material resources across each of our issues and then evaluate whether the individual organizations and the sides controlling more resources of various types are more successful in getting what they want.

Our measures of resources come from numerous sources and include information on the following indicators: lobbying expenditures, number of former government officials employed by the organization as lobbyists, campaign contributions, government allies, membership size, and overall financial resources (two indices, one for organizations and one for business corporations). Finally, we use two measures of outcomes, one assessing whether the group achieved what it wanted with respect to changing or maintaining the status quo and the other reflecting a broader range of goals that the group may have had.[6]

The Distribution and Effects of Resources

When we compare the level of resources that different types of organizations enjoy, we confirm the results of virtually every previous survey of U.S. interest groups by noting that occupational interests, especially businesses and trade associations, are the wealthiest in terms of material resources and lobbying staff. Table 10.1 compares citizen groups, unions, trade associations, professional associations, and businesses to assess how commonly, on average, they register to lobby or hire a lobbyist, how many of them have a lobbyist who was recently a decision-making government official, and how much they spend on lobbying and campaign contributions.

Under the Lobbying Disclosure Act of 1995, organizations that spend at least $20,000 on lobbying during any six-month period must register with the House and Senate as a lobbying organization.[7] In this biannual lobbying report, organizations must disclose the amount they spent on lobbying (including salaries paid to employees who regularly contacted government officials), the issue areas in which they lobbied, and the specific bills and regulations on which they lobbied. Grassroots lobbying—the mobilizing of citizens to contact their members of Congress—is not included

TABLE 10.1 **Average Resources by Group Type**

Group type	Percentage registered to lobby	Percentage with hired lobbyist	Average number of covered officials	Average spending on lobbying	Average PAC spending	N
Business corporations	70	79	.91	$1,051,985	$965,132	181
Trade associations	73	69	.56	$1,274,502	$439,204	275
Professional associations	67	44	.18	$973,333	$884,844	141
Unions	87	45	.14	$475,559	$4,265,099	77
Citizen groups	61	25	.24	$177,814	$187,354	329
All others	20	28	.07	$34,485	$55.168	241
All groups	59	47	.36	$628,632	$662,042	1,244

Note: Entries provide percentages or mean resource levels for the interest group participants identified as having played a major role in one of our 98 issues.

under the definition of lobbying, nor is testifying at public hearings or providing information under formal procedures such as filing a comment with an agency during a notice-and-comment period. Table 10.1 shows that unions were most likely to have filed a lobbying report; 87 percent of them did so, compared to only 61 percent of citizen groups. (Note that our list of groups is limited to those identified by other policy actors as having played a major role in one of our ninety-eight issues, so there is reason to expect these numbers to be uniformly close to 100 percent. However, clearly some groups, especially citizen groups, either avoid engaging in what the Lobby Disclosure Act defines as lobbying or spend little money as they do so.)

The Lobbying Disclosure Act also requires each organization to list the names of all of the employees who acted as lobbyists on behalf of the organization and to indicate whether any of these lobbyists previously had jobs as members of Congress, congressional staff members, or high-level agency officials during the past two years. These so-called covered officials are people who themselves likely were lobbied just a short time ago. We created a count of these covered officials to track the effects of the revolving door that often connects government jobs to lobbying jobs. These revolving door relationships are another resource in which businesses are especially well endowed. Table 10.1 shows that the average business in our sample has about one recent former covered official working on its behalf. This former official may be on staff in the corporation's Washington office, but more likely he or she has been hired by one of Washington's many lobbying firms, and that lobbying firm in turn has been employed by the corporation. The frequency with which corporations employ outside lobbying firms also leads to an increased frequency for those corporations to have friends in high places. Unions are the least likely to have such hired friends. Businesses, on average, employ six times more covered officials than labor unions do and more than three times as many as citizen groups.

The general imbalance in resources in favor of business is clear when we look at lobbying expenditures. Corporations, trade associations, and professional associations all average about $1 million in lobbying expenditures, whereas labor unions report about half that amount and citizen groups less than one-fifth the amount.

To examine the role of campaign contributions, we take the mean of all of the campaign contributions and all of the soft-money contributions to parties that each type of organization gave during two successive two-year election cycles just before and during our study. In the electoral arena, unions far outspend all other types of actors, but there are many fewer unions active in Washington than there are businesses. While unions on

TABLE 10.2 **Average Number of Governmental Allies by Group Type**

Group type	Number of government allies:			
	Low-level	Midlevel	High-level	N
Business corporations	2.38	2.72	0.74	181
Trade and business associations	2.25	2.81	0.52	275
Professional associations	3.09	3.71	0.55	141
Unions	3.14	2.25	0.45	77
Citizen groups	3.20	2.30	0.33	329
All others	2.82	2.68	0.37	241
All groups	2.78	2.70	0.47	1,244

Note: Cell entries reflect the mean number of governmental allies who shared a side with an organization. Low-level allies are rank-and-file members of Congress or agency officials. Midlevel allies include committee and subcommittee leaders (chairs and ranking minority members and their staffs) and department-level political appointees and cabinet officials. High-level allies include congressional party leadership and the White House.

average have donation totals that are quite large, the sum of all of those totals does not approach the sum totals of all of the business PACs, because there are so many more businesses. While there were 77 unions named as important actors in our issues, there were 181 businesses and 275 trade associations (which represent groups of businesses). Citizen groups donate much less than the occupationally based groups. One reason for this—beyond a simple lack of resources—is that many of the citizen groups have 501(c)(3) tax status. This tax status allows gifts to the organization to be deducted by the donor as a charitable donation, but such tax status also prohibits an organization from making PAC donations, becoming directly involved in elections, or promoting a specific candidate for office. Many nonprofit groups shy away from politics altogether for fear of running afoul of the IRS.[8]

In all, we can see that groups of different types show distinctly different patterns of control over the most important material resources. Taken as a group, corporations, trade associations, and professional associations are well endowed compared to others. Labor unions have substantial resources of certain kinds, and they play a major role in electoral politics, as reflected in their large average campaign contributions. Citizen groups are active on a great many issues (see table 1.3) but support this work with fewer resources overall.

We have seen so far that groups of different types control substantially different levels of material resources. How does this affect their ability to get what they want? We begin looking at this question in table 10.2, which looks at the ability of groups of each type to work with government allies.

The table shows that, while citizen groups on average have higher levels of low-level allies (rank-and-file members of Congress and bureau-level agency officials), the opposite is true when it comes to high-level allies (including party leadership and White House officials).[9] Businesses are more likely to have a friend in a high place than are other types of groups. The table makes clear that unions and citizen groups are quite successful in working with the rank and file but rarely get to take advantage of the highest level of government support. Businesses enjoy much greater access and cooperation at this level, more than twice the level of the citizen groups.

Resources and policy success

The tendency of resources to be concentrated in the hands of occupational and business groups is potentially troubling in terms of representation, but less so if those resources do not increase those groups' chances of political success. With this in mind, we first look to see whether groups with more resources are more likely to win their policy disputes. To measure success in these policy debates, we rely on two different measures of success and consider them at two different points in time. The first measure assesses whether the policy actor in question got all of what it wanted, part of what it wanted, or none of what it wanted, because this relates to changing the status quo policy. An organization that was trying to prevent any changes to existing law would be coded as getting all of what it wanted if there were no changes in the law. This variable is coded both for the end of the initial Congress in which we conducted our interviews and then again after the next two-year Congress immediately following our interviews.[10] The second measure asks essentially the same question—Did the actor in question get all, some, or none of what it sought?—but weights this consideration in terms of how extensive a change was sought. The measure is an additive index of a series of questions about possible changes to (1) the federal budget, (2) state and local budgets, (3) costs assessed to private actors, (4) existing law or policies, (5) the creation of new law or policies, or (6) the scope of government authority.[11] The more of these types of goals an actor sought and managed to achieve, the greater the actor's score on this index of policy success. This measure also is assessed at the end of the Congress in which we conducted our interviews and then again after the following Congress, two years later. Table 10.3 shows the correlation between these different outcome measures and the level of resources an interest group enjoys.

TABLE 10.3 **Money and Power: The Correlation between Advocate Resources and Outcomes**

Outcome	PAC spending	Lobby spending	Covered officials	Association assets	Members	Business assets
Initial win	−.01	−.01	.04	−.02	−.04	.06**
Initial outcomes index win	−.03	−.02	.06**	−.01	−.01	.05
Win in subsequent Congress	.01	.01	.06**	−.03	−.04**	.05**
Outcomes index win in subsequent Congress	−.02	−.01	.04	−.001	−.02	.08**

Note: $N = 1,242$. Cells entries are Spearman's rho or Pearson's r coefficients. (Spearman's rho correlation coefficients are used with the ordinal measures of whether a side won; Pearson's r correlation coefficients are used with the outcomes indices.)
**Correlation between resources and outcomes is statistically significant at $p < .05$.

The table shows the simple bivariate correlation between the various resources listed in the column headings with the four different measures of policy success.[12] In the first row, we look at whether the group achieved what it wanted with respect to changing the status quo, and we look only at the period of the initial Congress when our interviews were conducted. At the end of that period, the status quo was either changed or not, so each group can be scored for whether it was pleased or displeased with this outcome. The correlations with various resource measures range from −.04 to +.06. None is far from zero, and only the coefficient for business assets is statistically significant. The other rows present the results for a broader range of outcomes in that initial congressional session, as well as results for the subsequent congressional session (both the simple outcome and the index of outcome measures).

For the most part, resources have no significant correlation with a positive policy outcome. The exceptions to the general pattern are the cases of business assets and the number of former covered officials working for an advocate. In the case of business assets, the results are statistically significant for three of the four measures of outcomes. Businesses with high levels of resources are slightly more likely to achieve their preferred policy position. Of course, there are only 185 businesses in the sample. Thus, the finding that business assets matter might be simply a reflection of a preferred position of business in the policy-making process. Indeed, if we look simply at whether an advocate was a business or not a business (that is, no matter what level of assets), we find correlations that are roughly the same in magnitude as those that reflect the assets controlled by the business.

This implies that businesses as a group gain in the process, not only the wealthiest corporations. Likewise, for two of our outcome measures, organizations with more covered officials working with them are statistically significantly more likely to get their preferred policy outcomes. It is important to note, however, that these correlation coefficients, for both business assets and for covered officials, are quite low. The advantage they indicate may be statistically significant, but substantively their impact is small.

While business status and covered officials seem to lead to a slight increase in gaining one's preferred outcomes, we find a slight *negative* relationship between membership size and outcomes.[13] This implies that organizations with larger memberships were actually slightly *less* likely to get what they wanted in the issues we studied. But again, even in the one case where the correlations we observe are statistically significant, they are substantively so small that it is best to think of table 10.3 as a wash. In all, this review of the bivariate relations between financial assets and lobbying success suggests that the relationships are systematically close to zero, almost across the board. No matter which measure of resources we use and across four different measures of policy success, we find very weak correlations. Some of these reach levels of statistical significance, but none reaches even the level of 0.10 correlation. We find virtually no linkage between resources and outcomes.

Strange bedfellows and issue advocacy

Considering the characteristics and resources of individual advocates and their correlations with outcomes is a first step, but advocates do not work alone in policy debates. The resources of an individual organization are much less important than the aggregated resources on their side of the issue; after all, all advocates on a given side will get the same outcome, by definition, and few groups work alone in Washington. In fact, we find that the advocates sharing the same side of any one of our ninety-eight issues were often quite diverse. Large corporations sometimes worked with representatives of ethnic minorities. Huge pharmaceutical companies sought out patients' rights groups or others who have a more favorable public image. Citizen groups often were part of coalitions with wealthier organizations of different types.

It has often been noted that politics makes strange bedfellows. The financial arrangements of such partnerships and the implications for studies of who wins in Washington are less often discussed. Interest groups that would not normally be allies may come together because each holds a resource that the other lacks. As mentioned above, constructing a successful team implies recruiting players who have complementary, not duplicative, skills. The monetary and staff resources of large corporations paired with the membership and representational legitimacy of citizen groups and charities can be a powerful combination. In the case of the 3 percent excise tax, dozens of citizen groups were recruited to join the coalition formed by the telecommunication companies and trade associations: "It was a very important decision at the beginning of this whole process, that for it to be successful you have to put a human face on this," a member of the excise tax coalition told us. "And it can't be transparently thin that this is just for your own self-interest. This is for consumers." That is, according to this advocate, the creation of a broad and diverse coalition cannot be simple window-dressing with a few "consumer" groups bought and paid for by powerful industrial lobbyists. Reputable consumer groups would not lend their names to such efforts, and policy makers would see through it. Many of the issues that we studied really did mobilize diverse and sometimes surprising mixtures of consumer, business, and professional groups on various sides of the issue. Government officials were also involved in different elements of the same debates.

To continue with the excise tax example, the telecommunication companies that spearheaded the push to abolish the tax (and paid for it in its entirety) asked a series of citizen and consumer organizations to sign on with their coalition, add their names to the letters being sent to members of Congress, and show up at the press conferences. The organizations included consumer groups and several representing Mexican-Americans— because Mexican-Americans say they have among the highest long-distance bills of any demographic and are disproportionately affected by the tax. Those organizations that were recruited and agreed to participate were not simply dupes; they also agreed that it was a good idea to eliminate the tax and that doing so would help their constituents. The citizen groups brought a public face to the issue that the phone companies could never rival. On the other hand, the phone companies had the money. It was a good combination, a strong team.

Even groups that often find themselves on opposite sides of the debate in their area can sometimes find common ground on particular issues. When this happens, members of Congress often take note. In the annual allocation for the AIDS Drug Assistance Program (ADAP), pharmaceutical companies and AIDS activist organizations joined forces to convince

Congress to provide funds for drugs for those who don't have adequate insurance (or any insurance at all). In terms of public policy, the AIDS groups and the pharmaceutical companies are usually on opposite sides of the fence, with the activists campaigning for lower drug prices and the pharmaceutical companies hoping for longer patents and limited government regulation. Here, however, there was a shared goal. The pharmaceutical companies each contributed $5,000 and the activist groups each contributed $500 toward coalition lobbying expenses, and the case was made to the appropriations committees. Even the powerful combination of money, members, and a lack of explicit opposition does not automatically equal success, however. In the case of the AIDS funding, the efforts to gain additional funding were ultimately successful, while the efforts to end the excise tax were not.

Does the side that puts together the greatest *combined* resources achieve its policy goals? We've already seen that with the exception of business resources, bivariate correlations show only the slightest linkage between an individual organization's resource levels and whether that organization will be successful. Table 10.4 shows the correlation between a side's combined resources and getting one's preferred outcome.

As in table 10.3, the numbers in table 10.4 represent the correlation between the resource listed in the column heading with the measure of policy success listed in the row. None of the measures of financial resources or membership is statistically significant. When we look at outcomes based on sides of the issue, only one type of resource has a statistically significant relationship: the number of governmental allies on that side. In the initial Congress in which the issue is introduced, the presence of low-level governmental allies seems to help a side get what it wants, and having midlevel governmental allies (subcommittee and committee chairmen in Congress, or department-level officials in an agency) helped a side get the policy outcome it sought in three of the four types of outcome measures. These allies seem to matter, but levels of all other types of resources tend to cancel each other out. The ability to recruit or work together with government allies at the highest levels of the political system shows no systematic correlation with policy success. Although sometimes such high-level allies can be the deciding factor in a policy debate—as the support of the National Credit Union Administration was in the credit union debate—often both sides of an issue have allies in high places. The most fundamental result of our initial review of the linkages between money and power is that there is not much to talk about. The links, to the extent we see any in this bivariate analysis, are extremely weak.

TABLE 10.4 **Money and Power 2: The Correlation between a Side's Total Resources and Outcomes**

Outcome	PAC spending	Lobby spending	Covered officials	Members	Association assets	Business assets	Low-level allies	Midlevel allies	High-level allies
Initial status quo win	−.04	.05	.09	.06	.10	.06	−.14**	.15**	.09
Initial outcomes index win	−.001	.03	.08	.01	.05	.10	−.07	.10	.03
Status quo win in subsequent Congress	.09	.07	.10	.01	.11	.10	−.06	.17**	.13
Outcomes index win in subsequent Congress	.001	.10	.09	.05	.05	.13	−.01	.18**	.02

Note: $N = 191$. Cells reflect Spearman's rho or Pearson's r coefficients. (Spearman's rho correlation coefficients are used with the ordinal measures of whether a side won; Pearson's r correlation coefficients are used with the outcomes indices.)

**Correlation between a side's resources and outcomes is statistically significant at $p < .05$.

TABLE 10.5 **Issue Outcomes: The Richer Do Not Always Prevail**

Type of Resource	Percentage of issues where the side with greater control of this resource gained its preferred outcome	Number of issues
High-level government allies	78***	23
Covered officials lobbying	63***	35
Midlevel government allies	60***	48
Business financial resources	53	34
Lobbying expenditures	52	58
Association financial resources	50	58
Membership	50	58
Campaign contributions	50	58

Note: Cell entries are the percentage of issues in which the side with the greatest amount of that type of resource achieved its policy goals. *N* varies because not every issue had multiple sides and in some issues, none of the sides used that type of resource. Cases are included in the table if at least one side containing organized interests controlled the resource and if the outcome favored one of the groups over the others (that is, the outcome was not a tie). For example, there were 23 issues in which at least one of the sides had high-level government allies, and the side that had more of them got the outcome it wanted 78 percent of the time. Issues where no side had any high-level government allies or issues with no opposing interest groups are excluded from that calculation.
***Difference is statistically significant at $p < .01$.

Those simple correlational analyses are interesting in part because they demonstrate what political scientists and Washington insiders know but the stories of scandal sometimes make us forget: the relationship between money and power is not simple, and the richest side does not always win. We need to delve deeper, however, to answer our broader question about money and political outcomes, in part because the structure of policy conflict is so complex. For one thing, on some types of issues—health care, for example—there typically are multiple sides that all enjoy fairly high levels of resources. Other issues, such as questions of social justice, might have fewer sides, all of which have limited funds. The proper method of analysis, therefore, is to compare the sides within each issue, to see whether sides with more resources were more likely to succeed with their policy goals compared to sides with fewer *on the same issue*. To do this, we took each side and compared its levels of resources to the other sides on the same issue. Table 10.5 shows the percentage of cases where the side with the greatest amount of resources got what it wanted in terms of changes to the status quo.[14]

Table 10.5 presents the simplest way of thinking about the question of resources and success. Comparing the sets of actors active on the same issue, we simply ask whether the side with the most resources won. The results are striking in that the usual types of resources that are often assumed to "buy" public policy outcomes—PAC donations, lobbying expenditures, membership size, and organizational budgets—have no observable effect on the outcomes. The percentage of times the wealthier side won ranges from 50 to 53, which means that the side with fewer resources won with about the same probability. Thus, at the issue level, there seems to be no relationship between the level of these types of resources that a side controls and whether it obtains its preferred outcomes. The wealthier side sometimes wins and sometimes loses.

There is a kind of resource that does seem to matter: support of an allied government official who is actively involved in the cause. Here we are considering not simply those officials who supported the issue and may have voted in favor of it; rather, these allies are officials who themselves took a leading role in trying to push an issue onto the agenda and to get results. High-level government officials, defined here as officials at the level of congressional leadership and the president, are not active advocates on every issue, but when they do become involved in pushing an issue forward, they are likely to win. Twenty-three of our issues involved high-level governmental allies, and in nearly three-quarters of those issues, the side with more high-level allies won. A similar advantage is evident for those sides that had a midlevel government ally (committee leaders and agency and department officials) also fighting for their cause. Those with more of that resource won 60 percent of the time. The influence of government officials does not end when they leave office, however. Our results show that sides that had more former government officials lobbying on their behalf won 63 percent of the time. There were only thirty-five such issues in our sample, but the pattern is troubling, because the services of these former covered officials is indeed a resource that money can buy.

One reason why most monetary resources may not translate directly into outcomes is that lobbying is so competitive. For example, earlier in the chapter we quoted from our interviews in two high-profile cases where outside lobbyists worked closely with members of Congress, including in one case where the entire Democratic House whipping organization was fully engaged in the issue of preventing China from receiving permanent status as a most-favored trading partner. Surely, one might think, with these kinds of high-level allies, lobbyists could get what they want. But in fact they did not in that case. The reason? The other side had the White House, three former presidents, large numbers of business interests, and the Republican Party caucus in both the House and the Senate. Trade with China was engaged as a major national debate, and *both sides* benefited from high-level allies, close connections with important government officials who shared their views. If the issue had not gained so much high-level attention, then *neither side* may have been able to get so much time on the calendar of such high-level government officials. But once the issue engaged, and it was clear that there would be a major fight, each side mobilized their natural allies within and outside of government. The competitive nature of lobbying, and the ability of groups to expand the conflict when they see that their rivals are successfully mobilizing, may be one of the most important sources of structure in the process. It provides one of the best explanations of the power of the status quo (since people may mobilize to defend it only in those cases where challenges to it pass some threshold of likely success) and of the lack of clear relations between material resources and policy success. The number of resources devoted to a battle depends on the battle: Is there a chance of success? Is the other side broadly mobilized? Answers to these two questions help explain the mobilization of resources in Washington. Resources are, therefore, endogenous to the policy dispute; that is, the decision to devote resources to an issue, or to get involved in it in the first place, to make it a priority, depends on the likelihood of success and the actions of rivals.

A second reason for the surprisingly low correlations between monetary resources and outcomes is the heterogeneity of the sides active on our sample of issues. As we mentioned above, if the wealthy allied only with the wealthy, it might be statistically possible to observe a correlation between wealth and policy success. (Whether the wealthy-only coalition would win or whether it might generate a countermobilization from other actors is a different question.) Where the wealthy often ally with the poor, however, and where all the members of a given side achieve the same outcome, then it is logically impossible to observe a strong correlation between wealth and success. So a key question, and a key missing link in previous studies of lobbying success, is the relative homo- versus heterogeneity of lobbying sides. A simple way to look at this is to compare the resources of each interest group in our study with the aggregated resources of all of their allies. That is, if a group is a member of a side with twenty members, we can correlate the control of material resources for each individual member with those of the nineteen others. If the wealthy allied with the wealthy and the poor with the poor, we would find high correlations in this way.

We have identified thirteen distinct measures of material resources that an organization or a corporation might control. For corporations we know their total annual sales, annual income, and number of employees; for organizations, their membership size, annual budget, number of staff, total

TABLE 10.6 **Correlations among Individual Resources and Those of Allies**

Type of resource	Correlation between individual and allied resources[a]
Annual sales[b]	.26***
Annual income[b]	.24***
Number of employees[b]	.23***
Lobbying expenditures[b,c]	.17***
Number of former officials lobbying[b,c]	.13***
PAC contributions[b,c]	.22***
Membership size[c]	.05
Organizational assets[c]	.11***
Organizational income[c]	.13***
Annual budget[c]	.22***
Total staff size[c]	.22***
Index of organizational resources[c]	.15***
Index of business resources[b]	.31***

Note: The table shows the correlation among each of 13 separate indicators of material resources controlled by each individual organization or corporation with the aggregated resources of the same type controlled by all other organizations on the same side of the issue.
[a]$N = 1,244$ for all Pearson's r correlations.
[b]Measure available for corporations.
[c]Measure available for organizations.
*** $p < .01$

organizational assets, and total annual income; for both organizations and corporations we also know the size of their PAC contributions, the total amount spent on lobbying, and the number of recent former government officials lobbying on their behalf. As described above, we also calculate an overall index of material resources, separately for corporations and for organizations. (More detail on all these measures is available in our appendix.) In sum, we have identified thirteen different measures of material resources, so this allows us to compare each group's control of these resources with their allies' control of that same type of resource. If the rich lobby in concert with the rich, then these correlations should all be quite high. Table 10.6 shows the results.

Correlations range from .05 to .31. Most of the correlations are statistically significant, and all are positive. So there is some tendency for the wealthy to work with the wealthy and the poor with the poor. However, as statistical correlations go, these numbers indicate that there is great heterogeneity in the lobbying coalitions we have identified. A correlation on the order of .2 implies that about 96 percent of the variability in lobbying resources controlled by allies is *unaccounted for* by the resources controlled by an individual group. Even our highest correlations, those associated with our index of business resources, is only .31. Given the low correlations among the resources controlled by the lobbyists who work together, and given the fact that all of them will achieve the same level of success in gaining what they want out of the policy process (since they are part of the same lobbying side), it is logically and statistically impossible to observe a high relation between resources and outcomes.

The results shown in this chapter lead to some surprising conclusions. While our analyses do not suggest that money is unimportant, they do show that money alone does not buy policy outcomes. The reasons for this are complex, but we believe they fundamentally have to do with the structure of political conflict. The construction of lobbying sides does not bring together only similar organizations; groups work with a diverse collection of allies. Similarly, as lobbying is a competitive process, the mobilization of one side can lead to the countermobilization of rivals. It remains to be seen whether the tendencies we see here will hold true as we add political factors into the mix: Was the side arguing to change something, or to keep the status quo? Changing something is always more difficult than working to prevent change. Also, how did partisanship factor in? Our study provides a chance to observe how policies can change as administrations shift from Democrats to Republicans. As these contextual variables are added into consideration, they may serve to intensify the effects of resources on outcomes or to erase them entirely. We describe this more complete model in a later chapter.

Why Resources Matter but Appear Not To

We have shown in this chapter some surprisingly low correlations between monetary resources and policy outcomes. In fact, across a range of issues, we are hard pressed to find much of a relationship between wealth and outcomes. These findings do not suggest that it is better in politics to be poor than rich; a large membership, an ample staff, sufficient budget to organize large events, and established linkages with policy makers that come from multiple contacts are the fundamentals of effective lobbying day-in and day-out. Rather, the findings in this chapter may suggest that the impact of resources alone is limited; one needs also to consider the issues on which groups are working, who else is active on those issues, and the construction of like-minded coalitions on the issue. This is not because resources are unimportant in politics, but rather because these other factors are so fundamental to the very structure and organization of politics. Of all the findings here, it is perhaps the heterogeneity of sides that is the most striking. If the well endowed worked only with similar groups, they might win. But if a side were to consist only of such organizations, it might well raise the eyebrows of others monitoring politics or the concerns of equally wealthy groups from a rival industry, so it is not certain even when the wealthy get together that they would prevail. But in fact, our analysis of the composition of over two hundred sides across all ninety-eight issues suggests that these tend to have substantial diversity of membership. This political imperative must inevitably dilute any impact of resources on outcomes, since all the members of a given side benefit or suffer from the identical outcome at the end of the day.

Mark Smith's study of the policy impact of the U.S. Chamber of Commerce, one of the most powerful business organizations in American politics, came to the surprising conclusion that the Chamber was largely unable to get what it wanted.[15] With its diverse membership, covering many industries and both large and small business, the issues on which the Chamber could take a strong position without alienating a large percentage of its own members were "business-wide" questions related to such topics as health care costs, labor issues, and workplace safety. But any issue that unites and allows the mobilization of the entire U.S. business community likely also unites and mobilizes rival groups, such as consumers, environmentalists, and labor officials, and it probably also has high ideological and partisan overtones. When political disputes erupt on such broadly mobilizing issues, of course, having more resources is better than having fewer. But even the substantial lobbying resources of a group like the U.S. Chamber of Commerce (which spent $31 million on lobbying in 2006) cannot guarantee results if the issue mobilizes dozens or hundreds of other equally well-endowed organizations, each with their own powerful political backers. So the links between money and power depend strongly on the nature of the issue and the competitive nature of the lobbying process.

Another reason for the apparent lack of impact of resources is that policy disputes almost always revolve around what we call a "continuing issue"—that is, issues are not created out of whole cloth, with no history. Rather, there is a long history and usually an established federal program which itself reflects the results of lobbying in previous years and decades. Changing policy from the status quo involves justifying a *shift* in the allocation of resources, moving it from a status quo position to a new position. But the status quo position was already the object of the mobilization of interest groups, members of the public, and political leaders in previous years. So to see that money cannot automatically purchase shifts in the status quo does not mean that the status quo might not already reflect important biases in politics.

Finally, it is important to note that many issues never get raised in the first place. Or, similarly, one of the most important questions for a lobbyist is whether they can count on their allies in government to make "their" issue the number-one priority, really to push it. Of course, the prioritization of issues and the allocation of time and attention across all the issues that could potentially merit attention is a difficult problem. Government leaders and interest groups have to allocate their attention partly based on their own preferences, but partly based on what others are doing around them. Still, let us close with a quote from one of our interviews, in which the interest group official we interviewed was essentially complaining about the lack of commitment from one of his own closest allies, and the lobbyist attributed this set of misplaced priorities to fund-raising concerns: "In the end he did vote against the bill [that is, in accord with the lobbyist's wishes], but he did not twist arms. Why not? I can't say exactly, but let me say that he is just so focused on [national electoral concerns] that he wants some business support, especially in the high-tech industries. So this was sacrificed for his bigger agenda. And if you think money doesn't matter in politics and lobbying, here is an example where it does. His desire to raise lots of money from the business [community], and the high-tech community in particular, made him unwilling to lead this fight." Money matters in politics, there is no question. But other things matter as well, and the direct correlation between money and outcomes that so many political scientists have sought simply is not there.

CHAPTER ELEVEN

Policy Outcomes

Since the early days of the Fidel Castro regime in Cuba, the United States has enforced an economic embargo and diplomatic freeze toward the former client state of the Soviet Union. For decades, American agricultural interests have pushed for liberalized economic relations with Cuba, which relies heavily on food imports. Despite the hostility of the U.S. government toward Cuba, American farmers would be delighted to sell their products in Cuba. The short distance between the United States and Cuba gives American exporters a competitive advantage over producers in the European Union and many other parts of the world.

Efforts to open up agricultural and other avenues of trade with Cuba have been promoted with greater vigor since the early 1990s, when the collapse of the Soviet Union ended the Cold War and forced Cuba to reform its socialist economy. For years, a coalition of farm interests, including producers of the most bountiful commodities grown in the United States, has pushed for a new trade policy with Cuba. Coalition members regularly testify before congressional committees and meet with legislators to make their case.

However, their efforts have been stymied by many Cuban-Americans who vigorously oppose any assistance to the Castro regime. Many thousands of Cubans fled the island after the revolution and settled in South Florida, eventually becoming a force in Florida politics. Vote-rich Florida, is, in turn, a key battleground in presidential politics. Neither Democratic nor Republican presidents have challenged the prevailing orthodoxy regarding Cuban-American relations. A Cuban-American lobbyist in Washington argued in 2001 that sanctions "are the best way we have to pressure [the Castro regime]." He added, "Castro is on his last legs. Succession is imminent. I expect the political situation to change dramatically in six months to a year. If we keep on being patient, then the regime may collapse on its own."

Over the years, there have been small changes to relax some pharmaceutical and agricultural sales to Cuba. However, continuing restrictions on financing keep trade with Cuba limited. When we began following this issue in 2001, agricultural interests and farm-state legislators proposed legislation to open up the Cuban market to American exports. But with Florida continuing to play a decisive role in presidential elections (especially in 2000), the legislation went nowhere. Agricultural interests remain undeterred. They have reintroduced the legislation to open trade with Cuba in each Congress since 2001, even though they have not come close to passing it. As of late 2008, Fidel Castro is ill but still alive and has transferred ruling authority to his brother, Raul.

In many important ways, the case of trade sanctions with Cuba is typical of the issues in our study and of the policy process more generally. It has been the focus of lobbying activity for many years, and lobbying on the issue will likely continue for many years. And yet the status quo continues to prevail. The policy-making process rarely produces quick resolutions, and advocates often toil for many years in search of the opportunity to achieve significant policy change. Policy advocacy is usually a long-term gig.

Incremental versus Dramatic Change

In previous chapters we have pointed to a number of important elements of the policy process that may contribute to the likelihood of policy success. Here we weave together these partial explanations into an overall model of what causes policy change. Starting first with a systematic discussion of how we measured policy change, we then develop a model to explain the presence or absence of policy change in our ninety-eight cases. What predicts the outcomes we observe? We saw in chapter 9, for example, that overarching changes in the frames associated with our cases are rare; the stickiness of established policy frames is an important source of the power of the status quo. On the other hand, the status quo did change in almost 40 percent of our cases, and when it did change, the change tended to be substantial, not just marginal. In addition, we show that in many cases, but certainly not all, interest-group resources tend to cancel each other out, often producing policy stalemate. By comparison, government officials, and especially the president, are important sources of policy change. The first step, of course, is to determine exactly what we mean by policy change.

We followed each issue in our study for four years and noted the policy outcome in each case. We divided our study into two-year increments coinciding with electoral and legislative cycles in Congress. Thus, we coded the policy outcome for each issue during the initial Congress in which we identified the issue and then during the subsequent Congress as well. We delegate the outcome of each issue into one of three categories: significant, modest, or no change. Issues marked as having "significant" policy change include cases where the policy change is likely to have a large impact on the targeted population. In addition, in cases of "significant" change, advocates for policy change tend to get most or all of what they wanted. For example, repeal of the estate tax, the adoption of normalized trade relations with China, the new prescription drug benefit for Medicare patients, and federal funding for the Yucca Mountain nuclear repository are examples of issues in our study with "significant" policy change. These are cases where a dramatic break from the status quo was achieved.

We categorized other issues as having "modest" policy change. In these cases, the policy change that occurred was relatively small and usually represented only a portion of what the advocates for change wanted. For example, one of the issues in our study involved an effort by some health professionals to include hearing screenings for infants in standard health insurance coverage. After many years of activity and negotiation on the issue, in 1999 advocates succeeded in getting Congress to appropriate money for 22 grants to states (worth roughly $150,000 per grant) to begin to help cover infant hearing screenings. Advocates saw this as a small initial step toward their broader goal. As one supporter explained, "In round two we hope to get more funding for the states. The federal legislation has really been a catalyst for state action. . . . We need, and hope to get in the next phase of our efforts, major backers in the insurance industry. We'll next be moving on to pursue state legislation." Thus, issues that we code as "modest" change tend to be cases of incremental changes in policy that result from some type of negotiation and compromise.

Finally, issues where no policy change occurred were coded accordingly. The project Web site lists the policy outcome we coded for each issue in the study.

TABLE 11.1 **Summary of Policy Outcomes**

Policy outcome	Initial 2-year period	After 4-year period
No change from status quo	68	58
Modest policy change	13	13
Significant policy change	17	27
Number of issues	98	98

Table 11.1 provides the basic frequencies for each of the three possible outcomes. As the table indicates, the status quo enjoys a decided advantage. No change in policy occurred during the initial period in almost seven out of every ten issues in our sample. When we expand the time horizon, a somewhat weaker status quo advantage still prevails. After four years, no policy change had occurred in six issues out of ten. In previous chapters, we showed that advocates mentioned several serious obstacles to policy change (such as difficulty gaining attention for the issue, concerns about a policy's costs to government and society, and partisan divisions in government). As we show in chapter 3, the sides in our study promoting policy change far outnumber the sides defending the status quo. In addition, chapter 8 (on advocacy tactics) indicates that challengers to the status quo are more likely than status quo defenders to engage in several advocacy measures (such as meeting with a legislator and mobilizing group members). Despite these numerical and advocacy advantages, the forces for policy change tend to fail.

Nevertheless, in cases where policy change occurs, we observe significant change more often than modest change. When the momentum builds to make new public policy, the result tends to be a major revision, not a small tinkering around the edges of the established policy. This is especially evident when we view the issues in our study over the longer four-year time horizon, in which "significant" change occurs on more than twice the number of issues with "modest" change.[1] Thus, table 11.1 appears to be more evidence of "fat tails" in the distribution of policy change, as discussed in chapter 2.

Despite the privileged position of the status quo in the policy-making process, advocates of policy change are not deterred by short-term failure. When scanning all of the issues in our study, we find a clear pattern of prolonged activity on most issues, as table 11.2 shows.

In two out of every three issues in our sample, the advocates we interviewed reported previous advocacy activity, at least as early as the

Congress before we began following the issue. In many cases, previous advocacy stretched back several years. Furthermore, 87 of 98 issues in our study experienced continuing activity after the two-year period when we began following it. This means that advocacy efforts ended during the initial phase of our study for only 11 issues. In sum, 62 issues (a majority of cases in our study) experienced lobbying action for well over four years, just as in the case of the Cuban trade embargo. On these issues, lobbying activity had begun before our study and continued after our four-year field period.

The relatively small number of issues that were not subject to continuous advocacy require some discussion, for these issues tend to share one or two characteristics in common. First, some issues that avoided long-term advocacy campaigns were matters of government reauthorization of legislation (often involving trade) that could not legally be revisited for several years. For example, United States membership in the World Trade Organization was renewed under a provision that allows reconsideration once every five years. Similarly, renewal of the president's fast-track trade authority passed in 2002, not subject to review for several years. Other examples in our study of issues that are revisited in regular intervals and thus not subject to continuous lobbying include passage of a farm bill in 2002 and renewal of the aviation trust fund in 2000.

Second, a few issues generated a high degree of consensus that obviated the need for advocacy in the near future. For example, a law requiring the Occupational Safety and Health Administration (OSHA) to write regulations to reduce needlestick injuries in hospitals passed the House and Senate without a single vote in opposition. No effort has been made to repeal the legislation. As another example, the Environmental Protection Agency issued new regulations to reduce the sulfur content in gasoline after a new report showed that lowering sulfur content in gas would reduce harmful auto emissions significantly more than other potential changes (such as redesigning car engines). The issue united environmentalists and

TABLE 11.2 **The Continuing Nature of Advocacy**

Nature of activity	Number of issues
Activity began and ended in the two-year cycle of our initial interview	6
Activity began before and ended during the two-year cycle	5
Activity began during the two-year cycle and continued beyond	25
Activity began before and continued beyond the two-year cycle	62
Total	98

auto manufacturers, and the scientific consensus behind the report was so strong that opponents of the low-sulfur regulation (primarily oil refineries) had trouble arguing against it. As a result, there was no serious legislative effort to repeal the regulations once they were enacted at the end of the Clinton administration. (The Bush administration later extended the regulations to diesel fuel.) On a small number of similar issues, advocacy efforts basically stopped once government action occurred.

The examples above, however, are exceptions to the pattern of long-term continuous lobbying found in most cases. While scholars such as John Kingdon note that reauthorizations and other nondiscretionary items are a significant part of the legislative agenda, we find that these issues are a relatively small part of the lobbying agenda.[2] Since the status quo tends to prevail in most issues, advocates for policy change have to dig in for the long haul. Even in many cases where major government action was taken, advocacy continued on the issue afterward. For example, after a law was passed in 2003 to phase out the federal estate tax, advocacy has continued by groups who want to revisit the decision and by groups who want the repeal to remain permanent.

What Predicts Policy Change?

Having shown the distribution of policy change, can we predict it? Previous chapters have demonstrated the great diversity in the issues in our sample. Issues vary in terms of salience, the number of competing sides, and levels of partisan conflict. Furthermore, there is variation in the venues of activity, as well as the tactics and arguments used by advocates. As a result, there appear to be many routes to policy change. Put differently, there is no simple predictor of policy change. For example, we saw in chapter 10 that the material resources controlled by the various sides were only weakly associated with policy wins. Similarly, the salience or degree of media and government attention is not strongly associated with policy change.

Table 11.3 shows the degree of policy change after four years across those issues with various levels of salience. For the low, moderate, and high salience categories, the modal outcome is no policy change, the same pattern we observe across all issues in table 11.1. For very salient issues, significant policy change is slightly more frequent than no change, but the number of extremely salient cases is so small that we cannot generalize from those few issues. Furthermore, the correlations between the overall

TABLE 11.3 **Policy Outcomes after Four Years versus Issue Salience**

Policy outcome	Level of salience				Total
	Low	Moderate	High	Very high	
No change from status quo	20	23	12	3	58
Modest policy change	2	6	5	0	13
Significant policy change	7	6	10	4	27
Number of issues	29	35	27	7	98

Note: The relationship between outcomes and salience is not statistically significant ($\chi^2 = 9.4, p = .15$).

salience index and policy change after two years and after four years are weak ($r = .04$ and $r = .11$ respectively) and statistically insignificant. Finally, there is some question about the direction of causation on highly salient issues. It is possible that media and government pay more attention to an issue when policy change is likely. The four highly salient cases with significant policy change were permanent normal trade relations with China, a prescription drug benefit for Medicare recipients, the No Child Left Behind law, and the 2002 farm bill. Three of these four issues were major presidential initiatives, and the president's active role likely attracted more attention to those issues.

In previous chapters, we noted that highly salient issues tend to be the scene of partisan conflict and attract more policy advocates and lobbying resources than less salient issues. While partisanship and intense lobbying activity do not necessarily foreshadow policy gridlock, they do not seem to predict more policy change either. As chapter 5 indicates, policy change is just as likely on partisan issues as nonpartisan issues. Thus, low-salience issues, which are quite common but not often examined by political scientists, generate policy change just about as often as high-salience issues that tend to receive more attention from the press and scholars. In addition, policy change is equally likely regardless of whether the proposal would alter the federal budget or change the scope or regulatory authority of the federal government. It is difficult to find aspects of the policy environment that consistently foreshadow policy change.

Resources and Getting What You Want

This leads us to examine the resources of policy advocates again. As chapter 10 shows, a lengthy list of advocate resources are poor predictors of policy success. However, most policy debates involve competing

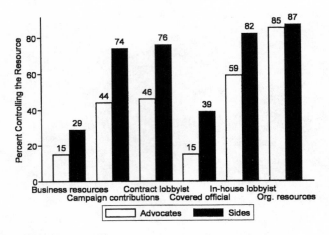

FIGURE 11.1. Control of resources by advocates and sides.

sides, groups of advocates pursuing the same policy goal fighting against another set of advocates who favor an opposing policy goal. In chapter 10, we note that policy sides tend to be quite diverse in their resources. One group's resources are only weakly correlated to the resources of the other groups sharing the same policy side. Therefore, we believe that policy sides help reduce the dramatic disparities in resources observed when comparing single-interest groups. In turn, the aggregated resources of an entire side may help determine success, especially if we compare these to the resources controlled by their rivals. Maybe the richest team wins the battle. We address these issues here, but before doing so we first consider how organizations with different types of resources come together to form teams or sides.

One reason for looking at entire sides rather than individual advocates, as we did in chapter 10, is that the composition of sides may be strategic. For example, those who control certain types of resources may actively seek out allies who complement rather than duplicate their own strengths. Figure 11.1 suggests that this may well be the case. It simply compares the percentage of advocates in our sample who control different types of resources with the percentage of policy sides in our study who control the same resources.

Many individual advocates lack certain kinds of resources, such as hired lobbyists, but few entire sides are without access to most kinds of lobbying resources. The figure shows, for example, that fewer than 60 percent of the interest groups in our study have their own lobbyist and less than half enjoy the services of a contract lobbyist. However, when groups are aggregated to a side, these resources are quite common. Over 80 percent of the sides in our study have their own lobbyist and three-quarters have a contract lobbyist. Similarly, fewer than half of the advocacy groups in our study made campaign contributions to any national candidates during a four-year period overlapping the time of our study, but three-quarters of the sides made such contributions. We see a similar pattern when we compare overall business and organizational resources. When we move from the level of advocates to the level of policy sides, the availability of resources is more widespread. The aggregation of advocates into policy sides helps provide a greater range of resources for the policy fight. Teams are stronger than individuals because of the diverse resources most teams bring to the table.

Do these resources relate to policy success? Table 11.4 shows the correlations between control of three types of resources and policy success. The resources are large numbers of members, the number of organizations with powerful reputations in the side, and an overall measure of aggregated resources across all the members of the side. In each case we find weak correlations with success, and none of the relations shown is statistically significant.

The first measure we consider is the number of advocates in a side. The figures in table 11.4 indicate that the size of a policy side is positively but weakly associated with policy success: the correlations fall short of statistical significance. When it comes to policy advocacy, we do not find compelling evidence to support the adage that there is strength in numbers. Rather, it is important to have a particular type of ally in a side. As chapter 10 demonstrates, and as we indicate below, having government allies is particularly important in achieving policy success.

We also examined whether having a renowned ally in a side improves the chances of success. Even though a number of resource measures are

TABLE 11.4 **The Correlation between Side Composition and Outcomes**

Outcome	Side size	Number of Power 25 allies	Side resource index
Policy success after two years	.09	−.03	.08
Policy success after four years	.10	−.02	.08

Note: $N = 214$ policy sides. Cells reflect Pearson's correlation coefficients. None of the correlations is significant at $p < .05$.

not strongly correlated with policy success, perhaps there are powerful organizations that have less tangible qualities (such as an experienced staff or an active membership) that make them effective policy advocates. Every two years *Fortune* magazine publishes the Power 25, a list of the most powerful lobbying organizations in Washington, based on a survey of legislators, congressional staff, White House aides, and lobbyists. The Power 25 list is merely a reputational measure, not a scientific indicator of influence. The list includes many well-known organizations, including labor unions (AFL-CIO, AFSCME, and the Teamsters), business peak organizations (such as the Chamber of Commerce and the National Federation of Independent Business), trade associations (American Hospital Association), and citizen groups (NRA and the National Right to Life Committee). For each side, we counted the number of participants listed on the Power 25 in 1999 or 2001.[3] Two-thirds of the sides in our study had no advocates on the Power 25 list. Just over half of the issues in our study (52 out of 98 issues) featured the advocacy of at least one member of the Power 25.

As table 11.4 indicates, the number of Power 25 organizations in a side is not associated with policy success. The Power 25 may help sell magazines, but they are no more likely to produce winners in the policy process than other organizations. This is consistent with other studies that fail to find a few powerful groups or individuals dominating national policy making.[4] As Mark Smith points out, many of these supposedly powerful groups do not share the same policy interests.[5] In fact, in seventeen issues in our study, Power 25 organizations squared off against one another, thus diluting their overall rate of success.

Finally, we create an overall index of resources for each policy side in our study. The resource index is based on the following measures: (1) the number of organizations in a side with their own lobbyist, (2) the number of organizations in a side with a contract lobbyist, (3) total lobbying expenditures by all organizations in a side, (4) the number of "covered officials" lobbying on behalf of organizations in a side, (5) the number of issue areas listed in lobbying registration reports by advocates in a side, (6) total campaign contributions by interests in a side, (7) the number of major policy advocates in a side, (8) the number of group members in a side, and (9) the organizational and (10) business resource indexes described in chapter 10. To create the resource index for each policy side, we first standardized each measure so that they share scales of equivalent magnitudes. Then we added the items and divided the sum by ten (the number of items). The resource index is a highly reliable measure; Cronbach's alpha for the scale is

.92.[6] Having an abundance of one resource suggests the presence of other types of resources, which implies that advocacy resources are fungible. (We do find a strong correlation between the resource index and the number of Power 25 advocates in a side [$r = .73, p < .001$]. Thus, the Power 25 rankings appear to be simply another indicator of organizational resources.)

Again, as table 11.4 indicates, overall resources are not a good predictor of policy success. The correlation between the resources of one side in a policy dispute and achieving the desired policy outcome is positive but weak and falls short of statistical significance. In sum, table 11.4 provides some surprising results suggesting that money, size, and prestige may be quite overrated in the lobbying game. One reason for these low correlations is that the wealthy often face off against the wealthy in politics. We consider these dynamics below, but first we consider the reasons why we see the particular patterns we observe.

It may appear to be a strange puzzle. When we examine a comprehensive assessment of the material resources controlled by individual advocates, we find little relationship with policy success (see chapter 10). When we isolate particular types of resources, we find little relationship with policy success. And when we aggregate our measure of resources to the side level, as we have done here, we have a better measure since many organizations work in alliances with groups that complement their skills and resources, but still we observe little association between resources and policy success. The reasons for the low correlations between resources and success have to do with competition. In short, large sides mobilize when necessary, not in the absence of powerful opponents. Similarly, the emergence of a powerful force for change can lead to other powerful groups moving into action to oppose them. Consider the linkage between resources and salience.

Resources help policy advocates in two ways. First, resources help policy advocates gain attention. There is a positive and statistically significant correlation between the overall resources of a policy side and the salience of the issue on which they are active ($r = .25, p < .001$). Policy sides with more resources are able to draw more government and media attention to their issues. In addition, policy advocates may use their resources to get the attention of government officials who are more effective at shaping policy. In a study of interest-group campaign donations and congressional committees, Kevin Esterling finds that groups tend to contribute more money to legislators with a high "analytical capacity," an ability to develop effective legislation.[7]

Second, resources help policy advocates gain a better understanding of the political environment and the knowledge community in which they operate. Consider the correlations in table 11.5. We find that resources are positively correlated with the level of active opposition and other obstacles mentioned by policy advocates on one side of an issue. At first blush this may seem counterintuitive. If sides with more resources are supposed to enjoy an advantage in policy disputes, then why do the resource-rich tend to mention more hurdles in their way? One answer is that resources tend to attract and mobilize opponents. However, we also find that resource-rich sides are more likely to cite a lack of attention from Congress, the administration, other organized interests, or the public. It is hard to imagine that sides with lots of resources attract more opposition and also face a problem of getting attention for their cause.

Another explanation is that sides with many resources have a better understanding of the policy process than resource-poor sides. With more resources come more allies, more members, more staff, and more connections to other knowledgeable advocates in Washington. This allows resource-rich sides to develop a more complete picture of their position in the policy process. They will have a better understanding of their strengths and weaknesses, where their opposition is coming from, and what arguments and tactics will be used against them. Thus, resource-rich sides are likely to mention more obstacles in their way, because they have a more complete understanding of the political and policy environment. In any case, the mobilization of one side of the fight is clearly related to the mobilization of the other side. Figures 11.2 and 11.3 show these relationships directly.

Using the resource index described in table 11.4, figure 11.2 plots the resources advocating for policy change against the resources defending the status quo in cases where no policy change occurred, excluding the issues with organized interests on only one side of the issue. A diagonal line

TABLE 11.5 **The Correlation between Side Resources and Policy Impediments**

Type of policy impediment	Resource index
Lack of attention	.14*
Active opposition	.19**
Other obstacles	.22**

Note: $N = 170$ policy sides. Cells reflect Pearson's correlation coefficients.
*$p < .10$ **$p < .05$

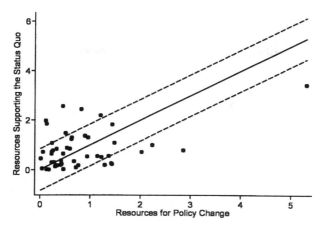

FIGURE 11.2. Resources mobilized for change versus resources supporting the status quo on issues for which no policy change occurred. A 45-degree line is superimposed on the graph. The dotted lines represent one standard deviation above and below the line on the resource index. $N = 48$ issues.

is overlaid on the graph, and observations close to the line indicate issues with evenly matched advocacy resources on both sides. The dotted lines indicate one standard deviation above and below the diagonal line for the resource index. In observations below the solid line, the advocates for policy change have more resources than the defenders of the status quo. In cases above the solid line, interests supporting the status quo control more resources than advocates for policy change. In a large cluster of typically low-salience issues in the lower left corner of the graph, both sides have roughly equivalent and relatively low levels of advocacy resources. We suspect that these are the kinds of issues that tend to be overlooked by journalists and scholars. Overall, the correlation between resources for the sides promoting policy change and the resources of sides defending the status quo is positive ($r = .44, p = .002$).[8]

There are certainly exceptions, but the overall pattern suggests that the forces for change and the forces defending the status quo tend to be fairly evenly matched. There are six observations above the top dotted line, where the resources defending the status quo are at least one standard deviation above the resources for policy change. The status quo was maintained on those six issues. There are also seven cases below the bottom dotted line, where the resources for policy change are substantially higher than the resources defending the status quo. Despite the resource

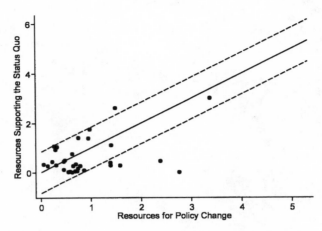

FIGURE 11.3. Resources mobilized for change versus resources supporting the status quo on issues for which policy change occurred. A 45-degree line is superimposed on the graph. The dotted lines represent one standard deviation above and below the line on the resource index. $N = 32$ issues.

advantage, policy change still did not occur on those seven issues. Most of the observations are between the dotted lines, meaning that the resources for one side are within one standard deviation of the resources for the other side. When interests with large resources organize to promote policy change, they are often met by an organized opposition with large resources as well.

Figure 11.3 plots the resources advocating for policy change against the resources defending the status quo in cases where policy change did occur. We see a similar pattern. Both sides tend to have similar levels of resources on most of the issues. Once again, there is a positive correlation between the resources for change and the resources for the status quo ($r = .40$, $p = .02$). Most of the observations fall between the dotted lines, although there is a cluster of five cases where the forces for policy change enjoyed a significant resource advantage and policy change indeed occurred.

Figures 11.2 and 11.3 suggest the limits of resources as determinants of policy outcomes. If resources strongly predict outcomes, then most of the observations of no change in policy in figure 11.2 should be above the main diagonal and most of the cases with policy change in figure 11.3 should be below the diagonal. For the most part, we do not observe those hypothesized patterns. Observations tend to fall on either side of the main diagonal in both figures, with the exception of small clusters of cases with large resource disparities that we describe more below.

Given the competitive nature of policy debates, it makes sense to control for the actions and resources of one's opponents in assessing the success of a given set of advocates. In a public-policy dispute the raw amount of resources held by one side is not as important as whether it has more than its opponents (and the magnitude of such a resource advantage or disadvantage). For example, in figure 11.2 and in figure 11.3, there is a highly salient case in the upper right portion of the graph (the debates over managed care reform in figure 11.2 and the prescription drug benefit for Medicare in figure 11.3). In both instances, both sides have vast resources, and in one of those cases (the prescription drug issue) the two sides are roughly evenly matched. There are twelve issues where the policy change sides had a significant resource advantage over the defenders of the status quo (at least a one standard deviation difference in the resource index). Policy change occurred in five of those twelve issues, suggesting that a large resource advantage may help, but is not always a sufficient condition for policy change. Conversely, there are seven issues where the forces defending the status quo had a significant resource advantage, and policy change occurred in just one of those seven issues. These examples suggest that resources matter in a relative sense.

Aggregating interests in policy sides and measuring resources in a comparative fashion are critical when considering the resource disparities common in interest-group politics. Previous studies compare the resources of individual interest groups and find a tremendously skewed distribution, with a relatively small number of resource-rich business groups and a large majority of resource-poor groups.[9] We find a similar pattern. Figure 11.4

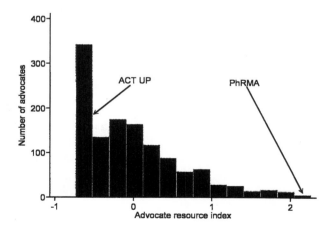

FIGURE 11.4. Distribution of advocate resources. $N = 1,263$ nongovernmental advocates.

shows the distribution of overall resources for the 1,263 advocacy groups in our study. The familiar skewed pattern is evident. A large number of groups clustered at the left end of the distribution have relatively few resources, while a small number of groups have substantially more resources than other groups.

In the figure we identify two interest groups that squared off over the issue of how to provide drugs to treat AIDS patients in Africa who had no way of paying for the medicine. One proposal was a "compulsory licensing" provision that would allow the production of generic AIDS drugs for use in Africa without paying a licensing fee to the original manufacturer. The issue pitted the AIDS community and human rights groups against major drug companies. Large drug companies that produced AIDS drugs opposed the compulsory licensing proposal. As one drug lobbyist argued, "It confiscates our patents and reduces the incentive to work on an AIDS vaccine." At the upper end of the resource distribution in figure 11.4, we identify the Pharmaceutical Research and Manufacturers of America (PhRMA), a large trade association of drug companies, a regular member of *Fortune* magazine's Power 25, and one of the major advocates against the compulsory licensing proposal.

At the lower end of the resource distribution in figure 11.4 is ACT UP, one of the advocates in favor of compulsory licensing for AIDS drugs in Africa. ACT UP is best known for acts of civil disobedience to increase AIDS awareness, precisely because it lacks conventional interest group resources. ACT UP has no lobbyists, makes no campaign contributions, and, according to the group's Web site, has no paid staff. If one views the compulsory licensing debate as a fight between PhRMA and ACT UP, it appears to be a very lopsided fight. However, PhRMA had few organizational allies in this fight. Meanwhile, ACT UP was one of many citizen groups arguing for the compulsory licensing provision. When all organizational resources on this issue are aggregated, the forces defending the status quo still have an advantage (as indicated in figure 11.5), but the disparity is far smaller than when only comparing PhRMA versus ACT UP.

When we examine the comparative resources of competing policy sides in our study, we get a very different picture than when we compare the resources of individual interest groups. The distribution of a comparative resource measure is presented in figure 11.5 for all 214 policy sides in our study. We compute a comparative resource measure by taking a side's resource index total and subtracting the combined resources of all opposing sides. For sides who face no organized opposition, the comparative

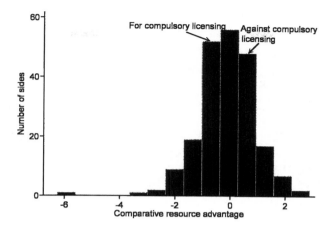

FIGURE 11.5. Distribution of comparative policy-side resources. $N = 214$ policy sides.

resource measure is the same as their score on the original resource index. Positive scores on the comparative measure indicate that a side has more resources than its opponents, while negative scores indicate that a side trails its opponents in resources. A score close to zero means that the competing sides are evenly matched in terms of their advocacy resources.

As figure 11.5 shows, some policy sides enjoy a resource advantage over their opponents, while other sides are at a disadvantage. Nevertheless, the vast majority of observations are clustered near zero, which means that most of the policy sides in our study faced organized opposition with roughly similar resources. There is one outlier at the far left end of the graph—noting the Federation of American Hospitals (FAH) on the issue of providing prescription drug coverage to Medicare recipients. FAH took the lonely position of trying to safeguard the long-term solvency of the Medicare program and found no organizational allies. As a result, its resources were swamped by the mammoth coalition supporting President Bush's prescription drug plan (including the pharmaceutical industry, the health insurance industry, the American Medical Association, and the National Association of Chain Drug Stores) and the equally heavy set of groups opposing President Bush's proposal (including the AFL-CIO, the American Federation of Teachers, the Consumer Federation of America, Public Citizen, the Grey Panthers, and Families USA). But aside from that unusual case, most issues in our study pitted competing policy sides that tended to be fairly evenly matched in resources. In sum, our evidence is consistent with the pluralist thesis that the involvement of resource-rich organizations (such as the Chamber of Commerce or AFL-CIO) pushing for policy change on an issue tends to provoke a countermobilization of other advocates to match the resources of the first side.

The resource story is complex. Where the mobilization of resources is unbalanced, we do find that the wealthy side tends to win; in 5 of 12 cases where those supporting change had a large resource advantage over the status quo supporters, change occurred. Similarly, where the status quo side had a large resource advantage, they got what they wanted 6 times out of 7. This is perhaps not surprising. The surprising thing is that we found only 19 cases out of 98 where there was such a large resource imbalance.

Predicting Policy Success

Now that we have established a way to measure the relative control of material resources, we can see whether a resource advantage is associated with policy outcomes: Does money buy power? In a final analysis, we test several predictors of policy success, including the comparative resource measures described above. We hypothesize that policy success is more a function of one side's resources relative to the resources of opposing groups. Our measures of policy success are the same ones used in table 11.5 and in previous chapters. They are coded 2 if the side fully achieved its desired outcome, 1 if the side had partial success in getting its desired result, and 0 if the side did not get its desired policy. We examine policy success after two years and after four years.

We first consider a model of policy success for sides defending the status quo. We control for factors identified in previous chapters as noteworthy aids or obstacles. For example, government officials act as advocates on almost all of the issues in our study. Furthermore, chapter 10 indicates that having midlevel allies in government (committee or subcommittee leaders in Congress or agency officials in the executive branch) is a correlate of policy success. We test that in the multivariate model below.

In addition, chapter 4 indicates that defenders of the status quo frequently mention opposition from organized interests, members of Congress, and the executive branch. Thus, we examine whether defenders of the status quo are more likely to fail when they face proponents of policy change from any of those three sources. Finally, table 4.2 identifies a series of other potential obstacles to policy success (including government

TABLE 11.6 **Statistical Model of Policy Outcomes for Sides Defending the Status Quo**

Independent variables	Policy success after two years	Policy success after four years
Comparative resource advantage for status quo	1.24**	0.64
	(0.50)	(0.39)
Midlevel government allies defending status quo	0.34*	0.28*
	(0.20)	(0.16)
Executive branch promoting policy change	−3.10***	−1.61**
	(0.89)	(0.65)
Members of Congress promoting policy change	0.22	0.51
	(0.73)	(0.59)
Organized interests promoting change	0.37	0.32
	(1.00)	(0.82)
Other obstacles to status quo position[a]	−0.52	−0.65
	(0.47)	(0.42)
Number of cases	63	63
Pseudo R^2	.29	.16

Note: Cell entries are ordinal logit coefficients (standard errors in parentheses).
[a]The "other obstacles to status quo position" variable includes cost concerns, insufficient data, divisiveness among allies, legislative logistics, jurisdictional disputes, electoral politics, partisanship, or a stigmatized target population.
*$p < .1$ (two-tailed)   **$p < .05$ (two-tailed)   ***$p < .01$ (two-tailed)

budget concerns, a divided coalition of allies, or a problematic legislative process). We total the number of these other obstacles mentioned.

The results in table 11.6 indicate that a resource advantage can help status quo defenders prevent policy change, particularly in the first two years. Holding other factors constant, increasing the comparative resource measure from the twentieth percentile to the eightieth percentile increases the expected probability of achieving a side's policy goal (maintaining the status quo) after two years from .76 to .94. Since the status quo tends to prevail overall, the magnitude of the resource effect is somewhat modest but still indicates that a resource advantage can help defenders of the status quo. We also observe a positive but weaker relationship between comparative resources and policy success after four years, although the relationship falls just short of statistical significance. Thus, a resource advantage does not appear to translate strongly into persistent policy success.

Our results also indicate that the executive branch is a force for policy change. Policy sides defending the status quo are more likely to lose when the administration is on the side of policy change. However, neither organized nor congressional opposition is a strong correlate of policy success for status quo defenders. When the administration is not pushing for policy change, the expected probability of maintaining the status quo after two years is .88, holding other factors constant at median values. In contrast, when the administration is a proponent of policy change, the expected probability of maintaining the status quo after two years falls to .29. Twelve issues in our study include the administration as an active opponent to the status quo. We observe significant policy change on seven of those twelve issues within two years; significant change occurs on eight of those twelve issues within four years, and on a ninth issue (building roads in national forests) a new president partially reverses a change in policy instituted by the previous president. Even though the White House is cited less frequently than congressional leaders as a source of opposition, the White House makes its presence felt.

The results in table 11.6 again suggest the importance of government officials as policy advocates. The more government officials defending the status quo, the greater the chance that the status quo position will prevail, although the effect is weak. Finally, the number of other obstacles mentioned by defenders of the status quo appears to be unrelated to their level of policy success. Combining as we do the activities of government officials and outside advocates into a single model, we find that government officials, in particular the president, play a predominant role, more important even than the wealthiest interest groups. This suggests that a strategic imperative for advocates defending the status quo is to avoid fights with the White House. The status quo may benefit when the president does not participate in a policy dispute.

We undertake a similar analysis of policy sides challenging the status quo, using a similar set of predictors of policy success. Chapter 4 indicates that challengers of the status quo more frequently mentioned lack of attention as a problem. Thus, we include an independent variable indicating whether the side faced any lack of attention from government officials, other organized groups, or the public. We find a weaker resource effect for challengers of the status quo than for defenders. But it is still a positive effect for the initial two-year period of our study. Holding other factors constant, increasing the comparative resource measure from the twentieth percentile to the eightieth percentile increases the expected probability of achieving modest or significant policy change after two years from .17 to .32. The greater the resource advantage a side enjoys over its opponents, the greater its chances of policy success over the first two years of our study. We observe no significant relationship between resources and policy success after four years for advocates of policy change. Thus, the impact of resource advantages for advocates of policy change may dissipate over a longer time horizon.

TABLE 11.7 **Statistical Model of Policy Outcomes for Sides Challenging the Status Quo**

Independent variables	Policy success after two years	Policy success after four years
Comparative resource advantage for challengers	0.54*	−0.02
	(0.30)	(0.22)
Midlevel government allies promoting policy change	0.02	0.09
	(0.08)	(0.08)
Executive branch opposition to policy change	−1.88**	−1.01*
	(0.84)	(0.62)
Congressional opposition to policy change	0.57	0.46
	(0.52)	(0.47)
Organized interests opposing policy change	0.21	−0.16
	(0.57)	(0.52)
Any lack of attention or interest mentioned	0.90	0.42
	(0.54)	(0.48)
Other obstacles to policy change[a]	−0.32	0.02
	(0.25)	(0.21)
Number of cases	107	107
Pseudo R^2	.09	.04

Note: Cell entries are ordinal logit coefficients (standard errors in parentheses).
[a]The "other obstacles to policy change" variable includes cost concerns, insufficient data, divisiveness among allies, legislative logistics, jurisdictional disputes, electoral politics, partisanship, or a stigmatized target population.
*$p < .1$ (two-tailed)   **$p < .05$ (two-tailed)

The results in table 11.7 again demonstrate the influence of the executive branch. When the administration is defending the status quo, policy change is less likely. When the administration is not defending the status quo, the expected probability of policy change after two years is .24, holding other factors constant at median values. In contrast, when the administration defends the status quo, the expected probability of policy change drops to .06. Eighteen issues in our study feature the administration as an active defender of the status quo. We observe significant policy change on just one of those eighteen issues within two years. Significant change occurs on only three of those issues within four years, and one of the cases of significant change (the nuclear repository in Yucca Mountain) involves a new president reversing the previous president's position.

As another example of the president's power, consider another issue where incremental change occurred. Efforts to reduce waste in mining operations have often proven contentious, pitting environmental interests against the mining industry. In 1997 John Leshy, the solicitor general in the Department of Interior (acting with the approval of President Clinton), rekindled the fires of mining policy debates. Leshy issued an opinion arguing that an 1872 mining law allows only one mill site (a facility used to process ore and support mining operations) per mineral claim (typically a twenty-acre plot of land). Environmentalists praised the new policy as a way to limit the environmental damage created by large-scale mining operations. The mining industry disagreed, arguing that allowing only one mill site on their properties would handcuff their businesses.

The mining industry then tried to get Congress to pass legislation undoing Interior's mill site policy. They were successful in the Senate, where western legislators supportive of the mining industry are more powerful, but not in the House. By the end of 1999, the best they could manage was an incremental change exempting a large proposed mine in the state of Washington from the new policy. But what appeared to be a policy victory for environmentalists and the Clinton administration was short-lived. After taking office in 2001, President George W. Bush's appointees in the Interior Department rescinded the policy restricting mill sites.

Finally, we note that other predictors of policy change appear insignificant. Overall, it is harder to predict success for sides advocating policy change than for those defending the status quo. This reinforces another advantage for the status quo in policy making. Among the issues in our study, opponents of policy change almost always unite into one side defending the status quo. In contrast, advocates for policy change sometimes fight against each other. As we note in chapter 3, twenty-two of the issues in our sample have multiple sides promoting policy change but working against one another. The forces for change are not always united, a condition that further limits the prospects for policy change.

Conclusion

Many features of the policy-making process (such as limits on government and public attention, continuity in policy communities, and multiple veto points) favor the status quo. Not surprisingly, the status quo tends to prevail among the issues in our study. However, we still observe policy change in 30 to 40 percent of our cases. Gridlock is not a uniform condition of the policy process.

In addition, when policy change occurs, significant change occurs more frequently than modest adjustment. This observation is more consistent with punctuated equilibrium theories of policy change than with incremental theories. For some issues, especially in heavily charged partisan policy disputes, incremental change does not appear as a policy option. Instead, government officials choose between significant policy change and the status quo. For example, in the case of trade relations with China, debated in 2000, the choice was between permanent normal trade relations and the status quo. There was little consideration of any incremental changes, such as a one-year extension of trade relations (as had been done previously) or normalizing trade for a limited list of goods. The legislation passed the House of Representatives without considering any amendments. We found other similar cases where little attempt was made at incremental change—rather, policy debate focused on proposals for substantial change versus defenses of the status quo.

First, we find that policy advocacy on a given issue is usually a long-term enterprise lasting several years. The vast majority of issues in our study involved lobbying activity before and after the period in which we closely followed the issue. Lobbying for policy change often takes time. Getting an issue on the political agenda, lining up support among other advocates, and working for government passage often takes years. But the passage of time increases the odds of policy change among our cases. We observe policy change on significantly more issues after four years than after just two years.

Second, it is difficult to find reliable predictors of policy change. The policy process is complex, and looking for solitary factors that predict policy change is a fool's errand. We observe policy change across a wide range of issues. For example, policy change appears equally likely on partisan and highly salient issues as on nonpartisan issues that receive little media attention.

Third, we employ three measurement strategies to estimate the impact of advocacy resources. We combine several resource measures into one index; we aggregate all the resources of advocates on the same side of an issue; and we measure resources in comparative terms, calculating a side's resources in relation to the resources of its opponents. When we employ all three measurement strategies, we find evidence that resources are a predictor of policy success, mainly during the initial two-year period of our study. However, the impact of resources is rather modest, partly because most of the issues in our study feature competing policy sides with roughly similar resources.

Business interests are thought to have a resource advantage in Washington lobbying. Our findings suggest that business power may be exaggerated. We have one caveat to add. In our sample of issues, labor unions are less successful than citizen groups in policy conflicts with business interests. Our study includes eleven issues where business and labor interests were on opposing sides, even though other advocates may have participated as well. Business interests prevailed in nine of those eleven issues, with labor succeeding on only two issues. By comparison, we identify sixteen issues that pit business interests alone against coalitions of citizen groups and unions or citizen groups and professional associations. These issues were fought to a draw, with business prevailing on nine cases and the citizen-group coalitions winning seven of the cases. These are a relatively small portion of the issues in our study, as business interests were found on opposing sides of most issues. However, as Berry argues, this suggests that citizen groups have become more effective than labor unions in checking the lobbying influence of business interests.[10]

Finally, we find that the president tends to be a powerful player in the policy process. The president did not get involved in many issues—the administration was an active player in roughly one-third of the issues in our study. However, when the executive branch takes an advocacy role in a public-policy debate, either defending the status quo or promoting change, it usually succeeds. Our results find common ground with Dahl's argument that "executive-centered coalitions" are common sources of policy change.[11]

We do not find evidence of similar influence among members of Congress. The president oversees a large bureaucracy and enjoys a number of formal powers and other tools of influence. As a result, the president weighs in on policy disputes with a heavy footprint and often makes the difference between policy change and the status quo. Earlier in this chapter we describe the debate between major pharmaceutical companies and several citizen groups over compulsory licensing of AIDS drugs for use in Africa. Despite a resource advantage for the drug companies, the groups in favor of compulsory licensing had an ace in the hole—several government officials on their side, including President Clinton. When Congress dropped the compulsory licensing provision from an Africa trade bill that was likely to pass, President Clinton instituted the provision by executive order. Comparing the role of the president and other government officials with those of interest groups in a single model, as we have done here, makes clear that the most powerful groups can achieve little without the support of government allies.

CHAPTER TWELVE

Rethinking Policy Change

Defenders of the status quo usually win in Washington. Policy frames are not revised and redefined willy-nilly. New information only rarely reorients how policy makers view the justifications for established public policies. Political conflicts often boil down to the budgetary implications of a given proposal. Material resources matter, but the link between wealth and policy success is attenuated because government officials intervene, because wealthy advocates attract wealthy opponents, and because the wealthy often work in concert with the weak in politics. Still, policy change, when it comes, can be dramatic.

Some of these findings may seem surprising, while others confirm long-held suspicions by scholars and journalists alike. But some of the most important results of our study of lobbying have to do with the fact that public-policy disputes are almost always related to existing public policies and that efforts to change an existing policy orientation usually fail. On the other hand, when policies do change they often upend decades of established ways of doing things, so these changes can have tremendous impacts on those people directly affected by them. No wonder lobbying is a multibillion dollar industry; the risks and opportunities associated with policy change are large, even if the probabilities are low.

There are many sources of bias in American politics; bankers are better organized than college students, for example. Therefore, when legislation regarding federal involvement in the student loan business is discussed, there is little surprise that the bankers have been able to place themselves at the center of the process: students take loans from existing banks (who charge a fee), and the federal government guarantees repayment of the loan. The net result is that students pay higher costs than they would if they borrowed from the government, and the industry benefits from the flow of billions of dollars on which individual banks take no risk. On the other hand, such a system avoids the creation of another significant federal bureaucracy.

Why is it that the banks continually win (at least so far), in each and every Congress? The answer is that the bias associated with the ability of some groups in society to mobilize more efficiently, and therefore to lobby with a louder and more effective voice in politics, is *already reflected in the status quo policy*. Note that the bankers win against the students, but they do not always win when they compete against credit unions. In contrast to students, who are largely unmobilized, credit unions can stand up and fight on a more equal footing with their rivals, the banks. In both cases, the status quo reflects the mobilization of the various interested parties, and this mobilization is not likely to change much in the short term. The vast bulk of lobbying in Washington has to do not with the creation of new programs, but rather with the adjustment of existing programs or with the maintenance of programs just as they are. Whatever biases are inherent in the system of interest-group mobilization (and these are substantial), these biases are already there, reflected in the status quo. The practical question, at any given time, is whether the status quo should be revised. Here, political science gives little indication about which side might win, if change is to occur. The equilibrium policy, reflecting the relative balance of forces, was presumably already attained in previous rounds of the policy process. The wealthy may have already achieved so much in previous rounds that policy makers do not feel the need to give them even more. And, indeed, we see in our study that the typical outcome of efforts to change public policy, even after following our issues for four long years, is that nothing occurs; the status quo is remarkably resilient. Further, we noted in chapter 11 that the correlations between material resources and policy outcomes were surprisingly modest; this may be because the wealthy already start out from a position of advantage.

But we note another important element. When change comes, it is often quite significant. The widespread acceptance of incrementalist theory has led to a misconception about policy makers, stereotyping them as technocratic tinkerers. If policy makers are going to actually go to the trouble of revising existing legislation on an important policy matter, there is little reason to expect that they will engage in only marginal tinkering. After all, before agreeing to devote time to this issue, they must be convinced that the problem is at least as severe as all the other policy priorities that are simultaneously clamoring for their attention. Why focus attention here if other problems are more urgent? When attention focuses on a given issue and when forces are strong enough to overcome the friction that supports the continued functioning of the status quo, policy makers may well reconsider some fundamental assumptions that justified the previous policy, resulting in substantial changes. Conditional on the occurrence of change, substantial policy changes were more than twice as likely in our sample as were marginal adjustments.

Are the wealthy advantaged by this process? To the extent that their advantages are already reflected in the status quo and that the status quo typically is not changed, undoubtedly the privileged are advantaged. Do the wealthy win in each round? Not at all. In fact, if the previous policy reflects an equilibrium of mobilized forces and what is on the table is adjustments from that equilibrium, there can be no prediction as to whether the next adjustment will be toward further advantage to the wealthy or away from that position. Like a stock value that oscillates around some average price reflecting its true worth, public policy may be moved sometimes in one direction, sometimes in another, with each individual shift not necessarily reflecting the overall bias in the system, but rather temporal fluctuations in power related to new information, attention-focusing events, and the crush of other issues on the agenda. The difference is whether we look at year-to-year changes or at longer-term patterns. Although students will never compete on an equal footing with bankers, legislation making student loans more attractive to students rather than to bankers can be adopted if attention focuses sufficiently on this issue.

The Power of the Status Quo

Undoubtedly, the most consistent finding throughout our book is that defenders of the status quo usually get what they want: No change. In spite of millions of dollars often spent on all the latest lobbying techniques and the involvement of some of the nation's most powerful corporations, consultants, and political leaders, most lobbying campaigns end in a stand-off, the status quo policy remaining in place. The sources of the bias in favor of the status quo are numerous, but some of the most important ones stem from the scarcity of attention and relate to the same processes that occasionally allow new policies to be adopted. Consider the distribution of policy change that we observed.

Across our 98 issues, we showed in chapter 11 that 58 saw no change, 13 showed just marginal adjustments to the status quo, and 27 saw significant changes during the four years that we monitored them. Further, when we looked at just the first two years of lobbying, the distribution was 68, no change; 13, moderate change; and 17, significant change. In the second two-year cycle, 10 additional cases moved from no change to significant change; none moved into the moderate change category. Why would the distribution of policy change be so skewed toward stalemate but simultaneously show such a high number of cases where serious changes took place? And if there is so much stalemate, why then do some lobbyists get so concerned about the threat of policy change (and why do those seeking change even bother)?

The answer is uncertainty about outcomes and the threat of significant change when it does occur. A purely incremental model of policy change suggests that when policy change occurs, marginal adjustments will be more common than substantial revisions. In fact, our findings are more consistent with what Jones and Baumgartner described as a friction model: a substantial tendency toward maintaining the status quo, but many large changes as well as marginal adjustments.[1] Looking at the numbers reported in the previous paragraph, of the 40 cases where change occurred, 27 saw substantial rather than marginal adjustments. Thus, almost 70 percent of the change that did occur was substantial rather than marginal, while over 60 percent of cases saw no change at all, even after four years.

These policy revisions may affect some people and companies very strongly, completely upending previous expectations about how a policy is administered and potentially translating into hundreds of millions of dollars in extra profits or expenditures. Freed of the constraints of incrementalist theory, there is no reason to assume a priori that a distribution of lobbying efforts would resemble a normal curve. Some scientists, for example, use catastrophe theory in their work on the natural world. Outliers like earthquakes, floods, avalanches, and forest fires are at the core of the theory, not what happens on a normal day. *Catastrophe* is too strong a term for what we observed, but the policy-making process in Washington is one in which it is not uncommon for a significant change to sweep aside years of equilibrium.

What this means to a lobbyist or a government official concerned, say, with the sulfur content allowed in gasoline, is that the amount of sulfur to be allowed in one year is likely to be identical to what was allowed in the previous year. Yet there is still some chance that it will be changed radically. Significant as opposed to marginal changes can put a company out of business, and lobbyists in Washington know that. If policy change is unlikely, but when it does come, 70 percent of the time it is catastrophic rather than marginal, that is enough to get one's attention. Indeed, in our case, the sulfur-content allowed in unleaded gasoline after the policy changes adopted by the EPA in the last year of the Clinton administration was reduced by 90 percent. This required expensive new refinery equipment to be installed and was expected to lead to the bankruptcy of many small refineries in the West. For those refiners, this was profound, maybe even a "catastrophe," and they lobbied hard (but unsuccessfully) with the help of the Western Governors Association for changes to the policy to reduce its impact on them.

Incrementalism or Friction?

What social scientists have learned about policy making is voluminous, but well-regarded theories of policy making are few and far between. Given that such a theory must encompass the vast array of processes and institutions that are part of government, it is understandable that scholars have shied away from trying to climb this mountain. Thus, a lack of competition and its own sharp insight into policy making have kept incrementalism front and center as perhaps the single dominant theory of policy making in American political science.

As detailed in chapter 2, the theory has its origins in a 1959 article, "The Science of Muddling Through," by Yale economist Charles Lindblom.[2] Lindblom provides a devastating critique of "textbook" policy making: the notion that policy makers go through a process that is comprehensive, reviewing all factors, and then tailoring the best solution to the problem at hand. He offers an alternative model which is closer to real-world practice. Policy makers operate not by synoptic or comprehensive analyses but by "successive limited comparisons." At any one time, policy makers compare only a set of small alterations to existing policy, and what modest changes are made build upon a base of current practices. The awkwardness of "successive limited comparisons" quickly gave way to the term "incrementalism." It is, at base, a theory of bounded rationality.

It may seem overly contentious to quarrel with an article written five decades ago, but the theory has been widely accepted as the conventional wisdom on policy making by generations of social scientists. Although there has certainly been criticism, Lindblom's conclusion that "policy does not move in leaps and bounds" seems commonsensical.[3] Yet once we conducted a thorough review of our ninety-eight cases, it was clear that incrementalism fails to explain what we observed. Most strikingly, the random draw of cases demonstrates that most issues before the Congress do not move incrementally. Rather, in any given year, the typical issue lobbyists are working on doesn't move at all. Instead, the status quo usually triumphs. This is not the same as incrementalism—it's stalemate.

A critique of incrementalism based largely on the basis that the status quo usually prevails raises two obvious objections. The first is that Lindblom was largely focused on administrative policy making, not congressional policy making. There's some justification in this objection. Most of our lobbyists were working on issues before the Congress, a consequence of a sampling procedure based on filings by lobbyists with the Congress. In contrast, most of Lindblom's examples involve agency administrators, and administrators formulate policy in the same areas on a more continuing basis than do legislators. Yet Lindblom reaches beyond agencies in his article, discussing political parties in addition to agency behavior. He claims that the nation's two political parties don't differ much, and he is direct in arguing that incrementalism is part of the fundamental nature of policy making in the United States.[4]

A second objection may be that the stability of the status quo is simply an artifact of the relatively short time horizon of our research design. After all, we ourselves have pointed out that achieving a change in Congress can take years. Moreover, it's often a sensible strategy for lobbyists to commit their organizations to the long-term, continuing to push an issue forward, mobilizing constituents, and promoting research, even when the short-term outlook is bleak.

Strategic as this lobbying approach may be, we reject the idea that continuing work on an issue while the status quo prevails fits the incrementalist model. Our distinction between status quo success in Congress and incrementalism is not a semantic difference; rather, they are fundamentally different views of the policy-making process. It's true that both status quo politics and incrementalism reflect some level of continuity in policy making. Still, while advocacy work may proceed for years, it may come to naught, and thus the continuity would reflect no movement over a long period of time. The database for this study is time-limited, and there is no way of knowing how many of the challenges to the status quo among the ninety-eight cases will eventually result in some degree of change. Given the modest increase in the proportion of issues that changed from the initial two-year period through the second two-year period, it's not overly pessimistic to assume that many challenges will simply fail to move policy. In this regard it's important to recognize that a good many of the issues that fell into the sample were on the periphery of the agenda, and there was no evidence to suggest that they would ever make it on to the agenda, much less to enactment.

Even in the situation where long-term advocacy eventually pays off sometime in the future with a degree of change sought by advocates, such an outcome is not necessarily an indication of incrementalism. Incrementalism is not a theory based on the idea that government *sometimes* makes changes in policy. Rather, it holds that there is ongoing bargaining within limited parameters of what might be possible and that the degree of change made is systematically modest and closely builds on existing statutes or regulations. This is not what we saw in Washington.

What we detected was a mix of proposals, some moving forward in a measured way, a considerably larger number moving in a dramatic new direction, and most moving not at all. In both Congress and agencies there are always many proposals pushing up against a set of barriers—friction—that restrict the flow of new policies. Congressional committee chairs and party leaders in Congress calculate what proposals should be taken up and which will be ignored.[5] The barbarians at the gates cannot always be ignored, but congressional policy making is very much a competition between what will be heard by legislators and what will be left aside, and there are vastly more proposals for change than there are opportunities to discuss them. Thus, calculations are continually being made as to what must be taken up and what is feasible to accomplish in the near term. Mobilization by advocates can push gatekeepers to promote their issues to active consideration, but most interests in Washington are not strong enough by themselves to force a proposal onto the agenda of a committee or an agency.

No one case can illustrate all these various scenarios, but consider a case we discussed in chapter 5, the Clinton administration's ergonomics regulations. Recall that labor unions had pushed for many years for a more extensive set of workplace protections for those who face demanding physical challenges in their everyday work. Despite its sympathies for organized labor, the Clinton administration did not issue the regulations until after the November 2000 election. These sweeping reforms incorporated rules for a wide range of different industries and different job descriptions. Business reacted in a fury, and, shortly after the Bush administration took office, the new regulations, which had not yet gone into effect, were revoked by the Republican-controlled Congress. President Bush's secretary of labor, Elaine Chao, said the administration would develop its own comprehensive set of regulations but then ignored the issue and left the much weaker pre-Clinton rules in effect.

There is nothing remotely incrementalist about this case. It is characterized by the two political parties not bargaining, opposing interest groups not bargaining, and policy not changing in a series of modest alterations. Rather, the ergonomics case has everything to do with who controlled which gates. One set of controllers unlocked the gates, brought labor unions inside. Sweeping changes were eventually put into place. Shortly thereafter, a new set of gatekeepers pushed unions back outside. (Business lobbies were always inside the gates.) The regulations were revoked, the status quo reasserted, and business allies pacified. Of course, this may have been an atypical case, but when we look across all ninety-eight of our cases, an incrementalist pattern is not apparent.

The general pattern of policy change that we observed fit Jones and Baumgartner's "friction" model better than the incrementalist one. At the core is the question of the allocation of attention. Attention is perhaps the scarcest commodity in Washington, and from what we observed this makes good sense. Information is freely flowing from policy advocates within well-organized professional communities and is widely available to any interested party. In fact, the problem is rarely the scarcity of information, but rather its overabundance—policy makers don't know how to make sense of it all, being overwhelmed with so much information coming at them from lobbyists on all kinds of issues. The friction that Jones and Baumgartner discuss stems from the idea that for any given issue, attention will typically be minimal; other priorities will be more urgent. During such a period, dramatic policy change is unlikely—if the status quo is to be changed, some serious bargaining is required. However, when attention is focused on the question (usually only after policy leaders have been convinced that the status quo policy is seriously, not just marginally, flawed), then substantial policy changes may be considered (and, sometimes, adopted). Jones and Baumgartner discussed their theory, as did the incrementalists, largely with reference to the U.S. budget, and they showed the distribution of policy changes that we reproduced in figure 2.1: a tremendous central peak associated with an extreme orientation toward the status quo, but also substantial "tails" in the distribution, reflected substantial, not just marginal, revisions. Marginal changes, in fact, were rare.

Neither Lindblom, the other incrementalists, nor Jones and Baumgartner conducted a study remotely similar to the one we have done here. Each camp has proposed theories that should help explain what we observed, however, if the theories are correct. Clearly, the distribution of policy changes and the process we have described, with its many obstacles to policy change, reflects some aspects of both models. But the fact is we saw little mutual adjustment and marginal change and a lot of the twin characteristics of a punctuated equilibrium or friction model: a strong status quo bias combined with a strong likelihood of dramatic policy change, when change occurred.

The friction model has practical application in what we have observed here. Policies move forward as proponents are able mobilize support sufficient to scale a threshold, or to overcome the friction associated with the scarcity of attention in Washington. The first threshold is to convince gatekeepers that a problem is worthy of being taken up. In practical terms this means convincing a small number of legislators—maybe only a single lawmaker at the beginning—to champion the cause. With competition for scarce space on the congressional agenda intense, many advocates will fail to gain a champion who is willing to spend significant time pushing the problem forward. Even among lobbyists who have succeeded in allying themselves with a congressional champion, the push forward to hearings and serious consideration will often be stymied by the lack of available space on the agenda or by outright opposition by subcommittee and committee chairs. To pass through the next gate, advocates must gain the support of the party leaders who decide what advances out of committee to a floor vote. Since this is Congress, every challenge is times two—two houses must advance legislation so that it may be enacted. It is a process full of resistance. Overcome the friction, and substantial policy change may follow, but it is not easy to overcome the high level of friction apparent in Washington policy making.

The Broad Sources of the Status Quo Bias

Lobbyists don't bother to work on just anything; like anyone, they prefer to spend their time on things that have some chance of success. As they typically have many goals, naturally they are more likely to expend their blood, sweat, and tears on those issues that have some chance of going somewhere, hopefully sooner rather than later. So when we interviewed our initial sample of lobbyists and asked them what they were working on, we were somewhat surprised to find out, four years later, that 60 percent of those cases had gone nowhere. Naturally, issues that were known to have no chance of ever going anywhere were excluded from our sample, since no lobbyist would have been working on them in the first place. This striking resilience of the status quo in American politics is worth some discussion; here we emphasize the most important reasons that we have found for it.

The first reason, one that we discussed in some detail in chapter 4, has to do with what we called "obstacles"—mostly, the inability of advocates to get on anyone's radar screen. Over 40 percent of the perspectives experienced what we termed "lack of interest, attention, or support" (see table 4.1). That is, before we even talk about officials or rival interest groups actively opposing one's goals, the initial hurdle is often just motivating anyone to pay attention. In short, the scarcity of attention, the crush of other problems, is obstacle number one that advocates face. Of course, for those who seek to protect rather than to change the status quo, the fact that leaders of Congress are swamped with even more important problems to worry about is a welcome thing; the crush of other problems or the scarcity of attention is the first of many powerful sources of support to the status quo.

A second source of status quo bias was detailed in chapters 6 through 8, where we reviewed the lobbying tactics and arguments that different types of advocates use. Those protecting the status quo engaged in fewer lobbying activities and systematically used different types of arguments. One particularly useful tactic was simply to sow doubt about any proposals for change: it might cost more than proponents say; it might not work as intended; any tinkering with the existing policy might have serious unintended consequences given the complexity of the policies already in place. We know from social psychology that raising doubts and focusing on costs rather than opportunities can be very effective, so these strategies often work.[6]

The difficulty of creating a bipartisan coalition was another problem, even though partisanship was often under the surface rather than at the core of explicit and vocal policy disputes. Party leaders may emphasize to rank-and-file members that a given proposal simply is not a party priority, even if it's something that the leadership would not necessarily oppose. In turn, this may be enough to prevent the creation of a bipartisan coalition. Even without active coaching by party leaders, we found many instances where proponents of change had trouble recruiting people from both political parties to play active roles as legislative champions, even though many of our issues were not particularly partisan. This "latent partisanship" reflects the presence of other more important priorities more than it reflects any active opposition. If these issues were suddenly thrust high on the agenda for some reason, members of both parties might well jump on board some proposal for change. But pushing an issue high on the agenda is easier said than done, and one of the reasons is the huge number of competing priorities for each individual political leader and party. Why should Republicans help champion a cause that is particularly dear to Democrats, even if they are not particularly opposed to it? Each side has its own priorities. A lack of enthusiasm or a different set of priorities, not outright hostility, dooms many policy proposals, further enhancing the status quo.

A fourth and very powerful source of stability is who sits in the gatekeeping positions. For most issues, given that they concern revisions to existing government programs, the gatekeepers were often involved in creating the existing policy, if not the primary authors of it. Naturally, it can take a lot to convince them that "their" policy doesn't work.

Perhaps the most important element that promotes stability in the policy process, however, is much more diffuse than just convincing a single gatekeeper of the need to revise an existing policy. As discussed in chapter 3, shared information is pervasive in diffuse policy communities surrounding each of the issues we investigated. Whether the concern was revising the rules concerning trade with China, preventing needlestick injuries for hospital workers, restricting the export of high-performance computers to rogue nations, or regulating mill sites in areas where mining takes place, scores if not hundreds or even thousands of professionals closely follow developments surrounding those particular questions. Each one of those issues, while they may seem esoteric to the rest of us, affect the day-to-day work lives of thousands of people. Administrators, professionals, union officials, citizen advocates, and business owners pay close attention to them, because they can affect the bottom line, personal safety, and livelihoods. Within each of these policy communities, information is widely shared. In our interviews, no matter what the particular angle that an advocate may have been pushing, all those to whom we spoke recognized certain common facts about the background and justification of the policy in place. While they may have disagreed about the value of various possible changes to the policy, there were few secrets. That is, they were commonly aware, as a group, of the facts and figures associated with the justification for the current policy, various proposals to change it, and research or experiences in states, communities, or foreign countries suggesting how any policy changes might be implemented. We call this an "information-induced equilibrium."[7]

Why does shared information induce stability? Because individual policy makers typically do not have the ability single-handedly to change the collective understandings of entire policy communities. Certainly they try. But when a new argument is introduced to the policy community, it is assessed by others who are equally expert on the background and technical details of the policy as the one making the proposal. Elements of the debate that the advocate promoting the new argument chooses to ignore can be quickly brought to the attention of others. In sum, a policy community is made up of experts, and they were not born yesterday; naive is not the operating rule within Washington, after all. A policy community, even if it is riven by deep divisions, provides the opportunity for experts to share common information and to develop common understandings of the shape, direction, and justification of public policy.

The broad base of participation in a policy community suggests that the stability that comes from the shared understandings of the current workings of a given public policy will likely be quite enduring. Individual policy makers may come and go. Presidential appointees may arrive with a mandate and an ideology that suggests dramatic changes to the status quo policy, and some of these proposals may succeed. In general, however, for most issues most of the time, the shared information and policy understanding that surround most public policies ensure that individual efforts to redefine an issue will be met with counterarguments and reminders of the dire consequences to many constituencies should that change be adopted. Because people are strongly motivated by threats as opposed to opportunities, it is easier for defenders of the status quo to mobilize opposition to proposed changes than it is for supporters of change to allay these fears.

The Complex Causes of Policy Change

But policy change does occur; stability is not the only possible outcome of the policy process. Just as the structure and shared knowledge that characterizes policy communities leads most of the time to stability, occasionally it can lead to entire policy communities moving en masse toward recognition that change is necessary, like it or not.

We have seen that stability is more common than policy change, but that significant change is more common than marginal adjustment. If policy change were the result of many independent forces, each having its own effect on the outcome unrelated to the other forces, then over time we would see an incremental pattern of change, with most things not changing much, some changing moderately, and a very small number showing significant alterations compared to the status quo. In fact, what we observe, and our own understanding of the policy process based on our interviews, suggests that the forces of policy change are not independent of each other at all. Indeed, their interaction is what makes the causes of policy change so complex, so interesting, and also so frustrating to those of us who would like to be able to understand and predict what happens in Washington.

We saw in chapter 11 that many of the factors we expected to affect the likelihood of policy success, based on significant studies done in the past, powerful theories, or simple common sense, simply had no impact or only a moderate one. Even elections had less of an impact than one might have expected. Money and material resources certainly had less impact than the literature would lead one to expect. The reason for this, we think, is not because such things as partisanship, leadership, elections, salience, or money are unimportant; indeed, they do matter. But the impact of any single variable is highly dependent on the context. The multiple and simultaneous events that must occur, the many variables that must align correctly, in order for policies to be changed generally ensure that policies do not change. Most of the time the combination of factors necessary for change simply is not there even if one variable, such as an election or a newly released study, is in place. Furthermore, for any single variable, say, having recruited an important political leader to one's side or having a newly published study available to demonstrate lower cost for one's proposal, there may be countervailing factors working in the other direction or there may simply be no space on the agenda. In sum, our results suggest that simple additive models of policy change are likely always to come up short. Combinations of factors, none individually, add up to policy change. Context matters.

But we do not mean to imply that the process is simply random or too difficult to explain, or that the "context" is just some undifferentiated mass of "other factors." Indeed, there are important elements of structure to the process. The most important element of structure has to do with the social nature of the Washington advocacy process and the reality that policy makers move in herds, not individually. This has many implications, but two stand out: First, attention is limited, so if the political agenda is already used up by other issues, there may be no space available to push a new item forward. Many of our cases ran up against this problem, in spite of well-heeled lobbying coalitions, bipartisan support, and other strong elements. Second, expectations matter; Washington policy makers are constantly looking around themselves, building expectations about what others are going to do, and acting accordingly.

Read carefully virtually any standard quantitative political science report about the causes of political change, and somewhere lurking in the footnotes is the Latin phrase *ceteris paribus*. This is the idea that the impact of each variable is assumed to be under the condition that "all else is equal"—that is, that the impact of one variable on the outcome is independent of the impacts of all the other variables. Any statistical regression equation has this as one of the (often unstated) assumptions, and it is absolutely necessary in order to interpret the results of such an analysis. But in Washington, things are often not independent. Each of the actors is monitoring the environment, trying to determine what others may be getting ready to do. Interest groups are looking for issues that might be "ripe" so that they can focus their efforts on those with the greatest chance of actually being enacted. Political leaders similarly are anxious to be involved in newly developing issues that appear to have "legs." Even those who are opposed to change may sometimes conclude that fighting the change is a losing battle and it is better to gain a seat at the bargaining table by signaling conditional cooperation than fighting to the bitter end.

In situations where people are basing their decisions not just on their own sense of what is desirable, but also on their sense of what other people around them are likely to do, we can see a phenomenon of "social cascades." Social cascades include things such as fads where for no apparent reason clothing styles come and go, or restaurants that suddenly become "hot" not so much because the food is so much better than elsewhere but because people hear so much about it they expect that if others are saying so it must be true. But social cascades are not limited to such trivial applications; they also apply to the policy process.[8] One need only to look at the presidential selection process to understand the importance of "momentum" in the primary season; early victories demonstrate that a candidate has true viability, whereas initial defeats can demonstrate that a candidate is a lost cause.[9] These results, of course, can be self-fulfilling prophecies, as anyone who has ever tried to predict which candidate will emerge at the top after the primary season knows. Similarly in the policy process, initial actions may have powerful effects on subsequent actions, and the actions of key players in the process may send cues to scores of others, all of whom may change their behavior when they see which way the process may be moving. For example, presidents want to be known for policy proposals that will have a significant impact and that will work. Which proposals to pick? Social activists have many proposals of interest to them, some of which have more compelling evidence than others, or allow for the creation of larger political alliances. Which ones to focus on? People inside and outside of government are constantly monitoring their peers to see which new studies are being received with great credibility, which key actors are showing interest in which proposals, and which legislative vehicles may be taking shape. They want to be associated with initiatives that have a chance of passage, not to waste their time working on proposals (even ones they like) that are likely to go nowhere. The result of all this is that it is indeed very difficult to predict which policy proposal may become the object of attention. But we can make strong predictions about the overall pattern of a system of social cascades: such processes follow a pattern of all or nothing, exactly as we have observed.[10]

We see a combination of order and randomness in the process we have described. The randomness comes in because we can't predict how policy makers will respond to new information. They may ignore it because there are too many other priorities, for example. Or a given press release may get more than its fair share of attention, potentially galvanizing support for some new proposal. Opponents to this proposal may conclude that it has so much momentum that it is better to get on board and attempt to water the proposal down (if possible), or they may mobilize to kill the proposal outright. We can't tell ahead of time which of these scenarios may take place, because these decisions may be made with reference to many other decisions or observations made virtually at the same time. But in looking at a large number of policies over time, as we have done here, we know that each of these things will occur. We see complex interdependencies, interactive effects of many variables, strategic actors responding to one-another; we don't see a single actor or key explanatory variable, even money, that explains a large percentage of what occurs, on its own. Simple explanations come up short.

On the other hand, we see a lot of patterns. The most important, and perhaps the most surprising, is the all-or-nothing nature of the policy process. This suggests social cascades, that the same forces that combine to produce stability occasionally align to allow for substantial shifts, as large numbers of policy makers recognize, all at the same time, that a new study will be taken seriously, that a powerful coalition has been formed and has great political backing, that the president indeed intends to make a given issue his priority, or some other relevant political fact. When these expectations are updated, sometimes a countermobilization occurs, and we should not forget that even after four years the most common outcome we saw to all these efforts to change public policy was that it was not changed at all, not one iota. However, we also observed about 40 percent of our cases where, over four years, some changes occurred. When change occurred, it tended to be substantial, not marginal. This may be because entire policy communities simultaneously recognize that the other side has won. Veterans of the Washington policy process know that sometimes when a train is leaving the station, it is better to get on board rather than to be run over. Much can be done to stop a train from getting close to being ready to leave, but occasionally that momentum builds and the policy shift is clear for all to see.[11]

Agenda Bias

Our close examination of the issues in our sample leads to one final question about the nature of the agenda: What wasn't there? The research design allowed us to capture a range of issues lobbyists were trying to convince Congress or an agency to pay attention to, but what of problems that weren't even on the periphery of the agenda?

The methodological problems in analyzing what's absent and not directly observable are manifest. Yet we're not talking about "missing" data. The research design allows us to compare what lobbyists are pushing for against the broader range of problems faced by Americans. There is, of course, no master list of what *should* be on the agenda, but we can proceed by contrasting the agenda documented here against the most significant problems and conditions that existed at the time of the fieldwork. We will do so by considering obvious and enduring problems as well as by consulting polls that ask Americans what they believe the most important problems are.

The research design did skew the resulting sample toward domestic policies. For example, we saw in chapter 1 (table 1.4) that international affairs and foreign aid captured 11 percent of congressional attention (at least as measured by the number of committee hearings), but we had few cases in our sample from those areas. And America was at war during much of the time of our fieldwork. Even defense-related matters, which were indeed represented in our sample, were not of the large-scale strategic kind that one could potentially imagine. Rather, the defense-related issues we saw tended to relate to such issues as weapons procurement or military personnel issues (four of the eight defense issues in our sample were procurement-related). Given the importance of foreign and defense policies (and the fact that America was at war during at least some of the time when we were in the field), it may seem surprising that few such issues appeared in our sample. This pattern surely reflects the centrality of the president in these policy areas. Much in foreign policy isn't directly legislated, and much isn't subjected to significant lobbying by interest groups. Defense is a bit different, because arms contractors are heavily involved in the legislative decision making over weapons systems. Lobbyists certainly are active on issues of procurement, about military pensions or health care, and on many defense-related issues. But it would be a severe misunderstanding of American politics to suggest that large-scale strategic decisions such as whether to go to war or whether to leave Iraq are usually driven by the same kinds of lobbying campaigns and interest-group mobilization as we see, for example, on the issue of reimbursement rates for health care professionals in the Medicare program. Defense and foreign policy are different.

Equally conspicuous is the relative paucity of issues relating to the poor and to the economic security of working-class Americans. For the poor, there is no shortage of reasons why they don't organize, but the lack of disposable income and modest political skills are the most obvious ones. If they had sufficient disposable income for dues or contributions and there were organizations competing for their support, the collective action problem would also be a formidable obstacle. Although some marginalized constituencies—ethnic and racial minorities, gays, women—have organized with beneficial results, the same cannot be said of those who are simply poor. As Kay Schlozman and her colleagues note, "The level of political inequality in America is high. The expression of political voice is strongly related to social class."[12] There could be no more vivid evidence of the relationship between class and voice than the nature of the issues in our sample.

Direct representation of the poor by lobbyists from their own interest groups is not the only path to a lobbying voice before government. Labor has traditionally served as an impassioned voice on behalf of low-income Americans and not just for those who formally belong to unions. Unions were evident in the sample and were a powerful force behind one of the most controversial of our issues, the Clinton administration's midnight regulations on workplace ergonomics. Despite its decline, organized labor still possesses substantial resources and maintains influence in Washington. It's also the case that on some issues directly affecting the poor (health reform, job training), labor is highly involved. Yet the results of our study do not dispel the widespread belief that unions are much weaker today than they were prior to the conservative resurgence that began with Ronald Reagan.

The poor also received some proxy representation from professional groups who push government to initiate or expand various social or health-related services. For many such issues, contraceptive coverage or chiropractic coverage, for example, the benefits of such lobbying by health professionals would likely accrue to both middle-class and low-income citizens.

Given the high level of lobbying activity by citizen groups, one might expect that some of that energy on the liberal side would be devoted to issues affecting low-income Americans. This is clearly not the case. Liberal citizen groups, which were the vast majority of all citizen groups identified in our fieldwork, display little interest in the problems of low-income Americans.[13] This is no small loss to those on the bottom of the income distribution. The passion of the liberals, important to the passage of the Great Society legislation in the 1960s, is today primarily directed at environmental and consumer issues. We see mobilization by environmental groups to ban the sale of bear organs and to limit the building of logging roads in the national forests, but we see no efforts to expand benefits to the unemployed, raise the minimum wage, improve social or educational services in disadvantaged neighborhoods, or promote other issues where one could easily argue that substantial social needs exist. There is a difference between social concern and the mobilization of an organized lobby in Washington; these issues simply have too few lobbyists in Washington actively promoting change. We did, of course, see mobilization around the issue of "criminal justice reform," a case cited by a Washington organization representing ethnic minorities. But the case went nowhere for lack of a broad coalition of supporters. Clearly, the universe of issues in our sample reflects the mobilization of interest groups in Washington, and this mobilization is highly skewed away from the disadvantaged.

We found in chapter 1 that our set of issue identifiers showed significantly more class bias and corporate connection than did our sample of advocates overall. The good news there from a perspective of democratic representation is that when noncorporate and professional interests get involved in an issue, they are taken seriously. The bad news is that the wealthy seem to set the agenda. We found that our issue identifiers controlled significantly more material resources than others involved in the same issues. Further, the sides associated with these advocates were also significantly wealthier. Largely, we believe these differences are associated with the simple fact that corporate, trade, and business groups simply are wealthier than citizen and labor groups. But the findings do strongly suggest that even if they do not always win, corporate, professional, and trade interests have a distinct advantage in setting the lobbying agenda.

Despite the highly visible role of conservative citizen groups and religious lobbies in Republican party politics, such groups were noticeable by their absence in the policy making related to our set of ninety-eight issues. There were a few issues, including late-term abortions, where such groups surfaced, but their numbers in the roster of groups we identified as active were tiny. Their relatively low level of activity is all the more surprising because Republicans controlled the Congress at the beginning of our study and then captured the White House before our fieldwork ended. In short, they had friends in power and still didn't do much direct lobbying of Congress. It may be that the conservative groups are effective at influencing public opinion and convulsing ideologues, but their active presence as a lobbying force in Washington appears rather limited.[14]

We can make a systematic comparison of the issues in our sample, reflecting the concerns of the Washington lobbying community, with the concerns of average Americans by looking at the list of issues mentioned in the Gallup Poll's periodic question asking Americans "What is the most important problem facing the country today?" Figure 12.1 compares Gallup's poll results with the distribution of issues from the sample.[15] At a glance it's obvious that there's little overall correspondence between the congressional agenda and the public's agenda. At the time of our research, the top public concerns were crime, the economy, international affairs, education, health, and social welfare. The top issues our lobbyists were working on are, by contrast, health, environment, transportation, banking, defense, science and telecommunications, and foreign trade.

There are many reasons for these differences. Gallup's open-ended question surely elicits the first issue that comes to mind; thus, the most visible

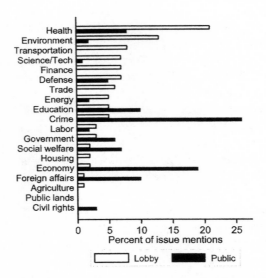

FIGURE 12.1. The lobbying agenda versus the public agenda. The figure shows the percentage of lobbying cases compared to the average responses to the Gallup poll question "What is the most important problem facing the country today?" Public opinion data were calculated from the Policy Agendas Project (www.policyagendas.org).

problems facing the country will score highly. The poll also asks about the most *important* problem, while the actual congressional agenda will always represent issues of varying levels of significance. The lobbying agenda we documented embodies the pluralism of our political system; the Gallup Poll offers a measure of majoritarian instincts. Ultimately, though, the disconnect between the public's priorities and Congress's agenda is largely a consequence of who is represented in Washington. For better or worse, interest groups are central participants in policy making in our political system. For any constituency, representation by one or more lobbies does not assure policy responsiveness by government, but lack of representation makes action considerably less likely. It may be that political systems built around majoritarianism work better for lower income citizens. It's certainly the case that in the United States the inequities of social class are sharply exacerbated by the organizational bias of interest-group politics.

The Continuing Nature of Public Policy

The most important conceptual issue regarding our research approach, beyond the need to study a broad range of issues, not just those in the headlines, is the easily forgotten reality that policy debates are almost always about what direction to *shift* the status quo. If the status quo already reflects the constellation of political forces from a previous iteration of the policy process, it is by no means clear that it will necessarily move further in a direction of perceived bias. This subtle difference between the status quo and efforts to change the status quo (what lobbying is about) has tremendous implications both for how to interpret our results and how to assess previous research. Much of the literature on the structure of bias in U.S. public policy and the mobilization of interests is based on an unstated idea that the point of evaluation is the degree to which a given policy benefits which social groups. Cases of privilege and disadvantage are easy to point out, of course: Farmers do better than the unemployed; bankers do better than college students; college students do better than their peers who chose not to attend school. But when we study lobbying, we are typically looking at efforts to *change* the status quo policy, not to create it from whole cloth, as if it had no history. Therefore, studies of lobbying should not always be expected to show the continued power of the wealthy over the weak, the mobilized over the unmobilized, as these biases should already be apparent and there is no reason why the next step in the process should point in one direction or the other.

If the status quo reflects decades of accumulated efforts by various constituencies to mobilize for effective representation in the halls of government, and greater success by some groups than others, what does that say about efforts at any given time to change the status quo? Should it be pushed even further toward the interests that dominate? Or should policy makers pull back from this bias and push policy in the opposite direction? If the policy already reflects some equilibrium of political power, there is no reason to think that movements to shift the policy will be in one direction or another. Hence, we see what appear at first to be surprisingly weak relations between resources and outcomes. The continuing nature of the policy process can help explain that. This does not imply that resources don't matter; we know that they do. But, on any given day in Washington, it is hard to tell which way the wind will blow. Typically, of course, it doesn't blow at all, and the status quo remains just where it was the day before.

Our review of the success of policy advocates to get what they want has revealed that none of them typically has much control over the collective outcome of the Washington policy debates we studied. Those who seek to protect the status quo can rest assured that their opponents have a hard row to hoe, because policy change is rare. On the other hand, change can be quite substantial when it comes about, upending long-standing practices and disrupting policy subsystems built up over decades. While individual lobbyists may not control the process single-handedly, they participate in a collective process which, as a whole, can lead to dramatic changes.

In the short run, individual lobbyists and even national political leaders have little control over how a policy will be understood or defined. They try to spin their issues, but opponents fight back, ensuring that for most issues most of the time, a stable equilibrium continues. As we have discussed, this equilibrium is held in place by the very communities of policy experts that implement the policies and who are the most knowledgeable about their every nuance and implication; these people are true experts. But in the long run, issues do indeed evolve, and the public and the communities of experts who are involved with the issues each day do change their views on the relative importance of the different elements of the debate. Through a process that none controls single-handedly, but to which all contribute, the issues are associated with shifting issue-definitions. Sometimes, changes are helped along by events or new studies that focus attention on a given dimension of the debate. In any case, policy change follows a pattern of stasis for the most part, but the dramatic policy changes that occasionally occur make it clear that those who are in it for the long term may indeed prevail in the end.

Methodological Appendix

R esearch reported throughout this book reflects work collectively done by the five authors with the assistance of more than fifty student collaborators over seven years, including four years of data collection and interviews. We have made extensive use of publicly available information for our research project and have archived and organized all this information systematically on our Web site, http://lobby.la.psu.edu, including supporting documentation, codebooks, datasets, and a full description of every one of our cases, with links to a complete archive of all publicly available newspaper articles, congressional hearing transcripts, interest-group statements, and related legislative proposals.[1] But the core of the research project derives from a set of confidential interviews that we conducted with a sample of lobbyists and other policy advocates from 1999 to 2002. Our methods are not so much complex as they are multifaceted, driven by a concern to construct a project that would be generalizable and allow systematic tests of various hypotheses from the literature. We hope that others will want to build on this approach, so we provide a complete description of our methods here.

Overview of Sampling, Case Selection, and Interviews

We began by drawing a random sample of interest groups active in Washington from the reports that lobbying organizations file with the House and Senate.[2] The sample was weighted so that organizations were selected in direct proportion to their level of lobbying activity. Specifically, the greater the number of issues mentioned in its lobby disclosure reports, the greater the chance of being selected in our sample. We then made an appointment with an individual lobbyist at these organizations and set up an interview. We asked these *issue identifiers* to discuss the most recent issue on which they had spent time, to describe what they had done and what their organization was trying to accomplish on the issue. If the respondent was working on more than one issue, we then asked them to talk about the issue that was related to the most recent phone call they made or paper that crossed their desk. The issues that they chose became one of our case studies. During the interview, we asked who else was working on the issue, asking about both allies and opponents, as well as any members of Congress, agency officials, or members of the administration who were involved. This enumeration formed the basis of our list of major participants. Typically the respondent would identify both allied and opposed organizations, as well as the relevant congressional committees, and possibly an administrative agency. If names were not offered, we asked for them. We held subsequent interviews with a selection of these additional participants. The number of interviews per case was not fixed, but our guiding principle was that we wanted at least one interview on each side of the interest-group equation. We also tried to obtain at least one interview with someone in government working on the issue. Most typically a case would involve interviews with representatives of two opposing interest-group sides and a staffer for a committee or agency. But complex issues, especially those where the issue was being actively debated, sometimes led to five, six, or more interviews. Overall, we interviewed 315 respondents across ninety-eight issues, or an average of over three sources per case.

By asking our issue identifiers to note the most recent issue dealing with the federal government that they or their organization had been involved in, we elicited a wide range of responses. Sometimes, what we got had been the object of a massive lobbying effort by an entire office, as, for example, when we talked to people about the Clinton administration's proposal to grant permanent normal trade relations status to China. Huge numbers of lobbyists spent months working on nothing else, so naturally this massive issue fell into our sample since we were in the field at the time. But other issues, because of the nature of our sampling design, were not even on any governmental agenda; the groups involved were trying to put them there, often unsuccessfully. On the periphery of the agenda, we heard about such issues as limiting the commercial trade of bear organs and a worker compensation matter that revolved around the respective definitions of "boat" and "ship." The vast majority of our issues fell in between the cataclysmic and the obscure.

We supplemented our interviews with a comprehensive document search, including texts of bills, hearings, and statements on the Library of Congress's Thomas database; online press releases and statements from interest groups; and media coverage available through Lexis-Nexis. In a few cases these searches led to additional major participants being added to the list. We continued to follow these issues throughout the current Congress and throughout the subsequent Congress, making use of publicly available documents and news coverage, and checking back by phone with at least one of our interview subjects whenever possible. (Our Web site incorporates every bit of publicly available information we were able to obtain about each of our issues.)

Our interviewing strategy was to ask a limited number of basic questions, relying on probes when necessary to extend discussion into fuller responses. This was a form of elite interviewing, relying on semistructured interviews with open-ended questions.[3] For example, when we asked an interest-group representative who was working against them, our question ran something like "Tell us about your opposition on this issue." This was truly open-ended, inviting the lobbyist to tell us what they thought was important on the issue. For qualitative research in American government, this is a common method. This approach relies on informants who offer extensive guidance on the intricacies and complex history of an issue, election campaign, or set of deliberations by policy makers.

Yet we converted our interviews into quantitative data. In short, our qualitative case studies were a means to a quantitative end. When political scientists interview elites for a study to be built around quantitative data, much of the questioning will rely on much more restrictive questions. Instead of asking, "Tell us about your opposition on this issue," there might be a series of specific inquiries such as "How many groups were on the opposing side?" or "Did the opposition use a grassroots campaign?" Why, then, did we choose open-ended questioning? There are a number of reasons, not the least of which is that we wanted to keep the inquiry open to whatever we might find. We also wanted to gain insight into the history and context of each issue, as that added to our confidence that each issue was accurately translated into quantitative values. Perhaps most importantly, we wanted to use the sheer breadth and detail of these answers to be able to describe the subtle, nuanced phenomenon of influence in politics. The loose, conversational nature of the interviewing facilitated circling back later in the questioning to a topic that the respondent did not completely answer, even with some initial probing. Often, asking in a different fashion, in a different context elicited a more helpful answer.

Overall, the open-ended questioning with probes and a less-scripted format than standard survey questioning generated long, richly detailed narratives about the issue at hand. The conversational tone put respondents at ease, conveying to them that they were free to tell us what they thought was important. Together with the documentary evidence (hearings, reports, media stories and the like) gathered by our assistants, we completed each case study with an impressive amount of information.

Too Many Cases, Too Few, or Just Right?

There is a classic trade-off in social science research between the number of cases and the depth of knowledge about each. The more cases—the larger the N—the more generalizable the results. But what is known about each of those cases may be superficial or limited. Unless scholars are able to use an already completed data file, the costs associated with collecting original, in-depth data can be substantial. As a result, choices as to what data are collected may be strongly influenced by what can be gathered expeditiously or inexpensively. Out of necessity, scholars may opt for what is available rather than what is most appropriate to their research question. For example, the number of corporations that testify at congressional hearings tells us something about who participated, but it says very little about the actual influence of corporations. Nevertheless, it's easy to count who testifies and one does not have to travel to Washington to conduct interviews. And since who participated does tell us something and we can build large N data sets from congressional testimony, it may be deemed "good enough" as one of many variables for a multivariate analysis.

In contrast, more in-depth analysis of public-policy making in Washington may involve interviewing participants, collecting and digesting primary documents, and tracking events over a long period of time. A common research design is to compare a small number of cases along a small number of critical variables. With a limited number of cases, the data will be presented qualitatively, and powerful generalizations are problematic in the absence of an emphatic and consistent finding. Kevin Esterling's study of the impact of expertise on congressional policy making is built around three richly detailed case studies.[4] His research was extensive and his interpretation of each convincing, but the significant variation in the impact of expertise on each of the three issues suggests caution in making generalizations. As with all such research with a limited N, the representativeness of the cases is problematic.[5] Nevertheless, Esterling's research design was appropriate, because policy expertise is not a subject that has been extensively studied by students of Congress and it is difficult to quantify the most relevant variables.

Our project works to blend some of the benefits of case-study research with benefits from quantitative analyses of large numbers of cases. While case studies can be useful because of the researcher's depth of knowledge about the policy and its history, it is always difficult to know how much should be made of insights drawn from a single case, or even a handful of cases. How typical are the cases? Would the patterns that occurred in those cases hold true in other policy decisions? On the other hand, large-scale quantitative analyses pose an opposite problem and offer a contrasting benefit. Although in most quantitative analyses there are too many cases for the researcher to know much about any individual case, the trade-off is that, with so many cases, the researcher can be better assured that the conclusions of the study are not simply the result of happenstance or an unusual issue. But many important elements about what happened and why may be missed in a large, quantitative study. Cases must be shoehorned into predetermined coding schemes, regardless of how well or poorly they fit.

We sought the detail and insight of case-study research, but combined with a large number of randomly selected cases. The combination was designed to give us insight into the patterns of the policy-making process, while ensuring that the conclusions we drew were not the result of the particular case we selected. By selecting cases randomly and selecting a large number of cases, we worked to create a more accurate picture of the way policy making works in Washington and the role of interest groups within that process.

This trade-off between quantity and depth of information per case was foremost in our minds as we planned our study. We wanted to be able to document and identify basic patterns of policy making, answering a series of complex questions about the governmental process. If the initial goals were clear, the path was still muddy. King, Keohane, and Verba point to the difficulty researchers have in determining the number of cases:

"The more the better, but how many are necessary?"[6] Although any answer to the question "how many" will be imprecise, some guidelines are useful. King, Keohane, and Verba emphasize that "the larger the fundamental variability" of the dependent variable, "the more observations must be collected."[7]

The decision to research a number of cases (ninety-eight) falling in between a large-N study and a case study also reflected an underlying belief that a powerful study of policy making had to be both quantitative and qualitative. At an intuitive level, we believed it was important to talk with participants and to learn a good deal about each case before making judgments (coding decisions) that could be quantified. As noted above, many of the questions being asked in this study are nuanced. For example, we coded each case according to what each of the competing sides was trying to accomplish. Often coding decisions had to be made whether a position promoting policy change involved just one side or two or three different options. Were those options different enough that they were really alternative solutions, or just variations on a theme? There is no way of making such an interpretation unless one is immersed in the case history and understands the issue at least to the degree that policy options could be differentiated with some sophistication.

Our initial conception was that a relatively large number of case studies would be the best design to yield convincing answers to the questions we had in mind. There was no adequate substitute for going to Washington and talking to participants working on each of the policy problems that emerged in our sample. Many issues were simply too obscure and could not be researched from afar. Not through the Library of Congress's Thomas, not through Lexis-Nexis, not through Google, not through any existing database could we have found out what was going on. Clearly, we probably would not have known that clinical social workers were lobbying to be excluded from bundled payments to skilled nursing facilities in the Medicare program unless the randomized selection process had brought this and other similar issues to our attention.

Being on the ground in Washington was crucial, but we also searched the published record. For each of our issues, we and our research assistants conducted an exhaustive search of news reports, congressional hearings, and organizational and governmental Web sites to collect publicly available information. (These documents remain available on our Web site.) And, for each interest group or corporation involved, we scoured through available databases to find out their total PAC contributions, their lobbying expenditures, their membership size, staff size, or annual corporate sales. We did this for over two thousand advocates we identified across all our issues. So we have a mix of quantitative and qualitative work here. The interviews and our sampling strategy remain, however, at the core of our research. The interviews identified policy issues that we would not have known even existed had we relied solely on published information. The interviews also provided insight into the decision-making process that is not written down in any public place. For the handful of issues that were most prominent, extensive news coverage meant that anyone could read about how insiders viewed the issue and what was going on behind the scenes. But for the majority of our issues, that information was available only in the memories and the files of the policy makers and interest-group advocates involved in the case. Even when published information was available, interview subjects often pointed us to resources we probably would not have otherwise found.

Sampling Procedures

Our Web site lists the ninety-eight issues that form the basis of our study, and these are listed in table A.1 below (at the end of this appendix). These ninety-eight issues reflect a random sample of the issues lobbyists registered with Congress were working on during the period of our study. We are confident of the representativeness of these issues because of our careful sampling procedures. Here is what we did.[8]

Congress in 1995 passed new legislation requiring organizations above a minimum level of activity in lobbying the federal government to register in each of seventy-four policy areas in which they are active, every six months. Working from microfiche copies of the 1996 reports made available to the public through the U.S. Senate Office of Public Records, Frank Baumgartner and Beth Leech compiled a database consisting of all of these reports. Groups must file a report in each separate issue area in which they are active, and in each report they must list each issue on which they were active. In total, Baumgartner and Leech identified 5,907 organizations, which collectively filed 19,692 reports and mentioned 49,518 issues.[9] The number of issues mentioned by each organization, like the number of reports filed, ranges substantially. We took advantage of this, because the number of distinct issues mentioned by a lobbyist is a good indicator of the level of activity of that organization in the lobbying process.

We treated the total number of issues mentioned as an indicator of the intensity of lobbying activity.

Gathering the data necessary to count the particular issues mentioned in almost twenty thousand reports was extremely time consuming, and, to our knowledge, such research has not been repeated in spite of the availability of the reports on the U.S. Senate Web site. Once we had these data, however, our sampling strategy was relatively straightforward: We drew a sample of lobbyists weighted by the frequency of their lobbying activity as measured by the number of issues they mentioned. Groups that filed fifteen reports mentioning fifty-six issues had fifty-six times the chance of being included in our sample compared to groups that filed only one report indicating activity on just a single issue. The result of this procedure was a sample of lobbying organizations weighted so that the odds of a group being selected at random were exactly proportional to the intensity of their lobbying activity.

The next step was to move from a sample of organizations to a sample of issues. After randomly selecting the organizations we wanted to interview, we searched through publicly available sources to identify the individual who was most likely to be aware of government relations activity; typically this was the executive director or the director of government relations. We wrote and requested an interview, and we followed up by telephone. We phoned several times in those cases when we had trouble scheduling the initial interview.

During the initial interview, our first substantive question was "Could you take the most recent issue you've been spending time on and describe what you're trying to accomplish on this issue and what type of action you are taking to make that happen?" If necessary, we noted in the follow-up discussion that we were interested only in issues dealing with the federal government, not any that might come up dealing with state, local, or other authorities. Legislative, executive, or judicial federal issues were all open. Further, we asked about what issue they were working on, not what individual federal official they were in contact with. In this way, if a group was active working on an issue, but was mostly working through contacts with other groups, this would still fall into our sample. (After all, we wanted to know the issues on which lobbyists are active; knowing which federal officials are the objects of this lobbying would follow once we had a random sample of issues that lobbyists were active on.) Finally, because we were often dealing with lobbyists who headed large offices dealing with many issues simultaneously, we were strict about limiting ourselves only to the "most recent" issue on which the organization had been active. (Many respondents wanted to discuss a "more interesting" issue that was not the most recent one; we listened politely but got the interview back to the most recent issue.) The result of this procedure, taking just one case from each lobbying organization, but weighting the sample of groups by levels of activity, is a random sample of the issues on which lobbyists are active.[10]

Political scientists must develop methodologies for drawing random samples in the study of public policy if we seek to generalize, but this is an extremely difficult research problem because there is no preexisting list or "universe" from which to draw. Indeed, it is not even clear sometimes where one issue stops and the next one begins. In our sampling procedure, we allowed the lobbyists themselves to identify the issue, and our issues therefore vary quite dramatically in size and scope (as well as in the number of others involved in them). If our initial respondent indicated that they were working on "the farm bill," then that entire bill became one of our cases. If, by contrast, that initial respondent said they were working on assuring that the peanut subsidy program be discontinued during the negotiations over the farm bill, then this smaller issue became the focus of our study. Lobbyists are sometimes involved in small parts of large issues, sometimes in the passage of the entire bill. Our sample reflects the diversity of these actions.

Our sample reflects the full range of activities dealing with the federal government that are the objects of lobbying activities. But because we weighted our initial sample of lobbyists by breadth of lobbying activity, doesn't that mean that we really have a sample of what the "big lobbyists" are interested in? In a word, no. Our sample has a double, or inverse, weighting mechanism built into it. This is because if our initial sample of lobbyists led us to interview a group with only one issue on their docket during the past twelve months, we would have discussed that one issue. On the other hand, in interviewing an organization involved in 150 issues over the past year, but picking only the most recent issue (as we did), we effectively sampled just 1 from the 150 issues that this group was involved in. For those with few issues, we sampled with high probability; for those with many issues, we sampled with low probability. That is, our initial list of lobbying organizations is directly weighted by the number of issues each group lobbied on, but the second stage is weighted by the inverse of this same factor. If in our initial sampling procedure we chose a group active on 5 issues, the chance of picking any one of those issues was 20 percent; if we picked a group active on 100 issues, the likelihood of picking any particular issue was 1 percent. The more active *group* was more likely to fall into our initial sample, but any *issue* had an equal chance of falling into our eventual list of issues. The result is an unweighted random sample of those issues on which lobbyists were active. The more lobbyists were active on the issue, of course, the more likely the issue was to fall into our sample. This is exactly what we wanted. In sum, our sample can be taken as representative of those issues dealing with the federal government that any given lobbyist may be involved in on any given day.

We contacted 173 individuals for these initial interviews and completed 98 interviews and had 75 refusals, for a 57 percent response rate. Reasons for refusals included "office policy" not to give interviews, the office having closed, scheduling problems, a preference not to talk about an issue while it was pending, and some outright refusals to identify an issue and participate in the project, even after scheduling an interview.

During each interview, we asked questions about who were the "major actors" in the issue, and we identified each distinct "side" on the issue, where a side was defined as any actor or group of actors seeking a particular policy outcome. Subsequently we made efforts to interview at least one leading player from each side (and in each of these interviews we further refined our list of actors and sides, adding new actors as we went). Typically, after two or three interviews and extensive online and documentary searching, we had a complete view of who was involved and any further interviews were of sharply diminished value. In all, we interviewed 315 individuals, an average of just over 3 per issue. Often there was more than one appropriate person who would be knowledgeable about the activities we were interested in, so if we could not schedule an interview with one, we attempted to get another person representing the same side. In this way we achieved interviews with leaders of almost every side we were interested in reaching. Thus, while our initial response rate was 57 percent, our response rate in this secondary part of the sample was 85 percent.[11]

Our sample is best thought of as a random sample of issues (with a 57 percent response rate), and then, within issues, something approaching a census, not a sample, of all the major sides on the question. In this secondary part of the interviewing process, we did not identify our respondents randomly at all. Rather, we sought one of the leading players most knowledgeable about the activities and points of view of those in each side. Table A.1 shows that, across the 98 issues, we identified 214 active sides and 2,221 major actors; we interviewed 315 individuals, at least one from each of 172 sides. (In 35 of the 42 cases where we failed to interview any members of the side, these were very small sides, with four or fewer members.

There were just 7 cases out of 214 for which we could not schedule an interview with a leading representative of the side, if the side had five or more members.)

The ninety-eight issues that constitute our sample range dramatically in size and in the level of interest that they generated in the Washington lobbying community. A modest number of issues were so small that a single interview sufficed to give us a good understanding of what was happening. (For example, in several cases, lobbyists identified an issue they were working on but indicated that it had not gone anywhere and no one else was working on it.) We could generally confirm the lack of broader activity from our documentary evidence. Just as the total number of active participants across our range of issues ranges from small to large, so does the number of interviews we conducted on each issue. This ranges from 1 to 15 with a mean of 3 (typically the number was between 2 and 4; just 6 cases had one interview, and only 14 had 5 or more interviews). Note that while most of our respondents were lobbyists working outside government, many were government officials from the executive or legislative branch. This is because in the secondary portion of our sample, we were interested in contacting leaders of each important side on the issue, and these individuals were often government officials. (This is one reason we often use the word "advocate" rather than the more restrictive "lobbyist," because lobbyists are generally understood to be acting on behalf of private- or nonprofit-sector interests outside of government. "Advocates," though, are sometimes government officials themselves attempting to sway other government officials, just as any other lobbyist would do.) Typically, we did not interview members of Congress but rather the staff member whose name was mentioned as playing a role on the issue. Our goal was to interview a leader of each major side or position on the issue. As we discuss in chapter 1, over 40 percent of all the advocates we identified were government officials, not outsiders.

Table A.1, at the end of this appendix, lists the ninety-eight issues that resulted from these procedures, short names of the various sides on the issue that we identified, the number of interviews that we conducted on the issue, and the total number of "major actors" within each side.

Interview Procedures

With only a few exceptions, our interviews during the first round were done in person in the subject's office in Washington. A small number were done over the phone when cancellations prevented one of us meeting the interviewee in Washington. The average length of the interviews was about 45 minutes, though many ran an hour or so. For each issue all interviews were conducted by a single member of the team, who also took responsibility for building on the initial interview to build a complete set of interviews on the issue.[12] The secondary interviews largely followed the same template of questions used in the first one, in which the issue was first identified. A key difference, however, was that the secondary interviewees were told at the beginning we were studying a particular issue and they had been identified as an expert on that matter. Thus, they did not choose the central topic of the interview, as was the case for issue identifiers.

At a point in the next Congress, typically around eighteen months later, each member of the research team did a follow-up interview for each of the cases they were responsible for. Because the follow-up interviews were short, with questions directed solely at updating the case, we did not feel it was necessary to travel to Washington to conduct them in person. These phone interviews took about 15 minutes, and almost all were with people we had interviewed face-to-face during the previous Congress. In a small number of instances, with cases that had a very limited number of original interviewees, we were unable to reinterview an earlier subject. More than a few times during the follow-up phase, we called and asked to speak to an individual only to be told by an icy voice that the person no longer worked there. In such instances we tried to find the person at their new job, but we did not always succeed.

All interviews were done on "background." For the uninitiated, "background" means that the scholar or journalist can use the interview responses, even quote from them, but cannot identify the source. "Background" is easily confused with "off the record." If an interview is off the record, it cannot be quoted or used in any overt manner; the information gathered by the interviewer is only for his or her own understanding of the issue. Our interviews, on background, gave subjects anonymity and the freedom to say things that were critical of other people or organizations. At the same time, we could still use the material.

On a broader level, we relied on background interviews because it eased the matter of trust. We had no prior acquaintance with any of our subjects and, when we walked into their office, it would be natural for them to be on guard. They had little idea of what we wanted or of how the information they gave us would be used. In our original letter requesting an interview and in the subsequent phone conversation scheduling an interview, we were deliberately vague about our research project.[13] After walking in cold and exchanging a few pleasantries, indicating that the interview is on background reduces the pressure on the subject to figure out what information the interviewer can be trusted with. Even on background, though, subjects surely deemed some information as proprietary or too awkward to release, and as we noted in the section on sampling above, some simply refused to participate.

Because the interviews were done on background, they cannot be released to others who might want to utilize our data. There is simply no way of maintaining any value to the transcripts if they are redacted to remove all information that could lead an informed reader to correctly identify the speaker or organization. However, we have released a wealth of information about each of our cases, and we hope that students and other scholars can re-create the vast bulk of whatever information they might like to find. It is indeed surprising how much information is publicly available. If we found information in a publicly available source, we archived it on our Web site and have quoted freely from it in this book. Only our interviews, not the rest of our research, was "on background."

Readers who examine our interview protocol (see table A.2, at the end of the appendix) will surely notice that we asked very few questions. The basic template, used for issue identifiers, has just seven questions. This limited number of formal questions written out in the protocol may be misleading, as the interviews were far richer than this brief list might suggest. The set of questions were actually designed to be entry points, with the interviewer using probes to gain more information or to move to tangential topics that might seem rewarding. The interviews were intentionally conversational in tone, and we asked the questions in a more informal way than the language on the template suggests. The template was more a reminder of all the topics we needed to cover, and we didn't even always follow the order of questions one through seven. If a subject brought up one of the topics sequenced later in the protocol, we would just deal with the matter then.

This informal, conversational approach might appear problematic. With differently worded versions of key questions, questions asked out of sequence, and a heavy reliance on unscripted probes, how do we know that subjects answered the questions with the same understanding of what was being asked? The method we used surely raises *reliability* issues. In the words of King, Keohane, and Verba, "Reliability means that applying the same procedure in the same way will always produce the same measure."[14]

There's no question that we didn't apply "the same procedure in the same way."

Every interviewing method has strengths and drawbacks. The trade-off is that, while we gave up something on reliability, we gained greater confidence in the fundamental accuracy of what we did elicit. Had we gone strictly in order, avoiding conversation between questions and wording every question exactly as written down on in the interview protocol, the result would have been shorter answers, less overall information, and, most likely, more guarded responses. The conversational tone, with our open-ended questions, encouraged respondents to tell us what *they* thought was important. Joel Aberbach and Bert Rockman note that open-ended questions allow "respondents to organize their answers within their own framework." They add, "Elites especially—but other highly educated people as well—do not like being put in the straightjacket of close-ended questions. They prefer to articulate their views, explaining why they think what they think."[15]

Still, relying on probes to push conversations in the right direction is not a foolproof approach. Jeffrey Berry has written, for example, "Open-ended questioning—the riskiest but potentially most valuable type of elite interviewing—requires interviewers to know when to probe and how to formulate follow-up questions on the fly. It's a high-wire act."[16] We did, in fact, depend on probes to push the subject gently toward topics not adequately covered or to gain more information about a matter than the interviewee volunteered. We also used probes and follow-ups to loop back to questions that were not fully answered. Probes allowed us to pursue what we hadn't anticipated but seemed fruitful. We sat in offices to learn how advocates go about their job, and in our body language, question wording, and informal, conversational style, we tried to convey that we were there to learn and the interviewee was to teach us.[17] Conversely, we tried not to communicate that we had a lot of boxes to fill in our questionnaire and that they needed to give us concise responses that fell into category A, B, or C.

Looking back at the interviews, we're convinced that our strategy paid off in lengthy, detailed answers that offered us a great deal of background and context. This better enabled us to understand these advocates' strategies, how their organizations operate, and how the policy-making process channels proposals forward or into limbo, if not into oblivion. We're also convinced that we did gather the essential information we were after: arguments, participants, coalitions, impediments, lobbying tactics, and so on.

During the interviews, we took partial notes, trying to maintain eye contact to further the conversational tone. Two of us used a tape recorder;

the others chose not to. Those who didn't use a tape recorder wrote up interviews in detail immediately after finishing them. All the interviewers organized their interview transcripts into the same template, organizing the responses by topic: who was involved, what arguments were used, who were the targets, what tactics were used, general background on the issue, and so forth. We called these "advocate summaries," and they were later used to code the data, translating the advocates' lengthy, evocative answers into electronic impulses in our computers. Our overall assessment of these interviews is that they were enormously rich both in detail and insight. As we sat in the Washington offices of hundreds of lobbyists and government officials, we found our interviewees to be wonderful teachers on the subject of policy making.

Supplemental Research

We made extensive efforts to supplement the interviews with document searches. Once our interviews were complete and we had a good sense of who was involved in the issue, we searched organizational Web sites, congressional Web sites, newspaper and TV archives, and other sources for information relating to the case. Our students followed strict protocols, working under the supervision of the person who had conducted the interviews, so that they systematically collected relevant documents from interest groups, congressional sources, executive branch agencies, and other sources. These are available on our Web site. Despite the obscurity of some of the ninety-eight issues, in virtually every case we assembled information that was already being made public through "member alerts," press releases, speeches or testimony in Congress, published regulations, or other sources, and we archived all that information on our Web site. In contrast to the confidential nature of our interviews, the information we found through these Internet searches was, of course, in the public domain, and we have quoted from it freely in this book and in other publications. Further, we archived all relevant primary legislative materials, such as the text of amendments, relevant sections of bills, testimony in hearings, speeches on the floor of the House or Senate, and other materials available through congressional sources. Where appropriate, we also searched executive branch agency Web sites and archived relevant documents, such as proposed and final regulations, comments, information sheets, and press releases. The result of this large Internet-based research effort is a fully documented set of primary source materials that allows anyone to read the full set of raw materials for our study, with the exception of the interviews themselves. In all, our Web site consists of approximately 258,000 files in almost 20,000 directories, relating to our ninety-eight issues. (We give more detail on the structure of our Web site below.)

In the years after our original interviews were conducted, we followed up on each issue by following publicly available sources to find out if relevant legislation passed, was defeated, or remained somewhere in between. We documented as best we could continuing debate on the issue, sometimes including contacting those who were involved for a follow-up interview. For congressional issues, we paid attention to what happened at the end of the two-year Congress in which the issue was discussed, coding its "initial outcome" and then again two years later to assess the "subsequent outcome" of the case. For administrative or regulatory issues, we followed a similar process, attempting to know what happened to the issue in the short term as well as in the longer term.

We gathered extensive information about each of the advocates we identified. If they were government officials, we noted their organization type (congressional leadership, committee staff, department or agency staff, White House staff), their partisanship, and so forth. For interest groups, we used publicly available sources such as the *Encyclopedia of Associations* and their own Web sites to gather information about their membership size, budget, and staff size; we also looked at publicly available summaries of IRS tax forms (form 990) for all nonprofit organizations that fell into our sample to gain information about their budget and assets. For corporations, we used Fortune.com and Hoovers.com as well as other Internet-based resources to gather similar information about overall size and resources, annual revenues, number of employees, and so on. We used the Lobbying Disclosure Reports available at the U.S. Senate Web site to gather information on lobbying expenditures for each of those identified as a major participant in our cases as well as the FEC Web site to gather information about their PAC contributions. In all, we were able to gather tremendous amounts of information about the vast majority of those identified as major actors in each of our cases, and we did so systematically.

Variables and Measures

We have taken pains to be as systematic as possible in defining an issue, an advocate, a side, and several other key analytic concepts that we use throughout this book. Here is a list of definitions.

ISSUE. From the initial interview, we took whatever the respondent described as the issue on which they had most recently been active. Note that some issues are extremely broad and some are defined narrowly.

MAJOR PARTICIPANT. During each interview, we asked who were the most important actors involved in the debate. We also used our Internet searching and documentary sources to identify the complete list for each issue of who was involved. Obviously, the distinction between a major and a less-important participant is somewhat of a judgment call. Our judgment was based on whether other advocates and policy makers involved in the same issue considered that the person or organization played an important role. Further, though we did occasionally identify what we call a neutral decision maker (we interviewed some of these individuals, because they were often good sources of information), we focused equally on governmental and nongovernmental actors in identifying major participants, and we found that government officials themselves constituted about 40 percent of the policy advocates; rare is the truly neutral government official involved in the policy process, outside of technical agencies of Congress and the executive branch.

SIDES. We define a policy side as an actor or a group of actors attempting to achieve the same policy outcome. Note that these advocates may or may not be working together as part of a coalition. Typically, however, most of the members of a given side do indeed coordinate their efforts informally or through a formal coalition. Sides include anyone attempting to promote the same goal, whether those advocates are within or outside of government. So a side may include private corporate actors, lobbyists, trade groups, executive branch officials, members of Congress, or even the president himself. While members of a given side typically work together, there may be important advocates working to achieve the same goal but with no coordination or even communication with the others. For us, then, a side is broader than a coalition. It includes anyone playing a significant role in the policy process who is actively attempting to achieve a given goal. The distinct goals that various policy advocates are attempting to reach on an issue define the sides associated with that issue. With this definition of a side in place, we can summarize the structure of conflict across our cases easily by noting the number of distinct sides in each case. Across our ninety-eight issues, we identified 214 distinct sides, or just over two per case, on average. Table A.1 lists these sides by issue.

ARGUMENTS.   During our interviews, we asked advocates, "So you're talking to these various people about why it's necessary to move forward on this issue [or, if relevant, why it's necessary to prevent something from happening, etc.]. What's the fundamental argument you use to try to convince people to do this?"

Our objective in coding the policy arguments advocates used was to distinguish them by their type (e.g., cost, implementation). Thus, we needed to define what constitutes an argument, so that only arguments and not descriptive statements, historical background, or other comments about the issue were coded. For our purposes, an argument is a statement that links a policy goal with either a justification for the policy or a discussion of its implications. In some cases, the linkage between the goal and the justification or implication is not explicit but can be gleaned from the context of the overall interview discussion. For a statement to be considered an argument, the policy consequences or rationale must at least be implicit in the discussion.

With this definition in hand, two coders independently read all of the interview summaries available for an issue. These coders highlighted any arguments they encountered in the summaries, distinguishing arguments offered by the advocate being interviewed from those arguments that were presented as being made by others interested in the issue.[18] Once all the arguments were identified, the coders (again acting independently) assigned each one to a "type" category, and any disagreements were worked out with one of the lead authors. We defined fourteen types of arguments, each with between two and six subtypes. These argument types are presented in table A.3, at the end of the appendix. The types are intended to describe, generally, the content of the appeal. The subtypes also distinguish systematically between positive and negative assessments so that we can observe the degree to which advocates directly contradict each other, raising opposite arguments along the same dimensions, or instead speak about different elements of the debate altogether, without necessarily engaging directly in a contradictory debate with their rivals.

TACTICS.   Respondents were asked to describe the actions they were taking to accomplish their objectives on an issue. With the responses to this question, and a series of follow-up probes, we documented as completely as possible the range of tactics that were used by advocates on a particular issue. Thirty-one categories of activities (plus one category for "other activities mentioned") were identified through prior research and a preliminary review of the interview summaries. One coder read through each interview summary to identify whether a tactic was undertaken by members of the side in which the advocate participated. Table 8.1 gives complete frequencies of use for each tactic that was reported by more than 10 percent of our respondents.

INTENT. For every issue side that we identified, we determined whether the side supported or opposed the status quo policy. The status quo was defined in one of two ways, depending on whether the policy issue in question was legislative or regulatory. The status quo for legislative matters was defined as the policy in existence prior to the start of the session of Congress in which the issue was identified. For regulatory issues, the status quo was represented by the policy in place at the start of the calendar year in which the issue was identified. Sides that sought to change the status quo policy—regardless of whether or not they proposed a clear alternative to it—were classified as status quo challengers. Overall, 81 (38 percent) of our sides are status quo supporters and 133 (62 percent) are challengers, as reported in the note to table 3.2.

MAGNITUDE AND TYPE OF POLICY CHANGE. Based on the information gathered through the interviews, each side was coded for whether it favored a proposal that would increase spending, decrease spending, maintain current spending, or have no implications for (1) the federal budget, (2) state and local governments, and (3) nongovernmental actors. We also assessed whether or not the issue dealt with an existing federal government program and, if so, whether their goal would involve abolishing, substantially reducing, marginally reducing, marginally expanding, substantially expanding, or maintaining the status quo. Table 6.1 summarizes the frequencies we observed.

ISSUE SALIENCE. In addition to the interviews we conducted, we searched for a wide array of publicly available information about each issue. Using a set of keywords developed for each issue, we gathered relevant print (major newspapers as well as the *National Journal*) and television news stories, information about congressional activity (bills, hearings, testimony, committee reports, member speeches, and Web-site postings), information about executive branch activities (regulations or proposed regulations), and materials posted by organizational advocates on their Web sites (e.g., press releases, reports).[19] We then created two standardized scales using Stata's "factor" command. The scale indicating "general sa-lience" is based on counts of congressional bills, congressional hearings, witness testimony at congressional hearings, documents and statements found on House members' Web sites, documents and statements found on the Senate Web site, floor statements, *National Journal* stories, news-paper stories, and television news stories (the index reliability score is .843). A scale designed to tap "inside the Beltway salience" does not in-clude the counts for newspaper and television news stories (the index reliability score is .830).

RESOURCES MEASURES AND DEALING WITH MISSING DATA VALUES.   Our analysis of group resources in chapters 10 and 11 makes use of twenty-one different measures of resources. Seven of these measures, collected from publicly available sources such as *Associations Unlimited* and Dun & Bradstreet's Million Dollar Database, suffered from high levels of miss-ing data, ranging from 14 percent to 50 percent missing. Simply ignoring the missing values and analyzing only the data that these research organi-zations collected would introduce selection bias into our analyses—only the type of organization that was likely to answer requests for information from the research companies would be reflected in our analyses. We thus used Amelia II software to impute these missing values.[20] For nonprofit organizations, we used missing data analysis on variables for membership size, organizational income, organizational assets, and number of staff members. For businesses, we used missing data analysis on variables for sales, net income, and number of employees. The variables created through this process were in turn used for our indices of association resources and business resources. Thus, we have thirteen measures of resources that have virtually no missing observations from the start and nine measures of resources with missing values imputed using Amelia II.

For the variables that are estimated using multiple imputation, Amelia II estimates (imputes) values for each missing cell in the data matrix and does this multiple times, creating multiple finished data sets. We estimated five parallel data sets, as recommended by King and his coauthors. Across these data sets, the observed values are the same, but the missing values are filled in with different estimates of the probable values of that missing data, with the estimates based on the observed values from similar cases. The variation that is seen across the five data sets reflects the uncertainty about the missing data. All five data sets are analyzed at once. (We used Stata and Clarify to do this.)[21]

The findings we report are robust. Whether we look only at those variables for which we have virtually no missing data (e.g., lobbying expenditures and related measures of lobbying activity, PAC donations, government allies, and Power 25 allies) or whether we look at the variables with missing values imputed, the conclusion is the same: higher levels of resources are not correlated with greater chances of success on an issue. If we rerun these analyses using the variables in their original form—without the imputed missing values—we have very similar findings, as well. While the imputed data that fill in for our missing values in some variables help us reach the most accurate parameter estimates, our results do not rely on those imputations.

Making the Most of Our Web Site

It should be obvious that our project involves much more than can be reported in this single publication. In fact, our Web site by itself constitutes a tremendous resource for research and teaching about American government, public policy, and lobbying, and we hope that all readers of this book will make extensive use of it to find out more about individual cases or just to get a "feel" for the substance of the complex issues on which we have based our study. The Web site is not just a depository for the data associated with this project, but rather, it is a window onto the process of lobbying, policy making, advocacy, and the U.S. government in general. Our issues range from defense matters to tax issues to health care reform to criminal justice to workplace safety to the environment; they cover the full range of activities of the federal government. Each of the ninety-eight issues we have studied is fully documented. By clicking on "Our Sample of Issues," one first sees the list of issues. Clicking on any one of those issues takes the user to a general overview of the issue. This is a short case history which we wrote based on our interviews and other materials that explains in general what the issue is about. At the left are a series of links, consistently defined and identical for each of our ninety-eight issues. These break out the supplemental information we have found into these categories:

1. Agency Activities (covering all federal executive agencies which may have been active on the issue).
2. Bill Information (copies of legislative texts related to the issue).

3. Committee Hearings (copies of abstracts and records of each hearing).
4. Congressional Statements (copies of statements from the *Congressional Record* or from the Web sites of representatives and senators, typically including their floor speeches or press releases on the issue).
5. News Stories (copies of articles from newspapers around the country on the issue).
6. Organizational Statements (what we have found on the Web sites of the organizations outside of government interested in the issue).
7. Television News (records of TV news stories on the issue, from the Vanderbilt Archive).

For each issue, in each of these categories, we provide original source documents as well as a record of where the document was originally found. Depending on the issue, there may be no relevant documents (e.g., Agency Activities for an issue that involves only a legislative proposal with no executive branch actions), or there may be hundreds of documents from many different sources (e.g., The Patient's Bill of Rights in the 106th Congress, in which we listed over fifty different interest groups, some of which had scores of relevant documents on their Web sites). The range of materials is striking and gives a feel for the range of what a member of Congress might be confronted with in any given period. Some issues clearly raise few eyebrows, whereas others become the objects of massive mobilizations by groups on many sides. This is all reflected in the number of documents on our site. Table A.4, at the end of this appendix, gives a sense of what is there.

Because of the comprehensive nature of our searches, readers can access a wealth of information on our various issues. Not only can they read the actual text of the various bills and amendments that may have been discussed in Congress, but they can see copies of press releases and "member alerts" sometimes from dozens of interested lobbying organizations. If the issue received any news coverage, the articles are available here. In sum, between our overview, which organizes the bulk of the information and explains how the case compares to others, and these primary materials, users can obtain a great range of information. And because our sample of issues is random, the Web site itself gives a generalizable picture of the workings of the U.S. government on any given day.

We have organized the site so that issues from the 106th Congress (the last two years of the second Clinton administration) are listed separately from those in the 107th Congress (the first two years of the first George

W. Bush administration). What changed? What types of issues were the objects of lobbying? What kinds of actors were involved? What types of arguments did they use? All these questions can be answered by anyone interested in systematically reading through the information we have made available. We look forward to seeing published analyses from people not involved in our project but who access its resources over the Web in the future. Further, we hope that the project will be useful for teaching courses on U.S. government, public policy, congressional processes, and lobbying.

Replicability and Future Research

We encourage others to build on the research that we have done, both for the U.S. federal government as well as in other political systems. Tremendous amounts of information are available from organizational Web sites, congressional sites, federal agencies, and public news sources, and these are freely downloadable (but most of these must be archived if one wants them to remain available in the future). However, this does not mean one can simply go to Google.com and conduct a complete research project. Limiting one's research only to highly salient issues would replicate many of the problems we have noted in the history of the study of lobbying. But clearly, the Internet and the tendency of so many interest groups to post information about the issues of public policy that concern them have made possible new opportunities in political science research. These must be used with care and do not substitute for the need to conduct in-person interview-based research. However, they can be invaluable, as we hope to have shown, in documenting and illustrating the substance of what these debates are about.

TABLE A.1 **Issues, Sides, Major Participants, and Interviews**

Issue and sides	Major Participants	Interviews
1. Managed care reform		
1 Supports a patient's bill of rights	54	11
2 Opposes a patient's bill of rights that contains employer mandates	19	4
2. Patent extension		
1 Supports granting patent extension to pipeline drugs	8	1
2 Opposes granting patent extension to pipeline drugs	15	2
3. Infant hearing screening		
1 Supports funding hearing screenings on newborn infants	29	3
4. Risk adjuster for Medicare+Choice		
1 Supports imposing a risk adjuster to limit overpayments (opposes 3, 4)	2	0
3 Opposes imposing a risk adjuster as currently envisioned by the Health Care Financing Administration (opposes 1, 5)	14	1
4 Opposes imposing a risk adjuster but believe there are bigger Medicare+Choice problems to address (opposes 1, 5)	5	1
5 Supports the idea of a risk adjuster but believe there are bigger Medicare+Choice problems to address (opposes 3, 4)	4	1
9 Neutral parties providing technical assistance	4	2
99 Unknown/missing data	3	0
5. Pap Smear screenings for cervical cancer		
1 Supports increased Medicare payments for Pap smear screenings	13	3
2 Opposes changing status quo	1	0
9 Neutral/no position	1	0
6. Coverage parity		
1 Supports coverage parity for the treatment of mental illness under Medicare (and generally)	29	4
9 Neutral	1	0
7. Clinical social workers		
1 Supports excluding CSWs from the bundled payment rules for Medicare	5	4
9 Neutral/no position	1	0
8. Appropriations for the AIDS Drug Assistance Program		
1 Supports funding ADAP at the level of ADAP Working Group estimate	38	4
2 Supports funding ADAP but not necessarily at the level of ADAP Working Group estimate	1	0

10. Providing health insurance for the uninsured

1	Supports a refundable tax credit for individuals (between 100 and 150 percent of poverty) that is large enough to purchase health insurance coverage (no direct opponents)	12	1
2	Supports refundable tax credits for individuals (who work but lack insurance) that would not cover the full cost of health coverage (no direct opponents)	3	0
3	Supports income-related refundable tax credits for everyone to purchase health insurance (no direct opponents)	4	1
4	Supports single-payer, universal health insurance coverage (no direct opponents)	2	1
9	Neutral/no position	3	0
99	Unknown/missing data	2	0

11. Funding of graduate medical education (GME)

1	Supports maintaining or increasing funding for specific segments of the allied health professions either through the status quo or other funding plan (no direct opponents)	7	3
2	Supports changing the rationale/conceptualization of GME from training to enhanced patient care but still funding GME through the status quo funding mechanism (opposes 3, 4)	1	1
3	Supports an all-payer (or Medicare and all-payer) trust fund to support GME (opposes 2, 4)	9	3
4	Supports funding GME through an annual appropriation from general revenues (opposes 2, 3)	4	0

12. Chiropractic coverage under Medicare

1	Supports coverage of chiropractic services	8	2
2	Opposes changing regulations to include chiropractic services	1	0

13. Contraceptive coverage

1	Supports mandating contraceptive coverage by insurance companies	18	4
2	Opposes mandating contraceptive coverage by insurance companies	9	0

14. Medicare coverage of medical devices

1	Supports revising Medicare coverage policies (for procedures, devices, etc.) to increase physician input (no direct opponents)	5	1
2	Supports revising the Medicare review process for assessing coverage of medical devices, imposing noncost review criteria, and instituting an appeals process (opposes 3)	9	2
3	Supports imposing a cost-related criteria for the Medicare coverage reviews of medical devices (opposes 2)	2	0
9	Neutral/no position	2	0

15. Disinfectant by-products

1	Supports regulations requiring water utilities to decrease disinfectant by-products in drinking water (opposes 2, 3)	8	1
2	Opposes significantly decreasing disinfectant by-product levels in drinking water; opposes switching to alternative (nonchlorine) disinfectants (opposes 1, 3)	1	1

TABLE A.I *continued*

Issue and sides	Major Participants	Interviews
3 Supports minimizing disinfectant by-product levels; opposes major changes in treatment or disinfectant technology (opposes 1, 2)	7	1
9 Neutral/no position	1	1
99 Unknown/missing data	3	0
16. Funding for CH-47 helicopters for the Army		
1 Supports increased funding for the CH-47 Chinook helicopter	11	1
17. Mine waste disposal		
1 Supports limiting the number of mill sites at mine sites	15	1
2 Opposes limiting the number of mill sites at mine sites	12	2
19. Broadband deployment		
1 Supports revising the 1996 Telecommunications Act to give regional/local phone companies access to other service markets without their opening access to the local service market (opposes 2)	14	0
2 Opposes revising the 1996 Telecommunications Act (opposes 1)	23	2
3 Position on 1996 Telecommunications Act unclear; supports policies designed to encourage deployment of broadband (no direct opponents)	3	0
9 Neutral/no opinion	2	0
99 Unknown/missing data	1	0
20. Compulsory licensing of drugs to treat AIDS and a tax credit for AIDS vaccine research and development		
1 Supports vaccine R&D tax credit; opposes compulsory licensing provision/executive order (opposes 2, 4)	8	3
2 Supports vaccine R&D tax credit; supports compulsory licensing provision/executive order (opposes 1)	1	0
3 Supports vaccine R&D credit; no formal or known position on compulsory licensing provision/executive order (no direct opponents)	20	2
4 Supports compulsory licensing provision/executive order; no formal or known position on the vaccine R&D tax credit (opposes 1)	13	1
99 Unknown/missing data	1	0
21. Postal service reform		
1 Supports modernizing the postal service (opposes 2, 3)	25	2
2 Opposes modernizing the postal service (opposes 1)	7	0
3 Supports modernizing the postal service in theory, but refuses to allow the proposal of perspective 1 to move forward (opposes 1)	1	0

Item		
22. Modifying the Food Quality Protection Act (FQPA)		
1 Supports modifying the FQPA of 1996 in a way that further regulates how and when the EPA releases and presents safety information about chemicals used in food preparation & production	18	2
2 Opposes modifying the FQPA of 1996.	6	1
23. CAFE standards		
1 Supports increasing the Corporate Average Fuel Economy standards for light trucks and vans	12	0
2 Opposes increasing the standards	15	2
9 Neutral/no position	1	0
24. Low-sulfur gasoline		
1 Supports EPA's proposed air-quality regulations limiting the amount of sulfur in gasoline	14	2
2 Opposes the low-sulfur regulations	4	1
25. Low-power FM licenses		
1 Supports granting low-power FM radio licenses	16	3
2 Opposes granting low-power FM radio licenses	12	2
27. Estate tax		
1 Supports repealing the estate tax (opposes 2)	19	3
2 Opposes repealing the estate tax (opposes 1)	3	1
3 Advocates various alterations to the tax, not repeal (not opposed to 1 or 2)	2	0
28. Government pension offset and the windfall elimination provision		
1 Supports repealing or reducing the government pension offset and windfall elimination provision for retired government workers.	21	2
29. Conservation and Reinvestment Act		
1 Supports permanent and mandatory funding of conservation programs via CARA/Lands Legacy Initiative with restrictions on how coastal impact funds are used (opposes 2, 4)	5	1
2 Supports permanent and mandatory funding of conservation programs via CARA/Lands Legacy Initiative but with no restrictions on how coastal impact funds are used (opposes 1, 4)	4	0
3 Supports permanent and mandatory funding of conservation programs via CARA/Lands Legacy Initiative, generally (opposes 4)	14	1
4 Opposes permanent and mandatory funding of conservations programs via CARA/Lands Legacy Initiative (opposes 1, 2, 3)	1	0
40. China trade (permanent normal trade relations)		
1 Supports permanent normal trade relations with China	16	2
2 Opposes permanent normal trade relations with China	15	4

TABLE A.1 *continued*

Issue and sides	Major Participants	Interviews
41. Defense line item		
1 For	5	2
2 Against	2	0
42. Predator control		
1 Supports ending funding for federal control of predators on private lands	15	2
2 Opposes ending funding for federal control of predators on private lands	25	1
43. Excise tax on telecommunications		
1 Supports ending the 3 percent excise tax on telephone and cable bills	16	4
9 Neutral/no position	2	0
44. Regulation of Internet prescriptions		
1 Supports developing increased regulations for Internet prescriptions (opposes 4, 5)	4	2
2 Supports increased federal regulations for Internet prescriptions—disclosure only of pharmacy licensing sought (opposes 4, 5)	1	0
3 Supports increased federal regulations for Internet prescriptions—FDA licensing of Internet pharmacies sought (opposes 4, 5)	1	0
4 Opposes increased federal regulations for Internet prescriptions—it is a state issue and additional state laws are needed (opposes 1, 2, 3)	2	0
5 Opposes increased federal regulations for Internet prescriptions—existing laws need to be better enforced and voluntary efforts encouraged (opposes 1, 2, 3)	9	1
6 Agrees illegal prescriptions are a problem, but wants to make clear that their companies are not to blame. Wants to ensure that any new regulations don't hurt business. Wants better enforcement of existing laws but vague on what other solutions are needed (no direct opponents)	5	1
7 Wants better patient education about Internet prescriptions, but is neutral regarding how this is done (no direct opponents)	1	0
9 Neutral	6	0
45. Credit union membership		
1 Supports making it easier to have broad credit union membership	3	2
2 Opposes making it easier to have broad credit union membership	3	1
46. Bankruptcy reform		
1 Supports bankruptcy reform legislation	17	2
2 Opposes bankruptcy reform legislation	4	0

9 Neutral— provider of statistics and other information	1	0

47. Needlestick injuries

1 Supports a federal law requiring OSHA to draft a regulation requiring hospitals to use "safe" needles so that needlesticks are avoided.	13	2
2 Opposes a federal law requiring OSHA to draft a regulation requiring hospitals to use "safe" needles so that needlesticks are avoided.	2	1
9 Neutral	2	1

48. Commuter rail subsidies

1 Supports forcing commercial railroads to give favored treatment to all commuter rail authorities throughout the country.	11	2
2 Opposes giving favored treatment to commuter rail other than Amtrak.	2	1

49. Criminal justice reform

1 Supports changes to the criminal justice system	7	2

50. Electric utility deregulation

1 Private utilities, which want to minimize the capital gains taxes for selling off part of their businesses as part of deregulation/restructuring; want to minimize the benefits public power receives, since they are in competition now.	2	1
2 Public power, which wants greater control over how bond money can be used; supports tax breaks for private utilities only if the spun-off electrical generation is sold to a public entity.	11	1
9 Neutral/no position. Supported the two groups coming to some agreement.	4	0

51. Nuclear waste disposal appropriations

1 Supports releasing funds that Congress has already collected from nuclear power plants to pay for developing a permanent disposal site.	3	1
2 Opposes releasing the funds.	5	0

60. Aviation trust fund

1 Supports requiring that money collected from airline tickets and other fees for an aviation trust fund be spent completely on aviation and not on unrelated projects.	8	3
2 Opposes changing status quo	2	0
9 Neutral/no position	2	0

61. Reauthorization of the Elementary and Secondary Education Act (ESEA), Title I

1 Supports reauthorization of ESEA, Title 1, which provides funding for school programs (no direct opponents)	11	2
2 Supports funding through a block grant (opposes 3)	1	1
3 Supports funding through categorical grants (opposes 2)	1	1

TABLE A.1 *continued*

Issue and sides	Major Participants	Interviews
62. Ergonomics standards		
1 Supports ergonomic regulations for U.S. employers	3	1
2 Opposes ergonomic regulations	10	2
9 Neutral/no position	2	0
63. Individuals with Disabilities Education Act (IDEA)		
1 Supports IDEA with full mainstreaming, access (no direct opponents)	10	2
2 Supports IDEA, general (no direct opponents)	2	0
3 Supports strengthening of rights to discipline kids (no direct opponents)	3	0
4 Wants greater funding of special education to help schools (no direct opponents)	4	1
64. Legal Services Corporation		
1 Supports funding for the Legal Services Corporation	7	2
2 Opposes funding for the Legal Services Corporation	4	0
65. Religious licenses		
1 Supports providing educational broadcast licenses to religious organizations rather than more expensive standard licenses	9	1
2 Opposes providing educational broadcast licenses to religious organizations rather than more expensive standard licenses	11	2
66. Creating a repository for spent nuclear fuel		
1 Supports locating the repository in Yucca Mountain, NV	1	1
2 Opposes locating the repository in Yucca Mountain	7	1
9 Neutral/no position	1	0
67. Rise in gasoline prices		
1 Opposes government intervention to lower gas prices (opposes 2)	2	2
2 Supports increasing Corporate Average Fuel Economy standards (opposes 1, 3)	3	0
3 Opposes increasing CAFE standards (opposes 2)	2	1
9 Neutral/no position	1	0
99 Unknown/missing data	3	0
68. Roads in National Forests		
1 Supports a moratorium on new road building in national forests (opposes 2)	13	3
2 Supports status quo, allowing new road building in national forests (opposes 1)	3	1
3 Wants access to forest roads maintained (no direct opponents)	3	1

69. WTO membership
   1   Supports renewed membership in the World Trade Organization   5   1
   2   Opposes renewed membership in the WTO   2   0

70. Airline merger
   1   Supports US Airways–United Airlines merger   5   1
   2   Opposes US Airways–United Airlines merger   5   2
   9   Neutral/no position   1   0

80. Internet sales tax
   1   Wants to allow states to collect sales taxes on purchases over the Internet   23   4
   2   Opposes any taxation of Internet commerce   11   2
   99   Unknown/missing data   1   0

81. Physician antitrust waivers
   1   Supports exempting health care professionals from antitrust laws   4   2
   2   Opposes exempting health care professionals from antitrust laws   17   4

82. Interest expense rules
   1   Supports changing the tax treatment of interest expenses for foreign subsidiaries of U.S. companies   9   1

83. Class-action reform
   1   Supports changing class-action law so that more cases are heard in federal court rather than state courts   20   3
   2   Opposes changing class-action law so that more cases are heard in federal court   10   1
   99   Unknown/missing data   3   0

84. Prevailing wage rules
   1   Wants to maintain prevailing wage laws like the Davis-Bacon Act   9   3
   2   Wants to move toward repeal of the Davis-Bacon Act   9   1
   9   Neutral/no position   1   0

85. Computer depreciation
   1   Wants to reduce the depreciation period for computer equipment, allowing more rapid tax deductions (opposes 2)   7   3
   2   Opposes changes in depreciation because of loss of federal revenue (opposes 1, 3)   2   0
   3   Wants to overhaul depreciation schedules for all industries (opposes 2)   1   0

86. Right to carry
   1   Favors bills that would broaden gun-rights laws and allow citizens to carry concealed weapons (opposes 2, 3, 4)   4   0
   2   Wants to allow off-duty and retired police officers to carry a concealed gun (opposes 1, 3)   9   2

TABLE A.1 *continued*

Issue and sides	Major Participants	Interviews
3 Opposes right-to-carry law for officers (opposes 1, 2)	5	0
4 Favors gun control but neutral on right-to-carry for police officers (opposes 1)	1	0
87. Late-term abortions		
1 Opposes a ban on late-term abortions	13	1
2 Supports a ban on late-term abortions	6	0
90. Export controls		
1 Opposes export controls on high-speed computers as an unnecessary constraint on the industry	10	3
2 Supports computer export controls as a national security necessity	10	0
91. Airline age 60 rule		
1 Opposes raising mandatory retirement at 60 rule for commercial airline pilots	5	1
2 Supports raising mandatory retirement at 60 rule for commercial airline pilots	13	1
92. C-130 procurement		
1 Opposes procuring new C-130 aircraft	2	1
2 Supports procuring new C-130 aircraft	13	3
93. On-board diagnostic (OBD) service		
1 Supports new regulations governing OBD systems in vehicles that would require manufacturers to share information about OBD	18	4
2 Opposes the new regulations	3	2
94. Right to know		
1 Opposes an amendment to the No Child Left Behind Act that would require parental consent for nonemergency health services in schools	29	2
2 Supports requiring parental consent	11	1
9 Neutral/no position	2	0
95. Cuba sanctions		
1 Supports complete repeal of trade sanctions with Cuba (opposes 3)	18	1
2 Supports partial repeal of trade sanctions with Cuba for food and medicine (opposes 3)	3	0
3 Opposes repeal of trade sanctions with Cuba (opposes 1, 2)	17	2
96. Newspaper crossownership		
1 Supports a new rule to allow newspapers and TV stations to be owned by the same company, in the same market	8	2

2	Opposes a new rule to allow newspapers and TV stations to be owned by the same company, in the same market	7	1
9	Neutral—FCC given rule-making authority in 1996 Communications Act	2	1
97. Steel safeguard		
1	Supports steel-safeguard investigation into possible instances of foreign companies "dumping" steel on the U.S. market; supports increased tariffs	13	2
2	Opposes steel-safeguard investigation and tariffs	1	1
9	Neutral—ITC investigating by presidential order	3	0
100. NAFTA foreign investment reform		
1	Supports renegotiating chapter 11 of the North American Free Trade Agreement to provide greater protection for state and local autonomy	8	1
2	Opposes renegotiating chapter 11 of NAFTA	5	1
101. Medicare prescription drug coverage		
1	Supports new Medicare prescription drug coverage, to be administered by private insurance companies (that would not institute price controls) (opposes 2)	34	1
2	Supports new Medicare prescription drug coverage, to be administered by HCFA/state Medicare agencies (that would have authority to institute price controls) (opposes 1)	30	1
3	Supports new Medicare prescription drug coverage, with concerns about solvency of overall Medicare program—service providers do not want to lose income source to new program (no direct opponents)	1	1
99	Unknown/missing data	7	0
102. Terrorism Reinsurance		
1	Opposes creating a terrorism reinsurance program to provide federal support for the reinsurance industry in case of terrorist attack and to allow class-action lawsuits related to such attacks to be heard in federal court	6	1
2	Supports creating a terrorism reinsurance program	9	1
103. Outsourcing reform		
1	Supports existing government contract practices involving outsourcing of government jobs	8	1
2	Opposes existing government contract practices; supports Truthfulness, Responsibility, and Accountability in Contracting Act	22	2
104. Military property movement		
1	Supports retaining the existing policies for military personnel moving and storage services	6	1
2	Opposes existing policies; want relocation services companies to be able to compete for military personnel moving and storage services	9	1

TABLE A.1 *continued*

Issue and sides	Major Participants	Interviews
105. Predatory lending		
1 Supports reforming the Real Estate Settlement Procedures Act, requiring more disclosure of fees/costs; opposes "bundling" realty/mortgage services	11	2
2 Supports reforming RESPA by "bundling" realty/mortgage services	10	1
9 Neutral/no position	3	0
106. Open Access 2		
1 Supports requiring owners of broadband infrastructure to give access to Internet service providers/other media	5	2
2 Opposes requiring owners of broadband infrastructure to give access to Internet service providers/other media	11	1
107. Maritime Security Act		
1 Supports reauthorizing and providing funding for the Maritime Security Fleet	12	1
108. Food allergen labeling		
1 Supports existing voluntary food allergen labeling	5	1
2 Opposes existing voluntary food allergen labeling	6	1
109. Bear protection		
1 Supports prohibiting trade of black bear viscera	7	1
2 Opposes prohibiting trade of black bear viscera	11	1
110. TANF employment training services		
1 Supports increasing the amount of vocational education training allowed under the Temporary Assistance for Needy Families program	24	2
2 Opposes increasing the amount of vocational education training allowed under TANF	6	1
9 Neutral/no position	2	0
115. Derivatives		
1 Supports Securities and Exchange Commission regulation of over-the-counter derivatives	12	1
2 Opposes SEC regulations of over-the-counter derivatives	16	2
116. Funding for water infrastructure loans		
1 Supports increasing funding for water infrastructure through state revolving funds	10	2
2 Opposes funding water infrastructure through federal funds	7	1
99 Unknown/missing data	5	0

Item		First	Second
117. Effluent limitation			
1	Opposes strict EPA regulations on effluent limitations for transportation equipment cleaning	7	1
9	Neutral/no position	2	1
118. Optometric funding			
1	Supports graduate medical clinical education training for optometry	2	2
9	Neutral/no position	1	0
119. Student visas and lab security			
1	Supports stricter regulations concerning national security and terrorism	28	4
2	Opposes strict regulation; supports moderate regulations concerning foreign students or laboratory security	12	1
9	Neutral/no position	12	0
120. Disabled TANF			
1	Supports special measures to aid disabled recipients of Temporary Aid to Needy Families (more moderate time requirements, lower maximum number of work hours, and including treatment time and care of disabled individuals as working hours)	22	3
9	Neutral/no position	3	0
121. Human cloning			
1	Supports a ban on all forms of human cloning	20	3
2	Opposes a ban on all forms of human cloning (but may support ban on reproductive cloning specifically)	16	2
122. EA-6B Prowler			
1	Supports increased funding of development and research for an alternative to the Electronic Attack aircraft—the EA-6B Prowler	11	2
123. Farm bill			
1	Supports price supports (opposes 2, 3)	37	2
2	Opposes price supports (opposes 1, 3)	12	2
3	Supports provisions protecting smaller (alternative) farmers (opposes 1, 2)	1	0
4	Supports environmental and animal welfare provisions within farm bill (no direct opponents)	25	1
124. Wind energy			
1	Supports renewing the tax credit for producers of wind energy	22	3
2	Opposes renewing the tax credit for producers of wind energy	1	0
125. Smart growth and transportation			
1	Supports funding "SMART" transportation programs in the transportation reauthorization	19	3
2	Supports funding all, and especially large, transportation programs	14	2

TABLE A.1 *continued*

Issue and sides	Major Participants	Interviews
126. Corporate Average Fuel Economy standards 2		
1 Supports increased CAFE standards	22	2
2 Opposes increased CAFE standards	17	1
127. Basic education funding for developing countries		
1 Supports increasing funding for international basic education programs	17	3
128. Public Utilities Regulatory Provisions Act		
1 Supports maintaining PURPA protections for cogeneration facilities	28	2
2 Opposes maintaining PURPA protections for cogeneration facilities	4	1
129. Recreational Marine Employment Act		
1 Supports excluding recreational marine facilities from longshoreman insurance requirements	10	2
9 Neutral/no position	1	0
130. Housing aid eligibility for federal public safety officers		
1 Supports extending eligibility for the Housing Affordability for America Act's federal housing programs to federal public safety officers	3	2
9 Neutral/no position	1	0
131. FERC regulation of affiliate relationships		
1 Supports proposed Federal Energy Regulatory Commission regulation of affiliate relationships between members of corporate families, in both the natural gas and electricity industries (opposes 2)	5	1
2 Opposes increasing regulation of affiliate relationships between members of corporate families, in both the natural gas and electricity industries (opposes 1)	9	2
3 Not opposed to all aspects of the FERC regulations, but seeking a special exemption (no direct opponents)	1	1
132. Math/science funding		
1 Supports increasing funding for math and science partnerships program, regardless of government body overseeing the program (no direct opponents)	46	2
2 Supports increasing funding for Department of Education's math and science partnerships program (opposes 3)	1	0
3 Supports increasing funding for NSF math and science program (opposes 2)	2	1
133. Cystic fibrosis research		
1 Supports increasing funding for Cystic Fibrosis Clinical Trials Network	4	1
9 Neutral/no position	2	1

134. Stock option expensing

  1 Supports requiring companies to report stock options on their end-of-year financial statements; to expense them, not just to footnote them   10   1

  2 Opposes requiring companies to report stock options as an expense on end-of-year financial statements   18   2

135. Title IX

  1 Supports efforts to revise the application of Title IX regulations to athletics   10   1

  2 Opposes efforts to revise the application of Title IX regulations to athletics   14   1

  9 Neutral/no position   1   0

136. Aviation security

  1 Supports giving the airlines compensation for enhanced security efforts, access to carrying the mail, access to war risk insurance at capped prices, and more time to implement security deadlines; opposes allowing pilots to carry guns on planes and requiring self-defense training for flight attendants (opposes 2, 3)   6   2

  2 Supports giving the airlines compensation for enhanced security efforts, access to carrying the mail, access to war risk insurance at capped prices, and more time to implement security deadlines; supports allowing pilots to carry guns on planes and requiring self-defense training for flight attendants (opposes 1)   3   0

  3 No position on giving the airlines compensation for enhanced security efforts, access to carrying the mail, access to war risk insurance at capped prices, and more time to implement security deadlines; supports allowing pilots to carry guns on planes and requiring self-defense training for flight attendants (opposes 1)   3   0

  9 Neutral/no position   1   0

Total   2,221   315

Note: The table identifies the 214 sides active on our issues, lists the number of major participants in each side, and indicates the number of interviews we conducted with leaders of each. In addition, 34 sides with 75 participants are listed as "neutral/no position"—these were typically government decision makers who played important roles in the issue but who did not actively advocate a given proposal to other government officials. This included agencies providing purely technical data or cost estimates and government decision makers who had final authority to decide but who did not actively engage in advocacy themselves. Finally, for 29 actors in 10 of the issues, we were unable to identify to which side they belonged. (They are listed as "99: Unknown/missing data" in the table).

Our 315 interviews were conducted with leading members of 172 of the 214 active sides (80 percent); 7 interviews were conducted with neutral decision makers. The number of interviews per side, as the table shows, ranges from 1 to 4, with one additional case for which we interviewed 11 members of the same side. We were unable to interview any major actors on 42 of our sides; of these sides, 35 had four or fewer members. Data in Chapter 4 are based on 171 sides because one interview produced no data on opposition.

TABLE A.2 **Interview Protocols**

Following are the questions we posed in our interviews.

1. Could you take the *most recent* issue you've been spending time on and describe what you're trying to accomplish on this issue and what type of action you are taking to make that happen?

   The issue we talk about doesn't have to be associated with a particular bill, rule, or regulation, and it doesn't have to be an issue that's been receiving coverage by the media—whatever issue you've most recently spent a significant amount of time on is fine so long as it involves the federal government.

   [*If the interviewee seems uncomfortable picking an issue or expresses concern about boredom, etc.*] How about if we talk about whatever issue most recently came across your desk?
   - *Probe about lobbying activities, lobbying targets.*

   (Note: For the subsequent interviews after the issue-identifier, we mentioned the issue that concerned us when we requested the interview. Therefore, our first question was as follows. All subsequent questions were the same. "As I mentioned on the phone, I'd like to talk about your efforts on [issue]. What are you trying to accomplish on this issue and what type of action are you taking to make that happen?")

2. *Recap what they're doing and what they're trying to accomplish.* So who else is involved in this issue, both inside and outside of government?
   - *Probe about coalition partners (formal or informal).*
   - *Probe about who they are speaking with about this issue.*

3. So you're talking to these various people [*be specific if it's relevant*] about why it's necessary to move forward on this issue [*or, if relevant, why it's necessary to prevent something from happening, etc.*]. What's the fundamental argument you use to try to convince people to do this?
   - *Probe about different arguments for different targets.*
   - *Probe for secondary arguments.*
   - *Probe for partisan differences in terms of how people respond to this issue.*

4. What impediments do you face in achieving your objectives on this issue—in other words, who or what is standing in your way? What arguments do they make?
   - *Probe for the arguments of opponents and others.*

5. I was wondering if you could tell me a bit about whether and how your organization uses research when you communicate with other organizations and people in government. From talking to people in organizations like yours, I've noticed that some emphasize research and try to supply their representatives with a steady stream of original research and data to be used in presentations with government officials, their aides, and others. Others say that if research or data are needed they can be gotten from think tanks, universities, research organizations, or consultants. And then there are others who don't spend a lot of time gathering issue-related research at all.

   Where along this continuum would you place this organization? Do you rely a lot on research when you talk to people in government or other groups? If so, do you do much research in-house?
   - *Probe for examples about the type of research they do in-house, whether and how often they gather it from outside sources, and what types of outside sources they rely on.*

6. Now I'd like to ask you a couple of general questions about your organization. How are you organized here in terms of people and units that are involved in public affairs and advocacy?
   - *Probe for the different units within the organization that play a role.*
   - *Probe for the number of people in these units.*

7. Before we finish up, could you tell me about yourself and how you came to work at this organization?

8. Those are all the questions I have for you, but I do have a favor to ask. I wonder if I could call you in about six months or so to follow up with you on this issue. I'll be back in [city] so it would be over the phone. I'd just like to see how things have progressed—since I have all this background, the follow-up should only take about 15 minutes.

   Also could I get a copy of [whatever they mention that I want a copy of]?

   [*Leave them a card.*]

1. Policy will promote/inhibit the achievement of some goal.
    101. Claims linking the policy to shared goals.
    102. Proposal is equitable; treats all fairly.
    103. Proposal will inhibit shared goals.
    104. Proposal is not equitable; does not treat all fairly.

2. Costs to government.
    201. Policy imposes costs to government; is inefficient.
    202. Policy reduces costs to government; increases efficiency.
    203. Not enough evidence to determine cost to government.
    204. Policy will not impose costs to government or decrease efficiency.
    205. Policy will not reduce costs to government or increase efficiency.

3. Costs to nongovernmental actors.
    301. Policy imposes costs on nongovernmental actors; is inefficient.
    302. Policy reduces costs to nongovernmental actors; increases efficiency.
    303. Not enough evidence to determine cost to nongovernmental actors.
    304. Policy will not impose costs on nongovernmental actors or decrease efficiency.
    305. Policy will not reduce costs to nongovernmental actors or increase efficiency.

4. Secondary consequences of the policy, other than cost.
    401. Whatever the value of the proposed policy goal, the policy will have some unintended negative consequence, other than cost.
    402. In addition to the primary goal, the policy will also have some secondary benefit, other than cost.
    403. Not enough evidence to determine what secondary consequences will result.

5. Policy implementation/feasibility issues.
    501. Whatever the value of the proposed policy goal, severe implementation problems.
    502. Policy will work as expected; no problems with implementation.
    503. Need more study; not enough evidence to determine the feasibility of the policy.

6. Equality of treatment/discriminatory impact.
    601. Policy will affect some groups unfairly.
    602. Rebuttal to this argument; this policy will not have unequal impact.

7. Magnitude of the policy.
    701. Policy will set a large precedent.
    702. Proposed change is moderate, prudent, or otherwise not radical.

8. Problem is bigger/smaller than estimated; is misunderstood.
    801. Problem is big or bigger than other side claims.
    802. Problem is small or smaller than other side claims.
    803. Problem is misunderstood.

9. Appropriateness of government action.
    901. Claims about market failure; government needed to solve the problem.
    902. Claims about government inefficiency; problem is not one for government to solve.

10. Window of opportunity.
    1001. A crisis looms; we must act now.
    1002. There is no crisis or threat; better to wait.

11. Proposed policy will enhance security; references to terrorism, national defense, public safety.

12. Policy supported/opposed by constituency or other group.
    1201. Positively viewed group or member of Congress supports.
    1202. Positively viewed group or member of Congress opposes.
    1203. Negatively viewed group or member of Congress supports.
    1204. Negatively viewed group or member of Congress opposes.
    1205. Supporting coalition is large or growing; momentum favors supporters.
    1206. Opposing coalition is large or growing; momentum favors opponents.

13. Partisan or electoral considerations.
    1301. Electoral benefits; votes to be gained.
    1302. Electoral costs; votes to be lost.
    1303. Partisan actions within government preventing/spurring action; no explicit reference to elections.
    1304. References to campaign contributions or grassroots/lobbying/mobilization campaigns.

14. Government procedures/jurisdiction.
    1401. Jurisdictional disputes between agencies and Congress; between other levels or branches of government; separation of powers; committee conflicts; turf fights.
    1402. Constitutional claims.
    1403. Congressional or other governmental procedures are not being followed or are not appropriate; policy has been set by previous court cases or clear precedent; misrepresentation of congressional intent.
    1404. Federalism issues; states versus local communities versus federal-level responsibilities.

TABLE A.4 **Documents Contained on Our Web Site**

Issues	98
Directories	20,575
Files	267,773
Bytes	2,472,639,091

Notes

Chapter One

1. See Albert-Laszlo Barabasi, *Linked* (New York: Penguin, 2005), on the 80/20 rule; see Frank R. Baumgartner and Beth L. Leech, "Interest Niches and Policy Bandwagons: Patterns of Interest Group Involvement in National Politics," *Journal of Politics* 64 (November 2001): 1191–213, for evidence that it applies to the distribution of lobbyists across a sample of issues.

2. See Beth L. Leech, Frank R. Baumgartner, Timothy La Pira, and Nicholas A. Semanko, "Drawing Lobbyists to Washington: Government Activity and Interest-Group Mobilization," *Political Research Quarterly* 58, no. 1 (March 2005): 19–30.

3. If one individual was listed for the organization in *Washington Representatives*, that person was selected for contact. If several names were listed, we looked for titles such as Government Affairs Representative, Director of Congressional Relations, Director of Regulatory Affairs, and Washington Representative. If multiple possibilities were available, one individual was chosen at random. We then checked by telephone to see whether that person was still employed by the organization. If not, we asked for the name of the individual who filled the same position.

4. This is much akin to the way those conducting telephone surveys will ask to speak to the person in the house who has had the most recent birthday. Our approach was also inspired by sampling approaches sometimes used in animal behavior studies, where, of course, there are no lists of animals from which to sample. For a discussion of an application of these behavioral scan techniques to the study of human behavior, see Monique Borgerhoff Mulder and T. M. Caro's "The Use of Quantitative Observational Techniques in Anthropology," *Current Anthropology* 26 (June 1985): 323–35.

5. Just as telephone surveys of households have known threats to randomness—older people and homemakers are more likely to be at home when interviewers call, whereas students and transient people are likely to be missed entirely—so

too can we recognize some potential threats to the randomness of our sample. For instance, respondents could have ignored our instructions to talk about the most recent issue and instead talked about the most interesting one. From our resulting list of issues, it does not seem like this is the case, but the possibility remains. Our study does not include many cases of lobbying for special earmark appropriations. Then again, in spite of all the controversies surrounding earmarks, they represent only a small fraction of the $3 trillion federal budget – about one percent or less of total spending, according to the Congressional Research Service. It also worth noting that earmarks are more important for legislators than they are for lobbyists. Legislators use earmarks to gain credit and build support in their districts; lobbyists' primary concerns tend to be less tied to localities. Our sampling method is not the best way to get at small, niche issues within the bureaucracy that are largely private in nature (that is, issues that do not become salient to Congress). However, this may be because not very many lobbyists are working on them, comparatively speaking.

6. Beyond the initial "issue identifier" interview, we were directed to hired lobbyists as leaders of coalitions or key actors in the process. When we interviewed them, we made certain ahead of time that they knew that their clients were aware of our interest, and we found them to be forthcoming.

7. Compare, for example, the approach of most interest-group scholars who emphasize this "two lobbyists and a legislator" model of advocacy (e.g., John M. Bacheller, "Lobbyists and the Legislative Process: The Impact of Environmental Constraints," *American Political Science Review* 71 [1977]: 252–63; Arthur T. Denzau and Michael C. Munger, "Legislators and Interest Groups: How Unorganized Interests Get Represented," *American Political Science Review* 80 [1986]: 89–106; David Austen-Smith and John R. Wright, "Counteractive Lobbying," *American Journal of Political Science* 38 [1994]: 25–44; or Scott Ainsworth, "The Role of Legislators in the Determination of Interest Group Influence," *Legislative Studies Quarterly* 22, no. 4 [1997]: 517–33) with the much richer and more realistic notions of Richard L. Hall and Alan V. Deardorff, "Lobbying as Legislative Subsidy," *American Political Science Review* 100 (2006): 69–84, which focuses on how outside lobbyists work with their government allies to get them more involved in the debate.

8. It is clear that we had to make some judgment calls in deciding where to draw the line between who was a "major" player in the debate and who played a lesser role, but this was actually fairly easy to determine. Certain actors were mentioned by virtually everyone we met with or appeared as the leading players in discussions of the issue in governmental hearings and in the news. Certain congressional offices generated all the "Dear Colleague" letters and the floor statements, and certain subcommittees generated the bulk of the hearings on the topic. So it was not difficult to separate out who was playing a driving role in the debate from who may have been interested and involved at some level, but not what others would have seen as a major actor.

9. Following Jeffrey Berry (*The New Liberalism* [Washington, DC: Brookings Institution, 1999]), we define citizen groups as those organizations that lobby or advocate around issues not linked to occupational or business interests. These groups either have interested citizens as members or claim to act on behalf of these citizens' interests.

10. For instance, Baumgartner and Leech found that 2 percent of the registered interest groups in Washington were unions ("Interest Niches and Policy Bandwagons"). Kay Lehman Schlozman and John Tierney's survey of interest groups (*Organized Interests and American Democracy* [New York: Harper & Row, 1986]), which was weighted so that those organizations that were more active were more likely to be interviewed, showed unions with 11 percent of the total.

11. The AFL-CIO was mentioned in connection with ten of the issues, the American Federation of State, County, and Municipal Employees was mentioned in connection with seven issues, the American Federation of Teachers, the National Education Association, and the United Auto Workers were each mentioned in connection with six issues, and the Teamsters were mentioned in connection with five issues.

12. The Chamber of Commerce was mentioned as a major participant in twelve of our issues, the National Association of Manufacturers was mentioned in eight of the issues, the Business Roundtable was mentioned in six of the issues, the Alliance of Auto Manufacturers and the Health Insurance Association of America were each mentioned in five cases, and the Edison Electric Institute and the American Hospital Association were each mentioned in four of the issues. For businesses themselves, the top six organizations make up an even smaller percentage: the top six businesses make up 8 percent of the overall mentions of business as a major participant in our issues.

13. Schlozman and Tierney, *Organized Interests and American Democracy*, 413.

14. Berry, *New Liberalism*.

15. Data come from *Associations Unlimited*, searched on October 14, 2007, through the Penn State University library electronic resources online.

16. For "issue identifiers" the mean score on our resource index is +.25, whereas it is −.02 for non-issue identifiers ($t = 3.99$, $p < .001$). Concerning the aggregated resources for all the members of the side that include the issue identifier, we also find they are wealthier: +.28 versus −.24 ($t = 5.44$; $p < .0001$). Later chapters explain in detail our index of material resources. These differences represent between one-half and two-thirds of a standard deviation on the index.

17. The issues were (*a*) permanent normal trade relations with China, (*b*) the Medicare+Choice program, (*c*) managed care reform (also known as the patients' bill of rights), and (*d*) late-term abortion.

18. Data from the Policy Agendas Project were collected with support of the National Science Foundation by Frank Baumgartner and Bryan Jones. The project categorizes all government activity by policy area from 1945 to the present. For a complete codebook, see www.policyagendas.org.

19. This percentage was computed using data available on the Senate's public information Web site: www.senate.gov/legislative/Public_Disclosure/LDA_reports.htm. The total number of reports filed in the end-of-the-year filing period in the areas of health issues, medical diseases and clinics, Medicare and Medicaid, and pharmacy were divided by the total number of reports filed during that period.

20. See Jack L. Walker, Jr., *Mobilizing Interest Groups in America* (Ann Arbor: University of Michigan Press, 1991), 59. Walker found in his 1985 survey of Washington groups that about three-quarters of all membership-based interest groups were based in the occupational sectors; just 24 percent were what he called citizen groups—that is, groups whose members joined for reasons unrelated to their occupation. Walker did not include businesses and institutions like hospitals and universities in his study; if he had, the percentage of interest groups that are occupationally based would have been even higher. The occupational basis of the group system is clear from our sample of issues and explains why the objects of lobbying are not the same as the concerns of the public or even the activities of Congress. Some issue areas (such as government operations or international affairs) see much congressional activity but little lobbying. Interest groups just are not mobilized in the same numbers in these areas.

21. Berry, *New Liberalism*.

22. See Frank R. Baumgartner and Beth L. Leech, *Basic Interests: The Importance of Groups in Politics and in Political Science* (Princeton, NJ: Princeton University Press, 1998).

23. The logic here is identical to what economists refer to as the efficient market thesis. In the stock market, if a certain company has a certain value, that value is assumed to already incorporate the market's information about the expected future performance of the company. Day-to-day or month-to-month fluctuations in the price of a given stock, given the efficiency of the market, are expected to be random (and indeed they have been empirically demonstrated to be close to this value). In our study, the *level* of power that a group has can be thought of as similar to a company's value, and *changes* in power are analogous to fluctuations in the stock price. Just as economists find no relation between the price and changes in the price, we expect no relation between preexisting levels of power or mobilization and changes in those levels. See Bryan D. Jones and Frank R. Baumgartner, *The Politics of Attention: How Government Prioritizes Problems* (Chicago: University of Chicago Press, 2005); and Eugene Fama, "Efficient Capital Markets: A Review of Theory and Empirical Work," *Journal of Finance* 25 (1970): 383–417.

24. We see a difference, then, between a case-study approach and a systematic review of dozens or more cases. While it may certainly be true (and we have observations in our study here) that short-term mobilization forces favored the wealthy side in a particular case, the more important question is whether there would be a systematic tendency for this to be the case across the board. Our analysis and

logic suggests that it can work in either direction. Of course, if it can go either way, individual case studies will sometimes show that "money matters." In *Basic Interests*, Baumgartner and Leech discussed the contradictory nature of the case-study evidence about the impact of money on policy outcomes. Beyond only the problems with generalizing from small numbers, the more fundamental point here is that measuring the effect of lobbying requires some control for the presence of the status quo policy. Since the outcome of interest is *change* in policy, the input that should be studied should logically be *change* in levels of mobilization, but this has rarely been done in the literature.

25. See Jones and Baumgartner, *Politics of Attention*.

26. It may make sense that so many retired government officials become lobbyists themselves. Certainly it is a relatively well-paid profession, but lobbying may also be attractive because the work is so similar to what they did as elected officials. Elected officials appear to be just as much involved in the advocacy within government as interest groups are from without.

27. David E. Price, *Policymaking in Congressional Committees: The Impact of Environmental Factors*. (Tucson: University of Arizona Press, 1978); and Robert H. Salisbury and Kenneth A. Shepsle, "U.S. Congressman as Enterprise," *Legislative Studies Quarterly* 6 (1981): 559–76.

28. Richard F. Fenno, *Congressmen in Committees* (Boston: Little, Brown, 1973).

Chapter Two

1. David M. Halbfiner, "Kerry Vows Fight for Equal Pay for Women and a $7 Wage," *New York Times*, October 23, 2004, A13.

2. http://reid.senate.gov/issues/yucca.cfm, accessed September 27, 2007.

3. Charles E. Lindblom, "The Science of Muddling Through," *Public Administration Review* 19 (Spring 1959): 79–88.

4. Aaron Wildavsky, *The Politics of the Budgetary Process* (Boston: Little, Brown, 1964).

5. Herbert Simon, *Administrative Behavior: A Study of Decision-Making Processes in Administrative Organizations* (New York: Macmillan, 1947); Simon, *Models of Man: Social and Rational; Mathematical Essays on Rational Human Behavior in a Social Setting* (New York: John Wiley, 1957).

6. Joseph White, "Almost Nothing New under the Sun," in *Budgeting, Policy, and Politics*, ed. Naomi Caiden and Joseph White, 111–32 (New Brunswick, NJ: Transaction Publishers, 1995).

7. Frank R. Baumgartner and Bryan D. Jones, *Agendas and Instability in American Politics* (Chicago: University of Chicago Press, 1993).

8. Jones and Baumgartner, *Politics of Attention*.

9. Ibid., 111–12.

10. Ibid., 55.

11. Jeffrey M. Berry, "Interest Groups and Gridlock," in *Interest Group Politics*, ed. Allan J. Cigler and Burdett A. Loomis, 6th ed., 333–53 (Washington, DC: CQ Press, 2002).

12. See Sarah A. Binder, *Stalemate: Causes and Consequences of Legislative Gridlock* (Washington, DC: Brookings Institution, 2003), 1–10.

13. Gary W. Cox and Mathew D. McCubbins, *Setting the Agenda: Responsible Party Government in the U.S. House of Representatives* (New York: Cambridge University Press, 2005).

Chapter Three

1. See Kenneth A. Shepsle and Barry R. Weingast, "Structure-Induced Equilibrium and Legislative Choice," *Public Choice* 37 (1981): 503–19; and Shepsle and Weingast, "The Institutional Foundations of Committee Power," *American Political Science Review* 81 (1987): 85–104.

2. E. E. Schattschneider, *The Semi-Sovereign People: A Realist's View of Democracy in America* (New York: Holt, Rinehart, & Winston, 1960).

3. In addition to Schattschneider, see also Michael Lipsky, "Protest as a Political Resource," *American Political Science Review* 62 (December 1968): 1144–58.

4. Roger W. Cobb, and Charles D. Elder, *Participation in American Politics: The Dynamics of Agenda-Building* (1972; quoting from 2nd ed.: Baltimore, MD: Johns Hopkins University Press, 1983).

5. John W. Kingdon, *Agendas, Alternatives, and Public Policies* (Boston: Little, Brown, 1984).

6. Baumgartner and Jones, *Agendas and Instability*.

7. Anne Schneider and Helen Ingram, "Social Construction of Target Populations: Implications for Politics and Policy," *American Political Science Review* 87, no. 2 (1993): 334–47.

8. Deborah A. Stone, *Policy Paradox and Political Reason* (Glenview, IL: Scott, Foresman. 1988).

9. Keith T. Poole and Howard Rosenthal, *Congress: A Political-Economic History of Roll Call Voting* (New York: Oxford University Press, 1997).

10. William H. Riker, *The Art of Political Manipulation* (New Haven, CT: Yale University Press, 1986); and Riker, "The Heresthetics of Constitution-Making: The Presidency in 1787, with Comments on Determinism and Rational Choice," *American Political Science Review* 78, no. 1 (1984): 1–16.

11. This idea has been traced back to Ernest Griffith's concept of "policy whirlpools." See *Impasse of Democracy* (New York: Harrison-Hilton Books, 1939).

12. No review of the literature will be offered here, but for a prime example of this school of thought, see Douglass Cater, *Power in Washington* (New York: Vintage, 1964).

13. This is a large literature, but see Kenneth A. Shepsle, *The Giant Jigsaw Puzzle* (Chicago: University of Chicago Press, 1978); Shepsle, "Institutional Arrangements and Equilibrium in Multidimensional Voting," *American Journal of Political Science* 23, no. 1 (1979): 27–59; Shepsle and Weingast, "Structure-Induced Equilibrium and Legislative Choice;" Shepsle and Weingast, "Institutional Foundations of Committee Power;" Keith Krehbiel, "Are Congressional Committees Composed of Preference Outliers?" *American Political Science Review* 84, no. 1 (1990): 149–63; Krehbiel, *Information and Legislative Organization* (Ann Arbor: University of Michigan Press, 1991); and Scott E. Adler and John S. Lapinski, "Demand-side Theory and Congressional Committee Composition: A Constituency Characteristics Approach," *American Journal of Political Science* 41, no. 3 (1997): 895–918.

14. For example, see Morris P. Fiorina, *Congress: Keystone of the Washington Establishment* (New Haven, CT: Yale University Press, 1977).

15. Hugh Heclo, "Issue Networks and the Executive Establishment," in *The New American Political System*, ed. Anthony King (Washington, DC: American Enterprise Institute, 1978), 87–124.

16. Ibid., 88.

17. Jeffrey M. Berry and Clyde Wilcox, *The Interest Group Society*, 4th ed. (New York: Pearson Longman, 2007), 14–32.

18. Jeffrey M. Berry, "Subgovernments, Issue Networks, and Political Conflict," in *Remaking American Politics*, ed. Richard A. Harris and Sidney M. Milkis, 239–60 (Boulder, CO: Westview, 1989); and Thomas L. Gais, Mark A. Peterson, and Jack L. Walker, "Interest Groups, Iron Triangles, and Representative Institutions in American National Government," *British Journal of Political Science* 14 (April 1984): 161–85.

19. See Paul Sabatier, "An Advocacy Coalition Framework of Policy Change and the Role of Policy-Oriented Learning Therein," *Policy Sciences* 21 (1988): 129–68; and Paul A. Sabatier and Hank C. Jenkins-Smith, *Policy Change and Learning: An Advocacy Coalition Approach.* (Boulder, CO: Westview, 1993).

20. John P. Heinz, Edward O. Laumann, Robert L. Nelson, and Robert H. Salisbury, *The Hollow Core: Private Interests in National Policy Making* (Cambridge, MA: Harvard University Press, 1993); and Michael T. Heaney, "Issue Networks, Information, and Interest Group Alliances," *State Politics & Policy Quarterly* 4 (Fall 2004): 237–70.

21. John E. Chubb, *Interest Groups and the Bureaucracy* (Stanford, CA: Stanford University Press, 1983).

Chapter Four

1. Maxwell McCombs and Jian-Hua Zhu, "Capacity, Diversity, and Volatility of the Public Agenda," *Public Opinion Quarterly* 59 (1995): 495–525.

2. Richard L. Hall, *Participation in Congress* (New Haven, CT: Yale University Press, 1996); and Richard L. Hall and Frank W. Wayman, "Buying Time: Moneyed Interests and Mobilization of Bias in Congressional Committees," *American Political Science Review* 84 (1990): 797–820.

3. A 2003 national opinion survey showed that of the majority of respondents who favored repealing the tax, 60 percent did so because they thought it affected too many people, and 70 percent agreed with the statement that the tax could affect them someday (Larry M. Bartels, "The Strange Appeal of the Estate-Tax Repeal," *The American Prospect*, May 17, 2004). Although these poll results pertain to a 2003 debate about the estate tax rather than the debate in 2000 that is described here, there is no evidence to suggest that public opinion on this issue shifted between 2000 and 2003 or that a change occurred in the public's rationale for support (Larry M. Bartels, "Homer Gets a Tax Cut: Inequality and Public Policy in the American Mind," *Perspectives on Politics* 3 [March 2005]: 15–31; Michael J. Graetz and Ian Shapiro, *Death by a Thousand Cuts: The Fight Over Taxing Inherited Wealth* [Princeton, NJ: Princeton University Press, 2005]).

4. This description of the supporters' post-Senate strategy was provided to one of us by an organization representative who supported estate tax repeal as CSPAN broadcast the introduction of and votes upon Democratic amendments.

5. Peter Bachrach and Morton Baratz, "The Two Faces of Power," *American Political Science Review* 56 (1962): 947–52; and Roger W. Cobb and Marc Howard Ross, *Cultural Strategies of Agenda Denial* (Lawrence: University Press of Kansas, 1997).

6. Schattschneider, *Semi-Sovereign People.*

7. Robert Salisbury, John P. Heinz, Edward O. Laumann, and Robert L. Nelson, "Who Works with Whom? Interest Group Alliances and Opposition," *American Political Science Review* 81 (1987): 1211–34.

8. A chi-square test of independence reveals that the two forms of opposition are statistically related but only for those sides seeking change (chi-square = 9.643, p = .002; and chi-square = 0.169, p = .681, respectively, for status quo challengers and defenders). Specifically, active opposition is more likely to be cited as an obstacle when a lack of support is not mentioned, whereas when active opposition is not present, inattention as a form of opposition is more likely to be noted as a problem.

9. Under our coding scheme, partisan obstacles could include advocates' direct references to partisan politics affecting their prospects for success (e.g., the majority party prevented legislative consideration of an issue), as well as less direct references to difficulties that resulted from Democrats or Republicans, liberals or conservatives, or the majority or minority party in Congress.

Chapter Five

1. David W. Rohde, *Parties and Leaders in the Postreform House* (Chicago: University of Chicago Press, 1991); Poole and Rosenthal, *Congress.*

2. John H. Aldrich and David W. Rohde, "The Consequences of Party Organization in the House: The Role of the Majority and Minority Parties in Conditional Party Government," in *Polarized Politics: Congress and the President in a Partisan Era*, ed. John R. Bond and Richard Fleisher (Washington, DC: CQ Press, 2000).

3. Binder, *Stalemate*; Pietro Nivola and David W. Brady, eds., *Red and Blue Nation* (Washington, DC: Brookings Institution and Hoover Institution, 2006).

4. Alan Abramowitz and Kyle Saunders, "Ideological Realignment in the U.S. Electorate," *Journal of Politics* 60 (1998): 634–52.

5. Marc J. Hetherington, "Resurgent Mass Partisanship: The Role of Elite Polarization," *American Political Science Review* 95 (2001): 619–31; David C. Kimball and Cassie A. Gross, "The Growing Polarization of American Voters," in *The State of the Parties*, ed. John C. Green and Daniel J. Coffey, 5th ed. (Lanham, MD: Rowman & Littlefield, 2007).

6. Larry M. Bartels, "Partisanship and Voting Behavior, 1952–1996," *American Journal of Political Science* 44 (2000): 35–50.

7. Binder, *Stalemate*; Gary W. Cox and Matthew D. McCubbins, *Legislative Leviathan: Party Government in the House* (Berkeley: University of California Press, 1993); C. Lawrence Evans and Walter J. Olezsek, "Message Politics and Senate Procedure," in *The Contentious Senate*, ed. Colton C. Campbell and Nicol C. Rae, 107–27 (New York: Rowman & Littlefield, 2002); Barbara Sinclair, *Unorthodox Lawmaking: New Legislative Processes in the U.S. Congress*, 3rd ed. (Washington, DC: CQ Press, 2007).

8. Cox and McCubbins, *Setting the Agenda*.

9. Charles Babington, "Hastert Launches a Partisan Policy," *Washington Post*, November 27, 2004, A2.

10. Raymond A. Bauer, Ithiel de Sola Pool, and Lewis A. Dexter, *American Business and Public Policy: The Politics of Foreign Trade* (Palo Alto, CA: Atherton Press, 1963); Hall and Deardorff, "Lobbying as Legislative Subsidy."

11. Burdett A. Loomis, "Does K Street Run through Capitol Hill? Lobbying Congress in the Republican Era," in *Interest Group Politics*, ed. Allan J. Cigler and Burdett A. Loomis, 7th ed. (Washington, DC: CQ Press, 2007).

12. In the "somewhat partisan" category, partisanship was typically described as one among several impediments to an advocate's desired policy, and often the partisan impediment came in the form of low enthusiasm or priority for an issue rather than outright hostility. For example, on some issues one party was more interested than the other party in introducing bills, cosponsoring legislation, holding hearings, or working on the issue in other ways. However, if votes were held on the issue, they did not always split along party lines.

13. Rohde, *Parties and Leaders in the Postreform House*; Barbara Sinclair, *Majority Leadership in the U.S. House* (Baltimore: Johns Hopkins University Press, 1983); Cox and McCubbins, *Setting the Agenda*; John H. Aldrich, Mark M. Berger, and David W. Rohde, "The Historical Variability in Conditional Party Government,

1877–1994," in *Parties, Procedure, and Policy: Essays on the History of Congress*, ed. David Brady and Matthew D. McCubbins (Stanford, CA: Stanford University Press, 2002); and Mark A. Smith, *The Right Talk: How Conservatives Transformed the Great Society into the Economic Society* (Princeton, NJ: Princeton University Press, 2007).

14. Matthew Potoski and Jeffrey Talbert, "The Dimensional Structure of Policy Outputs: Distributive Policy and Roll Call Voting," *Political Research Quarterly* 53, no. 4 (2000): 695–710.

15. Thomas E. Patterson, *Out of Order: How the Decline of the Political Parties and the Growing Power of the News Media Undermine the Way We Pick the President* (New York: Knopf, 1993).

16. James D. Hunter, *Culture Wars: The Struggle to Define America* (New York: Basic Books, 1991); Geoffrey C. Layman, Thomas M. Carsey, and Juliana Menasce Horowitz, "Party Polarization in American Politics: Characteristics, Causes, and Consequences," *Annual Review of Political Science* 9 (2006): 83–110.

17. Sinclair, *Unorthodox Lawmaking*.

18. Poole and Rosenthal, *Congress*; and Cox and McCubbins, *Setting the Agenda*.

19. Jeffrey Talbert and Matthew Potoski, "Setting the Legislative Agenda: The Dimensional Structure of Bill Cosponsoring and Floor Voting," *Journal of Politics* 64, no. 3 (2002): 864–91.

20. Berry, *New Liberalism*.

21. Poole and Rosenthal, *Congress*.

22. Glen S. Krutz, "Tactical Maneuvering on Omnibus Bills in Congress," *American Journal of Political Science* 45 (2001): 210–23.

23. A few of the cases stalled under President Clinton moved forward on the legislative agenda after President Bush took office but did not pass Congress until Republicans won back control of the Senate in the 2002 elections. These include the class action reform, bankruptcy reform, and late-term abortion issues.

24. Glen S. Krutz, "Issues and Institutions: 'Winnowing' in the U.S. Congress," *American Journal of Political Science* 49 (2005): 313–26.

25. Binder, *Stalemate*; and Jeffrey S. Peake, "Coalition Building and Overcoming Legislative Gridlock in Foreign Policy, 1947–98," *Presidential Studies Quarterly* 32 (2002): 67–83.

26. Our coding of policy change is explained in more detail in chapter 11.

27. Berry, *New Liberalism*.

28. Lindblom, "Science of Muddling Through."

29. Our findings that a change in party in the White House affects some issues but not others are similar to those in Heinz, Laumann, Nelson, and Salisbury, *The Hollow Core*.

30. Mark J. Rozell, Clyde Wilcox, and David Madland, *Interest Groups in American Campaigns*, 2nd ed. (Washington, DC: CQ Press).

31. John H. Aldrich and David W. Rohde, "The Transition to Republican Rule in the House: Implications for Theories of Congressional Politics," *Political Science Quarterly* 112, no. 4 (1997): 541–67.

32. John W. Kingdon, *Congressmen's Voting Decisions* (New York: Harper & Row, 1973).

33. Barry C. Burden, *Personal Roots of Representation* (Princeton, NJ: Princeton University Press, 2007).

Chapter Six

1. One exception is the study by Heinz et al. of issue networks. They emphasize that much of what lobbyists do is to monitor an unpredictable policy-making process. See Heinz, Laumann, Nelson, and Salisbury, *Hollow Core*.

2. Business Roundtable, press release, "Aggressive, Early Start & Local Education Efforts Key to Business Roundtable's Successful PNTR Effort," May 24, 2000, http://lobby.la.psu.edu/040_PNTR/Organizational_Statements/BRTable/Aggressive.htm.

3. Daniel Kahneman and Amos Tversky, "Choices, Values, and Frames," *American Psychologist* 39 (1984): 341–50.

4. We found 37 news stories about this issue during the 106th session of Congress, compared to a median of 16 news stories across our sample of 98 issues.

5. Kingdon, *Agendas, Alternatives, and Public Policies*.

6. An interesting consequence of one group waiting to see what the others do is that the distribution of advocacy across a sample of issues will be highly skewed, with few working on most issues but huge numbers working on a small number of issues where others have become active. Groups may engage because they see a threat to their interests (but only if the momentum for change is sufficiently high, which it usually is not) or because they see a true opportunity for change (again, only if it appears that the change will indeed occur). This explains why we observe veritable lobbying frenzies on a few cases but not that much action on most issues. Baumgartner and Leech ("Interest Niches and Policy Bandwagons") showed this peculiar distribution of lobbying in a sample of 137 issues in Washington. Forty-five percent of the lobbying activity was on just 5 percent of the issues. We see a similar pattern here.

7. David Mayhew, *Congress: The Electoral Connection* (New Haven, CT: Yale University Press, 1974).

8. Bacheller, "Lobbyists and the Legislative Process"; Kenneth M. Goldstein, *Interest Groups, Lobbying, and Participation in America.* (New York: Cambridge University Press, 1999); Ken Kollman, *Outside Lobbying: Public Opinion and Interest Group Strategies* (Princeton, NJ: Princeton University Press, 1998); Schattschneider, *Semi-Sovereign People*; and Mark A. Smith, *American Business and*

Political Power: Public Opinion, Elections, and Democracy (Chicago: University of Chicago Press, 2000).

9. Bacheller, "Lobbyists and the Legislative Process"; William P. Browne, "Organized Interests and Their Policy Niches: A Search for Pluralism in a Policy Domain," *Journal of Politics* 52 (1990): 477–509; and Schattschneider, *Semi-Sovereign People*.

10. Lipsky, "Protest as a Political Resource"; Schattschneider, *Semi-Sovereign People*; Kollman, *Outside Lobbying*.

11. See, for example, Austen-Smith and Wright, "Counteractive Lobbying"; and Hall and Deardorff, "Lobbying as Legislative Subsidy."

12. John Mark Hansen, *Gaining Access: Congress and the Farm Lobby, 1919–1981* (Chicago: University of Chicago Press, 1991); Austen-Smith and Wright, "Counteractive Lobbying."

13. Hansen, *Gaining Access*.

14. Hall and Deardorff, "Lobbying as Legislative Subsidy."

15. Kevin M. Esterling, *The Political Economy of Expertise* (Ann Arbor: University of Michigan Press, 2004); David Whiteman, *Communication in Congress* (Lawrence: University Press of Kansas, 1995).

16. Jones and Baumgartner, *Politics of Attention*.

17. Richard A. Smith, "Advocacy, Interpretation, and Influence in the U.S. Congress," *American Political Science Review* 78 (1984): 44–63.

18. Many theoretical accounts of lobbying also emphasize the cost to lobbyists of acquiring the information they seek to transmit. Both Ainsworth ("Role of Legislators") and Austen-Smith and Wright ("Counteractive Lobbying") argue that legislators are more likely to listen to and perceive as credible lobbyists' messages when those lobbyists present information that is costly or difficult for a lobbyist to collect. The provision of information that proved costly to collect also signals to the policy maker that the lobbying organization is truly committed to an issue, and the more costly the information, the stronger the signal of how important the issue is to the group. From information that is costly for lobbyists to acquire, policy makers may conclude that the group is committed to and will continue to devote resources to pursuing their policy goals. In this way, lobbyists may also reduce a policy maker's uncertainty about whether an issue is likely to gain traction and hence whether he or she should devote attention and other resources to it.

19. Cobb and Elder, *Participation in American Politics*; Cobb and Ross, *Cultural Strategies of Agenda Denial*; Murray Edelman, *Politics as Symbolic Action: Mass Arousal and Quiescence* (Chicago: Markham Publishing, 1971); Murray Edelman, *Constructing the Political Spectacle* (Chicago: University of Chicago Press, 1988); Charles D. Elder and Roger W. Cobb, *The Political Uses of Symbols* (New York: Longman, 1983); Albert O. Hirschman, *The Rhetoric of Reaction: Perversity, Futility, Jeopardy* (Cambridge, MA: Harvard University Press, 1991); Jan Kubik, *The Power of Symbols against the Symbols of Power: The Rise of Solidarity and the Fall*

of State Socialism in Poland (University Park: Pennsylvania State University Press, 1994).

20. Edward G. Carmines and James S. Stimson, "The Two Faces of Issue Voting," *American Political Science Review* 74 (1980): 78–91; Roger W. Cobb and James H. Kuklinski, "Changing Minds: Political Arguments and Political Persuasion," *American Journal of Political Science* 41 (1997): 88–121; Edelman, *Politics as Symbolic Action.*

21. Kollman, *Outside Lobbying*; John R. Wright, *Interests Groups and Congress: Lobbying, Contributions, and Influence* (Boston: Allyn & Bacon, 1996).

22. Gregory A. Caldeira, Marie Hojnacki, and John R. Wright, "The Lobbying Activities of Organized Interests in Federal Judicial Nominations," *Journal of Politics* 62 (2000): 51–69.

23. Bacheller, "Lobbyists and the Legislative Process."

24. Darrell M. West and Burdett A. Loomis, *The Sound of Money: How Political Interests Get What They Want* (New York: Norton, 1999).

25. Wright, *Interest Groups and Congress.*

26. Kollman, *Outside Lobbying.*

Chapter Seven

1. Specifically, we examine the arguments made by actors associated with each side. If one or more of the actors associated with a side makes a particular type of argument, we consider the side as having made that type of argument. We do not have arguments for all 214 sides, because we did not seek or could not obtain interviews with representatives of 42 sides, many of which were very small. The analysis reported here is based on 315 interviews across the 172 sides.

2. The category of noncost consequences includes arguments about any consequence—intended or unintended—that does not refer directly to governmental or private sector costs. For instance, on the issue from the 106th Congress about whether to raise CAFE standards for light trucks and vans, the side that opposed raising standards (i.e., supported the status quo) offered arguments based both on cost and noncost consequences: "If fuel efficiency standards are raised, then manufacturers will go with something lighter [to construct vehicles]. If lighter materials are used, safety and cost become an issue. Lighter cars tend to be less safe and steel is less expensive than alternative materials." The cost argument is explicit and the noncost argument, in this case, is the unintended safety impact.

3. Of course, contributions need not be mentioned explicitly to effectively determine policy choices. That is, the receipt of a contribution may be sufficient to explain the recipient's policy preference.

4. One might expect to see a relatively greater attention to cost in the arguments made after September 2001. In other words, advocates might have found it

beneficial to emphasize the cost savings associated with their policy priorities—or the cost increases associated with the preferences of opponents—given the rising costs associated with homeland security and the "war on terror" in the post-9/11 period. Our data show that, generally speaking, this is not the case. Overall, the relative frequency of arguments related to the costs borne by government, and the costs borne by private actors, actually declined a bit in the post-2001 period.

5. Berry and Wilcox, *Interest Group Society*, 98.

6. Kahneman and Tversky, "Choices, Values, and Frames."

7. Ibid.

8. See ibid., 348.

9. Note that the numbers listed in this table are lower than those for table 7.1 because we can include here only those issues where we have interviews in both sides of the debate; this causes us to lose many issues that were either small in scope or one-sided.

10. Gary Mucciaroni and Paul J. Quirk, *Deliberative Choices: Debating Public Policy in Congress* (Chicago: University of Chicago Press, 2005).

11. Intent is correlated with the three impact variables. Although it is not unexpected that those challenging the status quo would tend to support policy options that were relatively more likely than those supported by status quo defenders to have sizable impacts on the federal budget, private costs, or established programs, the linkages between these variables make it more difficult to determine each variable's individual effect on argument use.

Chapter Eight

1. In chapter 7 our analysis was typically based on 172 sides; that number is lower here (155 sides) because we exclude any sides whose membership was made up solely of government officials as well as those sides for which we have no interviews with nongovernmental actors. Analyses of tactics is limited to outside organizations because, with few exceptions (e.g., coalition participation), the tactics used by government officials were different from those used by outside organizations. For example, among congressional advocates, the use of "Dear Colleague" letters is quite common. Here we present only those tactics that were mentioned by at least 10 percent of all sides. Less common tactics not reported here include: filing suits (used by 9 percent of all sides); filing amicus briefs (5 percent); participating in protests (4 percent); and the distribution of voter guides (4 percent).

2. Baumgartner and Leech, *Basic Interests*. See also David Knoke, *Organizing for Collective Action: The Political Economies of Associations* (Hawthorne, NY: Aldine de Gruyter, 1990), 199; Schlozman and Tierney, *Organized Interests and American Democracy*; Walker, *Mobilizing Interest Groups in America*; Heinz,

Laumann, Nelson, and Salisbury, *Hollow Core*; Jeffrey M. Berry, *Lobbying for the People: The Political Behavior of Public Interest Groups* (Princeton, NJ: Princeton University Press, 1977); and Anthony J. Nownes and Patricia Freeman, "Interest Group Activity in the States," *Journal of Politics* 60, no. 1 (1998): 86–112.

3. See Heinz, Laumann, Nelson, and Salisbury, *Hollow Core*.

4. Daniel P. Carpenter, Kevin M. Esterling, and David M. Lazer, "The Strength of Weak Ties in Lobbying Networks," *Journal of Theoretical Politics* 10, no.4 (1998): 417–444.

5. Kingdon, *Agendas, Alternatives, and Public Policies*, 2nd ed. (New York: Harper Collins, 1995).

6. Schattschneider, *Semi-Sovereign People*.

7. To some extent our findings here overstate the level of activity by status quo supporters because, as we pointed out in chapter 3, there are a number of cases, seventeen to be exact, where no side supporting the status quo even mobilized. Surely in most cases this was not because no one was interested in protecting the status quo. In the case of criminal justice reform, for example, proponents of the proposed shift in policy were so far away from achieving any goals that it was unnecessary for anyone to countermobilize against them. The analysis in this chapter, of course, does not include those sides that had yet to take a position and mobilize. Thus, there are certainly many more status quo supporters who are solely monitoring the actions of status quo challengers than is revealed by our data.

8. Robert H. Salisbury, "The Paradox of Interest Groups in Washington—More Groups, Less Clout," in *The New American Political System*, ed. Anthony King, 2nd ed. (Washington, DC: AEI Press, 1990), 224.

Chapter Nine

1. Carl Hulse, "Fine Art of Debating a Point Without Getting to the Point," *New York Times*, March 30, 2004, A16.

2. See James N. Druckman, "On the Limits of Framing Effects: Who Can Frame?" *Journal of Politics* 63 (November 2001): 1041–44.

3. Donald R. Kinder and Thomas E. Nelson, "Democratic Debate and Real Opinions," in *Framing American Politics*, ed. Karen Callaghan and Frauke Schnell (Pittsburgh: University of Pittsburgh Press, 2005), 103.

4. Robert M. Entman, "Framing: Toward Clarification of a Fractured Paradigm," *Journal of Communication* 43 (Fall 1993): 51. Let us be clear about our use of terms. *Framing* is often associated with strategies designed to change public opinion. Our research was not designed to measure public opinion change and only a small percentage of our issues could, in theory, be directly analyzed by measurements of public sentiment. Most were, quite simply, invisible to the mass public. Rather, the research was focused on trying to understand efforts by interest groups

and allies in government to either raise the salience of one particular argument concerning a policy problem, or to bring a new argument into the debate over that issue. Typically, the target audience was a community of political elites. Some scholars use the term *issue definition* to describe the prevailing understanding of an issue. We prefer the verbs *frame* and *reframe* to make it clear that we are analyzing mobilization by advocates trying to influence the way a target audience in the real world of Washington politics understands a given issue.

5. George Lakoff, *Don't Think of an Elephant!* (White River Junction, VT: Chelsea Green Publishing, 2004), xv.

6. Amos Tversky and Daniel Kahneman, "Rational Choice and the Framing of Decisions," *Journal of Business* 59 (October 1986): 254–55.

7. Druckman, "On the Limits of Framing Effects."

8. Riker writes, "*Heresthetic* is a word I have coined to refer to a political strategy. Its root is a Greek word for choosing and electing." *The Art of Political Manipulation*, (New Haven, CT: Yale University Press, 1986), ix.

9. Ibid., 106–13.

10. William H. Riker, *The Strategy of Rhetoric* (New Haven, CT: Yale University Press, 1996), 9.

11. Riker, *Art of Political Manipulation*, 106.

12. Bryan D. Jones, *Reconceiving Decision-Making in Democratic Politics* (Chicago: University of Chicago Press, 1994), 78–102.

13. Joe McGinniss, *The Selling of the President 1968* (New York: Simon & Schuster, 1969).

14. Robert Pear, "In Medicare Debate, Massaging the Facts," *New York Times*, May 23, 2006, A19.

15. Bob Thompson, "Sharing the Wealth?" *Washington Post Magazine*, April 13, 2003, 23.

16. Admittedly, we have used a broad brush to paint political journalists. Although far too many stories assume campaigns or the policy-making process are easily manipulable, there is good journalism that recognizes the obstacles faced by those trying to alter a frame. See, for example, Matt Bai, "The Framing Wars," *New York Times Magazine*, July 17, 2005, 38ff; and Noam Scheiber, "Wooden Frame," *New Republic*, May 23, 2005, 14ff.

17. On the selling of the Contract with America and the Clinton health plan, see Lawrence R. Jacobs and Robert Y. Shapiro, *Politicians Don't Pander* (Chicago: University of Chicago Press, 2000).

18. Quoted by Laura Miller, "War Is Sell," PRWatch.org, www.prwatch.org/prwissues/2002Q4/war.html.

19. Jacobs and Shapiro, *Politicians Don't Pander*, 50.

20. Schneider and Ingram, "Social Construction of Target Populations"; and Deborah A. Stone, "Causal Stories and the Formation of Policy Agendas," *Political Science Quarterly* 104 (1989): 281–300.

21. See Kingdon, *Agendas, Alternatives, and Public Policies*, 1st ed. (1984).

22. White, "Almost Nothing New."

23. Druckman, "On the Limits of Framing Effects," 1061.

24. Note that we do not assume that an issue is likely to be associated with just a single frame. Rather, there may be a series of important frames associated with a given issue. In looking at reframing, we will consider whether the most commonly used frames or arguments changed, whether new elements entered (but did not necessarily come to dominate) the debate, or whether the mix of frames present in the debate remained constant over time.

25. The logic of this second calculation is that an issue cannot be reframed if it's no longer under discussion. In selecting out cases which, at the second stage of research, were no longer being actively considered, our criterion was a firm conviction that the particular issue was off the table for the immediate future. Given the ongoing nature of policy making, only 13 of our cases met this standard, leaving 85 that might have been susceptible to reframing. Yet there are counterarguments to using this second method. First, in American politics, are issues ever really off the table? If some advocates can think of a way of reframing an issue they've lost on, they may try to generate a new or altered frame no matter how "settled" the issue seems. Second, our 98 issues are a random sample of issues lobbyists were working on at one point in time. The first method tells us how many of those issues underwent reframing one Congress later. The 13 issues that reached a termination point are simply part of what happens to a set of issues drawn at any one time. Since the difference in the two calculation is tiny, it's clear that the substantive result of the research is unaffected by the alternative approaches.

26. Douglas Jehl, "Bush Will Modify Ban on New Roads in Federal Lands," *New York Times*, May 4, 2001, A1.

27. On the constraints and potential of reframing, see James N. Druckman, "Political Preference Formation: Competition, Deliberation, and the (Ir)relevance of Framing Effects," *American Political Science Review* 98 (November 2004): 671–86; James N. Druckman and Kjersten R. Nelson, "Framing and Deliberation: How Citizens' Conversations Limit Elite Influence," *American Journal of Political Science* 47 (October 2003): 729–45; and Philip H. Pollock III, "Issues, Values, and Critical Moments: Did 'Magic' Johnson Transform Public Opinion on AIDS?" *American Journal of Political Science* 38 (May 1994): 426–46.

28. Frank Rich, *The Greatest Story Ever Sold* (New York: Penguin, 2006); and Jacob S. Hacker and Paul Pierson, *Off Center* (New Haven, CT: Yale University Press, 2005).

29. Heinz, Laumann, Nelson, and Salisbury, *Hollow Core*.

30. Kingdon, *Agendas, Alternatives, and Public Policies*, 1st ed. (1984), 134.

31. Ibid., 173–204.

32. Stephen Power, "Companies Cry 'Security' to Get a Break from the Government," *Wall Street Journal*, May 29, 2003, A1.

33. As noted in chapter 7, we found that national security arguments were not abundant in our sample of issues. Because our analysis extended beyond 9/11, it may be that the window of opportunity for reframing after 9/11 was short-lived outside of direct military and security issues.

34. Jones, *Reconceiving Decision-Making*, 78–102.

35. Berry and Wilcox, *Interest Group Society*, 98.

36. Berry, *New Liberalism*.

37. Jones and Baumgartner, *Politics of Attention*.

38. See M. Smith, *The Right Talk*.

39. Frank R. Baumgartner, Suzanna L. De Boef, and Amber E. Boydstun, *The Decline of the Death Penalty and the Discovery of Innocence* (New York: Cambridge University Press, 2008).

40. Teena Gabrielson, "Obstacles and Opportunities: Factors That Constrain Elected Officials' Ability to Frame Political Issues," in *Framing American Politics*, ed. Callaghan and Schnell, (Pittsburgh: University of Pittsburgh Press, 2005), 76.

Chapter Ten

1. Advocates of eliminating the tax finally scored a partial victory six years later—after the official end of our study period—when a series of federal courts ruled that the tax could not legally be applied to long-distance calls as they are billed today. The Internal Revenue Service agreed to stop collecting the tax on long-distance, wireless, and bundled services and to issue a tax credit to individuals and businesses for excise taxes paid over the past three years. The tax on local telephone services remains, but advocates hoped to continue their fight against that portion of the 3-percent excise tax in Congress.

2. Data on PAC contributions and lobbying expenditures were provided by the Center for Responsive Politics, www.crp.org.

3. For a review of this literature, see Baumgartner and Leech, *Basic Interests*. Scholars have been more successful in documenting links between PAC contributions and congressional access, activity in committee, and policy expertise. See, for example, Laura I. Langbein, "Money and Access: Some Empirical Evidence," *Journal of Politics* 48 (1986): 1052–62; Hall and Wayman, "Buying Time"; and Kevin M. Esterling, "Buying Expertise: Campaign Contributions and Attention to Policy Analysis in Congressional Committees," *American Political Science Review* 101 (2007): 93–109. Even these findings are not clearly supported; for an opposing view on campaign contributions and access, see Marie Hojnacki and David C. Kimball, "PAC Contributions and Lobbying Contacts in Congressional Committees," *Political Research Quarterly* 54 (2001): 161–80.

4. There have been, of course, some prominent issues of corruption, where members of Congress have been prosecuted precisely for this kind of quid pro

quo relation between personal gifts or campaign contributions and official actions; outright bribery does sometimes occur. Our question is "How common are such occurrences?" If they are quite common, then the outcomes in our data should reflect that.

5. See, for example, Bauer, de Sola Pool, and Dexter, *American Business and Public Policy*. For more recent views on the tendency to lobby friends rather than foes, see Frank R. Baumgartner and Beth L. Leech, "Lobbying Friends and Foes in Government," in *Interest Group Politics*, ed. Allan J. Cigler and Burdett A. Loomis, 5th ed., 217–33 (Washington, DC: CQ Press, 1998); Marie Hojnacki and David C. Kimball, "Organized Interests and the Decision of Whom to Lobby in Congress," *American Political Science Review* 92 (1998): 775–90; and Hojnacki and Kimball, "The Who and How of Organizations' Lobbying Strategies in Committee," *Journal of Politics* 61 (1999): 999–1024. Hall and Deardorff also provide a useful way of thinking about the efforts of groups to mobilize activity on the part of like-minded legislators in their article "Lobbying as Legislative Subsidy."

6. All of these variables are described in more detail in codebooks available on our Web site, http://lobby.la.psu.edu.

7. The amount was adjusted first in 1997 and then every four years afterward to keep up with inflation. As of 2005, organizations that spent at least $24,500 in a six-month period were required to register; those who spent less were not. If a contract lobbyist represented the organization and the contract lobbying firm was paid more than $5,000 in a six-month period, then the contract lobbying firm must register and list its client. The numbers we show here reflect an organization's total reported lobbying expenditures during the last six-month period of the congressional session in which the issue was raised.

8. See Jeffrey M. Berry with David F. Arons, *A Voice for Nonprofits* (Washington, DC: Brookings Institution, 2003).

9. Low-level allies are rank-and-file members of Congress and bureau-level executive branch personnel who were actively working to further a particular policy goal. Midlevel allies are committee and subcommittee leadership within Congress and executive branch officials at the agency or department level who were actively working to further a particular policy goal. High-level allies are congressional party leadership and White House officials who were actively working to further a particular policy goal. In all cases, these were not simply officials who agreed with the perspective or who might have voted in favor of a policy advocated by the perspective, but officials who in their own right were prominent advocates of adopting a new policy (or preventing the proposed policy).

10. For these variables, status quo is defined as the policy that existed at the time of the initial interviews on the topic. The variables are coded as 2 if the advocate got the outcome it preferred (either the policy changed as it wanted or it didn't change, if that's what the advocate wanted), coded as 1 if the advocate got

part of what it wanted, and coded as 0 if the advocate did not succeed in achieving its policy goal.

11. These two indices thus vary between 0 and 12. Cronbach's alpha is .65 for the initial outcome index and .66 for the final outcome index.

12. Association assets is a measure of the overall financial resources of associations (including citizen groups, professional and trade associations, unions, and any other nonprofit, nongovernmental advocate). This index includes the organization's annual budget and staff size, coded from *Associations Unlimited*, and the organization's assets and annual income, coded from IRS documents. Cronbach's alpha for the index was .913. The index for business assets includes annual net income, annual sales, and overall employees, collected from Fortune 500 company profiles for large companies and Dun and Bradstreet's Million Dollar Database for small companies. Cronbach's alpha for this index was .82. Both indices have been standardized to vary between 0 and 1. Missing values for the variables underlying the indices were imputed using Amelia II software (James Honaker, Anne Joseph, Gary King, Kenneth Scheve, and Naunihal Singh, *Amelia: A Program for Missing Data* [Windows version] [Cambridge, MA: Harvard University, 2001], http://GKing.Harvard.edu/). See the appendix for a discussion of how we dealt with these missing values.

13. Total membership size was collected for membership organizations only (obviously, businesses and institutions such as universities and hospitals have no members) from *Associations Unlimited*. Missing values in these data were imputed using Amelia II software. See note 12.

14. The number of cases in the table is lower than our 98 issues because 17 of our cases had no active conflict, 8 resulted in the same outcome for all perspectives, and 8 cases involved one perspective made up of organized interests and a second perspective made up of government officials (which means that we can't directly compare the resources controlled).

15. M. Smith, *American Business and Political Power*.

Chapter Eleven

1. We also note "significant" policy change that occurred after the four-year period of our study on six additional issues (repeal of the 3-percent excise tax, bankruptcy reform, class-action reform, interest-expense rules, a right-to-carry law for off-duty police officers, and late-term abortions).

2. Kingdon, *Agendas, Alternatives, and Public Policies*.

3. Jeffrey H. Birnbaum and Russell Newell, "Fat & Happy in D.C." *Fortune* 143 (May 28, 2001): 94–100; and Jeffrey H. Birnbaum and Natasha Graves, "Follow the Money," *Fortune* 140 (December 6, 1999): 206–8.

4. Heinz, Laumann, Nelson, and Salisbury, *Hollow Core*.

5. M. Smith, *American Business and Political Power*.

6. If we instead use factor analysis to create a summary resource measure based on factor scores, we get almost the same results indicated in this chapter. The correlation between our resource index and one based on factor scores is .99.

7. Esterling, "Buying Expertise."

8. The correlation is weaker but still positive if we exclude outliers with very large resources ($r = .27, p = .02$).

9. Schlozman and Tierney, *Organized Interests and American Democracy*, 67; and Baumgartner and Leech, "Interest Niches and Policy Bandwagons," 1195.

10. Berry, *New Liberalism*.

11. Robert A. Dahl, *Who Governs?* (New Haven, CT: Yale University Press, 1961).

Chapter Twelve

1. Jones and Baumgartner, *Politics of Attention*.

2. Lindblom, "Science of Muddling Through."

3. Ibid., 84.

4. Ibid., 84.

5. Cox and McCubbins, *Setting the Agenda*.

6. See Daniel Kahneman and Amos Tversky, eds. *Choices, Values, and Frames* (New York: Cambridge University Press, 2000); George A. Quattrone and Amos Tversky, "Contrasting Rational and Psychological Analyses of Political Choice." *American Political Science Review* 82, no. 3 (September 1988): 719–36.

7. See Shepsle and Weingast, "Structure-Induced Equilibrium and Legislative Choice"; and Shepsle and Weingast, "The Institutional Foundations of Committee Power." These authors point to particular institutional causes of equilibrium, in particular the committee structure in Congress. In our view, the causes of stability in the policy process are much broader than only this (though the institutional causes that Shepsle and Weingast identify are indeed part of the broader story). If the institutional structures were changed, however, the policy communities would still be there. This is why we see similar policy equilibria in countries outside the United States where there are no important committees in the national legislature, for example.

8. A general class of "threshold," "cascade," and "mimicking" models is common in areas of economics, sociology, and the natural sciences. The general idea is that in those areas of life where choices are made less on the basis of one's own preferences (because one may not have strong preferences, for example, or because one seeks to "fit in" with those around one), then when small numbers of people begin to change, entire groups can "tip" quickly from one pattern of behavior to another. Some general citations are Mark S. Granovetter, "Threshold Models of Collective

Behavior," *American Journal of Sociology* 83 (1978): 1420–43; Sushil Bikhchandani, David Hirshleifer, and Ivo Welch, "A Theory of Fads, Fashion, Custom, and Cultural Change as Informational Cascades," *Journal of Political Economy* 100 (1992): 992–1026; or Alan Kirman, "Ants, Rationality, and Recruitment," *Quarterly Journal of Economics* 108 (1993): 137–56. For more popular introductions see Malcolm Gladwell, *The Tipping Point* (New York: Little, Brown, 2000), and Albert-Laszlo Barabasi, *Linked* (New York: Penguin, 2005).

9. See Larry Bartels, *Presidential Primaries and the Dynamics of Public Choice* (Princeton, NJ: Princeton University Press, 1998). Consider as well the philosophy of "Emily's List"—a fundraising campaign designed to support female candidates for office; *Emily* is actually an acronym for "Early Money Is Like Yeast," or the idea that initial success in raising funds can create the potential for a candidate to demonstrate viability and therefore attract increased support as a result.

10. For example, Nobel Prize winner Thomas Schelling constructed a simple model to explain the phenomenon of residential segregation. Assume that everyone wants to live in an integrated neighborhood, he wrote, but that people move if their neighborhood becomes strongly (that is, more than 80 percent) dominated by neighbors of another race. The results of that model, perhaps surprisingly, showed that virtually all neighborhoods would quickly converge to strongly segregated patterns. The key element in the model is that of a social cascade: once the cascade starts, individual actors are powerless to stop it. Further, they may participate in the cascade even if it is based on concepts with which they do not personally agree. Schelling's article is "Dynamic Models of Segregation," *Journal of Mathematical Sociology* 1 (1971): 143–86.

11. We have argued that there is a lot of stability in our cases, but some may suggest that if 40 percent of our cases changed, often quite substantially, over a period of four years, that is actually quite substantial. We do not disagree. The status quo is important, but it does not determine everything. Further, as we have stressed, when change comes, it tends to be substantial, not marginal. With regard to whether the percentage of cases with stability was high or low, however, we note that our sample is not a sample of public policies. The vast majority of public policies most likely remain unchanged in any given time period. Our sample is limited to the objects of lobbying. Some are lobbying on the issue because they see that others are already involved, and therefore we can expect that change would be more common in our sample than across all existing policies in government. In any case, the likelihood of change in our sample is certainly higher than would be observed if somehow we had a random selection of existing public policies, rather than a sample of the objects of lobbying, as we do.

12. Kay Lehman Schlozman, Benjamin I. Page, Sidney Verba, and Morris Fiorina, "Inequalities of Political Voice," in *Inequality and American Democracy*, ed. Lawrence R. Jacobs and Theda Skocpol (New York: Russell Sage Foundation, 2005), 69.

13. Berry, *New Liberalism*, 48–57.

14. See Jeffrey M. Berry and Sarah Sobieraj, "The Outrage Industry," paper presented at the conference "Going to Extremes: The Fate of the Political Center in American Politics," Dartmouth College, June 2008.

15. Because our sample was selected from issues on which lobbyists were active from 1999 to 2002, we use that same period as well for the Gallup Poll. Results show the average poll response from all polls over those four years.

Methodological Appendix

1. The only information we do not make available is that based on confidential interviews. Because we promised our respondents anonymity in their interviews, we cannot make public some of the information we have gathered, including, unfortunately, a full list of which individuals or organizations were active on each issue. However, we have made available all nonconfidential information on our Web site.

2. The universe we sample from is 1996, the last year for which these registration data were compiled in a usable format at the time we began the data collection. See Frank R. Baumgartner and Beth L. Leech, "Studying Interest Groups Using Lobbying Disclosure Forms," *VOX POP* 18 (Fall 1999): 1–3.

3. Beth L. Leech, "Asking Questions: Techniques for Semistructured Interviews," *PS* 35, no. 4 (December 2002): 665–68; Jeffrey M. Berry, "Validity and Reliability Issues in Elite Interviewing," *PS* 35, no. 4 (December 2002): 679–82.

4. Esterling, *Political Economy of Expertise.*

5. See John Gerring, "What Is a Case Study and What Is It Good For?" *American Political Science Review* 98 (May 2004): 341–54.

6. Gary King, Robert O. Keohane, and Sidney Verba, *Designing Social Inquiry* (Princeton, NJ: Princeton University Press, 1994), 216.

7. King, Keohane, and Verba, 214.

8. Readers interested in more detail on these questions can see our proposals to the National Science Foundation that lay out these plans at our Web site.

9. See Baumgartner and Leech, "Issue Niches and Policy Bandwagons," 1191–1213, for more detail on these reports. The database itself is available on our Web site in the "Related Projects" section.

10. Some readers might question whether the lobbying activities in 1996 (on which we based our sampling frame) would reflect the levels of activity in 1999 or later (when we did our interviews). While the levels of activity would certainly change marginally, there is great stability in which groups are extremely active and which groups are less active from year to year. We are confident that our sampling procedure produced as close to a random sample of the objects of lobbying as could be devised. Probably the biggest limitation to our sampling technique was that it produced no judicial cases. When asked about "lobbying," most respondents would not have understood that to include litigation, even though we would

have been pleased to talk about efforts to change U.S. government policy through the courts. Another reason for this is probably that we spoke to those active in government affairs offices, but litigation, even that associated with policy goals, is typically done in legal departments or by law firms hired for the task. We do not discuss litigation here, though we know it to be an important means of affecting U.S. government policy.

11. We conducted 98 initial interviews and 217 secondary interviews, for a total of 315. In the secondary part of the sample, we were unable to find a suitable replacement in 39 instances where we sought to interview a relevant leader of a given side. These secondary interviews were done, therefore, with 217 of the 256 respondents we sought, or 85 percent.

12. Our most senior graduate students, Christine Mahoney and Tim LaPira, conducted the interviews for 20 and 18 of our issues, respectively. Mahoney has also published extensively, using her interviews and comparing them to comparable research she conducted in Brussels with advocates involved in the European Union. See, in particular, Christine Mahoney, *Brussels vs. the Beltway: Advocacy in the United States and the European Union* (Washington, DC: Georgetown University Press, 2008).

13. The rationale for the vagueness was to avoid cueing answers. We didn't want our subjects thinking about what we wanted before we got there, because we believed that it was best that they not prepare answers in their mind. In short, we preferred their unscripted, off-the-cuff answers to ones where they might have first tried to figure out what the college professor would be most impressed by or most interested in hearing.

14. King, Keohane, and Verba, *Designing Social Inquiry*, 25.

15. Joel D. Aberbach and Bert A. Rockman, "Conducting and Coding Elite Interviews," *PS* 35 (December 2002): 674.

16. Berry, "Validity and Reliability," 679.

17. Leech, "Asking Questions," 665.

18. Although we gathered information about the arguments being made by rivals, we make no systematic use of this. Because we interviewed representatives from virtually every side, we use only the self-descriptions, not the descriptions of the arguments of the rivals. Often, these were crude caricatures.

19. All of these data are available on our project Web site.

20. See Gary King, James Honaker, Anne Joseph, and Kenneth Scheve, "Analyzing Incomplete Political Science Data: An Alternative Algorithm for Multiple Imputation," *American Political Science Review* 95, no. 1 (March 2001): 49–69; and James Honaker, Anne Joseph, Gary King, Kenneth Scheve, and Naunihal Singh, *Amelia: A Program for Missing Data* (Windows version) (Cambridge, MA: Harvard University, 2001), http://GKing.Harvard.edu/.

21. Michael Tomz, Jason Wittenberg, and Gary King, *CLARIFY: Software for Interpreting and Presenting Statistical Results*, version 2.0 (Cambridge, MA: Harvard University, June 1, 2001), http://gking.harvard.edu.

Index

Italicized page numbers refer to tables.